T0329657

PENSIONS IN THE HEALTH AND RETIREMENT STUDY

PENSIONS IN THE HEALTH AND RETIREMENT STUDY

ALAN L. GUSTMAN

THOMAS L. STEINMEIER

NAHID TABATABAI

HARVARD UNIVERSITY PRESS

Cambridge, Massachusetts, and London, England

2010

Library of Congress Cataloging-in-Publication Data

Gustman, Alan L.
    Pensions in the health and retirement study / Alan L. Gustman, Thomas L.
Steinmeier, Nahid Tabatabai.
      p.   cm.
    Includes bibliographical references and index.
    ISBN 978-0-674-04866-9 (alk. paper)
    1. Pensions—United States—Longitudinal studies. 2. Retirement income—
United States—Longitudinal studies. I. Steinmeier, Thomas L. II. Tabatabai,
Nahid, 1951– III. Title.
    HD7125.G87   2010
    331.25'20973—dc22   2009050759

To Janice, Diane, and Amin

Contents

Tables and Figures

Figures

Preface

In the late 1980s, retirement researchers were still using the brilliantly designed but rapidly aging Retirement History Study, a survey pioneered by
the Social Security Administration to explore the retirement behavior of a
cohort of men born from 1906 to 1911. Richard Suzman of the National
Institute on Aging (NIA), James P. Smith of the RAND Corporation, and
others recognized the pressing need to develop a new and expanded panel
survey and acted to bring that survey about. The new study would not only
update the analysis of retirement but explore the health, wealth, family
structure, and other key outcomes that would be of central concern to researchers and policy makers as the baby boomers approached retirement
age. With Dr. Suzman taking the lead at the NIA, a competition was launched
to identify a team to produce the new survey, the Health and Retirement
Study (HRS). F. Thomas Juster of the University of Michigan led the win-
ning team and became the founding principal investigator of the HRS. Co-
investigators included experts in labor markets, retirement, and pensions;
health; income and wealth; and demography and family structure. Two of
us, Gustman and Steinmeier, were lucky enough to be asked to participate
as co-investigators who focused on labor and pension issues. The other
members of the Labor Group included Olivia Mitchell and Charlie Brown.
Juster directed the HRS through 1996. He was succeeded by Robert Willis,
who suggested that we hire a full-time staff member to help run the labor
section out of Dartmouth College. Nahid Tabatabai came to work on the
HRS in 1998. In the last three years, David Weir has been the principal

investigator and has continued a remarkable tradition of research quality and innovation.

Over these years, we have explored the HRS labor and pension data. These data include respondents' answers to detailed survey questions, detailed pension plan descriptions produced by employers of HRS respondents, and Social Security earnings and benefit records of respondents who gave their permission for those records to be secured from the Social Security Administration.

Policy makers and pension providers continue to make things interesting for us. Rather than standing still, over the course of the survey, pensions have rapidly evolved. As a result, the HRS has had to modify the pension questions from wave to wave to keep up with this ever-changing environment, while still maintaining survey continuity. The HRS pension data provide a unique opportunity to understand the complex pensions covering the retirement age population in the United States, how they influence the behavior of the HRS population, and their implications for public policies.

Eight waves of pension data covering fourteen years and three distinct cohorts are now available from the HRS. Our aim is to summarize some of the most important lessons provided by the HRS pension data over this period. In the process, we want to make it easier for researchers to use the HRS pension data, to facilitate their use by policy makers, and to disseminate findings among pension experts and financial advisors. We also hope to encourage the use of the HRS pension data in a wide variety of future studies. Toward that end, the data files underlying the tables in this book will be made available to researchers on the HRS Web site.

We gratefully acknowledge research support for this book. Gustman and Tabatabai's efforts have been supported through a subcontract to Dartmouth College as part of the NIA grant to the HRS. Gustman and Steinmeier's time has also been supported by a grant from the NIA under a RAND program project, "Economic and Health Determinants of Retirement Behavior," IP-OIAG022481 (Arie Kapteyn is the principal investigator), under "Behavioral Analysis in Structural Retirement Models," R01 AG024337, and "Integrating Retirement Models" R01 AG022956. John Phillips has been in charge of our grants. All three of us have also benefited from research support to the Michigan Retirement Research Center from the Social Security Administration, with a subcontract to Dartmouth College, under UM09-09, "How Do Pension Changes Affect Retirement Preparedness?" Dartmouth and its Economics Department have provided a stimulating intellectual environment. Special thanks are due to Dartmouth's associate dean for the social sciences, Michael Mastanduno, and the director of budgets and fiscal affairs, Kate Soule, for fostering an institutional environment that has been highly supportive of our research.

Many members of the HRS have been helpful over the years. The three principal investigators, Tom Juster, Robert Willis, and David Weir, have provided brilliant leadership and have been very supportive of our efforts. HRS staff members Robert Peticolas, Helena Stolyarova, Kandice Kapinos, Dorothy Nordness, Mike Nolte, and Cathy Liebowitz have lent their expertise and support. Kory Hirak of Dartmouth was helpful in preparing the manuscript. We would also like to acknowledge the help and encouragement from our editor at Harvard University Press, Michael Aronson, and the assistance of his editorial assistant, Hilary Jacqmin.

Finally, we would like to thank seminar participants at RAND and Harvard for their helpful comments.

An early version of Chapter 7 was published as "Do Workers Know about Their Pension Plan Type? Comparing Workers' and Employers' Pension Information," in Annamaria Lusardi, editor, *Overcoming the Saving Slump: How to Increase the Effectiveness of Financial Education and Saving Programs* (Chicago: University of Chicago Press, 2008). Among other differences between the revised chapter here and the one in the Lusardi book is that only partial data were available for 2004 in the earlier version.

Abbreviations

After NR age	The year after the individual qualifies for normal retirement benefits
CPS	Current Population Survey
DB	Defined benefit
DC	Defined contribution
DK	"Don't know" response
DROP	Deferred Retirement Option Plan
EB	Early boomers—the cohort of the Health and Retirement Study ages 51 to 56 in 2004
ER age	The year during which the individual qualifies for early retirement benefits
ER–NR age	The period between the year during which the individual qualifies for early retirement benefits and the year during which the individual qualifies for normal retirement benefits
ERISA	Employee Retirement Income Security Act
HH	Household
HRS	Health and Retirement Study
HRS 51–56	The cohort of the Health and Retirement Study ages 51 to 56 in 1992
HRS 51–61	The cohort of the Health and Retirement Study ages 51 to 61 in 1992

IRA	Individual retirement account
IRS	Internal Revenue Service
90/10	The ratio of the value at the 90th percentile to the value at the 10th percentile
NR age	The year during which the individual qualifies for normal retirement benefits
R	Respondent
RF	"Refuse to answer" response
SCF	Survey of Consumer Finances
SPD	Summary plan description
SRA	Supplementary retirement account
WB	War babies—the cohort of the Health and Retirement Study ages 51 to 56 in 1998

Introduction

The baby boom population is just beginning to retire. Their support in retirement will depend in part on the proverbial three-legged stool: personal saving, Social Security, and pensions. The viability of all three has been subject to question. Social Security, which accounts for more than a quarter of retirement wealth, faces financial problems.[1] Personal saving is said to have been declining. In addition, some have expressed fears about the future prospects for pensions.

Our concern in this book is with the third leg of the stool, pensions. Pensions account for almost one-fifth of the total wealth of those approaching retirement. Over three-fourths of the families approaching retirement age have benefited or will benefit from a pension.

Even before the financial downturn of 2007–2009, analysts and policy makers had grown increasingly concerned with pensions. Some argue that pension coverage is too low; others suggest there is too much reliance on defined contribution (DC) plans. (Defined contribution plans, such as 401[k] or 403[b] plans, hold employer and worker contributions in an account, allowing investment returns to accrue on a tax-deferred basis until the worker retires.)

DC plans are said to have a number of faults, among them, that the plans require the participant, rather than experts employed by the firm or union, to decide whether to participate, how much to contribute to the plan, and how to invest contributions in stocks and other financial instruments. They also require retired participants to determine the optimal rate at which to spend down the assets in the retirement account, drawing down the accumulated balances left in the plan at the time of retirement. The goal is to avoid spending assets so rapidly as to be left with a number of years where there are no assets left in the account, while at the same time avoid being left with too many assets in the account at the time of death.

A number of critics argue that many participants are barely financially literate and thus are incapable of making these decisions, or of making them in a timely fashion. Recent legislation has attempted to address these issues, but the criticisms persist. Now with the financial downturn, a central concern is that those with such accounts are overexposed to risk from volatile stocks.

While these criticisms apply to all DC plans held by workers of different ages, plans held by those approaching retirement age are said to be of greatest immediate concern. Those nearing retirement are among the most vulnerable of the working age population because they have little time to adjust their spending or labor market participation in response to unexpected changes in financial markets or in personal circumstances.

This book marshals extensive evidence from the Health and Retirement Study (HRS) describing the pensions held by those approaching retirement age. Separate chapters focus on major features of pensions, including plan participation, plan type, ages of eligibility for retirement benefits, and values of pensions of different types. Also covered are how pension values are influenced by the choice of retirement age, how plans are settled when a worker leaves a firm, how well people understand their pensions, how important pensions are in retirement saving and as a share of household wealth, and how vulnerable the retirement age population may be to the financial downturn. The HRS is the best source of information available for integrating details on pensions covering a nationally representative sample of the retirement age population of the United States with related data on a variety of personal and household characteristics, including income, health, wealth, family status, and labor market activity and retirement. These measures help us to understand the importance of pensions to the retirement age population. Together, the pension and related information available in the HRS provides the basic facts required to determine how pensions are changing over time and who is most affected, to ascertain which policy concerns might be warranted and which are not, and to understand the environment that will determine the likely effects of new policy proposals.

Because our analysis is based almost entirely on the Health and Retirement Study, we now turn to a discussion of why this data set is so informative about the pensions held by the retirement age population.

The HRS: A Tool for Studying Pensions and Retirement Policies

The Health and Retirement Study is a large and comprehensive data set. At its core is a sample of households with at least one member born from 1931 to 1953. It covers a wide variety of topics on the aging population in the United States and probes deeply in each topic area.[2]

HRS data are longitudinal, obtained by questioning the same individuals every other year. During 1992, the first year of the study, there were over 12,500 respondents, all from households with at least one member between the ages of 51 and 61. Younger cohorts have been added to the sample every six years.[3]

Many questions ask about the features of the pensions held by this population. Pensions from previous jobs are tracked, and the disposition of pensions is reported at the time of job termination. Information is collected about pension incomes once a person is retired. When there are two earners in the household, each is asked the details of his or her own pension.

When available, pension plan descriptions produced by the respondents' employers are included. This is particularly important for defined benefit (DB) pensions, the plan type that bases periodic benefit payments after retirement on earnings and work history and that dominated the pension scene for the retirement age population through the turn of the century, and indeed continues to do so. Special software is produced by the HRS and used in this book to evaluate the detailed rules governing the timing of retirement eligibility and the level of pension payments.

Questions are also asked of respondents about their expected (or, if retired and collecting benefits, their actual) Social Security benefits. Matched earnings and benefit records are obtained from the Social Security Administration for the members of the sample who gave their permission.

A great deal of complementary data is collected from respondents. The labor section of the survey includes the standard set of questions on labor market activity that one finds in the Current Population Survey and elsewhere, as well as details about the characteristics of jobs, labor market activities, retirement expectations, work history, and other labor market variables. Separate sections of the survey report on the respondent and spouse's demographic characteristics, wealth, income, health, family structure, and finances. This makes it possible to relate the pensions of each individual to many other factors.

The HRS also provides a unique opportunity to study the pensions of individuals as their plans and benefits evolve over their work lives and into retirement. Because the HRS is a panel study, following the same individuals over time and interviewing them every two years, it allows us not only to measure the pension-related outcomes listed in the previous paragraph but to understand the role of changing pensions over time and to trace how pension changes have affected those on the verge of retirement. It also allows us to determine the fate of pensions held at some time over the lifetime and thus how pension coverage while on the job affects a respondent's pension income and wealth once retired. Given the very rapid changes in pensions over the past two decades, this is a particularly propitious time to have a mature panel data set available for analysis.

Among the wide set of dynamic outcomes that can be examined, the HRS describes how participation in a pension and pension values change over a lifetime in the labor market, how each person's pension changes during time on the job, what happens to their pensions if individuals leave a job before retiring, and how pension expectations before retirement compare with pension realizations after retirement. Information on their pensions is available for those following different courses during their work lives. Some people continue on the same job, and their pension rules remain unchanged; some remain on the same job but experience changes in their pensions; still others leave a pension job. Some of those who leave their jobs maintain their pensions at their old firms; others roll their pensions over, cash them out, collect benefits, abandon them, or take other actions affecting the future values of their retirement benefits.

Pensions vary widely among different groups of workers—between men and women, between private and public sector employees, between union and non-union workers, between employees and self-employed persons, and by education, income, and race. Rapid changes in the labor market and in pensions have caused major changes in some of these differences. When surveys ignore pensions, conclusions about compensation paid to employees and how compensation differs among various groups may not only be incomplete but systematically biased. Similar issues arise for studies of wealth and saving. When surveys of family income and wealth do not include detailed information on pensions, wealth measures derived from these surveys are incomplete, and conclusions drawn from these data may be quite wrong. Analogous problems arise for studies of retirement, the income distribution, and other topics that use data without adequate information on pensions. The information in the HRS is adequate for analyzing each of these issues.

An Introduction to Pensions

Pensions began to spread widely during and after World War II, a time when price or wage controls were often in place. Pensions were exempt from these controls, allowing employers to raise compensation in a tight labor market at a time when wage increases were limited. This strategy was particularly attractive to large unions that could spread the overhead costs of administering a pension among its many members.

Firms think of pensions as an important and expensive part of their compensation policies. They have paid increasing attention to pensions over the past two decades as pension costs have increased with the aging of the labor force, as changes in regulations required firms to offer benefits to a wider range of workers and to account for full actuarial costs, and with changes in the stock market and interest rates. As a result, firms have changed the array and characteristics of pensions offered to employees.

As implied by the three-legged stool analogy, pensions are a major part of the wealth people accumulate over their lifetimes. Pensions are an attractive vehicle for retirement saving because they receive favorable treatment under the tax laws.

Two major descriptors of pensions are pension participation and pension plan type. Typically about half of all current employees between the ages of 25 and 64 have a pension. This fact, that half of current workers are covered by a pension, has led some to the misleading conclusion that most people do not have a pension, or saving resulting from a pension, by the time they enter retirement. As we will see, among those approaching retirement age, many more people are covered or have been covered by a pension. Fifty-seven percent of respondents from the youngest HRS cohort, that is, not just of employees but of the total population, are approaching retirement with a live pension (i.e., a pension from which the respondent either is collecting benefits or expects to collect benefits in the future) from a current or previous job earned at some time over their lifetime. Sixty-eight percent of respondents were covered by a pension from their own employment at some time during their lifetime—with some of these previously earned pensions having entered savings or individual retirement accounts (IRAs) or in some other way having improved retirement prospects. If coverage of a spouse is counted, the figure rises to four-fifths of respondents.

Plan type is a major defining feature of pensions. We have mentioned the two major types of plans, defined benefit and defined contribution, but some further discussion may be helpful. Defined benefit plans typically provide a benefit for life, where the benefit amount is determined by a formula that bases the periodic payment on earnings history at the firm, time worked under the plan, and age. A very simple defined benefit plan might replace 2 percent of the average of a person's earnings over the last three years of work, for each year of service, thereby replacing half of the earnings for a person who worked twenty-five years. A defined contribution plan is an account held in the name of the employee, where the firm, the individual, or both may contribute to the account. The most common type of DC plan is a 401(k) plan, but there are other types. The account earns a return that depends on how the balance is invested. Once retired, the covered worker must decide the rate of withdrawal from the account.

The final column of Table 1.1 shows the frequency of each plan type as reported by HRS respondents with a pension in 2006. The continuing importance of defined benefit plans for those at or near retirement age is readily seen in the data. Altogether, half of all workers with a pension have a DB plan and two-thirds have a DC plan. (Because 17 percent of respondents with a pension have both plan types, the sum of these fractions exceeds 1.)

Despite the greater incidence of coverage by DC plans, we will see that the DB plans held by the retirement age population account for a larger share of pension wealth than do their DC plans. The main reason is that DC plans are

Table 1.1   Percentage of public and private sector employees by self-reported plan type on current job in 2006 (weighted)

Self-reported plan type	Public	Private	Total
DB only	57%	22%	34%
DC only	21%	59%	47%
Both	18%	17%	17%
DK	3%	2%	3%
Total	100% (895)	100% (1,843)	100% (2,738)

Notes: Respondents with a current job are asked if they are working for the government at the federal, state, or local level (KJ720). Note that notations such as KJ720 refer to question numbers in the HRS. Total number of observations is reported in parentheses.

not yet fully mature. The retirement age population has been covered by DB plans for almost all the time they have spent on the job, while those in the retirement age population have been covered for many fewer years by their DC plans.

The plan types held by public and private sector workers are also shown in Table 1.1. Three-fourths of public sector employees with a pension report that their plan is defined benefit, 57 percent report they are participating in a DB plan only, and 18 percent report they are participating in both a DB and a DC plan. Twenty-two percent of private sector workers with a pension report participating in a DB plan only. In contrast to public sector workers, 39 percent of respondents with a pension and working in the private sector report participating in a DB plan, while just over three-fourths have a DC plan. Of these two groups, 17 percent of private sector employees have both plan types.

When a worker's job is covered by a defined benefit plan, the worker is normally required to participate in the plan. For those who have not yet reached retirement age, each additional year of work under a DB plan adds more to benefits than the previous year's work. The closer one is to retiring, the less time one has to wait to collect benefits. Thus the closer one is to first becoming eligible for retirement, the greater the value of the increase in benefits from an additional year of work. Eligibility for receipt of benefits from a defined benefit plan is determined by the worker's age and work history. For example, to become eligible to receive benefits, a worker may be required to be at least 60 years old and to have worked at the firm for at least ten years or, if the individual will not have worked ten years before reaching his or her 65th birthday, but will have worked long enough for benefits to vest (typically five years), to wait until reaching age 65 before becoming eligible to claim benefits. More complicated formulas are also very common. Although there are some studies suggesting indirect links, benefits from DB plans are not linked directly to the funds that firms or government employers accumulate to back their DB pension plans, nor are they linked to earnings on investments of DB pension funds. Thus when returns are very low, or when for other reasons a plan is not well funded, a firm may consider changing or terminating the plan or, if in sufficient financial trouble, turning the pension over to the Pension Benefit Guarantee Corporation, the federal pension insurance agency. But there is no direct, mechanical link from stock market performance to benefits from DB plans. In addition, protective features in pension law (i.e., the Employee Retirement Income Security Act [ERISA]) prevent firms from simply reclaiming the assets already accumulated in a defined benefit pension plan, even if the firm is entering bankruptcy.

Many of those who worked for many years under a DB plan, and who are old enough, have the option of receiving their benefits early. Typically, benefits are reduced for retiring early, with the reduction depending on how early the covered worker retires and claims benefits. However, in many plans, there is only a modest reduction in benefits when a qualified worker retires early. Additional benefits are often paid to qualified workers who retire before Social Security benefits become available. To qualify for early retirement benefits, special Social Security supplements, or other supplements paid to early retirees, one must have accumulated sufficient tenure under the plan, have reached a specified age, or have satisfied a combination of age and tenure requirements. As a result, the present value of benefits, the lump sum required to generate the promised benefit stream, often jumps sharply in the year a person first becomes eligible for early retirement benefits.

In private sector jobs, defined benefit plans are typically supported by contributions made by the employer with no contribution required from the worker. Public sector employers also contribute to their pensions, but public sector workers with defined benefit plans are usually required to also contribute to their plans. Frequently, a separate account is kept representing the contributions made by public employees. Public employees who terminate their jobs before reaching retirement age have the option of waiting for payment under their DB plan until they reach the plan's retirement age or, upon leaving their job, they may roll their own contribution (sometimes together with the employer's contribution, plus a nominal interest return) into an IRA or withdraw the amount and pay a penalty.

Participation by workers in DC plans is typically voluntary. In some DC plans, the firm is the only contributor; in others, the worker is the only contributor. There are still others where there is some type of matching formula where the employer matches all or part of the worker's contribution, subject to a minimum and/or maximum firm contribution.

Discrimination rules prevent firms from confining plans to higher income workers or from having a disproportionate share of benefits accrue to high wage workers. So if high or middle income workers want to have a tax-deferred pension plan, these rules encourage firms to increase the participation of lower wage workers who might otherwise not participate.

Workers are most often given a choice as to which assets to purchase with their DC account balances. However, subject to certain restrictions, the menu of available investment choices is determined by the plan.

The value of a defined contribution plan is measured at a moment in time by the value of assets in the pension account that have vested—that is, that have become the property of the covered worker. Any contributions that will be made by the employer in future years of work will enhance the value of the pension at the time of retirement.

A useful step in comparing defined benefit and defined contribution plans is to calculate the equivalent *pension wealth* value of the DB plan, a single sum representing the account value that would be required to generate the stream of benefits promised under the DB plan. That measure of the expected value of a DB pension promise is calculated by discounting the periodic benefits expected to be paid from retirement age to death back to the age of retirement, while adjusting each future benefit payment by the probability that the worker will survive until that age. The expected sum of retirement benefits evaluated at retirement age is then further discounted back to whatever base year is under consideration (e.g., the year of the survey).[4] To make the calculations comparable, the value of the DB plan is adjusted to reflect work completed to date rather than including work between the date of survey and the date of expected retirement.

Changes in pension wealth from additional time spent on the job under a defined benefit pension affect the incentive to retire. Benefits typically begin to accrue a year or so after a person joins the firm, but they are not the property of the worker until they are vested, at which time the participant becomes entitled to them even if the person should leave the firm.[5] From the time the benefit is vested until the covered worker qualifies for early retirement (or normal retirement if early retirement is not available), the value of the benefit from an additional year of work is greater the longer a worker has been covered by a defined benefit plan. However, the rate at which the benefit accumulates with additional work, that is, the benefit accrual, is not always even over time. The benefit increase is typically greatest from working the year just preceding eligibility for early retirement. Benefits may also increase discontinuously when a person becomes eligible for normal retirement benefits. Thus a full description of the incentives created by defined benefit plans requires sufficient information to locate the discontinuities or spikes in the benefit accrual profile at the time of vesting and upon attainment of eligibility for early and normal retirement benefits. One more consideration is relevant. Benefit accruals may include not only the increase in pension wealth from working one more year but also, when analyzing retirement and saving incentives, the option value of working until qualifying for early retirement benefits or some other optimal point (Lazear and Moore, 1988). That is, when taking account of incentives from pensions, researchers also consider the value of being able to continue to accumulate benefits under the plan should one decide to continue on the job beyond the coming year.

Although for those who work under a defined benefit plan the yearly benefit increases for work undertaken after the age of normal retirement, the present value of the benefit does not always increase. When one postpones receiving a benefit by a year, to break even, future benefits must be increased so that the value of benefits received over the remaining lifetime compensate for receiving benefits for one less year. For older workers whose wage is not increasing rapidly from year to year and who have accumulated a great deal of service so that another year under the plan results in only a 3 or 4 percent increase in service, the yearly pension benefit from additional work may not increase by enough to compensate for postponing retirement by one year.

Recently, some DB pensions have been modified to encourage workers to delay their retirement. For example, Philadelphia offers a Deferred Retirement Option Plan (DROP) to those who have reached normal retirement age with at least ten years of service. The employee has the option of placing the monthly benefit as of the normal retirement age in a deferred retirement account plan while continuing to be employed. The annual benefit is frozen as of the date the DROP is chosen, but the benefits that the continuing employee would otherwise be entitled to are deposited in the DROP account, where they accrue interest. Moreover, the employee no longer has to contribute to the DB plan.

Further Discussion of the Pension Information in the HRS

Before the advent of the Health and Retirement Study, most data sets that provided detailed information on individual income and wealth did not provide all of the information required to calculate the value of a pension. As a result, studies of saving behavior and the distribution of wealth often ignored pensions entirely.[6]

In the 1970s and 1980s, most pension plans were defined benefit. To evaluate these plans, typically a researcher needed to know the pension formula, the worker's earnings in the last few years before retirement, and the worker's years of service. Initially, to measure pension values and retirement incentives from pensions, researchers relied on data provided by one or a few firms (Burkhauser, 1979). These data had the advantage of providing precise information on the rules governing pension plans. Moreover, cooperating firms provided information on the earnings of workers (Kotlikoff and Wise, 1985, 1987). Those who wished to use data sets that were nationally representative did not have precise information on pension plans together with the earnings of included workers until the Survey of Consumer Finances collected employer-produced plan descriptions for each of the respondents in its 1983 cross-section survey.[7]

In 1992, the Health and Retirement Study provided information on pensions held by workers in a nationally representative panel data set. Important panel data sets like the Retirement History Study and the National Longitudinal Survey of Older Men, fielded in the 1970s, had provided nationally representative data that followed men as they aged and moved from work through retirement. The surveys asked respondents about their pensions. But plan descriptions were available only from respondents, and those were incomplete. There were no matching pension plan descriptions available from the employers of these workers.[8] More recently, both the National Longitudinal Survey of Mature Women and the Panel Study of Income Dynamics have piggybacked on the HRS infrastructure to add employer-provided descriptions of pensions to their respondent data.[9] The HRS is the only survey to provide a panel of the respondents' description of their pension along with a panel of the employers' descriptions of their pensions.

The Health and Retirement Study built its approach to analyzing pension values on the approach taken in the Survey of Consumer Finances (SCF), which was also supervised by the HRS founding principal investigator, F. Thomas Juster. It is much easier to estimate the value of DC plans from respondent reports than it is to estimate the value of DB plans. The original idea of Juster and his colleagues was that DC plans would be evaluated by asking respondents how much they had in their account. DB plans would be evaluated from employer-provided pension plan descriptions, combined with respondent reports of their covered work history and final earnings. Nevertheless, DC plan descriptions were also gathered from employers. (DC plan descriptions obtained from employers in 2004 have not yet been coded by the Health and Retirement Study.)

Summary plan descriptions (SPDs) are detailed documents produced by the employer describing the provisions of the pension. The employer plan descriptions provide details about defined benefit plans that respondents might not know, especially since some of the important details pertain to choices the respondent did not elect. A full description of all options, whether chosen or not, is required to map out the full set of retirement incentives presented by the plan.

To evaluate the employer-provided pension plan descriptions contained in the SPDs, Juster and his colleagues constructed a template to house the key variables that determine pension values and to evaluate the resulting benefits. An updated version of that template and an accompanying program to evaluate benefits are available from the HRS. The program requires other inputs to calculate expected pension values, including the respondent's years of participation in the pension, earnings history, projected wage growth, interest rate, inflation and adjustments in plan value to inflation, and other values. These detailed descriptions of pensions by both employers and respondents are paired with unique information on work and earnings histories obtained not only from respondents but also from detailed Social Security and W2 earnings histories. The program uses relevant variables reported in the template to calculate expected yearly benefits at alternative retirement ages. It calculates the present value of benefits conditional on the date of retirement from DB plans, taking account of life expectancy.

For DC plans, the pension program calculates the value of a DC account as of a specified date. It requires information on the contributions made by both the respondent and the firm. Engelhardt and Kumar (2006a, 2006b) have shown that the Social Security and W2 data can be very helpful along with innovations in their own pension software in providing some of the missing information required to evaluate the DC pensions held by HRS respondents. Nevertheless, some of the information required to evaluate the DC plan is not available from the survey (e.g., yearly returns to investments).

The HRS traces pension values through the decades preceding retirement, gathers additional data at the time of retirement, and solicits information on pension incomes after retirement. Most of the information gathered before retirement is collected near the end of the employee's working life and thus provides a good indication of the total value of the respondent's pension or pensions accrued over the life cycle. The HRS also traces pensions from previous jobs, keeping track of the disposition of plans that do not enter pay status, or are not cashed out, when plan participants leave their employers.

HRS pension data are valuable for a number of reasons. First, the HRS provides a wide variety of information about pensions. Second, the HRS puts these data into context, allowing analysis of pensions together with family incomes and labor market activities. Third, the HRS contains information on demographic and employment characteristics of workers and collects information for a number of cohorts, allowing analysis of pension differentials and trends and changes in pensions over the life cycle.

Even today, with the exception of studies based on data from the Health and Retirement Study and in some cases the Survey of Consumer Finances, many surveys of wealth and saving do not provide sufficient information to evaluate defined benefit pensions, and in many cases they also ignore the value of Social Security.

Trends in Pension Plan Type

The past two decades have been a time of rapid change in pensions, and in particular in pension plan type. Although defined contribution plans were available for many years, helped to no small degree by changes in the tax law that introduced the 401(k) defined contribution plan, a very rapid trend in new DC plans began in the mid-1980s. At the same time, DB plans began to stagnate and then to decline. Roughly half the decline in coverage by DB plans observed in the 1980s can be attributed to a shift of employment away from manufacturing and union jobs that typically offered DB plans, toward industries and jobs in services and other areas where DB pensions were less commonly available than in the union and manufacturing sectors (Gustman and Steinmeier, 1992; Ippolito, 1995). Through the mid-1990s, few new DB plans were established. Although some DB plans at small firms were terminated, defined benefit pension plans held by employees of large firms remained (Ippolito and Thompson, 2000). There also has been a widespread increase in the availability of secondary 401(k) plans, so that in addition to the rise in primary DC plans, by 2004, half of those holding a DB plan in the Health and Retirement Study had a secondary DC plan. Near the turn of the twenty-first century, significant numbers of large firms began to terminate their DB plans (Beller, 2005).

Figures 1.1 and 1.2 provide a preliminary picture of changes in the level of pension participation and plan type among cohorts covered by the HRS. There is a small trend in plan participation, defined either as coverage among all workers, that is, those who work more than 100 hours per year, or as coverage among full-time employees.[10] These results are discussed in detail in Chapter 5.

Consistent with other data on trends in pensions, HRS data examined in Chapter 6 show a more modest trend in plan type. Because HRS respondents are older than the general population, they are much more likely to work in jobs that continue to offer DB plans than would be found in a sample of employed workers of all ages. HRS respondents show evidence of the trend to DC plans, of course. Figure 1.2 shows that there is a clear decline over the survey period of the HRS in the percentage of workers with a pension whose plan is defined benefit. Nevertheless, that decline is muted compared with the decline experienced by the general population. Similarly, the data clearly show the growth in DC plans.

Pension freezes have become more common in recent years. Munnell and Soto (2007a) find that about 15 percent of private sector DB plans were frozen over the period from 2000 through 2007. Depending on the nature of the freeze, a covered worker may no longer enjoy increased benefits due to additional service and perhaps also due to a further increase in wages. Instead, a

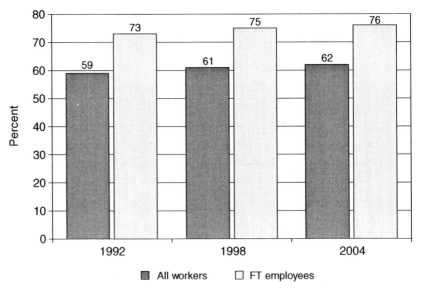

Figure 1.1 Trends in pension coverage for those ages 51–56, by year (weighted)

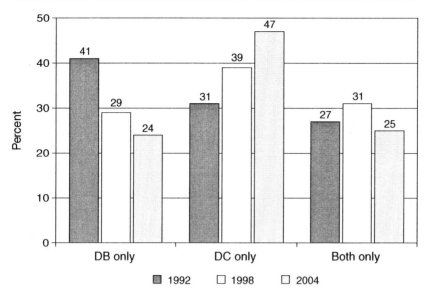

Figure 1.2 Trends in pension plan type for those ages 51–56, by year, for all workers (weighted)

defined contribution plan may be added or enhanced in value. Pension experts attribute the increased incidence of freezes of DB plans to a combination of factors. Many older firms are carrying an overhang of unfunded liabilities from pension and health insurance costs, including costs for retiree health plans. Costly benefits were adopted in an era when firms had market power, earning extraordinary rents (better than normal returns to their investments), and when there were strong unions. With market power and union strength now gone in many areas, the additional pension and health costs continue to haunt older firms, making some of those firms uncompetitive with newer entries that are not saddled with such legacy costs and with foreign firms whose access to U.S. markets has increased with globalization. Another factor raises the costs of DB pensions directly. There has been a continuing stream of costly pension legislation. The trend away from DB plans has been reinforced by changes in the labor markets brought about by the retirement of the baby boomers. To the extent that DB plans were adopted and modified to encourage earlier retirement by older workers, with the aging and looming retirement of the baby boomers, older workers have become more valuable. As a result, costly early retirement incentives are now less attractive to many firms (Schieber, 2007).

In recent years, defined benefit plans have been replaced not only by DC plans but also by hybrid plans. Hybrid plans contain elements of both defined benefit and defined contribution plans. A particular type of hybrid plan, called a cash balance plan, may create a *notional* account. The account balance is considered notional because it is based on a history of hypothetical contributions by the employer and either a specified but hypothetical return (say 6 percent) or a market-determined return (e.g., the one-year treasury bond rate) on those contributions (Clark and Schieber, 2001, 2002, 2004). For example, the value of the account may be based on a hypothetical yearly contribution of 5 percent of salary, which earns a hypothetical return specified by the plan to remain steady at 6 percent. Cash balance plans do not fund individual accounts. Instead hypothetical liabilities from all employees' accounts are aggregated, and the total of these liabilities is funded based on actuarial principles in the same way that pension liabilities from a defined benefit plan are funded, so that when fully funded, contributions by the firm cover the total of promised liabilities. This contrasts with a defined contribution plan, where each worker's funded account balance is determined by actual contributions made in the name of the worker, contributions that become the property of the worker. Once the contribution passes to the worker's DC account, there is no longer a firm liability.

A major point of contention with cash balance plans arises from the transition from a DB plan to the cash balance plan. Typically, the first step is to freeze the DB account. The wage and tenure used in calculating the DB benefit are held at their level at the time the cash balance plan is adopted. ERISA prevents firms from reducing the promised benefit below this amount. However, if the cash balance plan were simply substituted for the frozen DB plan, the overall value of the pensions at retirement is likely to be reduced. Such a reduction is most likely to affect older workers who have already accumulated high benefits, due to their high wage, high tenure, and a short time until retirement. However, under ERISA, a firm is not permitted to reduce a promised pension benefit below the amount that has already been earned.

An alternative some firms adopt when changing to a cash balance plan is to guarantee the value of the old DB plan as a minimum payment. This guarantee, in turn, creates an issue called "wear away." The problem is that the value of the DB account, when it is frozen, may exceed the value of the cash balance plan calculated under the assumption that the hypothetical contributions and interest accumulate from the first day of the person's pension participation. Since the benefit cannot be reduced below the value of the frozen DB pension, there is a prolonged period during which the worker's pension is frozen at the value of the old DB pension benefit. The value of the pension does not increase after the adoption of the cash balance plan until the value of the cash balance plan has increased to the level of the frozen DB benefit. Under the 2006 Pension Protection Act, wear away was outlawed for companies adopting cash balance plans after June 2005.

To deal with the wear-away problem, some firms grandfather the benefits of certain workers, those who were beyond a specified age or had accumulated a specified level of service at the time of plan adoption. For these grandfathered workers, wage and service credits continue to accumulate under the DB plan. In other cases, special benefits are offered to offset the wear-away problem. Another possibility is to have the cash balance plan begin with a balance equal to the value of the frozen DB pension. From that date forward, total benefits are then equal to the sum of frozen DB benefits plus any value in the cash balance plan accumulated from the date of plan termination, rather than having the cash balance plan valued from the first day of participation in the original DB plan.[11]

It is surprising given the very rapid growth of cash balance plans that the HRS finds very few cash balance plans in its sample. In 2004 and 2006, neither the survey of respondents nor the pension data collected from employers suggest that the HRS population will be greatly affected by cash balance plans. While that finding is less surprising for the HRS cohort, that is, those born from 1931 to 1941, where many were past their retirement age by the time cash balance plans were introduced in large numbers, the failure to find many cash balance plans is surprising for the younger cohorts, those born between 1941 and 1953. It would appear either that firms have held harmless most of the older workers who are sampled by the HRS, allowing them in many cases to receive the benefits based on their original formulas, or that perhaps their plans were subject to a freeze, but they were replaced by a 401(k) rather than a cash balance plan.

Trends in Pension Plan Characteristics

Over time, standard defined benefit plans have taken on some of the features of defined contribution plans. For example, in a growing number of DB plans, benefits may be claimed as a partial or full lump sum, rather than paid out in the form of an annuity, as had been typical for a DB plan. Conversely, some DC plans have always had certain characteristics of DB plans. There are DC plans where benefits vary according to a formula that links employer contributions to age or other factors. Under the Dartmouth College pension plan, for example, the employer's contribution varies from 3 percent to 17 percent of salary, with the rate of contribution increasing with the age of the employee. As another example, many DC plans in higher education pay benefits in the form of an annuity, although lump sum options are now more commonly available.

Even for those whose type of pension plan has remained the same over time, plan features have changed. For a number of years, retirement ages specified by DB plans declined (Gustman and Steinmeier, 1999a). For a sample of respondents to the 1983 and 1989 Survey of Consumer Finances, who were included in defined benefit pensions in both years, over the six-year period between surveys the early retirement age declined by a year. As of 1992, three-fourths of those in the Health and Retirement Study with a defined benefit plan were on the way to qualifying for early retirement benefits by age 55 (Gustman and Steinmeier, 2000a). This was a sharp reduction in early retirement age from decades earlier.

Between 1969 and 1992, changes in plan participation and plan generosity alone more than doubled the value of pensions held by older households (Gustman and Steinmeier, 2000b). That is, holding constant the effects of wage growth, the value of pensions increased by 145 percent. The median value of DB plans for respondents at age 55 was 40 percent higher in 1989 than in 1983. Using data from Watson Wyatt reporting on the pensions offered by thirty-nine of the fifty largest U.S. companies, other important changes were observed over the 1990–1995 period (Gustman and Steinmeier 1999a). Again, a sizable minority of firms experienced very large changes in their plans.

Other recent changes have been encouraged by the Pension Protection Act of 2006. Until recently, eligible workers who did not indicate a desire to participate in a DC plan typically were not enrolled. Under the new rules, employers are permitted to elect participation as the default, enrolling respondents in their defined contribution pension plan unless the respondent specifically elects not to participate. Moreover, employers are encouraged to choose a life cycle fund for those employees who fail to make an investment choice, so the share of account invested in the stock market declines with age. The new law protects an employer who chooses a prudent default, one that enhances the expected value of the pension the employee will receive even though the option carries some risk.

The Effects of a Changing Pension Environment

Using data from the Health and Retirement Study, it is possible to quantify the changes in pensions experienced by individuals over their lifetimes, to record changes in pension values over time, and to determine the reasons for the various changes. The HRS also allows us to measure the cumulation of pensions from different jobs held over the lifetime, as the values of new pensions are added to those from pensions held at previous jobs.

Defined benefit plans were designed by unions and firms to provide adequate benefits in retirement for long-term employees. There was little for the worker to worry about. Coverage was mandated and benefits were prescribed so that they would be adequate even for those who did not understand their pensions and how they worked. In many cases, between Social Security and their DB pension, workers with a defined benefit plan could expect to replace two-thirds or more of their preretirement earnings. Moreover, there was no need to manage the flow of expenditures. Benefits were annuitized and thus guaranteed for as long as the retiree lived. Indeed, if joint and survivor benefits were chosen, benefits would last for as long as either spouse was alive.

The current situation is very different. The defined contribution plans that predominate today require workers to decide how much to save in the form of a pension. Unlike DB plans, defined contribution plans typically do not offer an annuity option as part of the plan. As a result, once retired, the worker is also required to regulate the rate of withdrawal from pension saving. Thus the retiree trades off between two goals, an adequate replacement rate and the need for the pension to last throughout retirement.

A defined contribution plan asks the worker not only to manage the accumulation and decumulation of funds but to adjust to a changing pension environment, one in which the rules that will govern pensions (and Social Security) in the future are in doubt. If plan rules change before a worker reaches retirement, pension benefits that are received in retirement may differ considerably from the pensions that were expected. Even if pension rules remain unchanged, ill health, job loss, or other intervening events affecting work and earnings may create differences between pension benefits a person expected while still at work and the pensions realized after retirement.

Complexities of Pensions Lead to Imperfect Understanding

There are concerns that many workers do not understand their pensions well enough to effectively manage their plans. Innovative studies by Madrian and Shea (2001) and by Choi et al. (2004, 2005), as well as by other researchers whose contributions are noted in Chapter 7, all suggest that these concerns have a firm foundation. As a result, as we have noted, the pension law was recently revised (under the Pension Protection Act of 2006) to encourage firms to enroll workers in their plans as a default if the employee does not make an explicit choice as to whether to participate in a defined contribution plan, and to encourage enrollees to adopt asset investment policies that sensibly balance risk and return.

If workers do not understand their pensions well, there are implications not only for the welfare of the worker and for public policy but also for the reliability of data collected in pension surveys. If many people are poorly informed about their pensions, respondents' descriptions of their plans will be unreliable. Misidentification of plan type by the respondent is a particularly important problem affecting the quality of information gathered by the main HRS survey instrument. Plan type is identified by the respondent in an HRS question that asks whether the plan will provide a benefit on the basis of a formula involving age, years of service, and salary (defined benefit); or whether money is accumulated in an account for the respondent (defined contribution). Different follow-up questions are asked of those reporting a defined benefit plan than of those reporting a defined contribution plan. Consequently, if plan type is misidentified, respondents will be asked a set of questions relevant to a plan type that is different from theirs.[12]

The possibility that some people do not fully understand their pensions also raises a host of behavioral questions about what information people use to make their saving and retirement decisions, how well they use that information, how many people make mistakes, and what the effects of those mistakes are for those who do not plan well or are confused.

As would be expected if respondents do not fully understand their pensions or do not have full command over the details of their pensions, important discrepancies may appear when comparing plan features as reported in summary plan descriptions produced by employers with respondent descriptions of their pensions. Plan type, plan characteristics, ages of eligibility for benefits, and payouts at various ages may all differ when outcomes based on SPDs are compared with those based on respondent reports (Gustman and Steinmeier, 2004b). Even if people were well informed about what benefit to expect at a particular age—for example, the benefit at early retirement age—they often are poorly informed about options not taken. For example, they may have difficulty describing pension values that would be paid at retirement ages they are not considering. As a result, it is often difficult to obtain from respondent reports all the details required to understand how pension rewards vary with alternative retirement dates and other plan features that are not likely to be taken by the respondent.

To resolve questions about reporting error, imperfect knowledge of pensions, and their consequences, it helps to have access to the firm-based reports describing pension rules, together with respondent reports on workers' pensions. We will compare HRS data from both sources to learn more about imperfect information about pensions and its consequences.

Outline of the Book

Our aim in this book is to use the HRS to systematically answer a number of key questions about pensions, in the process providing as full a description of the pensions covering the retirement age population as possible. These questions are listed in Table 1.2.

The remainder of this book is organized as follows. Chapter 2 discusses theoretical explanations for pensions. Chapter 3 describes in greater depth the structure of the HRS survey, including basic information on sample sizes, labor market outcomes and different cohorts, and the different sources of information on pensions in the HRS. Various types of pension data available in the HRS are described in Chapter 4. Chapter 5 focuses on participation in pension plans. Chapter 6 analyzes data on pension changes and pension plan type. Issues in measuring plan type are discussed in Chapter 7. Chapter 8 presents data on retirement age, including ages of eligibility for early and normal benefits, and expected age of benefit claiming. Chapter 9 focuses on pension values, including the amounts in accounts under defined contribution plans and the present value of benefit streams promised by defined benefit plans at different retirement ages. Chapter 10 documents the retirement incentives created by pensions in the HRS by examining changes in pension values associated with leaving the firm before or at the early retirement age, the normal retirement age, or deferring leaving until after qualifying for normal retirement

Table 1.2   Key questions about pensions

Who has a pension?

How many plans?

From which employment and when?

What kinds of pensions do respondents have?

How do respondents' pensions change?

How well do people understand their pensions?

When can they claim pension benefits?

What do they do with their pensions when they leave a job?

What are their pensions worth?

How do pension expectations before retirement compare with pension realizations after retirement?

What incentives do pensions create to retire or save?

How are pensions accumulated over the lifetime?

How well do pensions cover the population in retirement?

How important is it to follow pensions from previous jobs in determining pension wealth?

How important are pensions in retirement saving and as a share of household wealth?

How vulnerable is the pension wealth of the retirement age population to the financial downturn?

benefits. Chapter 11 explores the various ways that pension benefits are paid out. Chapter 12 measures how pensions vary as a share of total wealth over the course of the Health and Retirement Study. Chapter 13 summarizes our findings and discusses some representative policy implications, including how the 2008–2009 downturn in financial markets is likely to affect the wealth of the retirement age population.

By now, a very large number of researchers has used the Health and Retirement Study. However, many researchers do not make full use of the pension data, even when these data are central to their studies of retirement or saving. Despite the rich detail available, they often will take a shortcut, including simple descriptive statistics of pension coverage or plan type but ignoring measures of plan value and indicators of how plan value changes with behavior.

Using HRS pension data requires a very large investment. The HRS has gone to great lengths to reduce the costs of that investment. One of our goals in writing this book is to further encourage the use of HRS pension data. Accordingly, we will make the files underlying the various tables in this book available to researchers. These files, which will be posted on the HRS Web site, update the available files to newer cohorts and provide information related to more dimensions of pension outcomes than have been available previously.

Those who wish to reproduce the tables in this book will find the data listed by individual and household identification number posted on the HRS Web site (http://hrsonline.isr.umich.edu/data/index.html).

2

Theories Explaining Pensions

Before turning to data on pensions, it is useful to discuss the reasons why workers and firms are willing to use pensions as a vehicle for saving for retirement. Studies explaining the demand for and supply of pensions began as a theoretical literature generating formal analyses of pensions and their role in the labor market. This literature, which dates from the 1970s and 1980s, drew on models from public economics, finance, and labor economics and tailored those models to analyze pension outcomes.[1]

It created a common view as to the forces shaping pensions held through the early 1990s. At that time, major changes in the pension landscape raised questions about some of these explanations. Nevertheless, some of the explanations for pensions produced by this literature continue to be widely accepted.

Explanations for Pensions from the 1970s, 1980s, and 1990s

One explanation for pensions is the special treatment they enjoy under the tax law. Returns to assets held in a pension plan are not subject to taxation until the benefits are paid. Effectively, the returns to pension investments accrue at a tax-free rate. Because this special tax treatment enhances the value of the pension to the worker while leaving compensation costs unchanged for the firm, it is in the firm's interest to offer compensation in the form of pensions (Ippolito, 1986).

If workers fully understand the rules of their pension plan and the effects of the special tax treatment of pensions, this should increase the demand for pensions at the expense of other forms of retirement saving (Gale, 1998). The evidence does not, however, uniformly suggest that pensions are treated by covered workers as a good substitute for other forms of saving.[2]

Pensions may also be demanded because they provide insurance that is of value to covered workers (Bodie, 1990). Defined benefit (DB) plans pay retirement income in the form of an annuity, which insures covered workers against outliving their retirement savings.[3] Pensions also provide other types of insurance. For example, early retirement benefits insure against wages lost due to disability in an employee's fifties or early sixties (e.g., Nalebuff and Zeckhauser, 1985), and together with early retirement buyout packages also insure against unexpected layoff (Hutchens, 1999; Bellman and Janik, 2007).

In the case of the firm, DB pensions make most sense in the context of a long-term employment relation. Benefits in DB plans are backloaded, with additional work adding more to pension value the closer one is to retirement. Benefits also accrue unevenly, with sharp increases in benefit value as benefits are vested, as one qualifies for early retirement, and as a covered worker qualifies for normal retirement benefits. These patterns, and especially the spikes in benefit accrual at key ages, do not accord with patterns of productivity. While the special roles of early and normal retirement ages make sense in the context of a lifetime employment contract and the retirement of a worker from a prolonged period of employment, they make little sense in the context of a spot labor market where compensation always matches the worker's productivity for the particular period of employment. Indeed, some of the strongest evidence we have supporting the existence of an implicit long-term employment and compensation contract was seen at the time of double-digit inflation in the late 1970s. Retired workers, who could not have contributed to productivity at all, received ad hoc adjustments to their pension benefits after they retired. These increases made up for half the value of lost benefits due to the unexpected increase in the cost of living (Gustman and Steinmeier, 1993a). Although some pension plans have explicit schedules spelling out how benefits are increased in periods of moderate inflation, there was no contractual obligation for the firms to grant these ad hoc increases in benefits for those who had already retired and were finding their benefits eroded by a large and unexpected inflationary shock. Clearly there was some type of implicit contract behind the defined benefit pension.

DB pensions are said to be valued by the firm as a human resource tool. Among other attributes, in their heyday, defined benefit plans were said to be very helpful in regulating retirement. In particular, DB plans created actuarial penalties for working after reaching normal retirement age. These penalties were said to be an important substitute for mandatory retirement provisions that have since been outlawed. A relatively simple mechanism led to a decline in the present value of pension benefits for those who remained at work after reaching normal retirement age. Even though eligible for benefit payments, a person who continued working would not receive any pension payments while still employed. At the same time, there would be no increase in pension benefits to be paid in future years to compensate for the foregone benefit. For example, consider a person whose pension would replace half his wage at normal retirement. By foregoing this year's pension benefit, without enjoying a compensating increase in the yearly benefits paid in all future years, the individual's net wage would effectively be cut in half. Today, in response to changes in age discrimination rules, when a person with a DB plan works another year, even after qualifying for normal retirement benefits, the yearly benefit that will be paid once the person retires is increased in recognition of the foregone benefit. The idea is that the present value of all pension payments will not be reduced for those who choose to work after the normal retirement age.

Researchers took an important empirical step when they documented the patterns of rewards from different defined benefit pensions. Detailed pension plan data were obtained from firms, along with payroll data. Present values of pension benefits were then calculated at alternative ages of exit from the firm.[4] Chapter 10 uses pensions from the Health and Retirement Study to document the incentives from pensions facing those nearing retirement today.

To encourage employees to accelerate their retirement, firms establish eligibility requirements for early retirement based on accumulated age and service. They then enhance the benefits of those who retire upon attaining eligibility for early retirement. Although those who retire early receive lower annual benefits than if they had retired at the normal retirement age, their annual benefits are reduced by a relatively small amount. The effect is to decrease the rate at which the value of the pension benefits they will collect over their lifetime grows with additional work. This reduces the net reward to continued work after the early retirement age and encourages additional retirements at the age of eligibility for early retirement benefits. In addition, some firms add special payments for those whose early retirement age is below age 62, supplementing their retirement incomes until they become eligible for Social Security benefits.

Availability of an early retirement supplement does not lead all workers to retire after qualifying for early retirement. Moreover, availability of an early retirement supplement may encourage some who would otherwise retire before attaining eligibility for early benefits to delay their retirement until they qualify for those benefits. Indeed, anyone who leaves a year or two before qualifying for early retirement benefits would pay a heavy penalty. This increases the number of people retiring at the early retirement age of a defined benefit plan.

Throughout the 1970s and 1980s, firms reduced the ages of eligibility for normal and early retirement benefits. This was one factor behind a trend toward earlier retirements (Anderson, Gustman, and Steinmeier, 1999).

Once the incentives from pensions were carefully measured, studies estimated how pension incentives influence retirement behavior. The sharply discontinuous reward structure produced by a defined benefit pension, especially around the ages of eligibility for early and normal retirement, played an important role in shaping retirement outcomes.[5] Retirements were highest at the ages of eligibility for early and for normal retirement benefits.[6]

These findings were taken as support for the view that pensions are an important tool for regulating productivity (effort) over the course of a long-term employment arrangement (Lazear, 1979, 1983). Specifically, it was argued that workers would increase their effort if wages started out low and then were increased rapidly with time spent on the job. An employee would not want to lose a job that would offer a wage premium in future years if the individual stayed with the firm. Therefore employees would not shirk or give their employer some other excuse to terminate their employment for cause. This type of contract called for paying a wage that fell below productivity in early years of employment but promised a wage above productivity in later years. Thus if the worker maintained employment, in many of the years until normal retirement age was reached the wage would exceed productivity. Finally, to terminate the contract, compensation would be allowed to fall below productivity. The DB pension was considered an efficient mechanism for reducing compensation near the end of the work life. As long as the firm stopped adding to the yearly pension amount after employees reached the age of 65, net earnings would decline sharply once workers reached that age. As a result, the pension would encourage retirement at age 65. The fact that the pension did indeed encourage retirement at this age led the pension to be incorporated in the implicit contract model as a mechanism for terminating employment contract, where otherwise compensation would exceed the productivity of those around retirement age.[7] (A weakness of this view is that many workers with pensions were union members or worked in public sectors jobs, where it is notoriously difficult to dismiss a worker for shirking. Another weakness is that jobs in the union sector and in large firms, which were more likely to offer pensions, do not pay very low wages in early years of employment and then high wages in later years. Wages paid to young workers in unions and large firms are also higher than workers can obtain elsewhere.)

It was also felt that pensions discouraged turnover by workers and thus were useful where firms invested in training. For example, Dorsey, Cornwell, and Macpherson (1998) argue that pensions help those firms that wish to invest heavily in the training of their workers to reduce losses from turnover. Because benefits accrue disproportionately in the years before a worker qualifies for early retirement benefits (see Chapter 10), defined benefit pensions discourage skilled, experienced workers from leaving the firm while they are still highly productive. Most important, DB plans provide a very high reward for a worker nearing retirement age from postponing retirement until becoming eligible for early retirement benefits.[8]

Considering these motivations as a package, pensions were thought to be part of an implicit employment contract between workers and firms. With a long-term employment arrangement where specific training and hiring costs tied a worker to the firm, at any moment in time wages did not always equal productivity. Instead they were equated over the course of the long period of attachment between initial hire and retirement. Unsecured or partially insured future benefits were promised by the firm as part of this long-term employment arrangement.[9]

Implicit pension contracts were not without risk. Firms could violate these contracts by terminating defined benefit plans. Under the law, a firm is obligated to pay a defined benefit pension based only on earnings and employment to date, an obligation termed the legal liability. The effects of possible future employment on the pension do not have to be taken into account. Thus if a worker with a vested defined benefit pension leaves a job today, the benefit owed to the worker at normal retirement age is calculated using the current wage rate and the years of service accrued to date. But if the worker is employed for a full career, the pension paid for each year of tenure is based on final earnings before retirement, rather than on a wage in the middle of the career. Similarly, if a firm terminates the defined benefit plan today or freezes the plan (in particular, adopts a hard freeze where neither a higher wage nor additional service increases the nominal benefit to be received upon retirement), the benefit is the same as if the worker left the plan today. This means there is a windfall to be gained by all firms offering DB plans by terminating the plan immediately. Benefits would be much higher if current workers were allowed to work through to retirement. It is important to understand that the benefit increases disproportionately with continued employment. When a person continues to work under a DB plan that bases benefits on the product of a generosity coefficient (say 2 percent), multiplied by a final average wage and tenure on the job, the total of years of work accrued to date are, in most cases, multiplied by an average of the final few years of earnings (Ippolito, 1986). The firm also has other incentives to violate the implicit pension contract. For example, with additional work, many workers would qualify for special early retirement benefits that are not fully reduced for retiring some time before qualifying for normal retirement benefits.

Reconciling Recent Changes in Pensions with the Theory of Implicit Contracts

Many explanations for pensions argue that the demand for defined benefit plans stems from their usefulness as a human resource tool when jobs are held over many years. Yet the past two decades have witnessed an accelerating decline in the prevalence of defined benefit plans, especially in the private sector. Do the rapid and fundamental changes in pensions, and in particular the sharp decline in defined benefit plans, call into question some of the prevailing explanations for the role of pensions in the labor market and as a vehicle for saving? Or have there been other changes that increased the cost of the implicit contract and made it less useful?

A number of regulatory, legal, and economic changes have reduced the value of DB pensions as a human resource tool. Ippolito (2003) argues that implicit contracts as we knew them were undermined by 1983 IRS regulations that permitted excess assets to revert to the plan sponsor, whatever the reason for the plan termination. He also argues that subsequent government efforts to impose taxes on plan reversions simply raised the cost of exposing workers to financial default risk, which is an inherent property of defined benefit plans.

There are a number of other reasons to believe that even if defined benefit pensions were just as useful as they were thought to be in the past, we would witness a strong trend away from them. To begin with, aside from the taxes on reversions, the costs of DB plans have increased. A likely culprit in this scenario once again is changes in regulations (Clark and McDermed, 1990). The period of stock market boom and then decline, accompanied by legislation that capped funding, has created a funding gap in recent years, which was made worse by interest rate declines that increased the value of pension liabilities (Schieber, 2007; Munnell and Soto, 2007a).

Changes in the composition of employment have also affected the likelihood of finding defined benefit pensions. DB pensions were often found in unionized or large manufacturing firms offering jobs characterized by long-term job attachment. As the market positions of unions and manufacturing eroded, there was less support for DB plans (Gustman and Steinmeier, 1992; Ippolito, 1995). Changes in the composition of employment, and the decline of monopoly power in the hands of union and manufacturing firms, also reduced the prevalence of jobs offering lifetime attachment. The more often workers turn over, and the fewer who have been at the same job for many decades by the time they reach retirement, the less valuable defined benefit plans are to workers. Even though there are many jobs in which workers continue to be attached to their employers for a very long term (Farber, 1998, 2000, 2008; Neumark, Polsky, and Hansen, 1999; Jaeger and Huff Stevens, 1999; Huff Stevens, 2005), the increasing likelihood that a job will not last until retirement lowers the expected benefit under a defined benefit plan.

Changes in pension law encouraged the growth of alternative tax-favored saving vehicles, the 401(k) plan and the individual retirement account. At the same time, changes in financial institutions, such as the rise of low-cost mutual funds, reduced the cost of managing stock portfolios in these alternative vehicles. This reduced the advantage that large firm pension plans, which were predominantly defined benefit, once had from economies of scale in investing. Moreover, once individuals became more familiar with financial markets as greater numbers of small investors were included in mutual funds, many individuals became more comfortable managing their own retirement investments outside of a DB plan, a trend encouraged by the stock market boom of the 1980s and 1990s.

It also has been argued that due to demographic changes, many firms, or at least those firms that are not in decline, may no longer wish to encourage earlier retirement, reducing the demand for DB plans with strong early retirement incentives. Thus Clark and Schieber (2001, 2002, 2004) focus on the looming retirement of the baby boom generation as a reason for the decline in defined benefit plans and the rise of cash balance plans. They posit that increases in the relative demand for older workers have encouraged firms to reduce the reward for early retirement, lengthening the implicit contract. In their view, cash balance plans are a sign that firms no longer wish to subsidize early retirements. These same arguments, that changing demography of the labor market explains the trend to cash balance plans, may also be applied to explain the trend to 401(k) plans.

Although the changing age structure of the workforce may make firms more willing to retain older workers in the face of a declining supply of new workers (Nyce and Schieber, 2002; Lofgren, Nyce, and Schieber, 2003), other labor market changes have also been noticed. For example, long-term employment contracts may be less valuable in an era of rapid technological change (Friedberg and Owyang, 2002; Friedberg, 2001). Thus the course of long-term job attachment continues to be the subject of debate (Huff Stevens, 2005), and the role of changing long-term job attachment in fostering changes in pensions remains unclear.

Another change may make defined benefit plans less effective as a human resource tool of use to firms as a mechanism for terminating a delayed compensation contract that enhances productivity. Benefit accrual rates no longer turn sharply negative after reaching normal retirement age. In contrast to the situation in earlier years, the Equal Employment Opportunity Commission and various court decisions have required that, except for those who have attained an acceptable replacement rate due to very long years of service, after a person qualifies for normal retirement, benefit adjustments must be actuarially fair. Available data clearly show that accruals after qualifying for normal retirement benefits were much more negative in the 1980s (Gustman and Steinmeier, 1989) than in the early 1990s (Gustman and Steinmeier, 2000a). At one time, defined benefit pensions may have been a useful device for terminating an implicit employment contract. Today that is no longer the case.

Recent Trends Raise Questions about Other Explanations for Pensions

Although some changes in pensions can be rationalized without overturning previous theories, other changes call some aspects of these theories into question. Consider the argument that DB pensions were valued because they typically provide an annuity, which defined contribution (DC) plans do not. With the decline of DB plans, a much smaller part of retirement income is annuitized.

Yet there is no reason why 401(k) and other DC pension plans could not offer benefits in the form of an annuity. They could be structured to enjoy the same advantage mandatory DB plans do in avoiding adverse selection into annuities. Indeed, private sector DB plans are becoming less annuitized. The probability that a DB plan will offer a full or partial lump sum to covered workers has increased. Moreover, workers today are more likely to accept a lump sum when offered. Clearly it is not the workers' demand for annuities that accounts for the strong demand for DB plans observed until the mid-1980s. A partial explanation is that the unions and firms, or the actuaries employed by unions and large manufacturing firms, acting on behalf of covered workers, were behind the perception that the workers themselves demanded annuitized benefits. With the decline of unions and manufacturing, the demand for annuitized retirement benefits fell.

Until recently, firms appeared to have adhered to an implicit contract when it came to delivering on the pension promise. They did not terminate defined benefit plans to gain a windfall by reducing their pension liabilities. Even during previous takeover waves, where terminating a defined benefit plan would be a source of cash for those taking over the company, it was rare to see this course of action. Today, however, we are witnessing greater abandonment of DB plans in the labor market. Munnell and Soto (2007a) find that 15 percent of DB plans were frozen between 2000 and 2007. The substitution of cash balance plans for DB plans leaves older workers with a promise of lower benefits.

To understand the causes of recent trends in plan type, it may be useful to consider differences between trends in state and local and private sector pensions.[10] In particular, there is very high pension coverage among state and local workers. Moreover, DB pensions continue to be an important plan type in the state and local sector but are of declining importance in the private sector.

Consider first how some of the factors used to explain the demand for DB pensions might also explain the relative decline in DB plan coverage in the private vis-à-vis the public sector. Changes in unionization are undoubtedly a part of the explanation for greater pension coverage in the state and local sector and for the relative decline in DB coverage in the private compared with the public sector. For decades we have known that public sector unions have a profound effect on both pensions and the wage structure (Gustman and Segal, 1977a, 1977b). Unions prefer defined benefit plans because of the disproportionate influence of older union members, who benefit the most from DB plans. The rapid relative decline in private sector unionization thus can explain some of the decline in the prevalence of DB plans in the private sector but not in the public sector. Similarly, trends in unionization have left state and local governments facing influential unions, while there has been a sharp decline in union employment and employment at large manufacturing establishments, the major sponsors of DB pensions in past years (Gustman and Steinmeier, 1992). The political influence of teachers in nonunion states may also have a similar but weaker effect, strongly mitigating the trend to DC plans in the state and local public sector.

Increasingly effective reporting requirements in the private sector could explain some of the relative decline in DB plans in that sector. Underfunding has become a major issue in the private sector, with firms required to report plan deficits more prominently. State and local plans may be more willing to tolerate defined benefit plans because there is a smaller immediate penalty from underfunding of plans. For many years, state and local governments shifted costs into the future by underfunding their DB plans. DC plans must, of course, be fully funded. Although there is increased pressure on state and local DB plans now that the bill for having habitually shifted costs into the future has come in, defined benefit pensions still provide an opportunity for state and local governments to defer a portion of current labor costs. Similarly, if falling interest rates and changes in stock market prices increased financial pressure on DB plans, increasing pension liabilities while reducing the value of pension assets, a greater ability of state and local plans to live with underfunding may account for the stronger trend away from DB plans in the private sector.

Consider next which factors used to explain the decline in DB pensions could not account for the differential changes observed between the public and private sector, and more generally fall silent on the reasons for the decline in DB pensions in the private sector. Tax advantages of pensions are a major explanation for the overall demand for these plans, but since tax advantages are similar for DB and DC plans, tax advantages from deferred compensation do not explain the demand for DB pensions or the observed changes in the relative demand for DB pensions in favor of the public sector. More specifically, in both sectors pensions defer taxes for covered workers. But there are no tax advantages to state and local governments from providing pensions, while there are for private sector employers. Thus unless the tax advantages of pensions to employers have declined, the tax benefits of deferred compensation cannot explain why the relative demand for pensions, and for defined benefit plans, has declined in the private sector. To summarize, tax incentives have not increased for public versus private sector workers in a way that would favor either increased relative pension coverage in the public sector or the greater relative popularity of DB plans in the public sector.

Higher initial pension coverage among state and local employees is undoubtedly influenced by their higher wages. But wage differentials have not grown in favor of public sector workers so as to explain the continuing support for DB plans in public but not private sector employment.

Theories about regulating shirking on the job would seem to have less force in the public sector. State and local government employees are unlikely to be fired for cause. As a result, withholding a portion of the reward from a pension until retirement as a bond to avert shirking, as DB plans do, is unlikely to provide a strong spur to productivity. Nor do public sector wages rise steeply with job tenure (Gustman and Segal, 1977b). With relatively flat wage profiles in the public sector, we are less likely to find a period just before retirement where wages greatly exceed productivity. This limits the usefulness in the public sector of a mechanism that would encourage retirement once early shortfalls in wages are paid back to the employee, as posited in Lazear's (1979, 1983) theory. This would lead us to expect fewer defined benefit pensions in the public sector. Yet most state and local government workers are covered by pensions, and their pensions are predominantly defined benefit.

Other theories also posit changes that should have generated the same trend away from DB plans in both state and local and private sectors. If DB plans were demanded because workers valued annuities, and for some reason the taste for annuities changed, one should see the same trend away from DB plans in the public and private sector. If demographic changes in the baby boom and bust cycle at first induced a demand for earlier retirements, and only subsequently a demand for later retirements, one should see in both sectors similar trends, first toward and then away from early retirement provisions in DB plans, and perhaps in the frequency of DB plans themselves.

Our findings in the HRS data will add to the puzzle. Although for the HRS population there has also been a trend from DB to DC plans, and the trend is pronounced, it is much weaker than the trend found for younger cohorts. For those in the youngest cohort of the Health and Retirement Study, a sample of respondents ages 51–56 in 2004, two-thirds of their pension wealth continues in the form of defined benefit plans. Only one-third of their pension wealth is due to defined contribution plans.

Certainly, no single explanation accounts for all the changes observed in pensions since the 1960s: the spread of pensions and extension of coverage to more than half the workforce; the initial primacy of DB plans; the fall in DB plans at small firms and absence of new DB plans; the coincidental rise of DC plans; the rise of hybrid plans; and more recently the freezing and sharp decline of DB plans, especially in the private sector. One can construct a theory based on the sequence of changing tax laws; the emergence of a variety of pension regulations; changes in cost structures for pensions, in demographics, and in industry structure; and other factors. But in the face of these many changes, the theoretical basis for explanations of the trends in pensions is much less unified and coherent than was the accepted body of theory that prevailed ten or twenty years ago.

Implications of Imperfect Understanding of Pensions for Life Cycle Models

We noted earlier that the life cycle model—the standard, or at least baseline, model used to explain retirement and saving—can explain many of the retirement outcomes observed in the data. This suggests that many people are making their retirement decisions in accordance with the life cycle model.

Planned saving is designed to smooth consumption over a person's lifetime, and in particular to support consumption after retirement. For reasons explained earlier, the pension is a preferred vehicle for saving. Thus the demand for pensions is seen to have its roots in the need to smooth consumption over the life cycle.

There is a great deal of disagreement, however, as to whether saving decisions are actually made in accordance with the life cycle model. Many argue that patterns of saving, patterns of consumption, including the consumption decline after retirement, and the presumed failure of some to save adequately for retirement are inconsistent with the life cycle model. Others argue that the life cycle model does a much better job in explaining saving once various subtleties are included in the model. These include uncertainty as to length of life, interactions of decisions in the household and the substitution of time for money after retirement, allowance for heterogeneity in time preference, and other considerations that, if ignored, leave the model unable to explain certain patterns in the data.[11]

The life cycle model typically assumes that workers are fully informed about how their benefits will vary with their future employment and that workers are forward looking and plan the future course of their work and savings years ahead. Once again, consistent with the life cycle model, workers seem to be aware of many of the various types of information that are required to calculate outcomes under the life cycle model. For example, workers seem to know roughly how long they will live and make plans that are consistent with these expectations (Hurd and McGarry, 1995, 2002).

Yet when surveys solicit information about pension rules, and especially the effects of these rules on patterns of benefits, many individuals do not know or are misinformed about how their pensions work. A substantial number of people say they do not know what kind of plans they have, at what ages they can or will claim benefits, what their benefits will be worth, and what the effects would be of postponing claiming (Gustman and Steinmeier, 2004b). Many of those who claim to know the answers make errors when describing plan features.

The results reported in Chapters 12 and 13 indicate that many people are adequately prepared for retirement. But a sizable minority is not. Of these, some will fully understand the consequences of their actions. They heavily discount the future and thus are unwilling to save, even though they know what the consequences will be once they retire. Others may not have the self-control to save for retirement, although pensions are one vehicle for overcoming self-control problems (Laibson, 1997; Diamond and Koszegi, 2003). Still other members of this minority either do not understand how much they need to save, perhaps because they are financially illiterate, or do not focus on how failing to save adequately over their lifetime will reduce consumption opportunities in retirement.

Although those with pensions may be imperfectly informed, the early literature on pensions and saving suggests that having a pension may improve one's knowledge of the need for and the value of retirement saving. It also suggests that having a pension may lead to greater total saving as each dollar added to a pension does not cause the covered individual to reduce other forms of saving by an equal dollar amount. Employers with pensions have an interest in schooling their employees about their pensions. They also try to improve their employees' financial literacy and financial planning. Work by Bernheim and Garrett (1996), Bayer, Bernheim, and Scholz (1996), Clark and Schieber (1998), and others suggests that seminars run by firms to encourage greater use of and appreciation for pensions does increase participation in these plans. Because employers who offer pensions may improve their employees' knowledge of the mechanics of and need for retirement saving, Katona (1965) and others recognized that those with pensions could save more in nonpension vehicles than uncovered workers.

Clearly, many covered workers learn about their pensions and understand how their pensions work. Others of those with DB pensions may be entitled to such high benefits in retirement that they have little incentive to learn the detailed mechanics of their pensions. What they know is that their plan will provide an adequate benefit, whatever the precise details. Such persons will leave their firms after qualifying for early retirement benefits while depending on the firm to explain the particulars of the pension at the time of retirement.

Brigitte Madrian and her colleagues suggest that if left to their own devices, many covered workers with 401(k) plans will make poor decisions on whether to participate in the plan as well as on the amount and type of saving to choose. Their choices can be improved if the firm suggests which choice is most reasonable or provides an appropriate default option for those who cannot or will not make a choice. More specifically, Madrian and Shea (2001), Choi, Laibson, Madrian, and Metrick (2004, 2005), and other studies by various combinations of these authors show that choices made by those eligible for 401(k) plans as to whether to participate in a pension, to what extent to participate, how to take full advantage of employer matching contributions, and how to allocate investments depend heavily on the default positions adopted by employers. Pension saving will be highest if there is a default whereby all covered workers are enrolled in the plan unless they choose explicitly not to participate. Similarly, retirement account balances will be higher if the plan has a default contribution rate that is high enough to ensure that the maximum employer contribution is made to the plan. If a plan does not specify defaults, fewer covered workers will participate and pension balances will be lower. It also appears that workers can be coaxed into balancing their contributions among stocks and bonds. If one default is a life cycle fund, participants are more likely to allow the composition of their portfolio to become more conservative as they age. Related work shows that people have a great deal of trouble choosing how to invest when they are given too many investment choices (Brown, Liang, and Weisbenner, 2007; Huberman and Jiang, 2006). Workers will be less confused if the plan allows only a few key choices, rather than a very large number of choices.

These findings were influential in shaping the provisions of the Pension Protection Act of 2006. That act allows firms to take action on behalf of employees who do not explicitly choose whether to participate, how much to save in their pension, and how to invest those funds.

Similarly, some recent work claims that people are relatively well informed about their Social Security benefits (Rohwedder and Kleinjans, 2006) and that many claim optimally in view of their life expectancy (Delavande and Willis, 2007). In contrast, early work on the retirement earnings test showed that people stop working when they earn an amount that triggers a benefit reduction under the earnings test, reducing their benefits by fifty cents for every dollar earned (Gordon and Blinder, 1980; Burtless and Moffitt, 1984). Yet they would have been compensated for their lost benefits. That is, many of those who stopped working once they earned an amount equal to the level that would trigger the earnings test would have had their benefits increased in the future to make up for any benefits lost due to excess earnings. The authors concluded that many people did not understand that future benefits would be increased to compensate for benefits lost to the earnings test. Gustman and Steinmeier (2004b) show that there are many aspects of Social Security rules that covered workers do not understand. They compare respondent reports about Social Security benefits with the amounts they are entitled to by formula and consider benefit reductions under Social Security rules. Some of the findings on the amounts of benefit adjustment from postponed retirement in Delavande and Willis (2007) are consistent with this result. Dominitz, Manski, and Heinz (2001) examined knowledge about Social Security and also found understanding of the rules to be imperfect. The Employee Benefit Research Institute (2004) has done some work along the same lines. Their 2004 Retirement Confidence Survey suggests that most people do not know when they can receive full Social Security benefits and that they do not know that the Social Security retirement age is rising. Finally, work by Lusardi (1999) and others suggests that very few workers have done any formal planning for retirement.

So it appears that some are as knowledgeable as the life cycle model assumes; others are not. Some behave consistently with the life cycle model; others do not. Thus Chan and Huff Stevens (2008) suggest that retirement behavior conforms to the incentives from pensions only for those who understand how their pensions work. Poorly informed agents make their retirement decisions based on their incorrect perceptions of pensions, while well-informed agents follow perceptions that conform to the true incentives created by the plans.

Those people who are imperfectly informed, who are illiterate or semiliterate in financial matters, or who cannot do the calculations visualized by the life cycle model are not protected by actuaries or others who work for their unions to insure that their retirement income will be adequate. Because there are people who, for these and other reasons, cannot or do not maximize in accordance with the standard model, models that assume retirement and saving outcomes are always the result of a well-functioning maximization process with all agents fully informed will have to be revised. That effort is well underway. Newer models are exploring the effects on retirement and saving of imperfect knowledge, nonmaximizing behavior, procrastination, and other behavioral characteristics that are not consistent with current models.

One issue we will consider in the course of our analysis is the question of how knowledge about pensions should be measured and, when measured properly, how it is distributed in the population. In particular, we will ask whether discrepancies between respondent reports and those of their employers are adequate indicators of pension knowledge. Or as Rohwedder (2003) has argued, do employer plan descriptions and respondent reports sometimes fail to agree because of flaws in the procedure used to collect employer-produced plan descriptions and match them with HRS respondents? To answer this question, we will use data from the Health and Retirement Study covering individual respondents over time, matched employer data taken at various times, information for different cohorts, and related information gathered in special experiments and through special supplements. We also will use other special survey data from the Watson Wyatt company that have been matched with administrative data from employers.

Another issue is how to deal with changes in pensions. Virtually all empirical studies of the effects of pensions on retirement and saving that measure pension incentives with employer pension plan descriptions use data from only a single year. They simply assume that a pension plan covering a worker remains unchanged over time.

What is the best way to represent retirement and saving behavior when pensions change as sharply as they have over the past two decades (Gustman and Steinmeier, 1999a; Anderson, Gustman, and Steinmeier, 1999)? When the pension plans do change over time, one cannot rely on pension data from a single year to determine how pension values will vary with continued work.

Indeed, for many people the evidence suggests that their pensions changed just as they approached retirement.

The Health and Retirement Study provides unique data for exploring all of these issues. The next chapters will analyze many dimensions of the HRS pension data.

3

Employment and Retirement in the Health and Retirement Study

This chapter sets the stage for the analysis of HRS pension data. It begins with a description of those sections of the HRS that are relevant to an analysis of pensions, then shifts to data describing the labor market activities and retirement behavior of the HRS population.

The Structure of the HRS

Questions about pensions are largely contained in the labor market section of the HRS, although information on income from pensions is also contained in the assets and income section of the survey. The labor section begins with a Current Population Survey (CPS) style section asking about labor market activities and earnings. It then contains a large set of questions on pensions. Respondents are asked about pensions at both current and previous jobs. Pensions may be traced throughout the respondent's work life. If a respondent mentions a pension in one wave and conveys an intention to collect benefits from that pension at some future time, the HRS asks about the status of that pension in subsequent waves. Using the data from the pension history and throughout the panel, a researcher may piece together a complete picture of pension wealth held over time and the value of pensions at retirement.

Because the HRS population is age 51 or older, the information needed to estimate the value of pensions held at the end of the work life will be particularly reliable. There is no need to project outcomes for decades into the future, as is required when estimating pension wealth for younger workers.[1] Information gathered in the assets and income section on the value of nonpension assets allows the researcher to put into perspective the relative importance of pensions as a source of retirement wealth.

HRS respondents are observed as they transition into retirement. This information allows the researcher to estimate the influence of pensions on retirement and to compare that influence with other factors shaping the retirement decision.[2] Observing the course of pension spend-down also allows the researcher to understand the role played by pensions in the asset decumulation stage that follows retirement.

The Health and Retirement Study began in 1992 with a single cohort born from 1931 to 1941, a group that was 51 to 61 years old at the start of the survey. This original cohort bears the name of the study and is called the *HRS cohort*.[3] At the time this book was written, eight waves of data were available for the HRS cohort, covering the period from 1992 through 2006.

Cohorts representing the population born before 1931 were added to make the HRS panel representative of the U.S. population over the age of 50.[4] New cohorts of respondents 51 to 56 years old are added every six years so that the HRS remains representative of the population over the age of fifty. In the intervening years until a new cohort is added, the minimum age of the HRS population rises above 51.

This study uses data for respondents to three cohorts: the original HRS cohort; the *war babies* cohort (born from 1942 to 1947), and the *early boomer* cohort (born from 1948 to 1953). Members of the last two cohorts were 51 to 56 years old in 1998 and 2004, respectively. To allow calculations of cohort and time effects, those 51 to 56 in the original cohort in 1992 can be used as a baseline group. Thus in addition to reporting results for the full HRS cohort, those 51 to 61 in 1992, we also report results for a subset of that cohort, those 51 to 56 in 1992. Together, then, when searching for differences by cohort, there are three comparable groups available in the HRS, all the same age when they entered the Health and Retirement Study, one in 1992, the others in 1998 and 2004.

To be more precise about the age groups included in this study, it should be noted that age is defined according to the month and year of birth from the pension tracker file provided by the HRS. An individual is included with a cohort if at the time of the interview the respondent's age falls in the specified age range, 51 to 61 in 1992, 51 to 56 in 1992, 51 to 56 in 1998, and 51 to 56 in 2004.[5]

The three HRS cohorts are sampled at different rates. Figure 3.1 shows the number of respondents in each of three HRS cohorts by year of the survey, as well as the number of those in the original HRS cohort who were 51 to 56 in 1992. By the design of the survey, the HRS cohort is much larger than are the other two cohorts. The large size of the original HRS cohort helps to analyze the basic behaviors of interest to those who would use the HRS, while the smaller subsequent cohorts helps to isolate cohort differences in behavioral responses.

The HRS was originally constructed from a sample of households with at least one member who was 51 to 61 in 1992. In some households, one spouse or the other was out of that age range.[6] One group of spouses who were out of age range includes husbands who were older than their 51- to 61-year-old wives in the initial year of the survey in 1992 and were also older than 61. A second group of spouses who were out of age range includes younger wives of men who fell within the HRS age range, that is, women who were younger than 51 in 1992.

Out of age range spouses affect the relative size of each cohort and foster differences in the composition of each cohort. Thus some members of the war

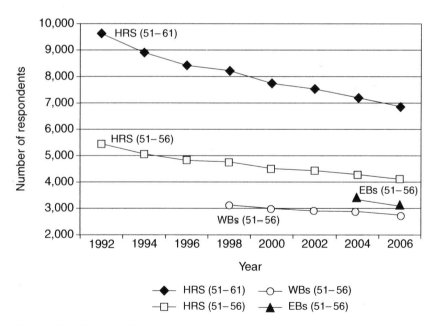

Figure 3.1 Number of respondents by cohort and survey years

baby cohort, those born from 1942 to 1947, did not enter the survey in 1998. Rather, they entered in 1992.[7] In 1992 these younger spouses, who were mainly wives, fell below the lower limit age cutoff for inclusion with the original cohort. Although sampled in 1992, they were given a survey weight of zero from 1992 through 1996. These younger spouses did, however, come within the age range of the war babies, and were included with the war baby sample with a positive weight as of 1998. Because the original cohort has many more members than the war baby cohort, the survey weight of these younger spouses first sampled in 1992 is reduced compared to the weight given to comparable individuals who were first sampled in 1998. Similarly, some members of the early boomer cohort entered the survey before 2004.[8] This makes it particularly important to use respondent level weights in most calculations, particularly when comparing outcomes for members of different cohorts. The respondent level weight is scaled to match the number of individuals in the March CPS. Out of age range spouses also affect outcomes for households. Thus when we examine pension coverage and wealth by household by cohort, out of age range spouses are included, but they do not enter into comparable comparisons based on individuals who are members of the specified cohorts. It is useful to remain aware of the complications created by out of age range spouses.

The number of respondents in the HRS cohort declines over time both because some of those who remain alive leave the survey and because some of the original cohort members die.[9] The unweighted number in the original HRS cohort declined from 12,521 in 1992 to 8,878 in 2006. Given the smaller size of the war baby cohort and its later year of birth, a smaller decline is observed for the younger war babies, from 2,529 in 1998 to 2,237 in 2006. For the early boomers, the corresponding figures are 3,330 in 2004 and 3,035 in 2006.

Employment in the HRS over Time, by Cohort and Sex

The absolute number of respondents who report having a pension in the HRS depends on how many people in the population were targeted for inclusion in the survey, on their rate of participation, on attrition rates over time, on patterns of employment and retirement among respondents, and on rates of pension coverage and other pension outcomes among the employed and the retired. Patterns of employment over the lifetime play a particularly strong role in shaping observed pension changes as a person ages. In this section, we consider patterns of employment and labor market participation by cohort and, given strong underlying differences, patterns of employment and participation by sex.

As they age over time, fewer members of a cohort remain employed. As seen in Figure 3.2, there is a larger decline in employment with age in the HRS cohort since that cohort is observed for a longer time span than other cohorts and because the war baby and early boomer cohorts were younger than the original HRS cohort in the initial year of inclusion in the survey (their average age is 53.5 compared with 56 for the HRS cohort). Unweighted employment in the HRS cohort falls from 6,469 in 1992 to 1,692 in 2006, a decline of 74 percent, while among war babies the number employed falls from 2,278 in 1998 to 1,429 in 2006, a fall of 37 percent. The corresponding figures for the early boomer cohort are 2,447 in 2004 and 2,156 in 2006.

Table 3.1 uses weighted data to report employment in each cohort separately for males and females. It also indicates the percentage of respondents at full-time work in each survey year.[10] The fraction of respondents from the

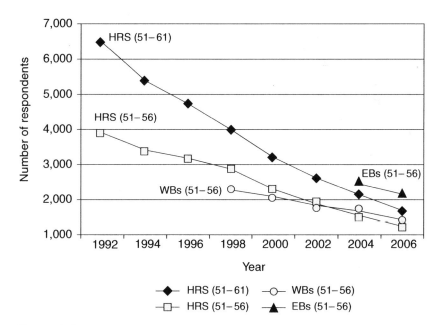

Figure 3.2 Number of respondents working, by cohort

Table 3.1 Percentage of respondents working and working full time, 1992–2006, respondent data (weighted)

Labor force activity, cohort, and sex	1992	1994	1996	1998	2000	2002	2004	2006
% of HRS respondents 51–61 in 1992 who are working	68	63	57	50	43	36	30	26
Males	78	72	67	58	49	42	36	30
Females	59	55	48	42	37	31	26	21
% of HRS respondents 51–56 in 1992 who are working	73	70	67	62	53	44	37	32
Males	83	79	77	71	60	50	43	37
Females	64	61	58	54	46	38	32	27
% of war baby (WB) respondents working (age eligible)	—	—	—	75	73	66	62	55
Males	—	—	—	82	79	73	69	62
Females	—	—	—	70	67	61	55	49
% of early boomer (EB) respondents working (age eligible)	—	—	—	—	—	—	75	73
Males	—	—	—	—	—	—	79	79
Females	—	—	—	—	—	—	71	67

% of HRS respondents 51–61 in 1992 who are working full time	59	53	46	38	28	23	17	13
Males	72	65	57	47	33	29	22	16
Females	47	42	36	30	23	17	14	9
% of HRS respondents 51–56 in 1992 who are working full time	64	61	57	51	39	30	23	17
Males	77	73	69	61	45	38	29	21
Females	52	50	45	41	32	23	18	13
% of WB respondents who are working full time	—	—	—	68	62	55	51	44
Males	—	—	—	77	71	66	60	51
Females	—	—	—	59	54	46	43	36
% of EB respondents who are working full time	—	—	—	—	—	—	66	63
Males	—	—	—	—	—	—	74	72
Females	—	—	—	—	—	—	58	54

HRS cohort working falls from 68 percent in 1992 to 26 percent in 2006, reflecting the course of retirements. The fraction of HRS cohort members who are employed and working full time declines even more steeply. As expected, there are less rapid declines in the younger cohorts.

Comparing employment data for the initial year when members of each cohort entered the survey, and confining the comparison to those who were 51 to 56 in the initial year, the employment rate of men fell from 83 percent in 1992 to 79 percent in 2004, while the employment rate increased for 51- to 56-year-old women from 64 percent to 71 percent. These changes narrowed the gap in the employment rate between men and women from 19 percentage points in 1992 to 8 percentage points in 2004. The analogous gap in employment at full-time work between men and women is wider. It falls from 25 percentage points in 1992 to 16 percentage points in 2004. The very rapid increase in labor market participation and full-time work by women in younger HRS cohorts will be accompanied by major trends in pensions.

Trends in Retirement Status, 51- to 56-Year-Old Men and Women

Comparable data on retirement, partial retirement, and nonretirement by cohort are presented in Table 3.2. Partial retirements change only slightly for both groups over time. The rates of full retirement are about 4 percentage points higher for men and 7 percentage points lower for women in 2004 than in 1992. The gap in retirement rates between men and women shrinks from 19 percentage points in 1992 to 8 percentage points in 2004.

Disaggregating Labor Force Status over Time

Table 3.3 further disaggregates the data to examine trends in retirement for subgroups of the population. Participation is measured by the labor force participation rate, the employment rate, and the rate of full-time employment. All three participation rates are higher for white males than for Hispanic males, which are higher than participation rates for black males. For females, whites have higher participation than do blacks, who have higher participation than do Hispanics. Measures of labor market participation and employment increase for those who are married and decline slightly for those who are unmarried. Participation rates are lower among younger cohorts for those with less than a high school education. Union and nonunion members, who are by

Table 3.2 Retirement status based on the number of hours worked per year for anyone ages 51–56 in 1992, 1998, and 2004 (weighted)

Retirement status	1992 survey			1998 survey			2004 survey		
	Males	Females	Both	Males	Females	Both	Males	Females	Both
Retired	17	36	27	18	30	25	21	29	25
Partially retired	6	12	9	5	11	8	5	13	9
Not retired	77	52	64	77	59	68	74	58	66
Number of observations	2,519	2,930	5,449	1,204	1,917	3,121	1,466	1,850	3,316

Table 3.3 Employment among subgroups of the population, ages 51–56, by year (weighted)

Subgroups	Labor force			Employed			Employed full time		
	1992	1998	2004	1992	1998	2004	1992	1998	2004
All	78	79	81	73	75	75	64	68	66
Males	88	86	86	83	82	79	77	77	74
Females	69	73	76	64	70	71	52	59	58
White	80	81	83	75	78	78	65	70	69
Males	90	87	88	85	84	83	80	79	77
Females	70	76	78	65	72	73	52	61	60
Black	72	70	75	65	66	65	57	60	58
Males	73	75	74	65	70	62	59	65	58
Females	71	67	76	66	63	67	56	56	58
Hispanic	69	71	73	61	64	65	54	57	54
Males	84	87	80	75	76	70	70	73	63
Females	55	59	67	48	55	61	40	44	46
Other	83	74	76	75	66	69	68	64	63
Males	90	89	83	84	79	76	78	76	75
Females	76	62	69	67	56	61	59	54	52
Married	78	80	82	73	76	77	64	68	67
Not married	79	78	78	72	73	70	64	66	62
Less than high school	68	59	62	59	54	52	52	47	43
High school grad	76	78	76	72	74	71	62	68	62

Some college	82	83	84	78	79	77	68	69	68
College grad	87	88	86	84	85	81	73	78	72
More than 16 years	92	92	91	88	88	88	80	80	77
Union	*	*	*	*	*	*	92	94	92
Not union	*	*	*	*	*	*	86	91	89
Large firm	*	*	*	*	*	*	92	94	91
Medium firm	*	*	*	*	*	*	92	93	90
Small firm	*	*	*	*	*	*	81	82	83
Missing firm	*	*	*	*	*	*	75	92	90
Public employer[a]	*	*	*	*	*	*	90	90	87
Private employer	*	*	*	*	*	*	87	89	87
Employee	*	*	*	*	*	*	89	92	90
Self-employed	*	*	*	*	*	*	79	80	78

a. When first interviewed, respondents were asked whether they had ever worked for the federal, state, or local government and the start and end date of such jobs. They were first asked directly whether they were working for the government at the time of the survey in 2006. Status as a public/private employee in 2004 is estimated from two sources. First for respondents who reported working at the same employment in 2006, the information is taken back to 2004. For the new interviewees, the public/private employee index is constructed by comparing the start date and end date of any reported government jobs with the start and interview dates of their current job in 2004. Respondents who were reinterviewed in 2004 and were retired or changed jobs since their 2004 interview are not included in the sample.

* These questions are asked only of those who report they are employed.

definition employed and in the labor force, do not show strong trends in full-time work. Nor are there strong trends in full-time work associated with firm size or employment status.

Employment-Population Ratios in the HRS versus CPS over time

Given the potential bias from attrition in the HRS, it is useful to compare employment population ratios in the HRS with rates from the Current Population Survey. To anticipate the results, we note that the trends are similar between the two surveys. Figures 3.3 and 3.4 report employment-population ratios for men in various age groups in the HRS and CPS, respectively. As above, for men in their early fifties, the employment-population ratio declines slightly between 1992 and 2004. For those in their late sixties, the employment-population ratio increases.[11]

Notice that the employment-population ratio increases in the HRS for those in their late sixties. In 1998, those 65 to 69 would have been born from 1929 through 1933. The only observations available for this age group in 1998 are from the HRS, which only includes those born from 1931. Thus the

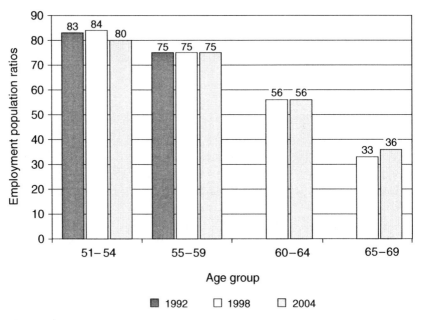

Figure 3.3 Employment population ratios for males in HRS data (not weighted)

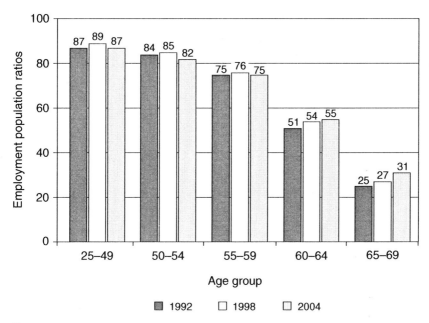

Figure 3.4 Employment population ratios for males in CPS data (not weighted)

group of those 65 to 69 in 1998 from the HRS data is older than the group labeled as 65 to 69 in the CPS. Nevertheless, those 65 to 69 in the HRS sample have a higher employment-population ratio than do those from the CPS sample. Those 65 to 69 in 2004 were born from 1935 through 1939. Thus all of this group comes from the 1992 HRS sample. Again, the employment-population ratio is higher for those from the HRS sample than for the CPS sample. In both cases, a likely explanation is attrition from the sample, where those who would have a lower employment-population ratio in their late sixties are more likely to have left the HRS sample over the twelve years between 1992 and 2004 than are those who would have been more likely to be employed in their late sixties. We return to the topic of attrition from the sample below.

Comparisons for women can be seen in Figures 3.5 and 3.6. They are consistent with the strong trend to increased labor force participation by older women. Given the strong trends in pension coverage and plan type to be seen in the data below, the very slight differences in trends in employment-population ratios between the HRS and CPS are unlikely to strongly influence our findings regarding trends in pensions.

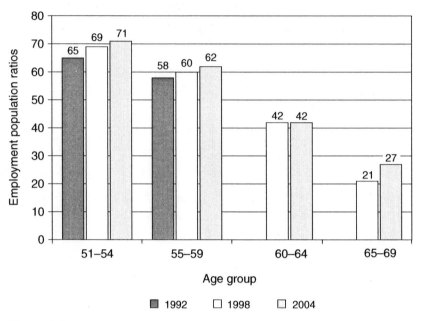

Figure 3.5 Employment population ratios for females in HRS data (not weighted)

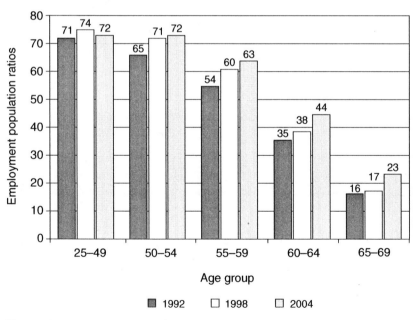

Figure 3.6 Employment population ratios for females in CPS data (not weighted)

Attrition in the HRS by Initial Labor Market and Pension Status

To examine the effects of attrition on trends in the HRS, Table 3.4 reports retention rates in the survey as of 2006 for members of the original HRS cohort. Specifically, the table reports the probability of attrition from the 1992 sample by employment status in 1992 (not working, working, working full time, working part time) and by pension coverage in 1992. The table calculates the number in the sample in 1992, the number of those retained in 2006, and the ratio of column 2 to column 1. Note that attrition includes mortality.

There is an 11 percentage point difference in the retention rate in the survey between those who were working in 1992 and those who were not. Starting with row 1, column 3, 59 percent of respondents who were not working in 1992 were interviewed in 2006, with the remaining 41 percent not interviewed. Among those who were working in 1992, 70 percent were interviewed in 2006. Retention rates are close whether the respondent was working full time or part time in 1992.

Among those initially employed, retention is 3 percentage points higher for those employed with a pension in the initial survey year compared with employees without a pension. Seventy-one percent of respondents working with a

Table 3.4   Attrition from 1992 to 2006 based on employment and pension coverage in 1992

Employment status in 1992	Number in 1992 (1)	Retained in 2006[b] (2)	Ratio (3)
Not working	3,149	1,855	0.59
Working	6,469	4,498	0.70
Working full time[a]	5,573	3,879	0.70
Working part time	901	623	0.69
Working with pension	3,597	2,558	0.71
Working full time with pension	3,376	2,393	0.71
Working without pension	2,872	1,940	0.68
Working full time without pension	2,194	1,483	0.68

a. Respondents working fewer than 100 hours per year are included in the not working category. Full-time status is measured by combining reported hours of work and self-reported retirement status. See Chapter 3, note 10.

b. Attrition includes mortality.

Table 3.5   Retention in the HRS between 1992 and 2006 by gender, 1992
employment, and pension status

Employment and pension status	Males	Females	Both
Not working	0.47	0.65	0.59
Working	0.67	0.72	0.70
Working full time	0.67	0.73	0.70
Working part time	0.63	0.72	0.69
Working with pension	0.69	0.74	0.71
Working full time with pension	0.69	0.74	0.71
Working without pension	0.64	0.71	0.68
Working full time without pension	0.65	0.69	0.68

pension in 1992 were still in the survey by 2006, while 68 percent of those working without a pension in 1992 were retained in the survey.

Retention rates vary with employment status much more strongly for men than for women. According to the data in Table 3.5, more than half the men who were not working in 1992 are missing from the sample by 2006. In contrast, a third of the women who were not working in 1992 are missing from the sample by 2006. Among those who were working, two-thirds of men are retained in the sample, while 72 percent of women are retained through 2006.

Among those who are working, men who were working without a pension in 1992 are about 5 percentage points more likely to be lost to attrition than are men working with a pension. Women without a pension are 3 percentage points more likely to be lost to attrition than are women with a pension.[12] Working full time rather than part time increases retention for men more than it does for women, but again the differences are not very large.

The weights used in the HRS poststratify to the March CPS each year, on average adjusting for differences in mortality and attrition among groups determined by birth cohort of the respondent and spouse, respondent gender, and race/ethnicity. (A description of sampling weights can be found at http:// hrsonline.isr.umich.edu/meta/tracker/desc/wghtdoc.pdf.) These weights do not adjust for differences in attrition according to differences in initial labor market status and pension coverage. As we have seen, some of the difference in attrition associated with initial labor market and pension status is closely associated with the demographic factors, such as gender, that are used by the HRS in constructing weights. To that extent, the HRS weights should be adequate.

Otherwise, there will be some remaining bias from attrition associated with initial employment and pension status.

Given the information in the CPS and limited cell sizes, it is not possible to adjust further for these factors. But one should be aware that any remaining bias might affect estimates of pension coverage. In particular, there may be some overstatement of pension coverage among those in the war baby cohort. This reflects the delay between the time the screener sample was administered and when the survey of new members of the war baby cohort was given. There were two screener samples administered by the HRS, one in 1992 and another in 2004. The screener sample covers the full population. Each household is asked about the age of each its members. Household members falling in the proper age range are then included with the corresponding cohort. In the first wave of the survey, the sample is fresh right after a screener sample and not subject to attrition. So none of the HRS cohort, and only part of the early boomer cohort (those first sampled in earlier years as younger spouses), is subject to attrition. But in 1998, the screener sample used to find members of the war baby cohort was 6 years old. Thus the members of the war baby cohort, either those who were younger spouses of members of the HRS cohort first included in 1992 or those first sampled in 1998, had been screened six years earlier. As such, attrition would take its toll even in the first wave of the survey. Because attrition is more likely among those without a pension, those remaining in the sample are more likely to come from those who had a pension, leading to an overstatement of pension coverage, especially for those in the war baby cohort.

Retirement Trends and Trends in Pensions

Explanations for changes in pensions are somewhat in conflict. Consider first conflicting explanations on the firm side. One set of explanations focuses on the retirement of the baby boomers. As boomers retire, there are too few workers from young cohorts available to replace them. Accordingly, firms adopt or change personnel policies to retain older workers in the face of a declining supply of new workers (Nyce and Schieber, 2002; Lofgren, Nyce, and Schieber, 2002). One example of such a personnel policy change is presented by Clark and Schieber (2001, 2002). They argue that the changing demography of the labor market has encouraged firms to substitute cash balance plans for defined benefit (DB) plans. Firms are said to adopt the cash balance plan because they

Table 3.6 Retirement status of males by age and year, using hours per year to define retirement (weighted)

Age	Not retired (%)			Partially retired (%)			Fully retired (%)		
	1992	1998	2004	1992	1998	2004	1992	1998	2004
51–56	77	77	74	6	5	5	17	18	21
56–62	66	63	61	7	9	9	27	28	30
61–67	—	34	37	—	13	13	—	53	50
65–67	—	22	25	—	15	15	—	63	61

Note: "Not retired" are working full time. "Partially retired" are working part time. Refer to note 10 for the full definition of these two categories.

no longer wish to subsidize early retirements. A contrasting argument on the firm side attributes the decline in DB pensions to technological change, such as increased computerization. Such changes are said to increase the demand for younger workers, who have more computer skills (Friedberg, 2001; Friedberg and Owyang, 2002). Both hypotheses generate the same prediction for pension changes: DB plans should be disappearing. But they generate the opposite predictions for retirement. If firms want more older workers, retirement rates will decline. If firms want their workers to have a high degree of computer literacy, retirement rates will increase.

Neither of these hypotheses is consistently supported by the retirement data. Rather, as seen in Table 3.6, trends for men in their fifties, their early sixties, and their late sixties were not uniform between 1992, 1998, and 2004. For those in their fifties in each of these years, there was a decrease in work over the period.[13] But those in their mid- and late sixties increased work effort. Thus at first blush, the trends in retirement are not nearly consistent enough to help in resolving conflicting explanations for trends in pensions. More detailed analyses of retirement behavior can help to resolve these apparent conflicts—for example, changes in Social Security rules encourage delayed retirement for those over 65 (Gustman and Steinmeier, 2009)—but one should be very cautious when attempting to determine the cause of trends.

Conclusions

When analyzing differences in outcomes using the HRS sample, in cross-section data, over time and among cohorts, the analyst must account for the complex sampling scheme of the HRS. The initial cohort covers a wider age range than do later cohorts. The cohorts differ in size. The out of age range sample from the original HRS cohort is carried over into later cohorts but primarily the war babies cohort, leading to a disproportionate representation for younger wives in that cohort. Attrition from the survey varies by employment status, pension status, and demographic measures. The screener samples containing a representative sample of the U.S. population are not fresh when samples are drawn for some cohorts, again primarily the war babies cohort, though they are fresh when other cohorts are drawn.

In analyzing pension outcomes, it will be important to weight observations from different cohorts appropriately. But in some circumstances, adjustment of weights to reflect attrition will not be adequate. One should also be careful to analyze observations from different cohorts separately and to analyze separately outcomes for men and women within cohorts. As long as pension outcomes are analyzed among those who are employed, rather than among all observations in the HRS, attrition from the sample would appear to have only limited effects on any conclusion reached about pensions.

Having set the stage with a discussion of the underlying sample, the next chapter begins with a description of the various types of pension data in the HRS.

4

Pension Data in the Health and Retirement Study

A number of features of the Health and Retirement Study make it a unique source of information for describing the course of pension outcomes, especially for the retirement age population. Respondents with pensions at their current job describe their plan(s) in detail. They provide updates on pensions from previous jobs that are still active. From the panel, that is, the answers to questions posed to the same respondent every two years, it can be seen how the number of pensions held by each respondent changes, how the rules of each plan change, and how the value of each continuing pension accumulates over time. Those who leave a firm where they held a pension describe in detail what happened to the pension when they left. This allows pensions to be traced through the years after the respondent leaves the firm and into retirement. By making comparisons for those of the same age, it is possible to isolate trends in pensions over time. The structure of the HRS also allows the researcher to compare expectations regarding the pension elicited before retirement with the values realized after retirement. Analogously, it is possible to compare respondents' understanding of their pensions, as reflected in their answers to detailed questions about their plans' features and values, with comparable outcomes generated from plan descriptions obtained from their employers. Comparisons of plan features and plan values from respondents and firms, and analyses of changes in pensions over time provided by respondents and obtained from employer plan descriptions, improve understanding of the pensions held by respondents and of respondents' knowledge about their pensions.

List of Pension Sequences in the Survey

Respondents' reports about their pensions are available in each wave of the HRS. As of the writing of this book, these include respondent self-reports from eight waves of the HRS cohort (born from 1931 to 1941), five waves of war babies (born from 1942 to 1947), and two waves of early boomers (born from 1948 to 1953).

When respondents first enter the survey, they are asked about pensions at their current job. If they are already retired when they first enter the survey, they are asked about pensions on their last job. Whether currently employed or retired, respondents are asked about pensions from up to three previous jobs—the most recent jobs held for at least five years that preceded their current job or, if not currently employed, preceding the last job they already reported on.

In their second and future waves in the survey, those who report they are continuing in the same job they held in the last wave are asked a number of questions to update information about their pensions. If they report that a pension has changed since the last interview or that they now are covered by a pension for the first time, they are asked the same detailed set of questions about the revised pension as is asked of new respondents when first reporting pension coverage.

Respondents who report that they have left a job at which they had previously reported having a pension are asked a set of questions to update knowledge about the pension from the old job.[1] Respondents are then asked what they did with the pension: withdrew the money, rolled it over into an IRA, left it to accumulate in the old plan, converted it to an annuity, expect future benefits, are receiving benefits, or received a cash settlement. These are followed by questions asking about the amount of the benefits received in each form and the dates of the reported action the respondent has taken.

Another sequence of questions is triggered by a preload to the survey. The preload takes account of the respondent's history of pension coverage and the disposition of old pensions reported in previous waves of the survey, allowing the current wave of the survey to update information on pensions from previous jobs that at last report were not cashed out, lost, or in pay status. Sometimes we will refer to the questions based on the preload as the "old pension sequence." The questions once again inquire about the fate of those pensions; about relevant values, including the amounts remaining in accounts, or pension payments; and, if the status of the plan changed from the last wave, the

dates when the respondent began collecting from the plan, rolled it over, annuitized it, or in some other way changed its status. To begin the "old pension sequence," the 1996 survey asked respondents a round-up question about plans
from last or previous jobs or other jobs held prior to the 1996 interview, where it
was previously reported they were expecting some future benefits or that the
assets in a pension account run by a previous employer were left under the care
of that employer.[2] Respondents were asked whether they were still expecting
future benefits; whether the account was still accumulating; whether they were
receiving benefits at the time of reporting; or whether they received a cash settlement, rolled the pension over into an IRA, converted it to an annuity, or
withdrew the money. Those who reported they were still expecting future benefits or that their account was still accumulating were asked again about the
status of those plans in 1998, 2002, and 2004. Basically, as long as a respondent's claim on a plan continues to be active, the respondent is asked in later
waves about the status of the plan.

Table 4.1   Available pension information by sources and survey year

Source	1992	1994	1996	1998	2000	2002	2004	2006
1. Current job								
Self-report	X	X	X	X	X	X	X	X
SPDs	X	—	—	X	—	—	X	X
2. Last job								
Self-report	X	X	X	X	X	X	X	X
SPDs	X	—	—	X	—	—	X	—
3. Previous job								
Self-report	X	X	X	X	X	X	X	X
SPDs	X	—	—	X	—	—	X	—
4. Job terminated since last wave	—	X	X	X	X	X	X	X
5. Follow-up on dormant pensions	—	—	X	X	—	X	X	X
6. Pension income from previous job(s)	X	X	X	X	X	X	X	X
7. Pension characteristics module	—	—	—	—	—	—	X	—
8. Experiment Y module	—	—	—	—	—	—	X	X
9. Supplementary questions	—	—	—	—	—	—	X	X

In the assets and income section of the survey, respondents are asked about the form and size of any pension income they are receiving. Special questions are also asked about pensions on a one-time basis. Most of these questions are meant to improve the identification of pension plan type.

Different types of pension information available in the HRS are summarized in Table 4.1. From this information it is possible to determine the characteristics of each pension and to value the pensions.

Information Obtained from Employer-Provided Pension Plan Descriptions

Beginning in 1992, the Health and Retirement Study collected names and addresses of respondents' employers and used that information to obtain summary plan descriptions (SPDs), which are detailed documents produced by firms describing each of their pension plans. SPDs were collected in the year following the baseline survey, in 1993, 1999, and 2005–2006. As a first step, the employer is contacted and asked for the pension plan description. When interviewers from the HRS contact an employer to request information about a pension plan, the firm is not given the name of the respondent because respondent confidentiality must be maintained. Plan descriptions are also collected from a number of other sources.[3] The Department of Labor has provided plan descriptions when they were on file and has also provided attachments to schedule B of Form 5500. Schedule B, filed annually with the Department of Labor, provides a detailed description of the pension plans. Plan descriptions for government employees are often available on the Web. In the 2004 survey, in addition to collecting plan descriptions from employers, the Department of Labor, or the Web, HRS began asking respondents to obtain SPDs from their employers. Last, plans are being formed to enhance the collection of plan descriptions from other forms filed with the Labor Department that summarize changes adopted in plans, as well as forms filed with the IRS.

Including plan descriptions available from files at the Department of Labor, using the 1993 employer survey, of the 4,344 HRS respondents who reported having a pension at a current job in 1992, there was an employer plan description for 2,929 of them, or 67 percent of respondents.[4] By 1999, firms were more reluctant to cooperate. In the 1999 employer survey, there were 1,754 respondents with a coded plan from a current job, with 3,347 reporting a pension, for 52 percent of respondents.[5] From the 2005 employer survey, there were 1,567 with an employer-provided pension plan description, out of 3,200 who reported having a pension, for a total of 49 percent. The HRS expects eventually to have pension plan descriptions for 56 percent of those with a pension in 1998 and 73 percent of those with a pension in 2004.

Gustman and Steinmeier (2004b) use data from 1992 to estimate the relationship of the probability of having a matched SPD to a number of individual and firm characteristics. Blacks, those with more schooling, homeowners, and those with a short planning horizon, long tenure, or a job in the nonmanufacturing sector are more likely to have a match.[6] Kapteyn et al. (2006) also find evidence of nonrandom matching of employer-provided pension SPDs for the original HRS cohort. More highly educated workers with a pension are more likely to have a matched SPD.[7]

When the firm has more than one pension plan, one must decide which employer plan description corresponds to which respondent. Where there is more than one plan, worker and job characteristics are used to facilitate matching. Account is taken of the respondent's job title, job description, union status, hire date, quit date, number of hours worked, firm size, and whether the worker is hourly or salaried.

In sum, the HRS provides information on pensions from a number of sources, for different cohorts, and over time. The wide variety of pension information provided by the HRS allows a user to evaluate pensions held at current jobs, at past jobs, and cumulatively over the lifetime. This information allows behavioral researchers to investigate how pensions and incentives from pensions are related to saving or retirement outcomes. These pension data also allow a user to compare respondent reports of pension characteristics and values with plan descriptions produced by employers, improving understanding of reporting error made by respondents, and related questions of economic literacy and comprehension.

For those readers who would like additional details on the pension information collected by the HRS, there are six appendixes to this chapter with additional information. The next conceptual step, undertaken in Chapter 5, is to examine pension coverage in the HRS.

Appendix 4.1: Tracing Pensions in the Panel

Start and end dates are recorded for each job and for pensions, allowing the jobs and the pensions on those jobs to be matched to the respondent. If a respondent has left a job by the first wave of the survey, there is an additional question asking when s/he left. If a respondent was employed at the time of the first wave, the employment history can be traced through the panel (the series of responses given every two years), with date of termination observed in the wave after the respondent left the job.

Start and end dates are then used by the HRS to identify pensions from previous jobs. Respondents are asked about the status of those pensions from jobs that the respondent had already left in previous waves but that were not yet in pay status, lost, cashed out, rolled over into an IRA, or annuitized. Using preloads that identify these dormant pensions, the respondent is quizzed about the fate of the pension, including whether it remains viable in the current wave. If it is not currently viable, the respondent is asked what happened to it and when. To create a pension history, each plan can be traced from the time it was first noted through the time when it goes into pay status or when the plan is cashed out, rolled over into an IRA, or taken as or used to purchase an annuity.

Unfortunately, questions about previously held pensions were not asked in every wave. In addition, in some cases the preload was not complete. In these situations, where a number of waves are skipped before the respondent is again asked about the old pension, the respondent is asked whether there were any changes in the status of the pension in the period since the status of the pension was last reported. By using the longitudinal information in the survey, it is then possible to identify all older pensions.

In addition, everyone who reported a pension at a current job and who in a subsequent wave reports leaving that job is asked what happened to the pension from the job they just left. Some will indicate immediately that the pension was in pay status, cashed out, lost, or rolled over. If the pension falls into one of these categories, it is no longer classified as dormant, and this is the last time the respondent is asked about the pension in the labor section. But if the respondent indicates that the pension was left with the old employer, the respondent will be asked about that pension in subsequent waves until its fate is resolved. If the plan is defined contribution (DC), the survey will ask about the balance.

Software developed in the course of our work for the HRS, called the pension tracker file, traces each plan reported in the labor section through each wave of the survey. The pension tracker file is described in the appendix to this book, as is other software that has been developed to aid those who have a need to understand pension coverage, plan values, or other aspects of the pensions covering HRS respondents. The software used to generate the pension tracker file is available on the HRS Web site.

Appendix 4.2: Further Details on Matching Employer Pension Plan Descriptions with Respondents

This appendix is meant to provide additional information for those readers who are interested in a more detailed discussion of the matching of employer summary plan descriptions to respondents. For each year in which employer plan descriptions were collected, Table 4.2 shows the number of respondents reporting a pension, the number of respondents with an SPD, and the ratio of the two. Columns 1, 4, and 7 (No. of Rs self-reporting a plan) report the frequency with which respondents report coverage by the indicated plan type. Columns 2, 5, and 8 (No. of Rs with an SPD) report the frequencies at which the indicated plan types are observed in the employer-provided plan descriptions. Thus from the figure in the first row and column, 1,857 respondents reported having a defined benefit (DB) plan only in 1992. From the first row, second column, for 1,342 of the respondents with a matched SPD, the SPDs collected suggested that the respondent had a DB plan only.

The figures in columns 3, 6, and 9 of the bottom row of the table can be taken as a match rate indicating how many respondents who reported having a pension have a matched employer plan description. (To obtain a match rate for 1992, we must first subtract 22 from the 2,929 people in column 2, representing the 22 respondents who had a matched SPD but reported they were not covered by a pension.) However, the ratios in the rows above the bottom one should not be read as indicating a match rate conditional on the respondent's reported plan type. Although in row 1 there are 1,857 respondents who report having a DB plan only, and from column 2, row 1, we see that 1,342 of all the respondents to the HRS had a plan match that turned out to include only a DB plan, these counts do not refer to the same respondents. For some of the 1,857 respondents who reported having a DB plan only, the matched plan may be DC, or their firm may provide both a DB and a DC plan. And some of the respondents whose matched plan is DB only may have reported having a DC plan or both plan types. Some of the tables explored in later chapters do restrict results to observations where respondent and employer plan descriptions correspond as to plan type, but that is not the case in Table 4.2.[8]

Consider the match rates reported in the last row of Table 4.2, columns 3, 6, and 9. In 1992, the HRS was likely to find an SPD in two-thirds of the cases, with matched SPDs in roughly half the cases in 1998 and 2004.

We also have created an employer pension tracker file, described in the appendix to this book, which contains relevant information about the employer-provided pension data for current, previous, and last jobs for 1993, 1999, and the 2005 samples of pensions at jobs that were held after the last employer survey. The first three rows in Table 4.3 show the number of respondents with one or more pension plans, those who were eligible, and the number of SPDs collected from all sources. Summary plan descriptions were also collected for previous and last jobs. Here the

Table 4.2 Availability of employers' plan descriptions by respondents' report of plan type for employees with a pension plan on current job

Plans	1992 survey			1998 survey[a]			2004 survey[a]		
	No. of Rs self-reporting a plan	No. of Rs with an SPD	Column 2/ Column 1	No. of Rs self-reporting a plan	No. of Rs with an SPD	Column 5/ Column 4	No. of Rs self-reporting a plan	No. of Rs with an SPD	Column 8/ Column 7
R has DB plan only	1,857	1,342	72%	1,288	703	55%	934	608	65%
R has DC plan only	1,289	699	54%	1,243	545	44%	1,482	496	33%
R has combination plan	1,089	806	74%	745	406	54%	695	389	56%
Other[b]	108	82	76%	71	100	1.41%	89	74	83%
R has a DB plan	2,952	2,314	78%	2,036	1,212	60%	1,635	1,157	71%
R has a DC plan	2,384	1,525	64%	1,997	1,420	71%	2,192	1,178	54%
Total	4,344	2,929	67%	3,347	1,754	52%	3,200	1,567	49%

a. In 1998 and 2004, results in columns 4 and 7 do not include respondents (Rs) who report a firm size of fewer than twenty-five employees at all locations.

b. The "other" category includes those who reported "don't know" (DK) or refused to answer (RF) on their second or third plan, 0/DK/RF on the number of plans, DK/RF for the type of plan, or did not have a pension plan but did have a coded SPD. In column 5 and column 8, those who had a matched employer plan but were from firms that reported having fewer than twenty-five employees are included under the "other" category.

Table 4.3   Match rates for employer plan description by job type and year of respondent survey

Respondents/plan descriptions	1992 survey	1998 survey	2004 survey
Current job			
No. of employees with pension	4,345	3,899	3,558
No. of eligible employees	—	3,460	3,293
No. of employees with matched SPDs	2,907	1,717	1,567
Match rate employees with pension	67%	44%	44%
Match rate for eligible employees	—	50%	48%
Previous job			
No. of employees with pension	2,862	708	—
No. of employees eligible	—	708	—
No. of employees with matched SPDs	977	257	—
Match rate	34%	36%	—
Last job			
No. of employees with pension	1,371	228	—
No. of employees eligible	—	183	—
No. of employees with matched SPDs	905	74	—
Match rate	66%	40%	—

Notes: Only employees are included in the survey of firms that collected summary plan descriptions. Those working in establishments or firms with at least twenty-five employees are deemed eligible for inclusion in the employer survey that collected summary plan descriptions. Firms with fewer than twenty-five employees were not included in the employer survey. In the 2004 survey, respondents' plan documents are included. Included in plan documents are statements/SPDs in the respondent's possession and reports collected from sources other than the respondent. There are twenty-two additional cases in the 1992 HRS survey for which a matched pension plan is provided but where the respondent did not report having a current pension. There are fifty-nine additional cases in the 1998 survey with matched plans who either reported zero for the number of plans or who denied having a current pension.

match rate is seen in Table 4.3 to be much lower than for current jobs. Data are not yet available for last and previous jobs for the early boomers.

Appendix 4.3: Identifying Plans When Respondents Report Having Both Plan Types

An issue arises when respondents report having both a DB and a DC plan from the same job. The problem is deciding which of the two plans types the respondent is talking about when asked to discuss the most important plan. Given the development and spread of the 401(k) plan in the late 1980s, one would expect that those older workers reporting on their most important pension held in the 1990s, and perhaps even later, would consider their DB plan to be their most important plan.

To determine which plan type is most important in HRS data, we have examined the data for respondents who have matched plan data and have reported both/combination plans. In 1992, about 25 percent of all respondents (1,089/4,344)

Table 4.4 Number of respondents with matched plans and both plans in the core in 1992, 1998, and 2004 by importance of plan type

Reported plan type and importance of plan type	1992	1998	2004
Reported combination/ both plans	437	208	175
Present value of expected DB benefits ≥ DC balance	81%	66%	72%
	(353/437)	(137/208)	126/175
DB: most important	84%	60%	68%
	(295/353)	(82/137)	86/126
DC: most important	9%	12%	9%
	(31/353)	(17/137)	11/126
Present value of expected DB benefits < DC balance	19%	34%	28%
	(84/437)	(71/208)	49/175
DB: most important	70%	28%	47%
	(59/84)	(20/71)	23/49
DC: most important	25%	32%	16%
	(21/84)	(23/71)	8/49

with a pension plan reported coverage by both plans. Table 4.4 shows that, among this group, 437 cases have a matched plan, and about 81 percent (353/437) of them have a DB plan with a present value of expected benefits that exceeds or equals the value in their DC account balances in the same year.[9] About 84 percent of this group (295/353) have actually reported that a DB plan is their most important plan. The other 9 percent reported DC as their most important pension plan.

Similarly, in the 1998 data, there are about 745 cases (22 percent=745/3,347 of all respondents) with pension coverage who reported both plans or a combination plan through their current job. There are 208 cases out of this group who have matched plans, 66 percent (137/208) of whom have a DB plan with the same or greater present value of expected benefits than their DC account balances in that year. About 60 percent of this group reported the DB plan as their most important plan. In 2004 data, the corresponding numbers are 695 (22 percent=695/3,200) cases with pension coverage who reported both plans or a combination plan on their current job. Of 175 cases with matched plans, 72 percent (126/175) reported having a DB plan worth the same or more than their DC plan, with 68 percent of this group reporting their DB plan as their most important plan.

We examined certain labor and pension characteristics of respondents whose DC plans were more valuable than their DB plans. Labor characteristics variables included job tenure, age, gender, race, industry, occupation, firm size, status as salaried or hourly workers, annual earnings, and respondent's education level. Pension characteristics variables included the number of years the respondent was included in the plan, the amount of the respondent's own contributions to DB and DC plans, and the amount of employer contributions to DC plans. These characteristics were not strongly related to whether one plan or the other was reported as the most important plan.

Appendix 4.4: Other Sources of Employer Plan Descriptions in the HRS

In addition to contacting employers directly or collecting employer plan descriptions from Department of Labor files, HRS researchers have made other efforts to collect employer-produced plan descriptions. This appendix describes some of those efforts.

For respondents working for private employers, the employers were contacted directly and their summary plan descriptions were requested. The plan descriptions for workers employed by the federal, state, and many local government agencies are now available on the Web. The federal and state plans and plans that state governments maintain for workers employed by their local governments were downloaded. Then these employers were contacted to confirm which of the plans obtained from the Web were relevant to the particular public employer and whether they were offering any additional plans that were not on their Web site. In cases where additional plans (mainly a DC) were offered, those plans were also requested.

Respondent Pension Document Request (Experiment Y). This experiment was initially administered to 400 individuals in the 2004 survey. Respondents in this sample had a pension in 2002. Half of these individuals were asked for any documents they had at home, including quarterly reports from their employers or pension providers. The other half were asked to request a summary plan description from the human resources department of their firms. They were paid $25 for any documents they had at home and $100 for obtaining the summary plan descriptions from their employers. The SPD request experiment was judged sufficiently successful that it was extended to 2004 interviewees among the HRS and war babies cohorts with a current pension who had not been interviewed roughly halfway through interview period. They were asked to obtain SPDs from their employers in exchange for a payment of $50.

Appendix 4.5: Other Sources of Pension Information in the Labor Section of the HRS

In addition to the pension questions in the core of the labor section, questions about pensions were added to the survey and asked of respondents on a one-time basis. The goal was to provide additional information that would be useful in re-designing the questions in the pension sequence. The redesign was ultimately adopted in the 2008 wave of the HRS.

Experimental Pension Characteristics Module. This is a set of questions about the characteristics of the plans covering respondents. It was distributed in 2004 to all respondents who reported they were currently covered by a pension. Questions were asked about various characteristics of their pensions. The idea was that these characteristics could be related to plan type and whether the respondent had a DB or a DC pension, and that they could perhaps be used to identify plan type without asking the respondents whether their plans were defined benefit or defined contribution.

The plan features that these questions sought to identify included whether enrollment is automatic, whether the individual receives periodic (quarterly) reports indicating an account balance, whether the employer contributes to the plan, whether the individual can guide the investment of his or her own contributions and of the firm's contributions, whether the individual can borrow on the plan, whether the respondent would be eligible for a lump sum payment upon leaving the firm before reaching the early retirement age, whether at retirement the respondent would receive periodic payments for as long as he or she lives, and the technical name for the plan.

Table 4.5 reports the percentages of responses in the pension characteristics module indicating the plan had the specified characteristics. Each characteristic is arrayed by plan type, DB, DC, or combination. In this table, the plan type is taken from matched 2004/2005 plan documents. All respondents who have gone through the module and have a matched document are included in the table. Questions such as whether there is automatic enrollment in the plan (67 percent of those with a matched DB plan, 49 percent of those with a matched DC plan), whether one has the ability to make choices in the account's investment (27 percent of those with a DB plan, 61 percent of those with a DC plan), whether one can choose how one's own contributions are invested (26 percent of those with a DB plan, 59 percent of those with a DC plan), and whether benefits are paid for the lifetime (90 percent of those with a DB plan, 63 percent of those with a DC plan)[10] are the characteristics that best discriminate among types of pension plan. Table 4.6 reports the same plan characteristics but arrays them by the plan type reported by the respondent in the module. The advantage of this second table is that it has many more observations than are available when plan type is determined from the matched employer plan. The disadvantage is that respondents report plan type with significant error, as we will see in Chapter 7.

Table 4.5 Number and percentage of responses reporting indicated plan characteristic in the plan characteristics module, arrayed by plan type reported in the plan documents collected in 2004/2005

Plan characteristic	DB plan	DC plan	Combination
Number of observations	829	456	41
Automatically enrolled	67%	49%	78%
Get statement	49%	75%	54%
Employer contributes	84%	91%	80%
Have choice on how account invested	27%	61%	22%
Have choice on how own contribution invested	26%	59%	20%
Allowed to borrow	25%	40%	24%
Lump sum allowed	60%	69%	61%
Expecting lifetime benefits	90%	63%	93%
Plan type in the module	32%	70%	3%

Notes: The DB and DC plan types are the plan types from matched 2004/2005 plan documents. Plan documents include documents collected from respondents. If respondents' documents were not available, we have used documents from their employers. It is assumed the DB plan is the most important plan if the employer offered it and it was matched with the respondent.

Table 4.6 Number and percentage of responses reporting indicated plan characteristic in module 6/7, arrayed by plan type reported in module 6/7

Plan characteristic	DB plan	DC plan	Combination
Any plan offered by employer	583	1,810	13
Automatically enrolled	80%	33%	46%
Get statement	40%	79%	62%
Any employer contribution	89%	88%	100%
Choice on how invested	16%	70%	54%
Choice on own contribution	14%	68%	69%
Borrowing allowed	15%	51%	38%
Lump sum allowed	44%	75%	54%
Lifetime benefits	93%	62%	85%
Know technical name	56%	86%	92%

Note: The module asked for information about two plans. This table provides information on the most important of those plans.

Appendix 4.6: Pension Data in the Assets and Income Section

The assets and income section of the HRS also provides detailed information on income received from pension plans by either spouse in the household. Questions about the value of pension accounts are also available in this section.

The financially knowledgeable respondent is asked whether the respondent or the respondent's spouse is receiving income from a retirement pension. If the answer is no, so that the pension is not in pay status, no further questions are asked. If the answer is yes, the respondent is asked about his or her own pension, the spouse's pension, or both if necessary. Questions ask about the number of pensions and about each, starting with the largest. The survey then asks about the amount of the pension payment; whether income tax was withheld; whether the amount of the pension payment can be adjusted (as is possible with a DC account); whether all of the money could be withdrawn this month if desired, if yes; and how much is in the account. It also asks when the respondent first received the pension and whether the payment is automatically adjusted for changes in the cost of living. The respondent is then asked whether the payment will continue as long as the respondent lives (a sign of a DB plan) and, if not, for how long the payments will continue; and whether, if the respondent dies, the payment would continue and at what level.

There are a number of issues that a reader should be aware of before using the pension information that is provided in the assets and income section. Although in many cases the financially knowledgeable respondent will also be the person who is covered by the particular pension in question, if the spouse who is not labeled as financially knowledgeable has a pension, the spouse without the pension will be the one providing the details. As a result, the person who is answering the pension questions will be less knowledgeable about the pension than the person who is directly covered by the plan, the person who is asked about the pension in the labor section.

A further problem is created for the panel. The same person is not always chosen in each wave as the financially knowledgeable respondent. When the financially knowledgeable respondent changes, the person who has direct knowledge of the pension will change. Thus the user must exercise care in matching the pension report in the assets and income section to the person whose plan it is.

A larger problem is that there is no crosswalk from the pension reported in the labor section to the pension reported in the assets and income section. It is straightforward to match a pension between the labor and the assets and income sections for those with only one plan. But matching becomes a very complex job once a person reports more than one plan on a particular job or when the person reports having pensions on more than one job.

One other dimension of care is required. Some pension questions (e.g., those that traced the fate of pensions that were reported in previous surveys) were moved from the assets and income section to the labor section as the study progressed.

5

Pension Plan Participation in the Health and Retirement Study

A first basic pension outcome is participation in a pension. To be a participant, a respondent's employer must offer a plan, and if participation is not mandatory, the respondent must choose to participate. In this chapter we will report very high rates of pension plan participation for HRS respondents.

Because the HRS is longitudinal, it allows us to measure participation and coverage in many different ways. It is possible to measure participation at a current job, coverage by an active pension at a current or previous job, whether a respondent has ever been covered by a pension at some time during the respondent's work life, and coverage by a pension based on the respondent's own work or a spouse's work. It is also possible to create other measures. Thus there are major advantages to being able to track pensions held over the life cycle in different jobs. It is also possible to trace changes in pension participation with age or over time.

The HRS also allows us to measure important trends in pension participation and coverage. A convenient comparison relates pension coverage for the cohorts who were 51 to 56 years old in the base year of the HRS with coverage in 1998 and 2004, the years new refresher samples were added to the HRS.

To describe patterns of participation in pensions, we begin with statistics reporting participation in current jobs, first by all members of each HRS cohort and then by members of different demographic and employment groups. Respondents who say they are included in the pension from a current job are classified here as participating in the plan.[1] The analysis then turns to patterns of participation by the employed at current jobs by cohort, by age, and over time. From there we take advantage of the panel information in the HRS, taking up the unique opportunity to trace the course of pension participation over the life cycle of employment.

If the plan is cashed out, rolled over, or lost at the time a person leaves a job, participation in that plan ends with the termination of the job. Plans that enter into pay status remain alive after employment is terminated. In other cases, the plan remains dormant after termination of employment, with the individual scheduled to receive a benefit at some time in the future. In tracing pension plan participation over the course of each respondent's work life, we report who participates at a current job, who has a pension from a previous job, and whether a respondent has a current plan, a dormant plan, a plan that is in pay status, or a plan that for other reasons may be classified as live. Once we trace participation over the course of the life cycle, later chapters will evaluate those pensions.

Pension Participation on Current Jobs

A majority of employed workers in the Health and Retirement Study, a group that is approaching retirement age, reports participating in a pension on a current job. As seen in row 1 of Table 5.1, this includes about 60 percent of employed individuals between the ages of 51 and 56 and almost two-thirds of those working full time.

To standardize for age, we confine the samples to members of the three HRS cohorts who were 51 to 56 in the year they entered the survey. In Table 5.1, we find only a small trend in participation among birth cohorts, with pension participation slightly higher for members of younger cohorts. As seen in the table, the trend is considerably stronger among women than among men.

HRS data reflect well-known patterns of participation by demographic and employment groups. Men have higher pension participation than do women. White men who are in the labor force, are employed, or are working full time have 1 to 18 percentage points higher pension participation than do black men, depending on the employment category and year. Both whites and blacks have higher pension participation levels than Hispanics. Depending on the cohort, the differential for employed black males over employed Hispanic males is 8 to 16 percentage points. Pension participation of employed black women is 16 to 22 percentage points higher than the participation level for employed Hispanic women. Gaps in pension coverage in favor of union employees are declining but remain very large, falling from 29 to 21 percentage points over time. The

Table 5.1 Pension plan participation in current jobs by employment status, cohort defined by year of entry into the HRS, and demographic group, population aged 51–56 (weighted)

Subgroups	In the labor force			Employed			Employed full time		
	1992	1998	2004	1992	1998	2004	1992	1998	2004
All	55	59	58	59	61	62	63	65	67
Males	58	60	59	61	62	63	64	65	66
Females	52	57	57	55	60	61	62	67	68
White	56	60	61	59	62	65	65	66	70
Males	60	61	63	63	63	66	66	65	70
Females	52	58	60	55	61	63	62	68	71
Black	56	56	51	60	59	59	64	64	64
Males	52	56	45	57	60	53	60	64	57
Females	59	56	55	63	59	62	68	63	70
Hispanic	40	43	38	44	47	42	46	51	47
Males	38	46	39	43	52	44	44	55	47
Females	42	40	37	46	41	40	49	47	45
Other	54	68	54	59	74	60	64	77	63
Males	53	61	53	57	69	57	59	72	59
Females	55	75	56	62	80	63	71	83	68

Married	56	61	61	59	63	64	64	68	70
Not married	51	53	52	57	56	57	61	60	62
Less than high school	40	40	27	45	44	32	48	49	37
High school grad	54	55	54	57	57	58	63	61	62
Some college	57	58	56	60	60	60	65	66	65
College grad	61	66	68	64	68	71	70	71	76
More than 16 years	72	75	73	75	77	75	78	81	81
Union	89	87	88	90	87	88	91	87	90
Not union	61	65	67	61	65	67	67	70	72
Large firm	84	84	85	84	84	85	87	86	89
Medium firm	75	76	75	75	76	75	77	79	79
Small firm	25	28	32	25	28	32	29	32	36
Missing firm	29	69	67	29	69	67	36	72	73
Employees	69	71	71	69	71	71	73	75	76
Self-employed	9	15	16	9	15	16	11	16	18

Note: The participation levels based on weighted data as reported in this table are about 1 to 2 percent higher than nonweighted levels for most of the subgroups. In contrast to Figure 1.1, participation levels are calculated for both employees and the self-employed.

probability of participating in a pension is even higher at 53 to 59 percentage points for employed workers from large firms compared with small firms. Those with higher levels of education have higher pension participation than do those with less education. The difference in participation between employed individuals in the highest and lowest education categories reaches as high as 43 percentage points, depending on the cohort and year. The widest pension participation differential is between employees and the self-employed, amounting to 55 to 60 percentage points in favor of employees.[2] By way of contrast, one of the smaller differentials is between married and unmarried persons. Pension participation is only 2 to 7 percentage points higher among employed married persons than among those who are not married, although the gap is widening over time.

Trends in Pension Participation within Demographic Groups

Reflecting the overall weak trend in participation by HRS respondents, as seen in Table 5.1, younger cohorts of employed men and of men employed full time have a 1 or 2 percentage point higher pension participation level than do members of older cohorts. As pointed out above, there is a greater difference in participation levels between younger and older cohorts of women. Employed women 51 to 56 in 2004 have a pension participation level on their current job that is 6 percentage points higher than the participation level for women who were 51 to 56 in 1992. With modest differences in participation of men but increasing participation of women in younger cohorts, the difference in pension participation levels between men and women is smaller in the youngest cohort, those entering the survey in 2004, than for older cohorts. As will be seen in coming chapters, the increasing participation of women is only the tip of the iceberg. Their plans and covered experience have changed in a number of ways that increase pension values of women relative to men.

Although there are no strong overall trends in participation, differentials among demographic and employment groups are changing among cohorts and over time. Pension participation levels shown in Table 5.1 are moving in favor of whites. Differences in participation between employed white and black males are higher in 2004, at 13 percentage points, than in 1992, when the difference was 6 percentage points. Moreover, although in 1992 pension participation levels were 8 percentage points higher for employed black women than for white women, the pension participation level for employed white women

51 to 56 years old in 2004 is 1 percentage point higher than for black women. The difference in pension participation levels between employed blacks and Hispanics has been widening for females and narrowing for males.

Pension Plan Participation with Age

Pension participation by those holding current jobs remains steady for the first few years a person is in the HRS but then gradually declines. As seen in Chapter 3, older persons reporting current employment are less likely to have remained in their long-term jobs. Moreover, their new jobs are more likely to be part-year or part-week. These jobs are less likely to offer a pension. As a result, with age the share of older workers who are partially retired increases, and the share of workers covered by a pension declines.

As shown in the first row of Table 5.2, the share of workers 51 to 61 in 1992 who had a pension on their current job declines from 56 percent in 1992 to 30 percent in 2006. For those who were 51 to 56 in 1992, there is a comparable decline in pension participation with age. The only noticeable decline for the war babies is in 2006. The first two observations for the early boomers show relatively similar rates of pension participation in each year.

Notice that in Table 5.2, where the column headings are years and the row headings are cohort, the baseline value for each cohort can be seen by looking at the first number in each of the bottom three rows. Thus as seen in Table 5.1, the percentage of respondents participating in a pension at ages 51 to 56 increases from 59 percent to 62 percent between the HRS and early boomer cohorts.

Even among full-time workers, pension participation at current jobs eventually declines with age. Participation declines more rapidly for men than for women, so that eventually pension participation levels for employed women in a given cohort exceed participation levels of men. Figure 5.1 shows pension participation among those reporting that they were in a full-time job at the time of the survey. Participation in each cohort is higher for men than it is for women. It stays that way for the first few years of the survey. Participation levels then fall faster for men than for women, so that after about ten years, the pension participation level for men working full time at a current job eventually falls below that for women. This can be seen most starkly in the right-hand side of the figure. Among the bottom four lines in 2006, the two lowest lines are for men from the HRS cohort, while the next two lowest lines are for women from the HRS cohort. The participation rates in pensions for women

Table 5.2 Percentage of respondents participating in a pension on a current job, among those working, by cohort: 1992–2006 respondent data (weighted)

Cohort	1992	1994	1996	1998	2000	2002	2004	2006
% of HRS working respondents with a pension	56	57	54	51	46	40	37	30
% of HRS working respondents with a pension among those 51 to 56 in 1992	59	60	58	57	54	46	41	33
% of war baby working respondents with a pension	—	—	—	61	64	62	60	52
% of early boomer working respondents with a pension	—	—	—	—	—	—	62	59

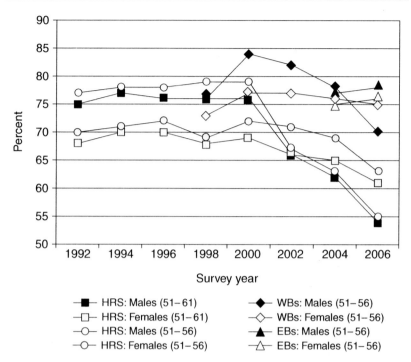

Figure 5.1 Percentage of full-time employees with pension on current job, by gender and cohort (weighted)

who were 65 to 70 in 2006 and were still working full time exceeded those for comparably aged men by about 8 percentage points.

Turnover from Pension Jobs

To increase understanding of trends in plan participation by age, it is useful to examine statistics on turnover from jobs offering pensions. As they age, increasing numbers of respondents leave the long-term jobs that were the source of their pension participation. Table 5.3 examines turnover for those who initially reported a pension in the first wave of the HRS. Row 1 begins with the number of persons in the initial wave of the HRS cohort who reported a pension at their current job. Almost half ([771+742+604]/4,456=0.48) of them left their 1992 jobs within six years. Much of this turnover is likely due to retirements. By 2006, fourteen years later, only 7 percent (320/4,456) of those employed in the first wave of the original HRS cohort remain employed

Table 5.3   Number of respondents with a pension plan in Wave 1 and the number of
           them leaving pension jobs in subsequent waves

Respondents (Rs) leaving by wave	Number of respondents
Number of Rs with a pension plan in Wave 1 (1992)	4,456
Left job before Wave 2 (1994)	771
Left job before Wave 3 (1996)	742
Left job before Wave 4 (1998)	604
Left job before Wave 5 (2000)	475
Left job before Wave 6 (2002)	441
Left job before Wave 7 (2004)	265
Left job before Wave 8 (2006)	174
Same job since Wave 1	320
Died before leaving 1992 job	121
Other attritors[a]	428
Total	4,341

Note: The difference between the total number of cases with pension (4,456) and the
number of cases accounted for after Wave 8 (4,341) results from missing values, DKs, and RFs.
Respondents' multiple jobs are not included. If a respondent moved to another job but had the
same pension, in this table that job and its pension are assumed to be terminated.

   a. Other attritors include those respondents who left the survey sometime after their initial
interview in Wave 1 but never reported having left their 1992 job.

in their same job. Attrition from the HRS sample (including deaths) accounts
for about 12 percent (549/4,456) of the decline in workers participating in a
pension since 1992, so that the rest of the decline is due to job leaving.

History of Pension Participation over a Lifetime of Work

In addition to pension benefits earned on their current jobs, some HRS respondents are entitled to benefits from pensions held on a previous job. Those
who held a sequence of jobs that offered pensions will have more than one plan
as they approach retirement.

   Over time some pensions from previous jobs enter into pay status. Others
are transformed into other forms of assets or are consumed and no longer represent a promise to pay future benefits in the form of a pension. Some smaller
pensions may be lost, and pensions that were not vested when the person left
the plan may never pay a benefit.

   A first approach is to count the number of respondents with a pension falling in one category or another. Eventually we will evaluate all of the pension
assets held, either in current jobs or remaining from jobs held in the past.

We use the HRS panel to keep track of how the number of respondents with different forms of pension holdings changes over time. It is useful to develop some terminology to summarize the current status of pensions that are owned, or have been owned, by a particular respondent. A *current pension* is one held on a current job that is accruing benefits to be paid in the future. Then there are the different states for pensions earned on previously held jobs. One possibility is that the plan is in *pay status*. Another is that the pension is *dormant*, a term we will use if a pension from a previous job will pay benefits at some time in the future but is not paying benefits currently. As a group, we categorize respondents with remaining pension rights as having *live pensions*, which include current pensions, dormant pensions, and pensions in pay status. Pensions from jobs held in the past may also be transformed into other forms of assets, fully cashed out, or lost (due to failure to vest or for other reasons). The total of pension rights ever accrued over the life cycle will include live pensions plus those that were transformed into other assets, cashed out, or lost. In tracing out pension participation over the lifetime, we also will encounter reporting errors. A plan will fall in this category if a respondent initially told us about, say, a dormant plan and then in some later wave says the plan never existed or reports that the dormant plan was actually cashed out sometime before it was reported as dormant.

Participants with Current Pensions

To place the data on current pensions on a comparable footing with data on dormant and other previously held pensions, Table 5.4 reports the fraction of all respondents with a pension at a current job. The relevant population differs from that reported in Table 5.1. There pension coverage rates were reported only among those who were currently employed. Similarly, Figure 5.1 reported the fraction of full-time workers on current jobs with a pension. Because Table 5.4 refers to coverage among all respondents instead of among those currently employed or working full time, not only are the pension coverage levels reported in Table 5.4 much lower than those in the earlier table and figure, but they fall much more rapidly over time. Pension coverage of the population declines not only because coverage is lower among older members of the population who are still at work but also because the fraction of the population at work declines rapidly as retirements increase with age.

Table 5.4 Percentage of respondents with current plans (weighted)

Group and cohort	1992	1994	1996	1998	2000	2002	2004	2006
At least 1 pension plan								
HRS: 51–61	38.7	35.8	30.8	25.8	20.2	14.7	11.5	7.9
	(9,623)	(8,899)	(8,416)	(8,226)	(7,740)	(7,530)	(7,203)	(6,870)
HRS: 51–56	43.0	41.7	38.9	35.5	28.6	20.4	15.5	10.5
	(5,448)	(5,064)	(4,818)	(4,766)	(4,511)	(4,435)	(4,287)	(4,109)
WBs: 51–56	—	—	—	46.2	46.9	41.6	37.5	29.1
				(3,126)	(2,992)	(2,899)	(2,878)	(2,747)
EBs: 51–56	—	—	—	—	—	—	46.8	43.4
							(3,326)	(3,081)
At least 1 pension plan: males								
HRS: 51–61	46.0	42.9	36.9	31.6	24.1	16.8	13.0	8.9
	(4,494)	(4,136)	(3,878)	(3,801)	(3,555)	(3,440)	(3,248)	(3,083)
HRS: 51–56	50.9	49.9	46.4	43.0	33.9	22.9	17.1	11.7
	(2,519)	(2,339)	(2,203)	(2,207)	(2,080)	(2,034)	(1,947)	(1,854)
WBs: 51–56	—	—	—	51.4	54.2	48.1	41.9	31.1
				(1,204)	(1,163)	(1,107)	(1,115)	(1,033)
EBs: 51–56	—	—	—	—	—	—	50.4	47.6
							(1,470)	(1,342)

At least 1 pension plan: females

HRS: 51–61	32.1	29.2	25.2	20.7	16.8	12.8	10.3	6.9
	(5,129)	(4,763)	(4,563)	(4,425)	(4,185)	(4,090)	(3,955)	(3,787)
HRS: 51–56	35.8	34.2	31.8	28.9	23.8	18.2	14.1	9.4
	(2,929)	(2,725)	(2,615)	(2,559)	(2,431)	(2,401)	(2,340)	(2,255)
WBs: 51–56	—	—	—	41.6	40.2	35.8	33.5	27.4
				(1,922)	(1,829)	(1,792)	(1,763)	(1,714)
EBs: 51–56	—	—	—	—	—	—	43.4	39.5
							(1,856)	(1,739)

Note: Total number of observations is reported in parentheses.

Two patterns are readily apparent in the first panel of Table 5.4 (At least 1 pension plan). First, looking across each row, the share of the members of each cohort that is participating in a pension on a current job declines over time. For example, for members of the HRS cohort who were 51 to 56 in 1992, 43 percent were participating in a pension at their current job in 1992, but only 10.5 percent of the population was participating in a pension on a current job by 2006. The second pattern concerns differences between cohorts of those 51 to 56 years old in 1992, 1998, and 2004. Here there was an increase in the proportion of the population 51 to 56 years old with a pension at the current job. This can be seen by comparing the first figures in each of the second, third, and fourth rows. The share of the population with a pension on a current job increases from 43.0 percent in 1992 among members of the HRS cohort who were 51 to 56 in 1992, to 46.8 percent among the early boomer cohort in 2004.

When the samples entering the survey at age 51 to 56 are divided into men and women, we see that the trend in the share of the cohort with a pension on a current job comes entirely from the sample of women. Looking at the third panel of Table 5.4 (At least 1 pension plan: females), the share of the population of women 51 to 56 years old with a pension on a current job increases from 35.8 percent in 1992 to 43.4 percent in 2004. There is no trend between the comparable cohorts of men.

Participants with Dormant Pensions

Having discussed current pensions, we turn now to Table 5.5, which presents some basic statistics on dormant pensions. On its face, comparing the first numbers in rows 2, 3, and 4, these data would suggest a strong trend in the percentage of respondents with a dormant pension. However, these statistics are not perfectly comparable across years because the questions about pensions from previous jobs were changed over time. Although precise corrections cannot be made for each number in the table, the effect of the changing definitions can be readily determined.[3] The bottom line for Table 5.5 is that once it is corrected for differences in methodology among cohorts, there remains a slight trend toward finding a larger fraction of respondents in younger cohorts reporting that they hold a dormant plan.

Table 5.5 Percentage of respondents with a dormant pension (weighted)

Cohort	1992	1994	1996	1998	2000	2002	2004	2006
At least 1 pension plan								
HRS: 51–61	9.1	11.3	10.2	10.4	11.2	12.2	8.9	7.8
	(9,623)	(8,899)	(8,416)	(8,226)	(7,740)	(7,530)	(7,203)	(6,870)
HRS: 51–56	10.3	12.4	11.9	12.1	13.6	14.8	12.0	9.6
	(5,449)	(5,064)	(4,818)	(4,766)	(4,511)	(4,435)	(4,287)	(4,109)
WBs: 51–56	—	—	—	13.4	15.4	18.3	15.7	14.2
				(3,126)	(2,992)	(2,899)	(2,878)	(2,747)
EBs: 51–56	—	—	—	—	—	—	15.9	14.9
							(3,326)	(3,081)

Note: Total number of observations is reported in parentheses.

Table 5.6 Percentage of respondents with dormant and/or current plans (weighted)

Cohort	1992	1994	1996	1998	2000	2002	2004	2006
At least 1 pension plan								
HRS: 51–61	44.3	42.6	36.9	32.6	28.2	24.3	19.2	15.0
	(9,623)	(8,899)	(8,416)	(8,226)	(7,740)	(7,530)	(7,203)	(6,870)
HRS: 51–56	49.0	48.7	45.1	42.3	37.4	31.6	24.6	19.2
	(5,449)	(5,064)	(4,818)	(4,766)	(4,511)	(4,435)	(4,287)	(4,109)
WBs: 51–56	—	—	—	53.4	54.4	52.4	46.1	39.0
				(3,126)	(2,992)	(2,899)	(2,878)	(2,747)
EBs: 51–56	—	—	—	—	—	—	54.1	51.2
							(3,326)	(3,081)

Note: Total number of observations is reported in parentheses.

Total Number of Respondents with Participation in Either Dormant and/or Current Plans

Since a respondent may have both a current and a dormant pension, we next consider statistics on the number of respondents expecting a benefit from holding one and/or the other plan. According to the data in row 1, column 1, of Table 5.6, in 1992, 44.3 percent of the respondents in the HRS cohort of 51- to 61-year-olds were expecting some future benefit from their previous/ current pension plans. By 2006, about 15 percent of the original HRS cohort had not yet begun collecting from a pension they expected would eventually generate a benefit in the future; the remaining 29 percent had started receiving their monthly benefits from their plans or had completely cashed out their pension.

Once again, members of younger cohorts have participation levels that are a few percentage points higher than the participation levels of those in the original HRS cohort. Thus from row 2, column 1, of Table 5.6, 49.0 percent of those 51 to 56 in the original HRS cohort, entering the survey in 1992, were participants in a current or dormant pension. In contrast, 53.4 percent of the war babies, who entered the survey in 1998, and 54.1 percent of the early boomers, who entered in 2004, had a current or dormant pension. Once again there is some exaggeration of the trend in coverage due to the wider scope of the questions about dormant pensions asked in later years and perhaps some offsetting bias from attrition, especially for members of the war baby cohort.

Respondents with Plans in Pay Status

The last of the elements comprising live pensions are those plans in pay status. Looking across the rows in Table 5.7, as would be expected the percentage of respondents with at least one plan in pay status increases over time. As the members of the cohort age, they are more likely to have claimed their benefits. For example, among members of the original HRS cohort listed in row 1, from 1992 to 2006, the percentage of respondents with a plan in pay status increased from 9.1 percent to 32.2 percent. Comparing the first figure in the row for each cohort of 51- to 56-year-olds, the fraction with a plan in pay status falls from 5.0 percent in 1992 to 3.5 percent in 2004, suggesting a very slight downward trend in the share of those in their early fifties who have already claimed benefits.

Table 5.7 Percentage of respondents with plans in pay status (weighted)

Cohort	1992	1994	1996	1998	2000	2002	2004	2006
At least 1 pension plan								
HRS: 51–61	9.1	11.8	16.6	20.1	23.4	25.9	30.4	32.2
	(9,623)	(8,899)	(8,416)	(8,226)	(7,740)	(7,530)	(7,203)	(6,870)
HRS: 51–56	5.0	7.0	10.8	14.2	18.5	21.9	28.2	30.7
	(5,449)	(5,064)	(4,818)	(4,766)	(4,511)	(4,435)	(4,287)	(4,109)
WBs: 51–56	—	—	—	4.5	7.6	9.7	15.5	19.3
				(3,126)	(2,992)	(2,899)	(2,878)	(2,747)
EBs: 51–56	—	—	—	—	—	—	3.5	5.5
							(3,326)	(3,081)

Note: Total number of observations is reported in parentheses.

Table 5.8 Percentage of respondents with a live pension from current/last or previous jobs by cohort (weighted)

Cohort	1992	1994	1996	1998	2000	2002	2004	2006
At least 1 pension plan								
HRS: 51–61	51.5	52.7	50.9	49.1	47.6	45.3	44.7	42.6
	(9,623)	(8,899)	(8,416)	(8,226)	(7,740)	(7,530)	(7,203)	(6,870)
HRS: 51–56	52.7	54.5	53.5	52.6	51.6	48.1	47.0	44.2
	(5,449)	(5,064)	(4,818)	(4,766)	(4,511)	(4,435)	(4,287)	(4,109)
WBs: 51–56	—	—	—	56.9	59.6	58.9	58.3	54.1
				(3,126)	(2,992)	(2,899)	(2,878)	(2,747)
EBs: 51–56	—	—	—	—	—	—	56.6	55.1
							(3,326)	(3,081)

Note: Total number of observations is reported in parentheses.

Pension Participation in a Live Plan

A live pension is a category that encompasses each of the three groups discussed so far. It includes pensions from current jobs, dormant pensions, and pensions in pay status. The share of respondents with a live pension is reported by year and cohort in Table 5.8. Looking across each row, and thus at respondents within each cohort, the number of respondents with a live pension falls slowly with age. For those in their early fifties, more than half of respondents have a live pension. For example, for members of the original HRS cohort, as shown in row 2 of the table, the share of respondents with a live pension at ages 51 to 56 decreases from 52.7 percent in 1992 to 44.2 percent in 2004. Once again this trend may be slightly exaggerated due to the increasing number of last and previous pensions included in later surveys. Coverage by a live pension is higher the younger the members of the cohort are, rising from 52.7 percent for those 51 to 56 in 1992 to 56.6 percent for those 51 to 56 in 2004.

Table 5.9 summarizes coverage for different types of live pensions and its course by year and cohort. As seen proceeding down the three rows representing participation in the key years of 1992, 1998, and 2004, the dominant change generating the decline in the number of live pensions with age is the decline with age in the number of respondents with a current pension. This decline is mainly fostered by increasing retirements with age from current jobs offering a pension and by increased claiming with age. As seen in column 3 of Table 5.9, the number of respondents with a pension in pay status increases within each cohort over time. Adding across each row, the share of respondents with a live pension declines over time within each cohort but remains substantial for all cohorts and years. The positive trend among cohorts in the share of respondents with a live pension upon entering the survey at ages 51 to 56 can be seen in the last column, comparing the first numbers for the second, third, and fourth cohorts.

Weighing the Importance of Pension Participation over the Lifetime

The fraction of the population participating in a live pension does not tell the full story. There will be some respondents who at some time participated in a pension but who are not participating in a live pension by the time they retire.

Table 5.9 Cohort differences in live pensions cumulated from work over the life cycle

	% of respondents with			
Cohort and year	Current pension	Dormant pension	Plan in pay status	Live pension
HRS: 51–61				
1992	38.7	9.1	9.1	51.5
1998	25.8	10.4	20.1	49.1
2004	11.5	8.9	30.4	44.7
HRS: 51–56				
1992	43.0	10.3	5.0	52.7
1998	35.5	12.1	14.2	52.8
2004	15.5	12.0	28.2	47.0
WBs: 51–56				
1992	—	—	—	—
1998	46.2	13.4	5.0	56.9
2004	37.5	15.7	15.5	58.3
EBs: 51–56				
1992	—	—	—	—
1998	—	—	—	—
2004	46.8	15.9	3.5	56.6

Note: Live pensions include any current pension, dormant pension, and pension in pay status.

Some will have cashed out, rolled over, or lost a pension but will still have another live pension at the time of the survey.

A larger share of wealth in retirement will be due to pensions than is represented by live pensions. Rollovers, annuitization, and cash-outs may have resulted in other forms of wealth that, while originating as a pension, are no longer held in the form of a live pension. We have discussed participation in live pensions. We now turn to past participation in pensions that are no longer live.

The percentage of respondents having been covered by a pension from a current, last, and/or previous job, irrespective of what happened to the plan at or after termination, are reported in Table 5.10. Thus the table includes plans that were transformed or cashed out.[4] By the final waves of the survey, two-thirds to three-fourths of all respondents report that they are participating in or have participated in a pension sometime in their work life.

Table 5.10 Percentage of respondents with any pension from current/last or previous jobs by cohort (weighted)

Group and cohort	1992	1994	1996	1998	2000	2002	2004	2006
At least 1 pension plan								
HRS: 51–61	61.1	63.1	63.6	63.0	63.3	64.4	64.4	64.3
	(9,623)	(8,899)	(8,416)	(8,226)	(7,740)	(7,530)	(7,203)	(6,870)
HRS: 51–56	62.4	64.6	65.5	65.5	66.3	66.8	67.0	66.9
	(5,448)	(5,064)	(4,818)	(4,766)	(4,511)	(4,435)	(4,287)	(4,109)
WBs: 51–56	—	—	—	68.7	72.1	73.3	74.2	73.1
				(3,126)	(2,992)	(2,899)	(2,878)	(2,747)
EBs: 51–56	—	—	—	—	—	—	68.0	69.6
							(3,326)	(3,081)
At least 1 pension plan: males								
HRS: 51–61	74.4	76.3	76.8	76.4	75.8	76.5	77.2	76.9
	(4,494)	(4,136)	(3,878)	(3,801)	(3,555)	(3,440)	(3,248)	(3,083)
HRS: 51–56	75.2	77.7	78.7	78.4	78.5	78.4	79.1	78.8
	(2,519)	(2,339)	(2,203)	(2,207)	(2,080)	(2,034)	(1,947)	(1,854)
WBs: 51–56	—	—	—	76.3	80.6	82.4	83.2	80.1
				(1,204)	(1,163)	(1,107)	(1,115)	(1,033)
EBs: 51–56	—	—	—	—	—	—	73.1	75.3
							(1,470)	(1,342)

At least 1 pension plans females

HRS: 51–61	48.9	51.1	51.6	51.1	52.4	53.9	53.4	53.4
	(5,129)	(4,763)	(4,563)	(4,425)	(4,185)	(4,090)	(3,955)	(3,787)
HRS: 51–56	50.8	52.6	53.5	53.9	55.5	56.5	56.4	56.2
	(2,929)	(2,725)	(2,615)	(2,559)	(2,431)	(2,401)	(2,340)	(2,255)
WBs: 51–56	—	—	—	61.8	64.2	65.2	67.7	66.8
				(1,922)	(1,829)	(1,792)	(1,763)	(1,714)
EBs: 51–56	—	—	—	—	—	—	63.1	64.3
							(1,856)	(1,739)

Notes: A pension from a previous job is included in this table whether it is still "live" or has been cashed out previously. Total number of observations is reported in parentheses.

As can be seen, it is important to consider the results separately for men and women. Pension participation is much higher for men, reaching almost four-fifths of the population, while for women maximum participation is two-thirds of total female respondents.

Looking at the first panel of Table 5.10, it appears that there is a trend in participation among cohorts. The percentage of respondents 51 to 56 years old reporting any pension from a current, last, or previous job increases from 62.4 percent for members of the original HRS cohort to 68.0 percent for members of the early boomer cohort.

However, most of the action is among cohorts of women. Among women 51 to 56 years of age, participation increases from 50.8 percent for those 51 to 56 in 1992 to 63.1 percent for those 51 to 56 in 2004.

With participation increasing for cohorts of women but not for men, the gap in participation between men and women narrowed over time. In 1992,

Table 5.11   Percentage of respondents with any/dormant/live pension from current/last or previous jobs by cohort (weighted)

Pension status	51–56	57–62	63–68	69–74
1992				
Current pension	43.0	32.8	—	—
Dormant pension	10.3	7.7	—	—
Pension in pay status	5.0	14.6	—	—
Live pension	52.7	49.9	—	—
Ever held a pension	62.4	59.4	—	—
1998				
Current pension	46.2	35.5	13.1	—
Dormant pension	13.6	12.2	8.6	—
Pension in pay status	5.0	14.2	30.5	—
Live pension	56.9	52.8	46.1	—
Ever held a pension	68.7	65.5	61.6	—
2004				
Current pension	46.8	37.5	15.5	6.3
Dormant pension	15.9	15.7	12.0	7.3
Pension in pay status	3.5	15.5	28.2	36.0
Live pension	56.6	56.3	47.0	43.9
Ever held a pension	68.0	74.2	67.0	62.8

Note: Live pension includes any pension on current job, dormant pension, and pension in pay status.

24.4 percent more men than women ages 51 to 56 had been covered by a pension. By 2004, the gap had narrowed to 10 percent.

Within cohorts, panel 1 of Table 5.10 suggests that there is a slight increase in participation over time. As seen in the first row of the table, 61.1 percent of respondents from the original HRS cohort had a pension from a current, last, or previous job in 1992. By 2006, the figure had risen 3.2 percentage points to 64.3 percent. Again, as can be seen by looking across the rows in the bottom panel of the table, the increase is larger for women than for men.

Summarizing current and past participation in pensions, Table 5.11 reports differences in participation in current or dormant pensions, pensions in pay status, those with live pensions, and those who ever held a pension, reporting by age and cohort. The table shows the percentage of respondents with the indicated type of participation by age group and does so for each of three years. For example, from columns 1 and 2, row 4, of Table 5.11, in 1992, 52.7 percent of HRS age-eligible respondents were participating in at least one live pension plan. As seen in the first two rows of the bottom panel, there are sharp declines with age in participation in current pensions and dormant pensions. As seen in row 3, there is a sharp increase in pensions in pay status. The bottom two rows of the table indicate that there are gradual declines in participation in live pensions with age and more modest declines in the percentage of respondents who ever participated in a pension.

Table 5.12 Percentage of households and respondents with any own/spouse/
partner pension from current/last or previous jobs by cohort: ages
51–56 in 1992, 1998, and 2004 (weighted)

Household members	1992	1998	2004
All respondents	78.8	81.2	80.4
All households	76.9	79.3	78.4
Couples	83.9	87.1	87.5
Males	74.8	76.6	75.4
Females	49.2	57.9	62.4
Singles	58.8	62.1	59.2
Males	64.8	62.8	61.1
Females	55.1	61.6	58.0
No. of households	4,533	2,662	2,770

Note: Married respondents whose spouses were not interviewed are included in the couples category.

Coverage through a Spouse

Many couples have only one spouse working, or at least only one spouse with a prolonged history of labor market activity. It seems unreasonable to judge pension coverage for members of these households by focusing separately on each individual. Accordingly, in addition to their own coverage, Table 5.12 reports respondents as being covered or having been covered by a pension not only if the respondent was covered in his or her own right but also if that respondent's spouse is or was covered.

By 2004, using that definition of coverage, over four-fifths of HRS respondents in the early boomer cohort had been covered or were currently covered by a pension. Over 78 percent of households were covered using that same definition. Among couple households, again by 2004 75.4 percent of the coverage comes from the man; 62.4 percent of women are covered based on their own work. By 2004, the difference in coverage between single men and single women, 61.1 percent for single men and 58.0 percent for single women, is much smaller than the gap between men and women in couple households. In both couple households and in single households, the gap in coverage between men and women has narrowed substantially over the 1992–2004 period.

Having analyzed pension participation in the Health and Retirement Study, Chapter 6 turns to a discussion of plan type. Later chapters will deal with ages of benefit receipt and pension values.

6

Pension Plan Type

Plan type is the most important single pension feature and, perhaps only after pension coverage, is the most important pension outcome to document and to understand. As the discussion of pension plan determination in Chapter 2 indicates, there are very sharp differences between defined benefit (DB) plans, which determine benefits based on a formula, and defined contribution (DC) plans, which provide benefits in the form of an account. In turn, DB and DC plans create different economic incentives that serve very different purposes.

Consider the type of pension held by HRS respondents who were 51 to 56 years old in 2004.[1] About a quarter of early boomer respondents indicated that the type of plan they held on their current job was defined benefit only. Another quarter indicated they had both a defined benefit and a defined contribution plan (see Table 6.1, columns 3 and 9, row 1). Almost half of this age group reported coverage by a defined contribution plan only.[2] Thus in 2004, half of those in the early boomer cohort with a pension had a defined benefit plan; three-quarters had a defined contribution plan.

Pension Plan Type by Cohort, Demographic Group, and Job Characteristics

To document the differences in the types of pensions held by those in different demographic groups and in different jobs, Table 6.1 reports plan type separately by gender, race, marital status, education, union status, firm size, and employer characteristics. In a number of cases, the differences in the plan type

Table 6.1 Differences and trends in plan type among subgroups, population aged 51–56 with a pension (weighted)

Subgroups	DB only			DC only			Both			Don't know/refuse		
	1992	1998	2004	1992	1998	2004	1992	1998	2004	1992	1998	2004
All	41	29	24	31	39	47	27	31	25	2	2	3
Males	39	28	22	29	36	46	31	35	29	1	2	2
Females	43	31	27	33	42	48	21	26	21	3	2	4
White	40	28	23	31	40	47	28	31	27	1	1	3
Males	38	27	21	30	36	46	32	36	31	1	1	2
Females	42	28	25	33	44	49	23	27	22	2	1	4
Black	48	49	35	28	27	44	22	22	18	2	2	2
Males	48	46	32	22	25	46	27	26	18	3	3	4
Females	49	51	37	31	28	43	18	18	19	2	2	2
Hispanic	39	28	28	39	37	49	16	26	16	6	9	7
Males	37	26	27	36	38	52	24	31	16	3	5	4
Females	42	32	30	42	35	45	5	19	15	11	14	10
Other	41	20	22	32	41	51	25	35	25	2	3	1
Males	52	12	27	28	43	50	20	38	23	0	7	0
Females	29	27	17	36	39	51	30	33	28	5	0	3

Married	41	28	24	31	39	46	26	31	26	2	2	3
Not married	39	31	26	31	39	50	28	29	22	1	2	2
Less than high school	49	29	20	36	51	60	11	18	11	4	2	9
High school grad	44	29	25	30	38	48	25	32	23	2	1	5
Some college	33	28	21	37	40	51	30	29	25	1	2	2
College grad	33	27	26	29	38	48	36	34	31	2	0	1
More than 16 years	41	32	27	24	33	39	35	33	31	1	2	3
Union	57	47	39	16	17	28	35	35	24	1	1	3
Not union	32	22	19	39	47	53	26	30	32	2	1	3
Large firm	40	32	24	25	29	41	27	38	21	1	1	2
Medium firm	44	28	28	33	48	46	33	23	10	3	1	5
Small firm	38	18	23	49	66	65	20	15	24	2	1	3
Missing firm	27	34	23	49	34	48	21	29	26	3	3	5
Employees	41	30	25	30	38	46	27	31	24	2	1	3
Self-employed	30	14	16	51	69	74	15	14	6	4	2	4

reported by members of different groups with pensions are substantial. For example, looking down column 9 in the table, in 2004 men with a pension were 8 percentage points more likely than women (29 percent vs. 21 percent) to have both a defined benefit and a defined contribution plan, rather than one plan type alone. Similarly, whites were 9 percentage points more likely than blacks (27 percent vs. 18 percent) to have both plan types. As of 2004, union workers were 20 percentage points more likely to have a DB plan only (39 vs. 19) and 25 percentage points less likely to have a DC plan only (28 vs. 53) compared with nonunion workers. Similarly, large differences are found between employees of large and small firms. By 2004, employees of small firms were 24 percentage points (65 vs. 41) more likely to have a DC plan only and 22 percentage points (10 vs. 32) less likely to have both a DB and a DC plan than were employees for large firms. Adding together those with DB only and both types of plans, by 2004 70 percent of union members still had a DB plan, whereas only 43 percent of nonunion members had a DB plan. Large-firm employees were also much more likely than employees of small firms to have a DB plan (56 percent vs. 33 percent) in 2004 and about equally likely to have a DC plan. Employees with a pension are much more likely to have both plan types than are the self-employed (26 vs. 6 percent in 2004). DB coverage among those with a pension in 2004 was 29 percentage points higher for employees than for the self-employed, while the self-employed had an 8 percentage point higher probability of having a DC plan.

Married and unmarried individuals reported similar levels of coverage by DB or DC plans. Similar results were also found for high school and college graduates with a pension. Most differences in plan type among groups are smaller than the corresponding differences in pension coverage that were discussed in the last chapter.

Plan type varies noticeably between public and private sector workers, with public sector workers more likely to have maintained a defined benefit plan. The HRS has data on differences in plan type between public and private sector employees for 2006. It is interesting to consider differences in plan type by sector separately for men and women. From the number of observations listed in the bottom row of Tables 6.1A and B, in 2006 28 percent (329/1,160) of men with a pension are public sector employees, while 36 percent (564/1,576) of women with a pension work in the public sector. Eighty percent (61+19) of men and 72 percent (54+18) of women in the public sector report having a DB plan, either alone or together with a DC plan. In contrast, 44 percent (25+19)

Table 6.1A Percentage of public and private employees by self-reported plan type in 2006: males (weighted)

Self-reported plan types	Public	Private	Total
DB only	61%	25%	35%
DC only	18%	53%	43%
Both	19%	19%	19%
DK	2%	2%	2%
Total	100% (329)	100% (831)	100% (1,160)

Note: Total number of observations is reported in parentheses.

Table 6.1B Percentage of public and private employees by self-reported plan type in 2006: females (weighted)

Self-reported plan types	Public	Private	Total
DB only	54%	19%	32%
DC only	23%	65%	50%
Both	18%	13%	15%
DK	5%	3%	3%
Total	100% (564)	100% (1,012)	100% (1,576)

Note: Total number of observations is reported in parentheses.

of men and 32 percent (19+13) of women with a pension in the private sector have a DB plan. In sum, women are more likely to work in the public sector, where DB plans are more common, while men are more likely to have a DB plan within each sector.

These findings have implications for the difference in pension values held by men and women. We will see later that there is a smaller gap between the values of DB plans held by men and women than between the values of DC plans. An important part of the gap in the total value of pensions held by men and women will reflect the importance of DC plans in the private sector, with 78 percent (65+13) of women and 72 percent (53+19) of men holding a DC plan, where for 53 percent of men and 65 percent of women with a DC plan, the DC plan is the primary plan held. Given the importance of DB pensions in the public sector, the greater share of women whose pensions are from public sector employment, the fact that women in the private sector are much more likely to have DC plans where plans held by men are more valuable than they are for women, and the narrower difference in DB benefits between men and women that will be seen in Chapter 9, one factor accounting for a relatively narrow gap in pension values between men and women is the higher proportion of women with pensions who work in the public sector.

Changes in Plan Type

The sharp trend to defined contribution plans is evident in Table 6.1. Plan type is reported in the indicated years for those ages 51 to 56. By standardizing for age in each year, the table removes any changes in plan type due exclusively to aging. To determine trends in plan type, it is necessary to add up the percentages with DB only and both types of plans. For example, in row 1 of Table 6.1, the percentage of pension covered workers 51 to 56 years old with a defined benefit plan is seen to decline from 68 percent in 1992 (41+27) to 49 percent in 2004 (24+25). Similarly, coverage by a DC plan increases from 58 percent in 1992 (31+27) to 72 percent (47+25) in 2004 of pension-covered workers ages 51 to 56.

Changes in plan type do not differ very sharply among those with different demographic characteristics or holding different types of jobs. That means that the differentials observed in cross-section data were maintained over time.

By 2004, indicators of plan type reflect the declining popularity of defined benefit plans for both genders and similarly reflect the continued spread of defined contribution plans. Among men with a pension, between 1992 and 2004, as seen in row 2 of Table 6.1, there was a 19 percentage point decline ([39+31] – [22+29]) in the proportion with a DB plan, while for women who were covered by a pension, the proportion with a DB plan fell by 16 percentage points ([43+21] – [27+21]). The percentages of both men and women with a pension whose plan was defined contribution increased by 15 points over that period. The declines in DB coverage for blacks and whites were slightly higher than for Hispanics. Whites were more likely to gain DC coverage (increasing the share with a pension whose plan was defined contribution by 15 percentage points), compared with 12 and 10 percentage point increases for blacks and Hispanics, respectively. The decline in coverage by a DB plan was slightly larger for nonunion members (16 percentage points) than for union members (13 percentage points), while the rise in DC coverage for nonunion members (11 percentage points) was smaller than the increase for union members (17 percentage points). Employees of large and small firms experienced a similar decline in DB coverage through 2004 (15 percentage points) and a similar increase in DC coverage at 15 or 16 percentage points. Between 1992 and 2004, there were comparable increases for employees and for the self-employed in the proportion of those with a pension who had a DC plan, amounting to about 15 percentage points.

Next consider changes in plan type over time among members of each cohort who continue to work full time. These changes, which reflect trends over time and aging, can be seen in Tables 6.2 and 6.3. Thus rows 4 and 5 again reflect, for those in a full-time job, the declining likelihood of coverage by a DB pension and the increasing likelihood of coverage by a DC plan. Each year some people retire; others leave jobs offering pensions and take up jobs that do not offer a pension, while still others gain pension jobs. These various job changes are related to pension plan type, which has been shown to influence both job turnover and retirements (Gustman and Steinmeier, 1993b; Anderson, Gustman, and Steinmeier, 1999).

Tenure on the Job and in Pension Plans by Plan Type

To further clarify the patterns of change, it is useful to consider how trends toward DC plans affected the job tenure and pension tenure of those holding DB or DC plans. Table 6.4 examines time spent on the job and time covered by the pension plan, separating respondents according to their cohort and plan type. An individual who has both a DB and a DC plan may appear in both columns. Table 6.5 presents the same information but includes only those who have a DB plan only or a DC plan only, so a person with both a DB and a DC plan is not included.

In 1992, those 51 to 56 years old with a DB plan (having a DB plan only or both a DB and a DC plan) had been on their jobs 2.0 years longer than those with a DC plan (17.6 vs. 15.6 years). By 2004, those with a DB plan had been on the job 3.0 years longer than those with a DC plan (16.8 vs. 13.8 years). The 4.8-year gap in job tenure found in Table 6.5 for those in 2004 holding either a DB plan only or a DC plan only is even wider.

The relatively recent appearance and spread of 401(k) plans is one reason why respondents with DC plans report shorter tenure under their pensions than on their jobs. Those with DB plans report longer tenure on their jobs than do those with DC plans. One reason for this difference is that jobs offering DC plans are typically newer than jobs that offer DB plans. In addition, the data show that there is less turnover from jobs offering DB plans.[3]

Table 6.2 Pension plan type in 1992–2006 HRS respondent data, among full-time employees with a pension, HRS cohort, among those 51–56 in 1992 (weighted)

Pension characteristics	1992	1994	1996	1998	2000	2002	2004	2006
% with DB plan only	41	50	45	41	39	35	30	29
% with DC plan only	30	30	35	37	43	49	49	51
% with combination/both plans	28	18	18	19	15	14	17	15
% with at least 1 DB plan	69	69	63	61	54	49	48	44
% with at least 1 DC plan	58	48	53	56	58	63	66	66
% who respond don't know/refused	2	2	2	2	3	2	4	5

Table 6.3 Pension plan type in 1992–2004 HRS respondent data, among full-time employees with a pension, war babies and early boomer cohorts (weighted)

Pension characteristics	War babies					Early boomers	
	1998	2000	2002	2004	2006	2004	2006
% with DB plan	29	37	36	31	34	25	33
% with DC plan	38	39	40	44	45	46	46
% who have combination/ both plans	32	22	22	23	19	26	18
% who have at least 1 DB plan	61	59	58	53	53	51	52
% who have at least 1 DC plan	70	61	62	67	64	72	64
% who respond don't know/refused	1	3	2	3	3	3	2

Table 6.4 Average number of years of job tenure and pension tenure by plan type and cohort in 1992, 1998, and 2004 (weighted)

Cohorts	DB plans		DC plans	
	Job tenure	Pension tenure	Job tenure	Pension tenure
HRS: 51–61	18.5	17.0	16.3	8.4
	(2,481)	(2,481)	(1,873)	(1,873)
HRS: 51–56	17.6	16.4	15.6	8.1
	(1,540)	(1,540)	(1,197)	(1,197)
War babies: 51–56	18.5	17.4	14.2	8.4
	(622)	(622)	(629)	(629)
Early baby boomers: 51–56	16.8	16.3	13.8	9.7
	(755)	(755)	(990)	(990)

Notes: The sample includes respondents who have reported a start date of their current job. They have pension coverage and have reported a plan type and the number of years they have been included in that plan. The pension tenure in 1992 is coded as 1 in the data if it was less than a year. Therefore, job tenure in that survey year is also converted to 1 if it was less than a year. However, in 1998 and 2004 data, some of the variables for pension tenure are zero. That means they are not converted to 1 as they were in 1992. Therefore, the pension and job tenures remain as reported if they were zero in the data for the 1998 and 2004 survey years. Total number of observations is reported in parentheses.

Table 6.5   Average number of years of job tenure and pension tenure for those with
a DB plan only or a DC plan only, in 1992, 1998, and 2004, by HRS
cohort (weighted)

	DB only		DC only	
Cohorts	Job tenure	Pension tenure	Job tenure	Pension tenure
HRS: 51–61	18.0	16.8	13.5	8.5
	(1,524)	(1,524)	(1,074)	(1,074)
HRS: 51–56	17.1	16.1	12.9	8.1
	(936)	(936)	(686)	(686)
War babies: 51–56	18.5	17.5	11.2	7.2
	(294)	(294)	(391)	(391)
Early baby boomers: 51–56	16.7	16.2	11.9	8.5
	(364)	(364)	(680)	(680)

Notes: The sample includes respondents who have reported a start date of their current job.
They have pension coverage and have reported a plan type and the number of years they have
been included in that plan. The pension tenure in 1992 is coded as 1 in the data if it was less
than a year. Therefore, job tenure in that survey year is also converted to 1 if it was less than a
year. However, in 1998 and 2004 data, some of the variables for pension tenure are zero. That
means they are not converted to 1 as they were in 1992. Therefore, the pension and job tenures
remain as reported if they were zero in the data for the 1998 and 2004 survey years. Total
number of observations is reported in parentheses.

The process by which the share of those with DB plans declined also contributed to the difference in pension tenure between those covered by different
plan types. DB plans were not simply replaced by DC plans. Until the past decade, old DB plans, especially plans offered by large firms, were not canceled.
Rather, employment fell in older industries offering DB plans, reducing the
prevalence of DB plans in the overall population (Gustman and Steinmeier,
1992). However, because older workers with seniority continued to work at firms
offering DB plans, but there were no openings for younger workers, the prevalence of DB plans among older, longer tenured workers did not fall nearly as
rapidly as it did for the population as a whole. Thus because the HRS population is relatively old, DB plans are still very common among HRS respondents,
and their tenure under these plans is longer than pension tenure observed for
those with DC plans.

Next, consider the implications of a difference between job tenure and pension tenure, where most people are on their jobs for a longer period than they
are covered by a pension. The difference is small for those with a defined ben-

efit plan, but it is much larger for those with a defined contribution plan. For those 51 to 56 in 1992 with a defined benefit plan, job tenure averaged 17.6 years, while coverage under the defined benefit plan averaged 16.4 years (Table 6.4, row 2, columns 1 and 2). For those 51 to 56 in 2004, the gap declined from 1.2 years in 1992 to 0.5 years (row 5, columns 1 and 2). For those 51 to 56 years old in 1992 with a defined contribution plan, job tenure averaged 15.6 years, while the average length of pension coverage was 8.1 years (row 2, columns 3 and 4). In 1992, 401(k) plans were a relatively recent innovation. Over time, with the establishment and aging of defined contribution plans, for those 51 to 56 years old the difference between job tenure and years of pension coverage fell from 7.5 years in 1992 to 4.1 years in 2004. Roughly speaking, in 1992 those with a DC plan were covered by their pension only half the time they were on the job.

Turning to Table 6.5, where those who have both a DB and a DC plan are excluded from the sample, the gap between job and pension tenure is reduced, but it remains substantial. In 1992, the gap for those with only a DC plan is 4.8 years (row 2, columns 3 and 4). It remains 3.4 years for the early boomers (row 4, columns 3 and 4).

Thus the gap between job and pension tenure is smaller for younger cohorts than for older cohorts, falling from 7.5 years to 4.1 years (Table 6.4, row 2 vs. row 4, columns 3 and 4). The smaller gap is due both to a decline in job tenure over time in employment offering a DC pension and an increase in pension tenure as one looks at younger cohorts. For all the cohorts, the gap between job and pension tenure for those with a DC plan remains significantly greater than for those with a DB plan.

Differences between job tenure and pension tenure are analyzed in detail in Table 6.6. For example, for observations appearing in the bottom row of Table 6.6, job tenure exceeds pension tenure by at least twenty years. Thus in the bottom row of the table, column 4, we find that job tenure exceeds pension tenure by more than twenty years for 12.1 percent of those 51 to 56 with a DC plan in 1992. By 2004, it is much less common to find people with a DC plan who were on their job for many years and were not covered by a pension on their job for more than twenty years. The specific figure is 3.4 percent of those 51 to 56 with a DC plan in 2004.

As seen by summing the first three rows of Table 6.6, a sizable minority of people report a period of coverage by their pension that is longer than the tenure they report on their job. For example, summing the first three rows of

Table 6.6 Percentage of respondents with various pension and job tenures by plan types in 1992, 1998, and 2004 (weighted)

Years between pension tenure and job tenure	HRS: 51–61 1992 DB	HRS: 51–61 1992 DC	HRS: 51–56 1992 DB	HRS: 51–56 1992 DC	WBs: 51–56 1998 DB	WBs: 51–56 1998 DC	EBs: 51–56 2004 DB	EBs: 51–56 2004 DC
Pension tenure > job tenure by 20 years or more	1.8	0.4	1.8	0.2	2.4	0.4	2.2	0.3
Pension tenure > job tenure between 10 and 20 years	2.8	1.2	2.9	1.2	3.1	0.9	4.5	2.1
Pension tenure > job tenure between 1 and 10 years	10.9	3.8	11.2	4.4	10.1	5.1	13.2	7.7
Pension tenure = job tenure	44.9	17.5	45.4	17.5	54.0	22.9	38.1	24.9
Pension tenure < job tenure between 1 and 10 years	31.0	44.2	31.0	44.4	32.2	43.9	35.4	46.8
Pension tenure < job tenure between 10 and 20 years	5.7	18.6	5.5	20.0	5.7	20.2	5.0	14.7
Pension tenure < job tenure more than 20 years	2.9	14.2	2.2	12.1	2.5	6.5	1.5	3.4

Notes: The sample includes respondents who have reported a start date of their current job. They have pension coverage and have reported a plan type and the number of years they have been included in that plan. The pension tenure in 1992 is coded as 1 in the data if it was less than a year. Therefore, job tenure in that survey year is also converted to 1 if it was less than a year. However, in 1998 and 2004 data, some of the variables for pension tenure are zero. That means they are not converted to 1 as they were in 1992. Therefore, the pension and job tenures remain as reported if they were zero in the data for the 1998 and 2004 survey years. Total number of observations is reported in parentheses.

column 1, 15.5 percent of those with a DB plan in 1992 reported a longer period of coverage under their pension plan than they spent in their current employment. For those 51 to 56 years old, the share of those with DB pensions who reported longer pension than job tenure increased from 15.9 percent in 1992 to 19.9 percent in 2004. (Compare the sum of the first three rows of column 3 with the corresponding sum in column 7.) Misreporting may be responsible for some cases where pension tenure exceeds job tenure. In other cases, multiemployer plans or mergers and acquisitions may be responsible. Some in construction, trucking, and other areas where they work for multiple employers are instructed by the HRS interviewers to count this work as a single job. Similarly, a teacher who moved from one school to another in the same district might report a longer period of pension coverage than job tenure. In some cases, a respondent's original employer may have merged or been purchased by another firm, while the employees were permitted to keep their original plans.

Thus it is important to bear in mind that in some cases job tenure may be shorter than pension tenure. Specifically, researchers need to be careful in interpreting findings as to pension values estimated from employer-provided plan descriptions since the normal procedure in using the HRS pension software is to insert job tenure, rather than pension tenure, into the program.

Pension Changes Experienced by Those Holding the Same Job

To increase understanding of pension changes, Table 6.7 shows the high frequency with which HRS respondents who stay on the same job report that their pensions have changed since the last wave of the survey. According to the summary measure presented in the last column of the table, each year between a sixth and a quarter of respondents who were working at the same employment and covered by a pension in two adjoining waves report some change in their pension plan between waves—that is, over a two-year period. Either their old plan was changed, or they were offered a new plan.

Table 6.7 pools observations for all those who remain on the same job between adjoining waves, whatever cohort they belong to. Once a new cohort enters the survey, its members may report pension changes in subsequent waves. This causes the number of observations to grow after a new cohort enters. In addition, some of those who report their pensions changed between waves may have reported a pension change one or more times in the past.

Table 6.7 Pension dynamics between waves: number of respondents working at the same employment with the same and new pension cross-waves

Waves and job status	Same pension[a]	Changed pension	New pension[b]	Total	(Changed+new) / total
Wave 1			4,457		
Same job in Wave 2 as in Wave 1	2,786	279	303	3,368	.17
Same job in Wave 3 as in Wave 2	2,347	258	287	2,892	.19
Same job in Wave 4 as in Wave 3	2,082	224	215	2,521	.17
Same job in Wave 5 as in Wave 4	2,194	402	374	2,970	.26
Same job in Wave 6 as in Wave 5	1,784	258	213	2,255	.21
Same job in Wave 7 as in Wave 6	1,523	167	259	1,949	.22
Same job in Wave 8 as in Wave 7	2,114	250	270	2,634	.20

a. *Same pension* refers to those pension plans whose rules have not changed since previous interview.
b. *New pension* includes pension plans from those who reported no pension in the previous interview.

Table 6.8 Percentages of those with indicated plan types, by cohort, for the base and terminal year for the job held in the base year (weighted)

Plan type by base and terminal year	HRS: 51–61 in 1992	HRS: 51–56 in 1992	WBs: 51–56 in 1998
DB only			
Base year	41	40	31
Termination	52	51	44
DC only			
Base year	28	29	30
Termination	30	29	29
Both			
Base year	29	29	38
Termination	17	18	26
At least 1 DB			
Base year	70	70	69
Termination	69	69	70
At least 1 DC			
Base year	57	58	68
Termination	47	47	55
DK			
Base year	2	2	1
Termination	2	2	1

Note: Column 1 is based on 2,122 observations, column 2 on 1,382 observations, and column 3 on 628 observations.

A next logical step is to examine changes in plan type within cohorts for those who remain on the same job. Table 6.8 presents relevant data on plan type reported in the base year observed for members of the HRS and war baby cohorts and compares those with plan type in the termination wave of the survey, defined as the wave just before the respondent leaves that job.[4] For example, column 1, row 2, indicates that on average, in the wave just before leaving their 1992 job, 52 percent of respondents with a pension reported having a defined benefit plan only. As seen in row 1 of column 1, 41 percent of these same respondents reported in 1992 that they had a DB plan only. Surprisingly, the data suggest that the frequency of holding a defined benefit plan only increased over time.

On the basis of the data in rows 7 and 8, respondents reported that they were just as likely to be covered by a defined benefit plan in the last wave they were employed on their job as in the first wave they were observed on that job. Moreover, and more surprisingly, comparing the values in rows 9 and 10, they reported that they were less likely to be covered by a defined contribution plan in the wave before they left a job than in the first wave in which they were included in the survey.

These results suggest two things. First, it is likely that pension plan type changes much more slowly for those remaining on the same job than it does when we compare pensions held by different people over time. Second, it seems implausible that over this period, the frequency of holding a defined benefit plan only increased over time while the frequency of holding a DC plan declined, and that there were fewer people holding a supplementary DC plan over time. This suggests that in addition to slow changes in plan type among those on the same job, there must have been reporting error.

As will be seen in Chapter 7, much of this puzzling result is, in fact, due to reporting error. That chapter spends a considerable amount of time trying to understand the extent of and reasons for reporting error in plan type and the implications of that reporting error both for our understanding of pensions and for survey design, which depends so much on accurate reporting of plan type.

Transitions to Cash Balance Plans Are Infrequently Reported in HRS Data

The recent trend to cash balance plans discussed in the introductory chapters is not reflected in HRS reports of pension plan type. In a special pension module in 2004 (referred to as Module 6/7), respondents were asked to identify their plan type without first determining whether they have a DB or DC plan. They were free to identify their pension as a cash balance plan or to choose cash balance as one type among a list that was read to them. However, only about 0.7 percent of HRS respondents with a pension in the module, and about 3.4 percent of those with a DB plan, identified their plans as cash balance. (In addition, the module understates the number with a DB plan because 16–17 percent of those in the module either did not identify their plan type or identified their plan type as "something else.")

Two reasons may be suggested for the low frequency of reports of cash balance plans in HRS data. First, the HRS population is older than other nationally representative samples. As a result, HRS respondents may have been grandfathered into their old DB plans. Second, there may be reporting errors in reported plan type, an issue that has already arisen as we tried to explain trends in plan type. There are no employer-provided data that will allow us to determine what the true frequency of cash balance plans is for a population that is on the verge of retirement. As a result, we cannot determine which of these hypotheses is correct.

Implications of Pension Changes for Workers' Decisions

As we have seen, plan type and other plan features covering a particular worker may change for two key reasons. A worker may change jobs, where the two jobs offer different plans. Or the worker may stay in the same job, but the firm may offer a different plan. Each of these may lead to one or more changes in individuals' pensions over their work life.

The uncertainty as to whether pensions will change may affect a worker's planning for both saving and retirement. Defined benefit plans promise a known payout for the remainder of an individual's life. They sharply define a window for retirement. Their value depends on continued employment under the plan. Defined contribution plans require a person to plan how to draw down the amount in the account so that it lasts for the remainder of the covered worker's life. As the pension amount changes, the rate of drawdown may not change proportionately, depending on whether the individual is committed to certain expenditures that are difficult to vary, for example, his or her current home.

A person who knew a pension change was coming could plan accordingly. Someone who knew that there was some possibility of a pension change could treat the availability and amount of expected pensions as uncertain. But many of those approaching retirement today had thought that their pensions were secure and that the scheme governing the payout of benefits was clearly determined. They did not predict the changes in industry structure and competition that underlie many of the changes in their plans. Indeed, many were sufficiently confident in their retirement prospects that they felt little need to plan for retirement. They saw older neighbors, friends, and colleagues enjoying comfortable retirements from similar pensions designed to last a lifetime, together with Social Security.

When plans change unexpectedly, that introduces a need to reoptimize. When plan type changes, that requires reeducation to learn how to manage the benefit drawdown. When plan changes reduce benefits, one has to play catch-up or reconcile to managing with a lower level of retirement income than originally expected.

Pension changes also complicate many types of economic analysis. Both expected and unexpected changes in pensions must be accounted for in explaining retirement and saving behavior. Many studies still ignore the vast differences in incentives across pension plans, with relatively few taking account of the important effects of the location and size of the spike in benefit accrual that is a common feature of defined benefit plans when the covered worker reaches early entitlement age. Most studies ignore the effects of availability of benefits as well as differences in time preference, which affect how the promise of additional future benefits is traded off against current benefits.

The most sophisticated retirement studies available today, estimating structural models that separate preferences and opportunity sets, still fall short of modeling the complications introduced by pension changes. Typically they assume that incentives from the pensions in place at a single moment in time will hold throughout the lifetime. Our findings regarding pension changes suggest that there is a good deal of work that remains to be done in retirement modeling.

7

Imperfect Knowledge of
Pension Plan Type

The designers of the Health and Retirement Study felt that workers were unlikely to be able to fully describe the complex rules governing benefit eligibility and values under defined benefit (DB) plans. Following the approach that the principal investigator of the HRS, Tom Juster, had taken as principal investigator of the Survey of Consumer Finances, details about respondents' pensions were gathered both from respondents and from their employers. The idea was that information on defined benefit plans would be obtained from employer plan descriptions, while account balances of defined contribution (DC) plans would be obtained from respondent reports.

Evidence continues to accumulate that there are substantial differences between pension outcomes reported by some pension-covered workers and the corresponding outcomes gleaned from employer-produced data.[1] One such discrepancy is particularly troubling for survey design. Respondents often report plan type with error, which means that their remaining set of questions pertains to the wrong plan type. The possibility that some respondents do not know enough about their pensions to understand whether they have a defined benefit plan or a defined contribution plan is even more troubling to those who are trying to understand retirement and saving behavior. Virtually all models of retirement and saving estimated by economists assume well-informed agents. If some people do not know even this very basic fact about their pension—what kind of plan they have—this suggests a fundamental problem for the standard approaches to modeling retirement and saving behavior.

This chapter documents the extent to which reported pension plan type differs between respondent and firm-produced data in the Health and Retirement Study and discusses the reasons for these differences and their implications. Most important, we would like to know whether differences between respondent and firm reports of pension plan type are the result of respondents' imperfect knowledge and understanding of their pensions, or whether there are other reasons for these differences.

Different reasons for incorrect reports of plan type may have very different implications, both for our understanding of behavior and for the design of relevant policies. If respondent errors are common and are the main cause of discrepancies between respondent-reported pension outcomes and outcomes obtained from employer plan descriptions, and if the misreports are due to poor understanding of their pensions by covered workers, then questions would be raised about how well people do in determining the adequacy of their retirement saving, whether covered workers understand the choice set created by the complex rules governing retirement plans,[2] and whether people appropriately value the pension plans their employers provide as part of their compensation packages. Such errors will also raise concerns about appropriate policy solutions and the costs and benefits of various strategies for dealing with illiteracy, ranging from educational programs to restrictions on choices or adoption of default schemes that channel decisions of the least informed agents to the least harmful outcomes.[3]

There also are implications for survey design. Because surveys condition the questions they ask about pensions on reported plan type, if plan type is incorrectly identified, some respondents may be asked questions that do not pertain to the plan they hold. In response to a question that does not apply to their pension, some may fabricate answers to satisfy reviewers. Others may bring in information about additional plans they hold other than the one under discussion. Another consequence of imperfect identification of plan type is that some respondents will not be asked questions that are important for determining the value and properties of their pensions.

The HRS presents a unique opportunity for studying the extent of misinformation. Previous studies have had information on disagreements between respondent and firm reports in a single cross-section. The HRS allows these discrepancies to be examined in the context of the panel. That means we can ask not only about consistency of answers at a moment in time but whether answers are given consistently by the same person over time. Patterns of answers over time can be related to other responses—for example, whether the respondent believes the plan has been changed.

Background information on the changing situation over time is provided by the course of firm-produced pension data, collected from employers contacted by the Survey of Consumer Finances in 1983 and by the Health and Retirement Study in 1993, 1999, and 2005. These data allow us to document how the relationship of employer to respondent reports has changed over the course of three decades. Panel data within the Health and Retirement Study are examined for respondents who report no change in their pension plans. In a number of cases, despite reporting that their plans have not changed, respondents report a different plan type from a previous wave. As seen in the last chapter, trends in plan type for those who do not change jobs suggest an increase in the frequency of defined benefit plans over the course of employment, a trend opposite to the very strong changes observed for all workers. Similarly, among those reporting no change in plan type, there are those who first report a DC plan and then report that they have a DB plan in a later wave.

Supplementing the information from the HRS, the Watson Wyatt Company has made available comparisons between employer payroll data and respondent reports of pensions. It is sometimes argued that pension outcomes differ between respondent data and matched employer pension plan provisions because of errors in matching the employee to the appropriate pension plan provided by the firm. In particular, it is argued that the multiple steps involved in securing pension plan descriptions from employers create a problem in matching. Firms may not submit all the plans covering their workers, or the specifications of which workers are covered by which plan in firms that offer multiple plans may be inadequate for determining which of these plans covers the HRS respondent. With the payroll data available from Watson Wyatt, it is possible to perfectly match a respondent's pension plan to the covered worker, so that all discrepancies are due to errors in information provided by the respondent. Again the data suggest that respondent reports of plan type are subject to substantial error.

To further explore these issues, we first list a number of reasons why firm and respondent reports may contain errors. We then compare reports of pension plan type from respondent data with reports from employer-produced plan descriptions. Following that, we document the consistencies and inconsistencies in firm and respondent reports of plan type over time. We then turn to the survey and matched payroll data from Watson Wyatt. In addition, we analyze variation in self-reported plan type in eight waves of the HRS panel for

members of the original HRS cohort who report that their pension plan is unchanged over time. For those who report no change in their pensions over time,
we compare plan type at the time of the survey to plan type at the time a respondent leaves a pension-covered job. We also consider an experiment where
those who reported a DB plan were asked questions relevant to a DC plan and
vice versa. This suggests the nature of errors that would arise should questions
not be conditioned on plan type, so that people with one type of pension are
asked about pensions characteristics for a plan type they did not report. In the
course of our discussion of reporting errors in plan type, we report findings
from listening to interview tapes, where respondents informally discuss any
source of confusion. We also present findings from an experimental module
that asked respondents whether they knew the technical name of the plan, before presenting respondents with a list of plan types.

Reasons for Differences between Firm and Respondent Reports

There are a number of theories about why respondents' reports of plan type
differ from the reports submitted by their employers. A few of them are listed
here.

The Fault May Lie with the Respondent or the Respondent's Knowledge

1. Some respondents may be badly informed about their pensions because
their plans are too complex for them to understand. Other respondents may
be able to understand their pensions after some effort but may choose not to
exert the effort because the eventual benefits are not worth the costs (Lusardi,
1999). Either the costs may be high because of the difficulty of the calculation, or the benefits may be low. For example, low benefits may reflect a low
dollar value of the pension or, conversely, a good pension that, together with
Social Security, will provide a good replacement rate. In that case, further
investigation about the nature of the pension will not affect either retirement
or savings decisions.

2. When the respondent is included in more than one plan, there may be
confusion created by the strategy followed by the HRS and other surveys, in
which the respondent is asked to first describe the most important plan. We will
show that in most cases, the DB plan is the most important plan. Nevertheless,

some respondents may think the DC plan is more important. Even worse, the respondent may report that one plan is more important in some waves and that the other is more important in other waves. Again, this may be the result of the complexity of the pension calculation. To avoid this problem, it is possible to categorize the pensions covering a particular worker as "all plans are DB," "all plans are DC," or "there are both types of plans covering the respondent." By not focusing on each plan individually, the burden of trying to determine which plan is most important is lifted, but at the cost of aggregating results that could be analyzed on a plan-by-plan basis.

3. If some respondents do not participate in a plan and do not report being eligible for the plan, these respondents may report being covered by fewer plans than are listed by the firm. This could be a particular problem for those with a DC plan who do not contribute each year and consider themselves not to be covered by the plan in years they do not contribute.

4. Respondents may misreport whether their plan has changed over time, affecting plan type reported in different waves.

The Fault May Lie with the Survey Questions and Design

5. Survey questions that attempt to distinguish plan type may be poorly crafted. For example, the survey may present definitions of DB and DC plans and describe the properties of different plans, noting that a defined benefit plan provides a benefit that is determined by salary and years of service, while a defined contribution plan provides an account. These descriptions may be unclear to the respondent. Evidence presented below suggests that errors are likely to lead to overstatement of the frequency of plans that are dominant in the market, DB in 1983 and DC in 2004.

The Fault May Lie with the Process of Collecting and Matching
Employer-Provided Plan Descriptions to Respondents

6. As noted above, a firm may offer a large number of plans of different types and may have submitted many plan descriptions to the HRS. Summary plan descriptions list the characteristics of those workers who are covered by the particular plan being described—for example, full-time union workers hired in a specified window, say from 1990 to 2000. Still, the characteristics of the respondent and of the covered workers may not be precisely enough stated (Rohwedder, 2003). As a result, the wrong plan description may be selected

from the group of plans submitted by the firm to the HRS and attributed to the respondent.[4]

7. In some cases, the firm may not have sent in all the available plan descriptions for its employees, or the full set of plan descriptions may not have been available from the supplementary sources used by the HRS when collecting plan documents.[5]

8. There may be some matching problems based on the date of the SPD, whether received from the firm or from other sources.[6]

Consistency between Employer and Respondent Reports

Gustman and Steinmeier (1989) use matched respondent and employer data from the 1983 Survey of Consumer Finances (SCF) to document the extent of agreement between respondent reports of pension plan type and reports from firms indicating the type of pension covering the workers in the sample. If the respondent report of plan type agrees with the matching report obtained from the employer, an observation will fall along the diagonal of a table in which respondent reports of plan type are indicated by the row head, while firm reports are indicated by the column head. Summing the first three figures on the diagonal in Table 7.1A, 59.7 percent of respondents with matched plan descriptions report a plan type that agrees with the plan type gleaned from employer documents. As for the rest, the response is "don't know" (DK) for 16.4 percent of respondents (row 4, column 4, of Table 7.1A), with the remaining 23.9 percent of the cases having misidentified their plan type.

It also turns out that these disagreements are not randomly distributed. If they were, the average frequency of DB and DC plans reported by respondents and gleaned from employer data would agree. Instead the average frequencies with which each plan type is reported, as seen in the bottom row and right-hand column of Table 7.1A, are in disagreement. Although firm reports indicate coverage by a DB plan only in 88.1 percent of the cases, 58.9 percent of respondent reports indicate coverage by a DB plan only. Even adjusting for the DKs in the respondent reports, dividing 58.9 by .836, the fraction of respondents reporting a DB plan only, at 70.5 percent, is substantially lower than in the employer data. Conversely, the fraction of respondents reporting both types of plans is much higher in the respondent data, with 17.3 percent of respondents (20.7 percent of respondents who identified a plan type) suggesting they are covered by both types of plans. In contrast, only 3.5 percent of firm

Table 7.1A Percentage distribution of self-reported versus firm-reported plan type for current job held in 1983, including only those respondents with a matched pension plan

Provider report in 1983	Self-report in 1983 (%)				
	1. DB	2. DC	3. Both	4. DK	5. Total
1. DB	55.2	4.0	15.1	13.8	88.1
2. DC	2.4	3.1	0.9	2.1	8.5
3. Both	1.2	0.3	1.4	0.5	3.5
4. Total	58.9	7.4	17.3	16.4	100 (579)

Note: Total number of observations is reported in parentheses. Total percentage has been rounded.

Table 7.1B Percentages with self-reported plan type conditional on firm report of plan type for current job held in 1983, including only those respondents with a matched pension plan (percent of row total)

Provider report in 1983	Self-report in 1983 (%)				
	1. DB	2. DC	3. Both	4. DK	5. Total
1. DB	62.7	4.5	17.1	15.7	100
2. DC	28.6	36.7	10.2	24.5	100
3. Both	35.0	10.0	40.0	15.0	100
4. Total	58.9	7.4	17.3	16.4	100

Source: Gustman and Steinmeier (1989, table 6), using data from the Survey of Consumer Finances.

documents indicate coverage by both types of plans. These discrepancies create additional differences between the totals with a DC plan, whether due to coverage by a DC plan only or by a DC plan together with a DB plan, as reported by respondents and firms.[7]

Nevertheless, at a time when most people had a DB plan, most respondents who could answer questions about plan type told interviewers that they had a DB plan when their employer said they had one and that they had a DC plan when employer data suggested this was the case. This can be seen in Table 7.1B, which indicates the distribution of employee responses conditional on the plan type obtained from employer documents. Only 4.5 percent of those whose employers' documents said they had a DB plan only reported they had a DC plan only. Of the 8.5 percent of respondents whose employer documents said they had a DC plan only, as seen in column 2, row 2, 36.7 percent of respondents agreed, with another 10.2 percent of them suggesting they had both a DB and a DC plan. Although 28.6 percent (column 1, row 2) of those whose employers reported that they had a DC plan only reported having a DB plan only, that difference represented only 2.4 percent of all those with a pension.

Turn now to more recent data from the Health and Retirement Study. Table 7.2A includes respondent and employer reports from the 1992 wave of the HRS. Comparing the HRS data in Table 7.2A with the data from the Survey of Consumer Finances in Table 7.1A, the growth in defined contribution plans is obvious. According to the employer data from 1992, 52 percent (column 5 of Table 7.2A, sum of rows 2 and 3) of all respondents reported a DC plan, either held alone or in combination with a DB plan. This compares with 12 percent with a DC plan (Table 7.1A, column 5, rows 2 plus 3) in 1983.

In 1992, 2 percent of HRS respondents said that they did not know their plan type. This compares with a DK level of 16.4 percent recorded in the SCF survey from nine years earlier. Respondents to the Survey of Consumer Finances were younger than respondents to the Health and Retirement Study. This may be one reason for the higher DK frequency in the SCF data.

Unlike the case in 1983, the average frequency of each plan type reported by respondents agrees with the average frequency of plan type calculated from matched employer data. Looking at the column and row totals in Table 7.2A, 48 percent of provider reports indicate a DB plan only (row 1, column 5), roughly the same total (46 percent) as in respondent reports (row 4, column 1). The fraction with a DC plan only (row 2, column 5) is 21 percent in the firm data and 24 percent (column 2, row 4) in the respondent data. The fraction found with any DC plan in the employer data in 1992 (column 5, rows 2 plus 3) is the same as the fraction found in respondent reports (row 4, columns 2 plus 3). Similarly, 79 percent of employer reports indicate coverage by a DB plan, either via coverage by a DB plan only (row 1, column 5) or by both a DB and a DC plan (row 3, column 5), while 74 percent of respondent reports suggest coverage by a DB plan either alone or in addition to a DC plan (row 4, column 1 plus column 3).

As in the 1983 data, the agreement between respondent and firm reports frequently breaks down at the level of the individual. This can be seen by comparing the frequency with which observations fall along the diagonal of Table 7.2A, but do not involve a DK response, with the frequency with which they fall off the diagonal, indicating disagreement. The number of responses in off-diagonal elements is larger in 1992 than in 1983. Thus from Table 7.2A,

Table 7.2A   Percentage distribution of self-reported versus firm-reported plan type as reported by the respondent and the firm, for current job held in 1992, including only those HRS respondents with a matched pension plan

Provider report in 1992	Self-report in 1992 (%)				
	1. DB	2. DC	3. Both	4. DK	5. Total
1. DB	27	7	13	1	48
2. DC	6	11	4	0	21
3. Both	14	6	11	1	31
4. Total	46	24	28	2	100 (2,907)

Note: Total number of observations is reported in parentheses.

Table 7.2B   Percentages with self-reported plan type conditional on firm report of plan type for current job held in 1992, including only those respondents with a matched pension plan (percent of row total)

Provider report in 1992	Self-report in 1992 (%)				
	1. DB	2. DC	3. Both	4. DK	5. Total
1. DB	56	15	27	2	100
2. DC	26	54	18	2	100
3. Both	45	18	35	2	100
4. Total	46	24	28	2	100

only 49 percent of responses lie along the main diagonal in 1992 and do not involve a DK response, compared with 60 percent in 1983.

Another perspective on the extent of disagreement is provided when we condition on provider responses and ask how well respondents' answers agree. From Table 7.2B, row 1, column 2, among those whose firm report indicates a DB plan only, 15 percent of respondents report a DC plan only. Among those with a firm report of a DC plan only, 26 percent report a DB plan only (row 2, column 1). As seen in row 3, column 2, 18 percent of respondents whose employer documents report both types of plans instead report having a DC plan only. Most of the rest reported a DB plan only, with only 35 percent of those respondents whose firms reported both a DB and a DC plan reporting having both a DB and a DC plan (row 3, column 3).

From Table 7.3A, in 2004 we observe systematic differences in the average plan type reported by respondents and obtained from their employer

Table 7.3A   Percentage distribution of self-reported versus firm-reported plan type as reported by the respondent and the firm, for current job held in 2004, including private and public sector respondents with a matched pension plan

Provider report in 2004	Self-report in 2004 (%)				
	1. DB	2. DC	3. Both	4. DK	5. Total
1. DB	12	5	7	0	25
2. DC	4	18	4	1	26
3. Both	24	9	15	1	49
4. Total	40	32	25	3	100 (1,533)

Notes: Public and private plans include respondents' documents (statements and SPDs) and firms' plan documents. Total number of observations is reported in parentheses. Total percentages may not add up due to rounding.

Table 7.3B   Percentages with self-reported plan type conditional on firm report of plan type for current job held in 2004, including only those respondents with a matched pension plan (percent of row total)

Provider report in 2004	Self-report in 2004 (%)				
	1. DB	2. DC	3. Both	4. DK	5. Total
1. DB	50	20	27	2	100
2. DC	14	69	14	3	100
3. Both	48	19	30	3	100
4. Total	40	32	25	3	100

documents, but the differences are not as sharp as they were in the 1983 data. Overall, the difference between respondent and firm reports lies in the overstatement by respondents, relative to the firm documents, of the frequency of those with a DB plan only and the corresponding understatement of the fraction with both plan types. From row 1, column 5, we see that 25 percent of provider reports indicate a DB plan only, while 40 percent of respondent reports (row 4, column 1) indicate coverage by a DB plan only. Twenty-five percent of the respondent reports (row 4, column 3), and 49 percent of the firm reports (row 3, column 5) indicate coverage by both types of plans. Twenty-six percent of provider reports (row 2, column 5) suggest coverage by a DC plan only, while 32 percent of respondents (row 4, column 2) indicate coverage by a DC plan only. Altogether, 74 percent of firm reports indicate coverage by a DB plan, either exclusively (row 1, column 5) or in combination with a DC plan

Table 7.3C Percentage distribution of self-reported versus firm-reported plan type as reported by the respondent and the firm, for current job held in 2004, including only private sector respondents with a matched pension plan

Provider report in 2004	Self-report in 2004 (%)				
	1. DB	2. DC	3. Both	4. DK	5. Total
1. DB	10	3	4	0	18
2. DC	6	31	6	1	44
3. Both	17	10	11	1	38
4. Total	32	44	22	3	100 (831)

Notes: Only private plans are included. Plans include respondents' documents (statements and SPDs) and firms' plan documents. Total number of observations is reported in parentheses. Total percentages may not add up due to rounding.

Table 7.3D Percentages with self-reported plan type conditional on firm report of plan type for current job held in 2004, including only private sector respondents with a matched pension plan (percent of row total)

Provider report in 2004	Self-report in 2004 (%)				
	1. DB	2. DC	3. Both	4. DK	5. Total
1. DB	56	19	23	3	100
2. DC	13	70	14	3	100
3. Both	44	25	29	2	100
4. Total	32	44	22	3	100

(row 3, column 5), while 65 percent of respondent reports indicate coverage by a DB plan (row 4, column 1, plus row 4, column 3).

In 2004, less than half the observations (45 percent) lie along the main diagonal of Table 7.3A, with 4 percent fewer observations found in 2004 than in 1992 (49 percent). Agreement between respondent and firm reports was higher in 1983, where 60 percent of the observations lay along the main diagonal. In 2004, only 3 percent of respondents reported that they did not know their plan type.

The findings in 2004 raise a question about one hypothesis for explaining systematic disagreement between respondent and firm reports of plan type. To the extent that descriptions of secondary DC plans are more difficult to collect from employers than are DB plans, it might be argued that the frequency of DC plans is systematically understated in employer data. Instead, what we find in 2004 is that coverage by DC plans is understated by respondents at 57 percent (32+25) relative to coverage by DC plans in employer data at 75 percent (26+49).

Other discrepancies are reported in Table 7.3B. Of those whose firm reports coverage by a DC plan only, 14 percent of respondents report coverage by a DB plan only, and 14 percent report coverage by both a DB and a DC plan. Altogether, 28 percent (row 2, columns 1 plus 3) of those whose firms report that they are covered by a DC plan only report coverage by a DB plan. Among those whose firm reports a DB plan only, 20 percent report coverage by a DC plan only (row 1, column 2), while 27 percent report coverage by both types of plans (row 1, column 3).

It might be argued that respondents who have public plans have greatest difficulty in identifying their plan type. While they are most frequently covered by DB plans, they often have an account based on their own contribution that will return a balance equal to the sum of their contributions, plus a low interest rate. Accordingly, Table 7.3C confines the observations to those in private sector plans.

When 702 public sector employees are excluded from the sample, the frequency of DC plans increases by 18 percent within the sample of employer documents gleaned from the private sector, while the frequency of reports of both plan types declines by 11 percent. This can be seen by comparing Tables 7.3A and 7.3C, rows 1 and 3 in column 5. However, there is little change in the reported frequency of both plan types in the self-reported data, where we would have expected this frequency to decline if public sector employees were more likely to report both plan types when they had a DB plan only. Comparing Tables 7.3B and 7.3D shows that conditional on the employer reporting a DB plan only, there is only a very small difference in the likelihood of the respondent reporting both plan types between the samples that include both public and private plans and the sample that is confined to private plans only. Although when public plans are eliminated from the sample those whose firms report a DB plan are 4 percent less likely to report having both plan types, this difference is small enough to suggest little distortion due to confusion by public employees who hold a DB plan as to whether their plan is DB only or both.

We can draw a number of conclusions from Tables 7.3A and B, which pertain to 2004 data, and Table 7.4, which summarizes a number of the key findings over the three surveys:

1. From Table 7.3A and B, misidentification of plan type by respondents does not cause the overall fraction of those with a DB plan (DB only plus both) to be badly misstated. The error is about 9 percentage points in 2004. Nor does it cause the fraction of those with a DC plan only to be badly misstated. But it does cause misstatement of the fraction with a DB plan only and of the fraction with a DC plan (DC only plus both). Respondents whose employers identify them as having a DB plan reported having either a DB plan or both in over three-fourths of the cases in 2004 (row 1, column 1+column 3) and so would have been asked about that plan in most cases. There is a greater problem for those whose employers offer both plan types. In 2004 respondents would have been asked about a DB plan in 78 percent of the cases (row 3, column 1+column 3) but would have been asked about a DC plan in only 49 percent of the cases (row 3, column 2+column 3).

2. Findings for 1983, 1992, and 2004 are summarized in Table 7.4. The results in the first three rows contrast the frequency of plan type reported in employer data, with the data highlighting the trend to DC plans. The fraction of respondents who do not know their plan type is lower in later years (line 4). Some of this disparity probably reflects differences in the age of the sample, which was younger in the 1983 SCF data than in the HRS data collected in later years. However, in our analysis below, we do not find better matching of respondent with firm reports for those who are closer to retirement or have just retired.

3. The fraction of respondents who correctly identify their plan type has only a weak trend over time, with the share of observations falling on the main diagonal running about 60 percent in 1983 and about 45 percent in 2004 (Table 7.4, line 8). Trends in DK are mitigated but not offset by trends in other errors.

4. Those whose firm reported that they had a DB plan only were less likely to claim erroneously that they had a DC plan only in 1983 (row 9, columns 1 and 3) than in 2004. In 2004, with DC as the dominant type of plan, those whose firm reported a DB plan only reported with greater frequency (in column 3, rows 9 and 10) that they had a DC plan only or both types of plans than in 1983.

5. Errors are likely to lead to overstatement of the frequency of plans that are dominant in the market, DB in 1983 and DC in 2004. In 1983, when DB was the dominant type of plan, those who worked for firms reporting that their plan was DC only were much more likely to report that they had a DB plan (column 1, row 11) than was the case for those who worked for a firm reporting DC only in 2004 (column 3, row 11), when DC was the dominant type of plan.

Table 7.4 Summary of respondent and firm reports over time

Reported plan type or related characteristic from employer or respondent data	1983	1992	2004[a]
1. DB only: employer data	88	48	25
2. DC only: employer data	8	21	26
3. Both: employer data	3	31	49
4. DK	16	2	3
5. Frequency of DB only	Understated by 18 percentage points in respondent report, after excluding DKs	Understated by 1 percentage point in respondent report, after excluding DKs	Overstated by 16 percentage points in respondent report, after excluding DKs
6. Frequency of DC only	Overstated by .4 percentage points, after excluding DKs	Overstated by 3 percentage points in respondent data, after excluding DKs	Overstated by 7 percentage points in respondent data, after excluding DKs
7. Frequency of both	Overstated by 17 percentage points, after excluding DKs	Understated by 2 percentage points in respondent data, after excluding DKs	Understated by 23 percentage points in respondent data, after excluding DKs
8. Share on diagonal: employer and respondent agree	60 percentage points on diagonal (despite high DK)	49 percentage points on diagonal	45 percentage points on diagonal

9. Conditional on firm reporting DB only, respondent reporting DC only	4	15	20
10. Conditional on firm reporting DB only, respondert reporting both	17	27	27
11. Conditional on firm reporting DC only, respondent reporting DB only	29	26	14
12. Conditional on firm reporting DC only, respondent reporting both only	10	18	14
13. Conditional on firm reporting both, respondent reporting DB only	35	45	48
14. Conditional on firm reporting both, respondent reporting DC only	10	18	19

a. Data for 2004 as well as for 1983 and 1992 include public and private plans.

Difference in the Panel in Respondent and Firm Reports among Those Reporting No Change in Their Pensions

For further evidence on reporting error, we turn to a panel of those respondents who reported that their pension plans did not change between 1992 and 1998. Here we examine changes both in self-reports of plan type and in firm reports of plan type.[8]

If respondent reports were correct and plans matched correctly, there should be no change in plan type for anyone in this sample, because when asked in each wave whether their pension had changed, the respondents answered no. Given the discrepancies we found in the previous section, it is not surprising to find that reported plan types vary over time for a significant minority of respondents who report no change in their plan. Moreover, when respondents reported in 1998 a different plan type from the one reported in 1992, they often misreport the nature of the change.

There are a number of possible reasons why reported plan type changed even though the respondent said there was no change. The respondent may be wrong about the plan not having changed; or despite reporting correctly that the plan has not changed, the respondent may misidentify the plan type in one or another of the two years. A third possibility is that the respondent may have a defined contribution plan but may participate in some years and not in others, failing to report plan type as DC in a year when not participating.

By contrasting the changes for the respondent sample and the firm sample, the evidence suggests that plans have changed in many more cases than respondents think. Table 7.5A shows the distribution of self-reported plan types between 1992 and 1998 for those who report no change in plan type. Along the diagonal, we see that 58 percent of respondents report the same plan type in 1998 as they did in 1992 (32+16+10). From row 1 of Table 7.5B, among those who reported having a DB plan only in 1992, 72 percent continue to report a DB plan only in 1998, 16 percent report a DC plan only, and 11 percent report both. Thus there is a reported gain in DC plans only, replacing DB plans only, and an 11 percent increase in the frequency of both types of plans.

For the 25 percent of respondents reporting a plan type who reported a DC plan only in 1992, as seen from Table 7.5B, row 2, 22 percent of respondents report that their plan type switched back to a DB plan only, and another 14 percent claim that they gained a DB plan as their firm adopted both types of plans. Yet we know that there was almost no adoption of new DB pension

Table 7.5A Percentage distribution of self-reported plan type for respondents reporting the same pension plan from 1992 to 1998 and with matched 1992 and 1998 plan data

Self-report in 1992	Self-report in 1998 (%)				
	1. DB	2. DC	3. Both	4. DK	5. Total
1. DB	32	7	5	0	45
2. DC	6	16	4	0	25
3. Both	14	4	10	0	28
4. DK	0	1	1	0	2
5. Total	52	28	19	0	100 (450)

Note: Total number of observations is reported in parentheses. Total percentages may not add up due to rounding.

Table 7.5B Distribution of self-reported plan type in 1998 conditional on self-reported plan type in 1992, for respondents reporting the same pension plan from 1992 to 1998 and with matched 1992 and 1998 plan data (percent of row total)

Self-report in 1992	Self-report in 1998 (%)				
	1. DB	2. DC	3. Both	4. DK	5. Total
1. DB	72	16	11	1	100
2. DC	22	64	14	0	100
3. Both	50	15	35	0	100
4. DK	22	44	33	0	100
5. Total	52	28	19	0	100 (450)

Note: Total number of observations is reported in parentheses. Total percentages may not add up due to rounding.

plans over this period (Ippolito and Thompson, 2000). Similarly, from row 3 of Table 7.5B, 50 percent of those who claimed to have both a DB and a DC plan in 1992 claim to have lost the DC plan in the intervening six years, while 15 percent of those with both types of plans claim to have lost their DB plan over the intervening period.

Now consider the changes in employer-reported plan type for this sample, remembering that they claim that their plans were unchanged over the period. From Table 7.5C, only 55 percent (14 + 16 + 25) of the observations lie along the diagonal, suggesting that plan type changed for the remaining 45 percent of the sample. The changes found in this table, and examined further in Table 7.5D, are much more consistent with what is known about trends in pensions over the

Table 7.5C   Percentage distribution of firm-reported plan type for respondents
reporting the same pension plan from 1992 to 1998 and with matched
1992 and 1998 plan data

	Provider report in 1998 (%)			
Provider report in 1992	1. DB	2. DC	3. Both	4. Total
1. DB	14	3	30	48
2. DC	1	16	2	20
3. Both	6	2	25	33
4. Total	21	21	58	100 (455)

Notes: The sample includes respondents with the same pension since 1992 who have
matched plan documents in 1992 and 1998. Total number of observations is reported in
parentheses. Total percentages may not add up due to rounding.

Table 7.5D   Distribution of firm-reported plan type in 1998 conditional on
firm-reported plan type in 1992, for respondents reporting the same
pension plan from 1992 to 1998 and with matched 1992 and 1998 plan
data (percent of row total)

	Provider report in 1998 (%)			
Provider report in 1992	1. DB	2. DC	3. Both	4. Total
1. DB	30	6	64	100
2. DC	4	83	12	100
3. Both	17	7	76	100
4. Total	21	22	58	100 (455)

Note: Total number of observations is reported in parentheses. Total percentages may not
add up due to rounding.

period. Thus while only 30 percent of those with a DB plan only in 1992 have
employer reports suggesting that they are covered by a DB plan only in 1998,
the reason is that 64 percent of them now are covered by both types of plans.
More important, among those with a DC plan only in 1992, their employer-
provided data suggest that they are covered by a DC plan only in 83 percent of
the cases. In sharp contrast with the self-reported data in Table 7.5B, where 36
percent of respondents with a DC plan only reported gaining a DB plan over
the intervening period, only 16 percent (4+12) of those whose employer reported they had a DC plan only in 1992 were seen to gain a DB plan over the
six years. According to this sample of respondents, there was no change in their
plans between 1992 and 1998, yet the changes observed in employer-reported

plan types mirror the strong changes observed among general holders of pensions, suggesting that the plans did indeed change between the periods.

In sum, the evidence suggests that respondents are misreporting having no change in plan type over time and that they are further misreporting the plan type covering them in the survey year. Many changes are observed in plan type in employer-provided data for a subsample who say that their plans have not changed. Moreover, the changes observed in the employer sample correspond more closely to trends in pensions in the 1990s found in administrative data such as Form 5500 information from the Department of Labor, while those reported by respondents do not.

Turn now to the changes in reported plan type for a sample of 103 respondents who reported no change in their pension for the entire period between 1992 and 2004 and have matched plan data for both the 1992 and 2004 surveys. In Table 7.5E, 51 percent of the observations lie along the diagonal and are not DK. Except for the few DKs, this means that plan type changed for the remaining 49 percent of the sample even though they had reported no change in their pension. Among respondents who had reported DC only in 1992, in 2004, as seen in Table 7.5F, 48 percent of them reported that their plan is DB only, again an unlikely outcome given the trend from DB to DC plans. Another 7 percent gained a DB plan because their plan was converted from a DC plan in 1992 to a combination plan in 2004. Of the plan types identified in the 2004 plan documents, 60 percent of the sample was in agreement with the plan type reported in the provider reports in 1992 (Table 7.5G).

In contrast to the results from self-reports in Table 7.5F, in Table 7.5H, only 12 percent of the observations for plan documents suggested a transition from DC only to DB only between 1992 and 2004, and only 6 percent of observations imply a transition from DC only to both over that period.

Next, Table 7.5I considers respondent reports of plan type for a sample that includes observations where respondents reported the same pension in 1998 and 2004. About 61 percent of respondents reported the same plan type in both survey years. Table 7.5K reports analogous results for the sample's employer plan documents. According to the plan documents, 59 percent of respondents had the same plan type in 1998 and 2004, so that there was a disagreement in plan type from the plan document in about 41 percent of the cases in this sample. Table 7.5L shows that 5 percent of the sample who had a DB plan only in 1998 had plan documents that showed in 2004 they had a DC plan only.

Table 7.5E Percentage distribution of self-reported plan type for respondents reporting the same pension plan from 1992 to 2004 and with matched 1992 and 2004 plan data

	Self-report in 2004 (%)				
Self-report in 1992	1. DB	2. DC	3. Both	4. DK	5. Total
1. DB	32	10	8	0	50
2. DC	14	12	2	1	28
3. Both	12	1	7	0	19
4. DK	2	0	0	1	3
5. Total	59	22	16	2	100 (103)

Notes: The sample includes respondents with the same pension since 1992 who have matched plan documents in 1992 and 2004. The 1992 and 2004 plan documents include public and private plans from firms. The 2004 plan documents also include respondents' statements and SPDs. Total number of observations is reported in parentheses. Total percentages may not add up due to rounding.

Table 7.5F Distribution of self-reported plan type in 2004 by self-reported plan type in 1992, for respondents reporting the same pension plan from 1992 to 2004 and with matched 1992 and 2004 plan data (percent of row total)

	Self-report in 2004 (%)				
Self-report in 1992	1. DB	2. DC	3. Both	4. DK	5. Total
1. DB	65	20	16	0	100
2. DC	48	41	7	3	100
3. Both	60	5	35	0	100
4. DK	67	0	0	33	100
5. Total	59	22	16	2	100 (103)

Note: Total number of observations is reported in parentheses. Total percentages may not add up due to rounding.

Table 7.5G Percentage distribution of firm-reported plan type for respondents reporting the same pension plan from 1992 to 2004 and with matched 1992 and 2004 plan data

	Provider report in 2004 (%)			
Provider report in 1992	1. DB	2. DC	3. Both	4. Total
1. DB	30	1	22	53
2. DC	2	12	1	15
3. Both	12	2	18	32
4. Total	44	15	41	100 (106)

Notes: The sample includes respondents with the same pension since 1992 who have matched plan documents in 1992 and 2004. The 1992 and 2004 plan documents include public and private plans from firms. The 2004 plan documents also include respondents' statements and SPDs. Total number of observations is reported in parentheses.

Table 7.5H   Distribution of firm-reported plan type in 2004 conditional on firm-reported plan type in 1992, for respondents reporting the same pension plan from 1992 to 2004 and with matched 1992 to 2004 plan data (percent of row total)

	Provider report in 2004 (%)			
Provider report in 1992	1. DB	2. DC	3. Both	4. Total
1. DB	57	2	41	100
2. DC	12	81	6	100
3. Both	38	6	56	100
4. Total	44	15	41	100 (106)

Note: Total number of observations is reported in parentheses. Total percentages may not add up due to rounding.

Table 7.5I   Percentage distribution of self-reported plan type for respondents reporting the same pension plan from 1998 to 2004 and with matched 1998 and 2004 plan data

	Self-report in 2004 (%)				
Self-report in 1998	1. DB	2. DC	3. Both	4. DK	5. Total
1. DB	37	5	10	0	51
2. DC	7	15	4	1	25
3. Both	10	1	9	0	21
4. DK	2	1	0	0	1
5. Total	55	21	23	1	100 (238)

Notes: The 1998 and 2004 plan documents include public and private plans from firms. The 2004 plan documents also include respondents' statements and SPDs. Total number of observations is reported in parentheses. Total percentages may not add up due to rounding.

Table 7.5J   Distribution of self-reported plan type in 2004 conditional on self-reported plan type in 1998, for respondents reporting the same pension plan from 1998 to 2004 and with matched 1998 and 2004 plan data (percent of row total)

	Self-report in 2004 (%)				
Self-report in 1998	1. DB	2. DC	3. Both	4. DK	5. Total
1. DB	72	9	19	0	100
2. DC	27	58	15	0	100
3. Both	47	6	45	2	100
4. DK	57	29	0	14	100
5. Total	55	21	23	1	100 (238)

Note: Total number of observations is reported in parentheses.

Table 7.5K Percentage distribution of firm-reported plan type for respondents
reporting the same pension plan from 1998 to 2004 and with matched
1998 and 2004 plan data

	Provider report in 2004 (%)			
Provider report in 1998	1. DB	2. DC	3. Both	4. Total
1. DB	7	1	9	16
2. DC	0	13	3	16
3. Both	27	2	39	67
4. Total	35	15	50	100 (246)

Notes: The 1998 and 2004 plan documents include public and private plans from firms. The
2004 plan documents also include respondents' statements and SPDs. Total number of
observations is reported in parentheses. Total percentages may not add up due to rounding.

Table 7.5L Distribution of firm-reported plan type in 2004 (public and private)
conditional on firm-reported plan type in 1998, for respondents reporting
the same pension plan from 1998 to 2004 (percent of row total)

	Provider report in 2004 (%)			
Provider report in 1998	1. DB	2. DC	3. Both	4. Total
1. DB	42	5	52	100
2. DC	2	77	20	100
3. Both	40	2	57	100
4. Total	35	15	50	100 (246)

Note: Total number of observations is reported in parentheses. Total percentages may not
add up due to rounding.

According to their plan documents, another 52 percent appeared to gain an additional DC plan. Among respondents whose employer plans had indicated DC only in 1998, for a majority (77 percent) of them, their employer plans also indicated a DC plan only in 2004. Their plan documents suggested a gain in DB coverage for 22 percent of respondents, with most of the gain resulting from the conversion of a DC to a combination type of plan. In contrast, Table 7.5J, based on respondent reports as to plan type, indicates that of those with a DC only plan in 1998, 42 percent gained a DB plan by 2004, either by having DB only in 2004 or by having both types of plans in 2004.

To summarize the number of observations falling along the diagonals of the preceding tables, of the respondents who reported no change in their pension for the period from 1992 to 1998 and who have matched plan documents, 58 percent of respondent reports indicate the same plan type(s) in those two periods. According to their plan documents, 55 percent of respondents had the same plan type in both years. For the corresponding periods from 1992 to 2004 and from 1998 to 2004, for the respondent-reported plan types, the match rates are 51 percent and 61 percent, respectively. For the plan documents, the match rates over those two periods are 60 percent and 59 percent, respectively. The other problems of identification of plan type notwithstanding, respondents do a poor job of indicating whether their plans have changed over time.

Comparison with Watson Wyatt Payroll Data

There are a number of potential problems that may result from the process of matching firm reports of plan type to the covered worker in the HRS sample. The firm is asked to provide the HRS with all of the pension plan descriptions they offer. Although the summary plan description describes the characteristics of covered workers, and the HRS asks respondents about these characteristics and uses them to match SPDs with respondents—for example, by identifying whether respondents are paid hourly or are salaried, whether they are union members and white collar or blue collar, and what their history of employment and coverage is at the firm—there is always a chance for slippage in matching a plan to an individual. Moreover, despite requests that firms send the HRS all their plans, they may not have supplied a full set of matched plans.[9]

Payroll data matched with respondent reports of plan type would help to determine whether there are strong consequences from these limitations on the pension matching process used by the HRS. Although the HRS does not have payroll data for its covered respondents, the Watson Wyatt Company has made available a matched sample with both payroll and respondent survey data. Since the payroll data reveal with certainty which plans the worker is participating in, comparisons of respondent reports of plan type with the payroll data provide a baseline for evaluating the extent of misreporting of plan type by respondents. Because we find the same degree of misreporting by respondents whether the baseline is taken to be summary plan descriptions collected from respondent employers by the HRS or the payroll data collected by

Watson Wyatt, the suggestion is that most of the discrepancy between respondent and firm-produced data is due to misreports by the respondent.

Steve Nyce (2007) of Watson Wyatt has followed this methodology by matching payroll data from the human resources departments of a number of firms with data from pension questionnaires administered to workers covered by those plans. Moreover, he has, at our request, reformatted his findings using 2003 data to allow a direct comparison with Table 7.3C, which relates employer and respondent data for the 2004 HRS.[10]

In Table 7.3C, 52 percent of HRS observations (for private sector employers) are on the main diagonal where respondent reports match firm reports. In Table 7.6A, the comparable figure for the Watson Wyatt sample is 65 percent.[11] Because there are overall differences in the samples of covered workers, it is useful to focus on respondent reports of plan type conditional on the plan type reported in firm-provided data. These data from Watson Wyatt are reported in Table 7.6B, which is comparable to the data for private sector workers in the HRS reported in Table 7.3D. When we compare them, the two tables match remarkably well. We summarize these comparisons in Table 7.6C. Among those with an employer report of a DB only, in the HRS the percentages of respondents reporting DB, DC, and both are 56, 19, and 23, respectively. In the Watson Wyatt data, the percentages reporting DB, DC, and both are 62, 16, and 10, respectively, which when adjusted for the additional 10 percent responding DK in the Watson Wyatt sample still come relatively close to the HRS values. For those whose firms report DC only, the comparable fractions in the HRS are 13, 70, and 14, while the corresponding figures in the Watson Wyatt sample are 2, 68, and 24. There is a larger tendency in the Watson Wyatt sample to mistakenly pick DC only rather than to mistakenly pick DB only, as in the HRS. The largest discrepancy is in respondent reports of having both types of plans, conditional on the employer saying that they have both types of plans. In the HRS, from Table 7.3D, 29 percent of those respondents whose private employer reports both also report both. In the Watson Wyatt data, when the employer reports both, 64 percent of respondents report both (Table 7.6B).

It is obvious that the findings from the HRS and Watson Wyatt survey are highly complementary. The comparisons between the Watson Wyatt and HRS findings indicate that most of the discrepancy between firm- and respondent-reported data results from errors or misunderstanding by respondents. These comparisons also indicate the validity of findings to date with the

Table 7.6A Firm versus respondent reports of plan type using 2003 Watson Wyatt data purged of those with no pension coverage, ages 20–64

Provider report	Respondent report (%)				
	1. DB	2. DC	3. Both	4. DK	5. Total
1. DB	2	0	0	0	3
2. DC	0	18	6	2	26
3. Both	2	21	45	2	70
4. Total	5	40	52	4	100
Number of observations	344	2,958	3,876	253	7,471

Note: Total percentages may not add up due to rounding.

Table 7.6B Distribution of respondent-reported plan type conditional on firm-reported plan type using 2003 Watson Wyatt data purged of those with no pension coverage (percent of row total)

Provider report	Respondent report (%)				
	1. DB	2. DC	3. Both	4. DK	5. Total
1. DB	62	16	10	13	100
2. DC	2	68	24	7	100
3. Both	3	30	64	2	100
4. Total	5	40	52	4	100

Note: Total percentages may not add up due to rounding.

Table 7.6C Plan type misreporting seen in HRS data also seen in 2003 Watson Wyatt payroll data where true type is certain

	2004 HRS	2003 Watson Wyatt
Firm reports DB only		
R says DB only	56	62
R says DC only	19	16
R says both	23	10
Firm reports DC only		
R says DB only	13	2
R says DC only	70	68
R says both	14	24

Note: The HRS sample includes private sector employees only.

HRS data suggesting that the source of reporting error lies with the respondent. Accordingly, findings with Watson Wyatt payroll data suggest that HRS data can be used to estimate and model the effects of imperfect knowledge in analyses of retirement and saving.

The analysis with Watson Wyatt data suggests that much of the discrepancy remains between respondent and firm identification of plan type, even when the match is perfect between the respondent and the employer-provided plan description. Watson Wyatt data also clearly indicate that most of the discrepancy between plan type reported in respondent and firm data lies in errors on the side of the respondent.

For the first time, results based on Watson Wyatt data also provide an indication of underreporting of pension coverage. The HRS does not try to collect plan descriptions from those who report not having a pension. Findings with Watson Wyatt data suggest that underreporting of pension coverage amounts to about 5 percent. (The tables above remove this 5 percent from the sample to allow comparisons.)

Plan Type in the Full Respondent Panel

In this section we will take full advantage of the HRS panel to examine changes in reported plan type by respondents who report that their plans have remained unchanged. The data allow us to consider consistency across adjoining waves as well as cumulative consistency over a number of waves. Once again it will be apparent that many people who claim to have unchanging pension plans nevertheless change their reported plan types over time.[12]

Table 7.7 documents some of the inconsistencies that arise in the panel among respondent reports of number of plans and plan type, for a sample that reports that their pension plans have not changed since their previous interview. In this table we see differences over two consecutive interviews. Comparing adjoining waves, typically a fifth to a third of those reporting no change in their pensions nevertheless report a different number of plans or plan type than they reported in the previous wave. For example, row 1, column 2, of Table 7.7 indicates that there were 2,771 cases who reported how many pensions they held in Wave 2 of the HRS. Out of this group, there were 752 cases (27 percent) who reported a different number of plans than they had reported in their Wave 1 interview. Similarly, row 1, column 3, shows that there were

Table 7.7 Number of respondents reporting the same pension across HRS waves but reporting different plan numbers and plan types

Respondents with the same pension	1. Same pension	2. Number of plans[a]	3. At least 1 DB plan	4. At least 1 DC plan
1. Wave 2	2,786	2,771	1,790	1,110
Wave 2 different from Wave 1		752 (27%)	329 (18%)	251 (23%)
2. Wave 3	2,378	2,369	1,303	1,048
Wave 3 different from Wave 2		566 (24%)	267 (20%)	356 (34%)
3. Wave 4	2,125	2,098	1,019	983
Wave 4 different from Wave 3		599 (29%)	299 (29%)	308 (31%)
4. Wave 5	2,227	2,215	1,132	1,126
Wave 5 different from Wave 4		559 (25%)	317 (28%)	268 (24%)
5. Wave 6	1,817	1,809	875	862
Wave 6 different from Wave 5		519 (29%)	260 (30%)	230 (27%)
6. Wave 7	1,548	1,528	696	835
Wave 7 different from Wave 6		443 (29%)	217 (31%)	229 (27%)
7. Wave 8	2,144	2,135	959	1,165
Wave 8 different from Wave 7		635 (30%)	268 (28%)	220 (19%)

a. "Don't know" responses and refusals are excluded.

Table 7.8 Those with cumulative inconsistencies in respondent reports of number of plans and plan type for those reporting no change in their pensions since Wave 1

Respondents with the same pension[a]	1. Same pension	2. No. of plans[b]	3. At least 1 DB plan	4. At least 1 DC plan
1. Wave 2	2,786	2,771	1,790	1,110
Wave 2 different from Wave 1		752 (27%)	329 (18%)	251 (23%)
2. Wave 3	1,776	1,768	1,030	757
Wave 3 different from Wave 2 or Wave 1		635 (36%)	303 (29%)	353 (47%)
3. Wave 4	1,120	1,113	609	511
Wave 4 different from Wave 3, Wave 2, or Wave 1		473 (42%)	241 (40%)	282 (55%)
4. Wave 5	663	660	362	323
Wave 5 different from Wave 4, Wave 3, Wave 2, or Wave 1		298 (45%)	193 (53%)	195 (60%)
5. Wave 6	383	381	206	174
Wave 6 different from Wave 5, Wave 4, Wave 3, Wave 2, or Wave 1		169 (44%)	125 (61%)	112 (64%)
6. Wave 7	213	212	108	107
Wave 7 different from Wave 6, Wave 5, Wave 4, Wave 3, Wave 2, or Wave 1		100 (47%)	69 (64%)	78 (73%)
7. Wave 8	119	119	55	53
Wave 8 different from Wave 7, Wave 6, Wave 5, Wave 4, Wave 3, Wave 2, or Wave 1		51 (43%)	36 (65%)	40 (75%)

a. The sample in each wave includes respondents who were interviewed and reported the same pension since Wave 1. For example, the Wave 5 sample includes respondents who reported the same pension in Waves 2, 3, 4, and 5. Respondents who have skipped an interview are not included in the samples.

b. "Don't know" responses and refusals are excluded. Those reporting zero plans are not excluded.

1,790 cases who reported having at least one DB plan in Wave 2. Of those, 329 (18 percent) reported not having any DB plans in Wave 1. Row 1, column 4, shows the number of respondents (1,110 cases) reporting at least one DC plan in Wave 2. There were 251 cases out of the 1,110 (or 23 percent) who did not report any DC plans in Wave 1, even though they reported that their plan was unchanged since Wave 1.

Cumulative changes since Wave 1 are reported in Table 7.8. By Wave 7, roughly one-half to three-fourths were reporting a different number of plans or different plan type than they reported in at least one previous wave. For example, row 5, column 2, indicates that 383 respondents in Wave 6 were working at the same employment since Wave 1, reporting each period that there had been no change in their pension since the last period. Out of this group, 381 cases reported a plan number (excluding those who responded "don't know" or refused to answer), and 169 of them (44 percent) report coverage by a different number of plans than in at least one previous wave. Row 5, column 3, shows that there are 206 cases in Wave 6 who reported no change in their pension since Wave 1 and reported having at least one DB plan. There are 125 cases out of this group (61 percent) who did not report any DB plans in one or more of the previous waves. Row 5, column 4, shows the number of respondents (174) with at least one DC plan in Wave 6. Out of this group, there are 112 cases (64 percent) who did not report any DC plans in one or more of the previous waves.

To generalize the results in the panel, we have compared respondents' reports of certain pension characteristics as they vary across seams. A seam is defined as a connection between two waves, starting with Wave 1, over which respondents report no change in their employment and in their pension plans' rules. One seam is reported if there is no change in the pension between Wave 1 (respondent's first interview) and Wave 2 or the respondent's next interview if the Wave 2 interview was skipped. Over two seams there is no change in the pension from Wave 1 through the next two interviews. For six seams there is no change from Wave 1 through the next six interviews, and so forth.

The number of seams could be 0, 1, 2, 3, 4, 5, 6, or 7, where 0 indicates that a respondent reported a change in plan rules or change in the job after the Wave 1 interview; 1 indicates no plan change between the first and second interview, but that the third wave differs from the first; and 7 indicates the plan did not change over the life of the survey, from Wave 1 to Wave 8.

Each cell in Table 7.9 indicates the percentage of observations with a given number of seams of respondents who reported the indicated number of matches in plan type across those seams. The overall sample for the table includes 4,345 respondents who reported coverage by a pension in Wave 1. The number of seams is the number of waves starting in 1992 over which the respondent reported no change in pension plan.

The first row of the table indicates the zero seam category, where 1,491 out of 4,345 cases did not report having the same pension in the next interview after Wave 1. Therefore, all (100 percent) of the cases had a zero match for their plan type. An observation fell in the one seam category if respondents reported the same pension and no change in the pensions across the first two waves. Two seams are reported if the respondent had the same pension in the first three interviews and the pension remained unchanged. In 683 out of 4,345 cases, the respondent reported the same pension in three consecutive interviews, that is, that their plan did not change from the last interview in Wave 2 and Wave 3. About half of this group (49 percent) consistently reported the same plan type in all three interviews and about 31 percent in two interviews. About 19 percent reported a different plan type in adjoining waves each of the three times they were interviewed.

The six seams category includes those who were interviewed in seven waves and had reported no pension change in any of the interviews. About 25 percent of this group consistently reported the same plan type in all seven waves and another 12 percent across five of the six seams from Wave 1 to Wave 7. About 2 percent of the respondents did not have a match in reported plan type across any seam, although they may have reported the same plan type in different waves that were not adjoining.

These inconsistencies buttress the evidence from comparisons between plan types reported by respondents and in matched SPDs obtained from employers that there is considerable error in reported plan type, so that one cannot rely solely on respondent reports of plan type as an error-free indicator of what type of plan is held by the respondent. Although they add to the weight of the evidence, these results are not sufficient to establish that the respondent is responsible for any discrepancy.

A question arises because the plan type used for any wave is that of the most important plan reported in each interview. As shown in Appendix 4.3, in the HRS, when a respondent has both plan types, DB plans are selected as more valuable than DC plans in 60–80 percent of the cases, depending on the cohort.

Table 7.9 Percentage of respondents with a given number of seams reporting the indicated number of matches for plan type for their most important plan, DKs/RFs excluded

No. of seams	No. of respondents	No. of matches								% of total
		0	1	2	3	4	5	6	7	
0	1,491	100%								34%
1	1,021	31%	69%							23%
2	683	19%	31%	49%						16%
3	468	8%	28%	22%	42%					11%
4	287	4%	22%	22%	16%	36%				7%
5	182	1%	23%	21%	12%	15%	27%			4%
6	105	2%	16%	23%	11%	10%	12%	25%		2%
7	109	0%	15%	15%	13%	13%	13%	6%	26%	3%
Total number or % of total	4,345	46%	27%	13%	7%	4%	2%	1%	1%	100%

Nevertheless, if the respondent with two plans is well aware of the plan type but feels that a plan that was once considered secondary is now of greater value than the primary plan, one can see the reported plan type of the most important plan change between waves even though the respondent correctly reports that there has been no change in the pension.

Reliability of Respondent Reports before Retirement and at Retirement

Hurd and Rohwedder (2007, 2008b) impute values for missing pensions. They assume that people know the most about their pensions right after they leave their jobs. Chan and Huff Stevens (2006) make a similar assumption when they examine respondent knowledge and how it changes as the respondent approaches the wave in which employment is terminated. Chan and Huff Stevens's findings raise questions about whether people become better informed about their pensions, and especially about pension plan type, as they approach the time when they leave the job. They find: "Among those reporting pensions on a job that has just ended, almost one quarter indicated in the previous wave that they did not have a pension on this job, while another 30 percent are inconsistent in their pension type reports, didn't know their pension type, or refused to answer the question." They also find that consistency in answering the plan type question increases by only 1 percentage point between the ages of 50 and 60. Comparing reports of plan type between the wave following job termination and each wave preceding job termination, they also find that "individuals are not likely to be more consistent in the wave immediately preceding job termination."[13]

We examine the question of how information improves as respondents approach retirement age and look at the quality of information after retirement. Specifically, we use HRS data to compare respondent descriptions of their plan upon leaving with corresponding employer plan descriptions. Comparisons are confined to those who left their job between the time the plan description was collected from the firm and the wave following that year.[14] We use employer-provided plan descriptions for the years 1992, 1998, and 2004. The sample of pension leavers is limited to those who left their jobs between 1992 and 1994, 1998 and 2000, and 2004 and 2006.

The data in Table 7.10 report the results of these comparisons. Figures reported represent the percentage of cases where respondent and firm reports of

Table 7.10 Comparisons of plan type reported in panel, and at time of job termination, with plan type from firm plan descriptions

Core	Firm 1992 (%)	Firm 1998 (%)	Sample
Core 1992	47	42	The sample includes respondents
Core 1994	50	34	who reported no change in the
Core 1996	51	36	rules of their pension in 1994,
Core 1998	51	41	1996, and 1998. They left that pension job between 1998 and 2000.
Pension plan type at job termination between 1998 and 2000	51	40	Number of observations: about 190 in the 1992 sample and about 150 in the 1998 sample.
Core 1998		40	The sample includes respondents
Core 2000		37	who reported no change in the
Core 2002		43	rules of their pension in 2000 and 2002. They left that job between 2002 and 2004.
Pension plan type at job termination between 2002 and 2004		43	Number of observations: about 150[a]
Core 1992	44		The sample includes respondents
Core 1994	56		who reported no change in the
Core 1996	50		rules of their pension in 1994,
Core 1998	51		1996, 1998, 2000, and 2002. They
Core 2000	46		left that job between 2002 and
Core 2002	49		2004.
Pension plan type at job termination between 2002 and 2004	50		Number of observations: about 90[a]

Note: Number reported is percentage of observations where respondent reports and firm reports agree that the plan is DB only, DC only, or both/combination only.

a. These are respondents who reported the same pension over the reported period and have all the required information available.

plan type agree. There is agreement in roughly half the cases. These results suggest that the respondent does not do any better in identifying plan type in the survey taken just after job termination than in previous surveys. Nor does the level of agreement improve markedly as one approaches the time of job leaving.

Evidence of Imperfect Information from Interview Tapes and Pension Module

Evidence from the Interview Tapes

To further our understanding of the problems in reported plan type, we listened to forty-four HRS interviews covering the pension section, selected randomly. Our impressions from the tapes reinforce the conclusions reached from examining the data in the preceding sections. They also provide further insight into the reasons for respondent errors in reported plan type and in other information pertaining to their pensions. Some generalizations follow.

Respondents seemed to fall into three groups based on their knowledge of their pension and their consistency in reporting plan type. *Well-informed* respondents know their plan type/name and give consistent answers to three different versions of the plan type questions. They also give consistent answers about most of the other features of their plans. They account for 26 percent of the interviews. We would call about 49 percent of the respondents *informed*. Some of them know the plan type and/or some of their plan features. The *poorly informed* group accounts for 26 percent of the interviews. Members of this group do not know much about their plan, often giving contradictory responses or clearly guessing about their answers.

The interviews left us with the following impressions, which in general are not contradicted by our findings based on the overall sample. In general, respondents are more likely to know their plan name if it is a 401(k). Without prompting or availability of definitions, respondents would not report plan type as "DB/Type A" or "DC/Type B." A majority of respondents with a DB plan can identify it as such if a DB plan is defined for them. Respondents who do not know their plan type may know other features of that plan. Respondents may be confused about the number of their plans. This is true especially for cases where there was both an own and an employer contribution. Respondents may be confused about their coverage. Respondents whose company is being merged, whose plan is being frozen, or who are not making any contributions may not indicate in their responses that they are included in a plan. Respondents do their best to answer a question even if it is not relevant. A respondent with a DC plan may give a value that s/he expects to receive at retirement even if the plan will not produce a regular benefit.

We also considered the quality of the interview. A majority of interviewers are well informed. They know how to ask questions and how to probe when it is needed. However, there are some infrequent errors. In a couple of cases, the interviewer showed a lack of knowledge about the name of plans. A few interviewers also had problems in deciding how to deal with the situation when a respondent made contradictory responses. In one case, the interviewer clicked on a wrong plan type, as evidenced by a discrepancy between the respondent's answer on the tape and the plan type recorded by the interviewer in the data for that observation.

Evidence from the HRS Pension Module

With an eye toward developing a procedure to improve identification of plan type, in 2004 the HRS administered a special supplement/module to the core survey to inquire about detailed pension plan characteristics, including the plan's type or name.[15] In this module, in contrast to the core, plan types were not defined, but respondents were asked whether they knew the technical name or the type of their plan. (In 2008, a modified version of this approach was introduced into the regular pension sequence.)

If a respondent indicated that s/he knew the technical name of the plan, the respondent was asked to provide it. A respondent who did not know the technical name was presented with a list of such names to choose from. Those respondents who did not know the type of their plan and could not identify it from the list were read the definition of a defined benefit plan and asked if their plan is DB.

About 49 percent of respondents (Table 7.11, row 3, column 1) who reported that they knew their most important plan type reported it as a 401(k). For about 68 percent of respondents (Table 7.12, row 1, column 2) who reported having a 401(k) only and had a matched plan, the plan document indicated that the plan was DC only. Among respondents with a matched DC plan only, about 74 percent (Table 7.13, column 2, rows 1+2+3) reported a DC plan only. Among respondents who had a matched DB plan only, about 20 percent (Table 7.13, row 5) reported a DB plan only. About 3 percent of respondents with a matched DB plan only answer "don't know" when asked their plan type. In contrast, 1 percent of survey participants with a matched DC plan only give a DK response when asked their plan type (Table 7.13, row 6, column 2).

These findings again suggest that respondents have a good deal of information about their pensions but that a number do not know their plan type. The

Table 7.11 Respondents with reported plan type in the pension characteristics module

Respondents	Most important plan	Second most important plan
Know the plan name/type	2,255 (73%)	707 (81%)
Reported:		
401(k)	1,108 (49%)	253 (36%)
403(b), 457, thrift/savings, SRA, etc.	495 (22%)	283 (40%)
DB	280 (12%)	44 (6%)
Something else	351 (16%)	119 (17%)
DK	21 (1%)	5 (3%)
Do not know the plan name/type	847 (27%)	167 (17%)
Selected from the list:		
401(k)	57 (7%)	13 (8%)
403(b), 457, thrift/savings, SRA, etc.	213 (25%)	49 (28%)
DB	112 (13%)	11 (7%)
Something else	163 (19%)	28 (17%)
DK	302 (36%)	66 (40%)
Asked of Rs with DK if a DB plan:	334	81
Yes	191 (57%)	48 (59%)
Something else	53 (16%)	12 (15%)
DK	90 (27%)	21 (26%)

Table 7.12 Percentage of respondents with various plan types reported in the plan documents conditioned on the plan types reported by respondents in the module

Respondents' report in the module	Plan documents				
	DB only (%)	DC only (%)	Both (%)	Total	No. of observations
401(k) only	7	68	25	100	214
Other DCs only	33	22	45	100	239
401(k) & other DCs only	10	55	35	100	82
DB only	27	11	62	100	245
Both	38	12	50	100	126
DK	27	9	64	100	44
Other combinations	29	14	57	100	378

method used in the module may improve the accuracy of respondent answers. Nevertheless, it appears that respondent reports of plan type will continue to be characterized by errors. Indeed, as DB plans take on more of the features of DC plans, morphing through cash balance or related plans, and as DC plans take on more of the characteristics of DB plans, offering opportunities for

Table 7.13 Percentage of respondents reporting various plan types in the module conditioned on the plan types reported in the employer documents

Respondents' report in the module	Plan documents (%)		
	DB only	DC only	Both
401(k) only	5	44	8
Other DCs only	24	16	17
401(k) and other DCs only	2	14	5
Both	15	5	10
DB only	20	8	24
DK only	3	1	4
Other combinations	31	14	33
Total	100	100	100
No. of observations	329	332	642

Note: Total percentages may not add up due to rounding.

annuitizing benefits and imposing defaults and participation requirements, respondent confusion about plan type may only get worse.[16]

Effects of Asking Questions Pertaining to the Wrong Plan Type

Much of this chapter has focused on the reasons for discrepancies between respondent and firm reports of pension plan types, with much of the evidence pointing to reporting errors by respondents. There are a number of consequences of this finding for the design of surveys such as the Health and Retirement Study. In particular, one might ask whether it is possible to skip the step of identifying plan type altogether. Why shouldn't surveys simply ask all respondents all questions about pensions, whether the preponderance of evidence suggests they have an account or a DB plan?

One answer is contained in Table 7.14, which is based on an experiment the HRS conducted in 2006. People were deliberately asked questions appropriate for plan types they did not have. It appears that respondents will move outside the current sequence to provide an answer, whether appropriate or not.

When respondents who report that their plan is DB are asked for the account balance, 62 percent of them provide an account balance, either directly or indirectly by choosing a bracket specifying a range within which the account balance falls (Table 7.14, third column).

Table 7.14 Respondents with DB plans answering to DC questions and vice versa
            in 2006

Questions		Respondents	
Rs with DB: receiving quarterly report	Yes:	40%	(466/1,153)
Rs with DB/both/DK: receiving quarterly report	Yes:	43%	(595/1,382)
Rs with DB:	Reported:		
Account balances	No account:	5%	(61/1,138)
	Zero balance:	1%	(12/1,138)
	An amount:	27%	(300/1,138)
	Thru brackets:	36%	(410/1,138)
	Total:	62%	(710/1,138)
Rs with DC:			
Had automatic enrollment		30%	(451/1,497)
Rs with DC:			
Expecting lifetime benefits		49%	(727/1,497)
Rs with DC:	Reported:		
Expected amount of benefits	An amount:	36%	(534/1,497)
	Thru brackets:	19%	(281/1,497)
	Total:	55%	(809/1,497)

Among those respondents who indicated that they had a DC plan, 49 percent reported that they were expecting a benefit for life, and 55 percent reported an expected amount for the benefit (either directly or through brackets). Both of those answers are usually appropriate for a DB plan.

To further understand just what it means when someone who says they have a DB plan reports a plan balance, we did a preliminary analysis for three groups:

1. *Respondents who have both a DB and a DC.* Among the respondents who reported their plan as DB, the DC balance some of them supplied was appropriate for their second plan. That is, some of them had a DC or a combination plan for their second plan, and the balance they reported for their DB plan was the same or within the same range (if amounts were reported in brackets) as they reported for their other plan. More specifically, fourteen out of eighty-two in the selected sample report the amount in their secondary DC account when asked what their balance is in their primary DB account.

2. *Respondents who report an expected value of the benefit in 2006 and the value of an account balance, when a person with a DB is asked how much is in the account.* We would expect to see the account balance somewhere between ten and

twenty times the expected yearly benefit. Again in a selected sample, the ratios of account balance to expected yearly benefit range from less than 1 to 50. Many ratios are in the low single digits.

3. *Respondents who report different plan types in 2004 and 2006.* Seventeen out of fifty-nine of this group reported a DB balance in 2006 that was very close to their DC balance in 2004.

Thus a survey that is designed to very carefully separate the question sequences between different plans, trying hard to avoid any double counting, may hopelessly entangle the answers pertaining to different plans if they do not clearly separate the plans according to plan type. Moreover, some of the answers provided to irrelevant questions may simply be erroneous. One cannot skip the process of determining plan type, keeping the questions on topic for the plan reported. Given the centrality of the plan type question to the process of gathering information about a pension, the best alternative is to determine the information content of the question and to understand what types of errors will be encountered and what the consequences of these errors are. That is the task we set for ourselves in the preceding analysis.

In sum, without looking at each case, it is going to be very difficult to interpret what the respondent is reporting when s/he reports a DB plan and then a balance. To be sure, one might label the experiment as a success in that a number is reported. However, most of the numbers are of questionable value, especially since different people are using different concepts. By asking a respondent a question about the plan type s/he did not report, one is not getting consistent reports on a single concept, let alone on the present value of the account that would pay the benefit.

Summary and Conclusions

This chapter has used a variety of approaches to document and explain discrepancies between respondent reports of pension plan type and reports from respondents' employers. To be sure, many respondents report the same plan type as found in their employer-produced documents and in other ways appear to be well informed about their pensions. Nevertheless, in the surveys we analyze, reports by a third or more of respondents disagree with their employers' reports as to what type of pension they hold.

It is not just a discrepancy in any one cross-section that is of concern. Discrepancies between respondent and firm reports are found in cross-section data, over time, in panel data, and across different surveys. Findings for respondents who report that their plans have not changed run counter to the well-known trend toward defined contribution plans and well-documented evidence that firms have not been adopting new defined benefit plans. The evidence also includes repeated contradictions in panel data between respondent reports that their pensions have not changed over time, accompanied by differences in plan type reported at different times.

We have also found considerable evidence as to the reason for disagreement between respondent and firm reports of plan type, namely, that a significant fraction of respondents are imperfectly informed about their pension plan type. Although the process of matching employer-produced pension plan descriptions with respondents is not error free, in the case of disagreements in reported plan type, the employer-provided data appear to be a more accurate indicator of plan type than are respondent-provided data. Thus data produced by the Watson Wyatt Company support the view that discrepancies between respondent reports of plan type and reports obtained from employers are mainly due to errors in respondent reports. These data show the same types of discrepancies between respondent and firm reports of plan type as are seen when summary plan descriptions are matched to covered workers. The tapes of the interviews themselves further confirm the confusion of respondents. Some simply do not know very much about their pensions.

These errors are not easily removed by various changes in question sequence, wording, indexing based on plan features, or other approaches. Consequently, the HRS is justified in an approach to gathering pension data where respondent reports about their pensions are supplemented with plan descriptions obtained from their employers.

Nevertheless, our findings do suggest some changes that may reduce the discrepancy between respondent and firm reports of plan type. For example, those with a defined contribution pension do a better job of identifying their plan type if they are first asked whether they know the technical name of their plan. In contrast, respondents with a DB plan are more likely to accurately report their plan type if the characteristics of a defined benefit plan are first read to them. As a result of these findings, the 2008 wave of the Health and Retirement Study asked respondents first whether they knew the technical name or type of their plan and, if so, what it was. For those who did not know, they were read a list of technical names. This was all done before reading the definition of each plan type to the respondent. Next respondents were read the key characteristics of defined benefit and defined contribution pensions and were asked directly what plan type they have.[17]

Still another change in the pension sequence adopted on the basis of this evidence reduces the number of questions that are conditioned on reported plan type. A few key pension questions about the size of payments and plan balances continue to be conditioned on the answers to the revised plan type questions.

Another area of concern was raised by the finding that some respondents misreport whether their plan has changed over time. To save survey time, the Health and Retirement Study had conditioned the set of pension questions asked in particular waves on whether the respondent reported a pension change since the last wave of the survey. When the respondent reported no pension change, the set of questions asked was truncated. But some of those plans had changed. As a result, the new procedure asks the same sequence of questions whether or not respondents report that their pension has changed since the last survey.

The errors in respondent reports of other characteristics of their pensions undermine the usefulness of some other approaches that might have been adopted to help improve identification of plan type. One suggestion was that the HRS should base identification of plan type on particular features that are more likely to be found in one plan type than another. For example, respondents may be asked whether their plan provides a benefit for life (more typical of DB plans) or whether they receive quarterly reports (more typical of DC plans). However, because most features occur with differing frequencies in both plan types, and because these features are reported with error, an approach that would identify plan type from reported plan characteristics turns out to be impractical. Many respondents would continue to be sent down the wrong plan type branch if many questions continued to be conditioned on plan type.[18]

To the extent that the misreporting of plan type results because some respondents do not understand their pension plans, to accurately reflect behavior it will be necessary to modify models of pension plan determination, saving, and retirement to reflect the role of imperfect information. The models will have to explain who misunderstands their pension plans, what form this misunderstanding takes, and what such misunderstanding implies for each type of behavior. Thus to fully understand retirement and saving behavior, knowledge must be treated as an endogenous outcome. Having to jointly explain knowledge, retirement, and saving greatly complicates life cycle and related models, but the evidence presented here and related evidence suggest that these complications may be unavoidable if we are to thoroughly understand the behavior and policies influencing retirement and saving.

This chapter has produced a great deal of evidence on the frequency and importance of reporting error in plan type. All of that said, we do not want to overdo it. One must remember that although respondent reports of plan type are subject to substantial errors, much of the evidence presented here also shows that respondent reports do contain a good deal of useful information and that many respondents are well informed about their plan type.

The following chapters explore other features of pensions. In addition to a central focus on the basic descriptions of each of these features, we will be aware of the likelihood that some are poorly informed about the plan characteristic of interest. Where imperfect information seems to be substantial, we will measure the extent of the problem and explore its implications.

8

Pension Retirement Ages

Pension early and normal retirement ages are determined by formulas that depends on the covered worker's age and the number of years spent under the plan. The formulas vary among pension plans.

The Health and Retirement Study asks respondents with a pension to indicate their expected ages of eligibility for early and normal retirement benefits at the time they enter the survey and again whenever there is a report that the plan has changed. *Respondent's expected early retirement age* is the age at which a person expects to first become eligible to receive a pension benefit. *Respondent's expected normal retirement age* is the age at which the respondent expects to first be eligible to receive an unreduced benefit.

It is also possible to use the actual pension formulas collected in employer-produced summary plan descriptions (SPDs) to calculate *SPD based estimates of the ages of early and normal retirement* benefit eligibility. The employer SPDs report each formula used for eligibility for early and normal retirement benefits, and these formulas are applied to the respondents' reports of time spent on the job.

Respondents are also asked at what age they expect to first receive benefits. *Respondent's expected age of benefit receipt* is determined by the pension rules and the individual's decisions as to when to retire and when to claim benefits. *Respondent's actual age of first benefit receipt* may be reported in the wave after a respondent leaves a pension-covered job and is also reported in the assets and income section of the survey after the respondent retires.

This chapter examines and compares the values of the different measures of retirement age. It considers the differences in retirement ages reported by members of different demographic and employment groups. Trends in retirement age are examined. Retirement ages based on respondent reports are compared with those computed from employer-provided pension formulas. Expected ages of benefit receipt are also compared with actual age of benefit receipt. Appendix 8.1 provides an example that indicates the sensitivity of pension retirement age to age of hire in HRS employer-provided pension data.

Please note that the tables in this chapter often come from different samples. For example, one sample may include those with a defined benefit (DB) plan who also have a matched employer-produced summary plan description, while another similar table may not be restricted to those with a matched plan description. For the reader who is interested in the full set of reasons for differences among related figures reported in different tables, Appendix 8.2 provides the full description of the sample underlying each table.

Respondents' Expected Early Retirement Age

For those with defined benefit plans, the full value of the pension paid over the retirement period is often disproportionately higher for those who stay until early retirement age, discouraging workers from leaving the firm until they qualify for early retirement benefits. Workers covered by a DB plan who qualify for early retirement may receive an annual benefit that is only slightly reduced from the benefit that would be paid at normal retirement age. As will be explained in Chapter 11, the penalty imposed on a person with a defined benefit plan who leaves the firm before reaching early retirement age may be equivalent in value to a year of pay. In addition, when a worker stays until qualifying for an early retirement benefit, the benefit may be paid for more years than if the worker left before qualifying for early retirement and had to wait until reaching normal retirement age to receive a benefit payment. Early retirees may also receive additional benefits during the first few years of retirement, sometimes to supplement the benefits of those who are too young to qualify for Social Security until they reach the Social Security early entitlement age.

The strong influence of age of eligibility for early benefits on pension value makes the early retirement age in defined benefit plans a very important statistic for those who wish to understand retirement behavior. It becomes an even more important plan feature when one realizes, as emphasized very early on by Kotlikoff and Wise (1985, 1987), that defined benefit pension plans differ in their requirements for early retirement benefits.

This does not mean that pension receipt for those with a defined benefit plan will necessarily begin at the early retirement age. As we will see in Chapter 10, having qualified for early retirement benefits, there is no strong penalty to waiting until normal retirement age to claim one's benefits. What we can expect is that a person with a DB plan who is not subject to influences outside of the pension, such as an adverse health shock or involuntary layoff, should not be seen retiring before qualifying for early retirement benefits.[1]

Early retirement age may also influence the retirement decisions of those with defined contribution (DC) plans. Normally when a person withdraws benefits from a DC plan or IRA before age 59½, there is a penalty. However, as long as a person retires from a defined contribution plan after age 55, there is no penalty to drawing benefits that would otherwise apply to those who claimed benefits before age 59½. Any influence of the early retirement age on the retirement of a person with a DC plan is likely to be the result of increased liquidity once the pension funds become available to support consumption.[2] This influence will be of particular importance to those without other substantial saving beside their pension and Social Security, especially if they wish to retire before qualifying for Social Security early entitlement benefits.

Roughly speaking, HRS respondents who are 51 to 56 report an early retirement age of 58 if their plan is DB and 60 if their plan is DC. This can be seen in Table 8.1, which reports average early retirement age for respondents' most important plan. The population covered in this table includes those 51 to 56 in 1992, 1998, and 2004, and the data cover those three years when new cohorts were admitted to the survey.

There is not much variation in early retirement age with demographic or employment status. Men with DB plans qualify for early retirement about a year before women do. Other groups delineated by common demographic categories and job characteristics and covered by DB plans have very similar average early retirement ages, with the largest differences occurring where employees of small firms qualify for early retirement a year or two later than do employees of large firms (with the exception of those with both plan types in

Table 8.1 Respondent report of earliest age of eligibility for pension receipt, most important plan held by employees ages 51–56 (weighted)

Subgroups	DB only			DC only			Both			Don't know/refuse		
	1992	1998	2004	1992	1998	2004	1992	1998	2004	1992	1998	2004
All	57.9	58.4	58.2	59.5	60.1	59.7	57.1	57.8	57.7	59.5	61.8	58.7
Males	57.1	58.4	57.9	59.5	59.9	59.5	56.8	57.4	57.3	60.0	59.5	57.5
Females	58.8	58.4	58.6	59.6	60.3	59.8	57.9	58.6	58.2	59.4	63.6	60.2
White	57.9	58.4	58.2	59.6	60.1	59.6	57.2	57.9	57.7	59.2	62.6	58.9
Black	57.9	58.8	58.5	58.7	59.7	60.2	56.3	56.3	57.9	63.1	55.5	56.0
Hispanic	58.7	57.4	58.5	58.3	59.8	60.3	56.6	58.6	57.3	62.0	65.0	60.0
Married	57.7	58.5	58.3	59.4	60.0	59.7	57.0	57.6	57.6	59.6	61.8	58.8
Not married	58.4	58.0	58.0	60.0	60.2	59.5	57.6	58.7	57.9	59.2	—	58.5
Less than high school	58.8	58.3	55.8	59.6	59.3	61.6	58.0	59.9	58.8	62.0	65.0	60.9
High school graduate	58.3	58.8	58.7	59.3	59.4	59.7	57.3	58.4	57.5	57.4	61.9	57.2
Some college	57.0	58.5	58.8	59.9	60.7	59.5	57.6	57.6	57.6	63.4	60.1	55.0
College graduate	57.9	57.5	58.4	59.6	60.2	59.6	57.1	57.0	57.8	57.1	—	62.0
More than 16 years	56.6	58.1	57.6	59.1	60.7	59.2	56.2	57.6	57.6	—	—	59.8
Union	57.4	58.5	57.6	58.8	58.2	58.6	56.7	57.1	56.8	60.8	59.5	57.7
Not union	58.4	58.2	58.6	59.7	60.5	59.9	57.3	58.2	58.1	59.2	63.6	59.3
Large firm	57.5	58.1	57.7	59.3	59.3	59.1	56.9	57.4	58.1	57.9	63.9	54.3
Medium firm	58.2	59.5	59.0	59.3	60.8	60.9	57.8	58.3	57.7	62.3	51.0	61.3
Small firm	59.1	57.1	59.7	60.1	61.2	60.1	58.0	58.8	56.0	59.5	—	62.3

Note: For further details on the sample underlying this table, see Appendix 8.2.

Table 8.2 Respondent-report of normal age of eligibility for pension receipt, most important plan held by employees ages 51–56 (weighted)

Subgroups	DB only			DC only			Both			Don't know/refuse		
	1992	1998	2004	1992	1998	2004	1992	1998	2004	1992	1998	2004
All	60.6	60.0	60.7	—	—	—	60.5	60.5	60.0	61.7	62.5	60.6
Males	60.1	59.3	60.4	—	—	—	60.2	60.4	59.5	61.7	61.7	60.5
Females	61.2	60.9	61.1	—	—	—	61.1	60.7	60.7	61.7	63.4	60.7
White	60.5	60.1	60.7	—	—	—	60.7	60.6	60.1	61.6	—	60.9
Black	61.2	60.5	60.5	—	—	—	59.2	58.8	59.1	65.0	58.5	58.9
Hispanic	61.3	58.1	60.9	—	—	—	60.1	59.5	59.5	62.0	65.0	59.5
Married	60.6	59.8	60.6	—	—	—	60.3	60.3	59.7	61.9	62.7	60.4
Not married	60.9	60.4	61.1	—	—	—	61.0	61.3	60.9	60.9	62.0	61.4
Less than high school	61.5	60.9	62.7	—	—	—	59.0	60.2	60.4	62.6	62.0	59.4
High school graduate	60.9	59.7	60.3	—	—	—	61.2	60.8	59.5	60.8	62.0	62.1
Some college	60.2	59.7	61.2	—	—	—	60.6	60.4	60.6	65.0	62.9	55.0
College graduate	60.3	60.0	60.9	—	—	—	60.7	60.4	60.0	59.9	—	62.6
More than 16 years	59.7	60.4	60.7	—	—	—	59.7	60.3	59.7	—	—	61.0
Union	60.2	59.6	60.3	—	—	—	59.9	59.9	59.5	61.8	58.5	59.1
Not union	61.0	60.4	61.0	—	—	—	60.8	60.9	60.2	61.7	64.0	61.9
Large firm	60.4	59.2	60.3	—	—	—	60.4	60.5	60.3	61.7	65.0	59.9
Medium firm	60.8	61.6	60.8	—	—	—	61.0	60.7	59.8	63.4	55.0	61.1
Small firm	61.2	59.8	61.8	—	—	—	60.3	59.5	59.4	58.4	—	65.0

Note: For further details on the sample underlying this table, see Appendix 8.2.

2004), and where nonunion workers qualify for early retirement about a year later than union workers. In contrast to a strong negative trend in early retirement age for men covered by DB plans that was observed in the 1970s and 1980s (Anderson, Gustman, and Steinmeier, 1999), there is evidence of a very weak positive trend, amounting to about a half year increase between 1992 and 2004 in early retirement age.

Respondents' Expected Normal Retirement Age

Respondents with a defined benefit plan are also asked to report a normal retirement age. The averages of the normal retirement ages they report can be seen in the first three columns of row 1 of Table 8.2. They fall between ages 60 and 61, two to three years after the early retirement ages reported for DB plans. Once again there is little variation over time or with demographic and employment characteristics.

Comparing Respondent and Employer Reports of Early and Normal Retirement Age

Respondents think that they will become eligible for early retirement benefits about two years after these benefits will actually become available. As can be seen in Figure 8.1, which plots early retirement ages for those observations where the respondent reports a defined benefit plan and where the matched employer plan is also a defined benefit plan, this difference does not vary systematically with tenure. The two-year difference also corresponds to the difference in averages found between Table 8.1 and Table 8.3. In Table 8.3, early retirement dates, which average around 56 years old, are calculated from matched employer-provided pension plan descriptions applied to the respondent's self-reported employment history. In contrast, the early retirement ages reported in Table 8.1 average about 58 years old.

One might be uneasy that the differences between the results in Tables 8.1 and 8.3 are due to differences in sample size or composition. Table 8.1 includes the entire HRS population ages 51 to 56, while Table 8.3 pertains to those with a defined benefit/combination plan and a matched employer pension plan description. Specifically, employer data are only available for a subgroup of respondents, about two-thirds in 1992 and about half in 1998 and 2004. But adjusting for this difference does not change the basic finding: respondent

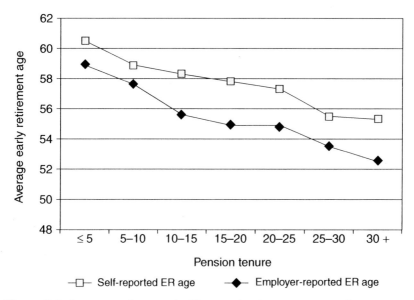

Figure 8.1 Average employer- and self-reported early retirement ages by pension tenure in 1992

reports of early retirement eligibility are at a later age than the early retirement age computed from employer data.

To investigate whether differences in the samples account for the higher age of eligibility reported by respondents, we make two different calculations. Columns 2, 4, and 6 of Table 8.3 use respondent-reported plan type and other covariates to impute results for those without a matched employer plan description. After including the imputed results for observations whose matched plan was missing, the early entitlement age moves up by only 0.3 percentage points in 1992. In 1998 the early entitlement age moves up to 56.2, a four-tenths of a year increase over the results based on the respondent sample with matched plans. Nevertheless, the early entitlement age reported by respondents is still roughly a year and a half later than the early entitlement age found in employer data.

To provide more detail about the distributions, in Tables 8.4A and B we compare the self-reports of early and normal retirement age with employer plan–based estimates, as in Figure 8.1 restricting the sample to those with matched employer data. Again the early retirement age is lower when calculated from employer plan documents. Fifty-two percent of respondents report

Table 8.3 Distributions of early and normal retirement ages for pension-covered employees with DB or combination plans and matched employer surveys, current job (weighted)

Age and plans benefits	1992 employer data		1998 employer data		2004 employer data	
	Matched plans	Matched plans with imputations	Matched plans	Matched plans with imputations	Matched plans	Matched plans with imputations
Average early retirement age	55.6	55.9	55.8	56.2	56.4	56.3
Number of observations	1,855	2,937	940	2,140	921	1,723
Percentile						
90	62	62	62	62	62	62
75	59	60	60	60	60	60
50	55	55	55	55	55	55
25	55	55	55	55	55	55
10	50	50	50	50	50	50
Average normal retirement age	61.2	61.8	61.2	61.7	60.2	60.7
Number of observations	1,854	2,937	940	2,141	919	1,723
Percentile						
90	65	65	65	65	65	65
75	65	65	65	65	65	65
50	62	62	62	62	61	61
25	60	60	60	60	58	58
10	55	55	55	56	55	55

Note: For further details on the sample underlying this table, see Appendix 8.2.

Table 8.4A Percentage of respondents with early retirement ages from the self-report and employer report for DB/combination plans in 1992, ages 51–56

Respondent report	Provider report								Total
	≤ 55	55–57	57–59	59–61	61–63	63–65	65–67	≥ 67	
≤ 55	44	3	1	4	1	0	0	0	52
55–57	4	1	1	1	0	0	0	0	6
57–59	4	0	1	1	0	0	0	0	6
59–61	3	1	1	3	0	0	0	0	7
61–63	12	1	1	5	2	1	0	0	22
63–65	2	0	1	1	1	0	0	0	6
65–67	0	0	0	0	0	0	0	0	0
≥ 67	0	0	0	0	0	0	0	0	0
Total	68	6	5	13	5	2	0	0	100 (882)

Note: Shaded cells indicate agreement between values from respondents and providers. Total number of observations is reported in parentheses. Total percentages may not add up due to rounding. For further details on the sample underlying this table, see Appendix 8.2.

Table 8.4B Percentage of respondents with normal retirement ages from the self-report and employer report for DB/combination plans in 1992, ages 51–56

Respondent report	Provider report								
	≤ 55	55–57	57–59	59–61	61–63	63–65	65–67	≥ 67	Total
≤ 55	10	2	2	5	3	6	0	0	26
55–57	1	1	1	2	0	1	0	0	6
57–59	1	0	1	1	1	3	0	0	6
59–61	1	0	0	5	1	3	0	0	10
61–63	2	0	0	4	5	11	0	0	23
63–65	1	0	0	4	5	16	0	0	26
65–67	0	0	0	0	0	0	0	0	1
≥ 67	0	0	0	0	1	1	1	0	2
Total	16	4	4	20	16	40	0	0	100 (852)

Note: Shaded cells indicate agreement between values from respondents and providers. Total number of observations is reported in parentheses. Total percentages may not add up due to rounding. For further details on the sample underlying this table, see Appendix 8.2.

an early retirement age of 55 or lower. When early retirement age is evaluated using employer-provided plan descriptions, the early retirement age is 55 or below in 68 percent of the cases. When SPDs are used to generate early retirement dates, there is also a small spike, consisting of 13 percent of the sample, falling in the 59- to 61-year age range (bottom row of Table 8.4A). Looking down the last column of Table 8.4A, the spike in respondent reports occurs between ages 61 and 63, involving 22 percent of the sample. Overall, half the cases fall along the main diagonal of Table 8.4A, indicating that respondent and firm reports fall within the same age range in half the cases. Otherwise, the early retirement ages calculated from employer reports almost always fall below the ages reported by respondents.

Although the respondent and firm reports of normal retirement ages are even less likely to fall along the main diagonal of Table 8.4B than are the reports for early retirement ages in Table 8.1A (38 percent of observations vs. 51 percent), the means and medians of normal retirement ages from both sources are in greater agreement than are the corresponding figures on early retirement ages.

Age at which Pension-Covered Workers Expect to Start Receiving Benefits

Respondents to the HRS who are covered by a pension also report the age at which they expect to receive benefits. This is an outcome that depends on the pension plan rules and the individual's expected retirement date, where retirement in turn is also influenced by plan rules. The expected age of benefit receipt from the most important plan held by those 51 to 56 years of age can be seen in Table 8.5. Over the period from 1992 to 2004, the expected age increases from 61.8 in 1992 to 62.6 in 2004.[3] (Compare row 2, column 1; row 3, column 2; and row 4, column 3.)

Next consider how the trend in plan type from DB to DC plans affects the age of expected benefit receipt. Table 8.6 reports ages of expected benefit receipt by plan type for those 51 to 56 in the indicated years. Scanning across rows 1 and 2, for those with a DB plan the expected age of benefit receipt increases by about four-tenths of a year over the twelve-year period. Looking across row 3, the increase in age of expected benefit receipt is about nine-tenths of a year for those with a DC plan.[4]

Table 8.7 shows the trend in expected age of benefit receipt within cohorts across all the waves of the Health and Retirement Study, for each cohort, and

Table 8.5 Self-reported expected age pension-covered employees will start receiving benefits from their most important plan (weighted)

Cohort	1992	1998	2004
Average expected age of benefit receipt: full-time employees in HRS cohort	62.2 (2,952)	—[a]	67.5 (376)
Average expected age of benefit receipt: full-time employees in HRS cohort, 51–56 in 1992	61.8 (1,858)	—[a]	66.9 (337)
Average expected age of benefit receipt: full-time employees in war babies cohort, 51–56 in 1998	—	62.1 (1,052)	64.1 (741)
Average expected age of benefit receipt: full-time employees in early boomer cohort, 51–56 in 2004	—	—	62.6 (1,184)

Note: For further details on the sample underlying this table, see Appendix 8.2. Total number of observations is reported in parentheses.

a. In 1998, only those members of the HRS cohort who reported a new pension were asked their expected age of retirement. In 1992 and 2004, everyone with a pension was asked about their expected retirement age.

Table 8.6 Self-reported age pension-covered workers expect to start receiving benefits, among employees ages 51–56, by plan type for their most important plan (weighted)

Cohort	1992	1998	2004
Full-time employees with a pension who have at least one DB plan	61.4 (1,304)	61.4 (722)	61.8 (639)
Full-time employees who have pension with DB plan only	61.5 (787)	61.3 (377)	61.9 (323)
Full-time employees who have pension with DC plan only	62.7 (530)	63.4 (318)	63.6 (521)
Full-time employees with pension who have combination/both plans only	61.2 (517)	61.4 (345)	61.8 (316)
Full-time employees with pension who respond don't know/refused only to plan type	61.9 (24)	63.9 (12)	62.6 (24)

Note: For further details on the sample underlying this table, see Appendix 8.2. Total number of observations is reported in parentheses.

Table 8.7 Average expected age of benefits receipt (weighted)

Pension characteristics	1992	1994	1996	1998	2000	2002	2004	2006
Average expected age of benefits receipt for most important DB plan: full-time employees in HRS cohort	61.9	62.3	62.8	63.4	64.4	65.8	67.0	68.6
Average expected age of benefits receipt for most important DB plan: full-time employees in HRS cohort who were 51–56 in 1992	61.4	61.8	62.3	63.0	63.9	65.1	66.3	68.5
Average expected age of benefits receipt for most important DB plan: full-time employees in war babies cohort	—	—	—	61.4	61.6	62.5	63.7	63.8
Average expected age of benefits receipt for most important DB plan: full-time employees in early boomer cohort	—	—	—	—	—	—	61.9	62.4
Average expected age of benefits receipt, for DC plan only: full-time employees 51–56 years old	62.7	—	—	63.4	—	—	63.6	—

Note: For further details on the sample underlying this table, see Appendix 8.2.

Table 8.8 Trends in expected age of pension receipt from most important plan, among subgroups, employees ages 51–56 (weighted)

Subgroups	DB only			DC only			Both			Don't know/refuse		
	1992	1998	2004	1992	1998	2004	1992	1998	2004	1992	1998	2004
All	61.5	61.3	61.9	62.7	63.4	63.6	61.2	61.4	61.8	61.9	63.9	62.6
Males	61.1	61.3	61.5	62.9	63.3	63.6	61.0	61.3	61.4	63.9	63.4	60.7
Females	61.9	61.4	62.2	62.5	63.4	63.5	61.7	61.6	62.3	61.2	64.6	63.9
White	61.5	61.4	62.0	62.9	63.5	63.7	61.3	61.5	62.0	61.1	64.7	62.6
Black	61.0	61.8	61.3	61.5	62.5	62.8	59.6	59.9	60.2	64.0	60.3	62.4
Hispanic	61.2	59.5	61.1	62.6	63.2	63.5	60.7	61.4	60.6	66.2	65.0	63.3
Married	61.4	61.3	61.6	62.5	63.3	63.5	61.3	61.2	61.6	61.7	63.7	62.5
Not married	61.8	61.3	62.5	63.4	63.4	63.6	61.1	61.9	62.4	64.2	65.0	63.0
Less than high school	62.2	61.7	63.1	62.4	63.0	63.2	60.7	62.0	60.3	62.7	65.0	65.0
High school graduate	61.5	61.5	61.4	62.5	63.1	63.5	61.4	61.6	60.9	62.1	64.8	61.9
Some college	61.2	60.4	62.5	62.7	62.8	63.2	61.2	60.9	62.2	63.6	62.9	63.4
College graduate	61.5	61.9	61.5	63.2	63.6	63.2	61.0	60.7	60.8	56.9	—	62.0
More than 16 years	61.0	61.6	62.1	63.6	64.8	64.7	61.4	62.0	62.7	65.0	62.0	62.8
Union	60.9	60.9	61.0	62.0	61.9	61.9	60.6	60.9	60.5	64.0	62.6	59.5
Not union	62.0	61.8	62.6	62.9	63.6	63.9	61.6	61.8	62.4	61.2	65.0	63.6
Large firm	61.3	61.2	61.4	62.4	63.0	63.4	61.1	61.2	61.9	61.1	64.8	61.0
Medium firm	61.6	62.2	62.2	63.0	63.7	63.5	62.1	62.4	62.1	62.8	59.7	63.9
Small firm	62.0	59.6	63.2	63.3	63.9	64.0	61.5	62.6	61.1	63.0	65.0	66.1

Note: For further details on the sample underlying this table, see Appendix 8.2.

by plan type. As seen in Table 8.5, holding plan type constant, the expected age of benefit receipt is increasing over time within cohorts, mainly because those who remain at work over time are aging (see note 2). That is, those who wished to retire early have left the sample as we move through time. Thus for members of the HRS cohort who were 51 to 56 in 1992, we see in row 2 of Table 8.7 that those at work in 1992 expected to retire at 61.4 years of age. Those from the original cohort who still remained at work in 2006 expected to retire after reaching age 68½.

There are a few cases where expected age of pension receipt differs between members of different demographic or employment groups. Thus in Table 8.8, expected age of pension receipt is higher for women with DB plans than for men, higher for whites with a DC plan than for blacks, and higher for non-union workers than for union members whatever their plan type. Some of these differences are at least partially due to differences in job tenure among members of these different groups, rather than to differences in pension rules.

Respondents' Retirement Plans

To understand retirement plans more thoroughly and how they differ by co-hort, Table 8.9 reports how respondents expect to proceed in the future. Re-spondents report whether they expect to stop work altogether, never stop, have not given it a thought, have no plan, plan to reduce hours, intend to change jobs, work for themselves, or work until their health fails. Perhaps not surpris-ingly given the indications of imperfect information found in Chapter 7, the most frequent answer, given by more than a third of respondents in each co-hort when interviewed at ages 51 to 56, is that they have not given it a thought. The fraction who have not given retirement a thought is lower in younger cohorts, declining from 40 percent who were 51 to 56 in 1992 to 33 percent of the war babies and 35 percent of the early boomers. Another 4 to 7 percent of respondents indicate in their first interview that they have no plan.

About a fifth of each cohort, when first interviewed, expects to stop working altogether. There also is an increasing share who expect to reduce their hours of work, rising from 18 percent for those 51 to 56 in the original HRS cohort, to 21 percent of the war babies and 23 percent of the early boomers.

Focusing on the expected retirement ages, Table 8.10 shows that those who have given retirement no thought or who have no plan actually expect to retire

Table 8.9 Percentage of respondents by retirement plan and cohort (weighted)

Retirement plans	1992	1994	1996	1998	2000	2002	2004	2006
HRS: 51–61								
Stop altogether	21	26	25	23	22	16	15	15
Never stop	8	7	7	6	7	4	7	8
Not given thought	37	32	31	29	28	30	36	36
No plan	8	7	7	9	9	12	10	13
Reduce hours	19	18	17	18	18	18	15	13
Change job	10	3	2	2	2	1	0	1
Work for self	1	1	1	1	1	0	0	0
Work until health fails			3	4	5	5	5	6
HRS: 51–56								
Stop altogether	20	24	25	24	24	18	16	16
Never stop	7	7	6	5	6	3	5	6
Not given thought	40	34	33	28	24	28	34	34
No plan	7	6	6	8	8	11	10	14
Reduce hours	18	18	17	19	21	21	18	15
Change job	10	2	2	3	1	2	1	1
Work for self	1	1	1	1	1	1	0	0
Work until health fails	—	—	2	3	4	4	5	5

WBs: 51–56

Stop altogether	21	20	21	20	21	—	—	—
Never stop	5	5	4	5	4	—	—	—
Not given thought	30	28	30	34	33	—	—	—
No plan	9	8	8	6	7	—	—	—
Reduce hours	22	24	20	20	21	—	—	—
Change job	2	2	2	3	3	—	—	—
Work for self	0	1	1	1	1	—	—	—
Work until health fails	3	3	3	3	3	—	—	—

EBs: 51–56

Stop altogether	19	19	—	—	—	—	—	—
Never stop	5	5	—	—	—	—	—	—
Not given thought	34	35	—	—	—	—	—	—
No plan	6	4	—	—	—	—	—	—
Reduce hours	23	23	—	—	—	—	—	—
Change job	2	3	—	—	—	—	—	—
Work for self	1	1	—	—	—	—	—	—
Work until health fails	4	3	—	—	—	—	—	—

Table 8.10 Average expected age of retirement by retirement plan and cohort (weighted)

Retirement plans	1992	1994	1996	1998	2000	2002	2004	2006
HRS: 51–61								
Stop altogether	61.8	62.1	62.8	63.6	64.6	66.4	67.5	69.5
Not given thought/no plan	—	—	—	66.6	67.9	69.7	71.6	73.5
Reduce hours	61.6	62.0	63.0	63.6	64.6	65.8	67.3	69.0
Change job	60.2	61.0	61.6	62.3	63.9	64.7	65.9	68.5
Work for self	60.4	60.2	62.0	62.4	63.8	64.3	66.5	68.6
HRS: 51–56								
Stop altogether	61.3	61.5	62.0	62.6	63.6	65.1	66.5	68.6
Not given thought/no plan	—	—	—	65.6	66.5	68.1	70.1	72.2
Reduce hours	60.6	61.3	62.2	62.9	63.9	65.1	66.3	68.4
Change job	59.0	60.2	60.9	61.7	63.1	64.1	65.7	68.2
Work for self	58.9	59.1	61.2	61.2	63.5	64.3	66.0	68.1
WBs: 51–56								
Stop altogether	—	—	—	60.7	61.1	62.3	63.4	64.0
Not given thought/no plan	—	—	—	64.4	64.6	65.6	66.3	67.2
Reduce hours	—	—	—	60.4	61.0	62.3	63.3	64.4
Change job	—	—	—	58.0	59.8	61.2	62.5	63.4
Work for self	—	—	—	58.4	59.9	61.4	62.4	63.5
EBs: 51–56								
Stop altogether	—	—	—	—	—	—	61.6	62.5
Not given thought/no plan	—	—	—	—	—	—	65.3	65.5
Reduce hours	—	—	—	—	—	—	61.1	62.2
Change job	—	—	—	—	—	—	59.7	60.4
Work for self	—	—	—	—	—	—	60.6	59.2

three or four years later than other respondents. Table 8.10 also shows that there is no trend among members of each cohort expecting to stop working altogether, with the expected ages varying between 60.7 and 61.6 years of age for those 51 to 56 in the original HRS cohort, the war baby, or the early boomer cohorts. For those who expect to reduce hours, the retirement age rises by half a year from 60.6 years for those 51 to 56 in 1992 to 61.1 years for those 51 to 56 in 2004.

Although the age of expected retirement increases as one looks across any row in Table 8.10, any apparent trend is likely to be the result of changes in the mix of those reporting in subsequent years. Typically, for a person covered by a pension, the median age of benefit receipt is in the person's fifties. Over time, those with earlier ages of retirement, either those with less education or those covered by more generous plans or with longer job tenure, leave the ranks of covered workers. That drives the age of benefit receipt up over time as members of a cohort age. Those with more education or those who have less generous plans or lower tenure remain within the pool of active workers. Also over time a person's expectations evolve. Those who expected an unrealistically early retirement date are forced to revise their expectations upward.

Expected versus Actual Age of Benefit Receipt

There are many reasons why expected and actual dates of benefit receipt may differ (Bernheim, 1988, 1989, 1990). Circumstances affecting the retirement decision may have changed between the time expectations were solicited and the time actual retirement was measured. For example, the respondent may have been laid off from work, the employer may have provided additional benefits to encourage earlier retirement, there may have been a deterioration in health or a change in family responsibilities, the pension itself may have changed, or there may have been other changes between the time that expected retirement date was reported and the time it was realized. To further complicate matters, when a person has more than one pension plan, there is no way to determine with certainty whether expected and actual values came from the same plan. For these and other reasons, differences between expected and realized dates of benefit claiming cannot be used as a direct measure of reporting error or respondents' misunderstanding of their pensions. Nevertheless, these comparisons are of interest.

Table 8.11 Percentage of respondents with a DB or combination plan by the expected age of first benefit receipt reported in 1992 and actual age of first benefit receipt reported in 2006 for the most important DB or combination plan, range of 3 years, age eligible

Expected age in 1992	Actual age in 2006							
	≤ 56	57–59	60–62	63–65	66–68	≥ 69	DK	Total
≤ 56	5	2	1	1	0	0	0	9
57–59	1	4	3	2	0	0	0	10
60–62	4	5	19	12	2	0	1	44
63–65	3	1	6	11	5	1	1	28
66–68	0	0	0	1	0	0	0	2
≥ 69	0	0	0	0	0	0	0	1
DK	1	1	2	2	1	0	0	6
Total	14	13	31	29	10	2	2	100 (1,083)

Note: Shaded cells indicate agreement between values from respondents and providers. The total number of cases is 1,083, and the sum of diagonal matches is 39 percent. Total percentages may not add up due to rounding. For further details on the sample underlying this table, see Appendix 8.2.

For purposes of discussion, we define a coincidence of expected date and actual date of benefit receipt as occurring if they both fall within a defined three-year range. Table 8.11 contrasts the expected date of benefit receipt as of 1992 against the actual date of first benefit receipt as reported in 2006 or earlier, for age-eligible members of the original HRS cohort.[5] There is overall agreement in 39 percent of the cases. These fall along the main diagonal of the table. For the remainder of the cases, there is no agreement. It appears that there is some tendency for the actual date of benefit claiming to fall after the expected date. About 63 percent of the sample expected in 1992 to receive some benefit by age 62. About 58 percent actually received a benefit by that age. All told, not counting DKs, 29 percent of the observations fall above the diagonal, indicating that the actual age of benefit receipt exceeds the expected age of receipt, while 21 percent of the observations fall below the diagonal.

It is also possible to compare directly the difference between when respondents actually left their job and the various indicators of retirement age. Of those with a defined benefit or combination plan, row 1, column 1, of Table 8.12 indicates that 14 percent of respondents left their 1992 job four or more years after their reported expected age of benefit receipt, that is, the age they expected to start receiving some benefits from their DB or combination plan. Moving to column 2, about 48 percent of these respondents worked at their 1992 job four or more years after their reported expected early retirement age; and in column 3, we see that 26 percent of them worked four or more years after their expected normal retirement age. In contrast, from row 9, column 1, about 19 percent of HRS respondents left their 1992 job four or more years earlier than their expected retirement age, about 10 percent left four or more years earlier than the reported early retirement age, and 21 percent left four or more years earlier than the reported normal retirement ages of their plans.

On average, respondents with any type of DB plan left their 1992 job about 0.47 years earlier than they had expected when surveyed in 1992. However, they stayed on their job about 3.25 years longer than the early retirement age they reported in 1992 and 0.42 years more than the normal retirement age they reported in the initial year of the survey.

Table 8.12 Percentage of respondents who left their 1992 jobs categorized by the number of years between the expected age of benefit receipt or early or normal retirement ages and age actually leaving the job (for the most important DB/combination or DC plan, 1992 survey)

Age in column head minus age respondent left 1992 job (no. of years)	DB/combination plan			DC plan	
	Expected age of benefit receipt	Early retirement age	Normal retirement age	Expected age of benefit receipt	Early retirement age
Left 1992 job 4 or more years after	14	48	26	14	41
−3	7	8	7	6	7
−2	12	10	10	9	8
−1	16	9	11	14	10
0	11	5	7	11	8
1	8	4	6	7	4
2	8	3	7	9	4
3	5	3	5	5	4
Left 1992 job 4 or more years before	19	10	21	26	14
Average of the differences	0.47	−3.25	−0.42	1.11	−2.27
No. of observations	1,993	1,993	1,993	1,041	1,041

Note: For further details on the sample underlying this table, see Appendix 8.2.

Comparing Estimates of Early and Normal Retirement Age and Expected and Actual Ages of Benefit Receipt

Table 8.13 summarizes the relations among the means of the various measures of age of pension benefit receipt whose distributions we have been discussing. The table is limited to 337 observations for which all measures of retirement age are available, but it is important to note that the results are not changed when the sample is expanded to include over 800 observations with matched employer and respondent-based observations on early and normal retirement age and over 600 observations with matched data on expected and actual ages of benefit receipt. Comparing the firm-based data with respondent reports, early retirement age in respondent data is higher by about 1.8 years, while normal retirement age is about 0.9 years lower in respondent reports. Expected age of first benefit receipt is about the same as actual age of first benefit receipt. Both expected and actual ages of benefit

Table 8.13 Means of self-reported retirement ages, retirement ages based on firm reports, and ages of first benefit receipt reported by respondents ages 51–56 in 1992 with a matched DB employer plan

Ages of benefit eligibility or benefit receipt	Ages based on respondent report	Ages based on SPD
Early retirement age	56.9	55.0
Normal retirement age	59.6	60.5
Expected age of benefit receipt	60.7	—
Actual age of benefit receipt	60.7	—

Note: For further details on the sample underlying this table, see Appendix 8.2.

receipt reported by respondents exceed the respondents' report of normal retirement age but are pretty close on average to the normal retirement age calculated from firm-provided formulas. Expected and actual ages of benefit receipt are closer to normal retirement age than to early retirement age. Last, remember that there is much greater disagreement within the distributions than there is in the means of the various measures of pension eligibility and acceptance.

Conclusions

Using both respondent and matched employer reports, the HRS data on retirement age reveal a number of intriguing results. There are no very substantial differences in early retirement age by demographic status or job characteristics. Women report eligibility for early retirement benefits about a year later than men, with less of a difference for members of younger cohorts. There also are later ages of qualification for nonunion workers and employees of small firms. In contrast to the 1970s and 1980s, where there was a sharp downward trend in age of eligibility for early retirement benefits among those who held defined benefit plans, there is no comparable trend in early retirement age from 1992 through 2004. Indeed, for 51- to 56-year-old men covered by a DB plan, there is perhaps a half-year increase over this period. Because the age of eligibility for benefits is about two years older for defined contribution than for defined benefit plans, the trend to defined contribution plans has increased the earliest age of eligibility for benefits by those with a pension. But within groups of those holding either a defined benefit or a defined contribution plan, the trend is very modest indeed.

When we examine the age at which respondents think they will first receive their benefits, respondents who are approaching retirement age think they have to remain longer on the job to qualify for early retirement benefits than is estimated using their plan's rules. Respondent estimates of early retirement age exceed the early retirement age calculated from plan features by almost two years. This result is puzzling for two reasons. First, we would expect most respondents to be relatively well informed about retirement ages from observing their colleagues. Second, although they might have more trouble estimating benefits, program rules regarding age of retirement are simpler than the rules governing benefits.

Age of expected benefit receipt has increased over time. Comparing cohorts of 51- to 56-year-olds, there is about a half-year increase in the expected age of benefit receipt for those with a defined benefit plan. The increase is closer to a year for those with a defined contribution plan. The change over time in plan mix toward defined contribution plans further increases the expected age of benefit receipt.

Comparing actual age of benefit receipt with the age of first benefit receipt expected fourteen years earlier, people collected earlier than they forecasted a decade previously. To be sure, there is important heterogeneity. Those who answer DK aside, while 39 percent forecast correctly, 29 percent collected their benefits after they had forecast they would, and 21 percent collected their benefits before they expected to. These differences may be due to different circumstances: a person who collects before expecting to may have been forced to leave the job early, while those who collected later than they expected may have found that postponing retirement increased their future consumption enough to make it worthwhile, they may have realized that they were not well enough prepared for retirement, or they may have delayed retirement and benefit claiming for other reasons.

The analysis of job and pension tenure in Chapter 6 highlighted the strong difference in years of pension tenure between those with defined benefit and defined contribution plans. Although those with defined benefit plans had almost six more years of pension tenure than did those with defined contribution plans, that difference declined but did not disappear over time. For analysts, a troubling finding from Chapter 6 is the small but not insignificant fraction of those who report being covered by their pension plan for longer than they have been in their job. Although this may in some cases reflect reporting error, it also may reflect opportunities to continue in the same pension after job transfer, for those with multiemployer plans, for teachers transferring among schools in the same district, and for others. Another finding is that although early retirement age varies with job tenure, the difference in early retirement age is much less than in proportion to any difference in job tenure.

From a policy perspective, the movement away from DB plans will be the major mechanism increasing the early retirement age in pensions. For older cohorts approaching retirement age who continue to be covered by a DB pension, there is little evidence that retirement trends will help to alleviate financial pressures on retirement programs.

Appendix 8.1: Sensitivity of Early and Normal Retirement Dates to Date of Hire

The later the date of hire, the later will be the early or normal retirement date that emerges from the pension formula. But the resulting differences in early and normal retirement dates are much smaller than the differences in dates of hire that brought them about. To illustrate the relationship between date of hire and early and/or normal retirement age, we estimate early and normal retirement dates using 1,070 employer-provided pension plan descriptions collected for the 1998 HRS survey. We apply these formulas to the same hypothetical individual, but we change the hypothetical dates of hire between the illustrative calculations. This allows us to examine the sensitivity of the retirement dates to the dates of hire, holding constant all other features of the pension plan as well as all other characteristics of the covered worker.

The simulated individual is assumed to have been born in 1944 and to have been hired at alternative ages: at age 25 in 1969, at age 35 in 1979, or at age 45 in 1989. In all cases, the individual is assumed to work full time (2,000 hours/year) at the same employer until retiring upon becoming eligible for early or normal retirement benefits in accordance with work histories and the rules of each particular plan.

Figure 8.2 presents the average early and normal retirement ages calculated across all the plans for the three different hiring ages, 25, 35, and 45. As is to be expected, the early and normal retirement ages are lower the earlier the start date for employment. The figure indicates that the average early age of retirement for the hypothetical individual hired at age 25 (in 1969) is 53.9. This age would increase to 54.9 if the starting age of employment was 35 (in 1979) and to 56.4 if the hire age was 45 (in 1989).

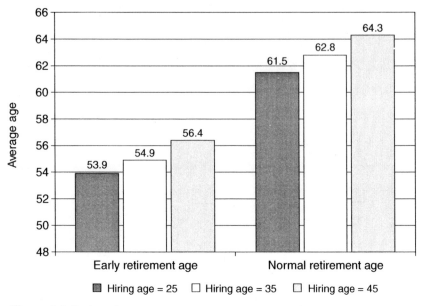

Figure 8.2 Early and normal retirement ages at alternative hiring ages

The normal retirement age is 61.5 if the individual was hired at age 25. The normal retirement age increases about 1.3 years if the age of hire was 35 and about another 1.5 years if the age of hire was 45.

The first column of Table 8.14 indicates that in 92.6 percent (22.4+3.3+66.9) of the plans, a person hired at age 25 would be eligible for early retirement by age 55. The rest of the plans have a later early retirement age. The percentage of plans allowing early retirement by age 55 declines to about 85.1 percent and 68.9 percent for hiring ages of 35 and 45, respectively. To provide a slightly different perspective, in the bottom three rows of Table 8.14, we consider the share of the population who must wait until they reach age 60 before they become eligible for normal retirement benefits. For example, according to the data in the bottom three rows, last column of the table, for about 95 percent (11.3+12.3+71.4) of the plans, workers hired at age 45 are not eligible for normal retirement benefits until after they reach age 60. These percentages decline in the last three rows of columns 5 and 4, respectively, to 90.1 percent and 74.4 percent for those hired at ages 35 and 25.

Table 8.14   Percentage of DB plans allowing early and normal retirement by indicated ages, for different ages of hire of hypothetical employee using matched defined benefit SPDs

	Early retirement age			Normal retirement age		
Age	Hired at age 25	Hired at age 35	Hired at age 45	Hired at age 25	Hired at age 35	Hired at age 45
≥ 50	22.4	12.1	6.0	5.2	2.9	2.6
51–54	3.3	1.6	0.9	2.6	0.4	0.2
55	66.9	71.4	62.0	14.8	2.6	1.0
56–59	0.7	1.8	2.3	0.7	4.0	1.0
60	4.0	9.5	20.4	6.4	14.8	11.3
61–64	0.9	1.4	2.6	7.8	11.2	12.3
65	1.7	1.9	5.5	60.2	64.1	71.4

Note: Retirement ages are based on employer-produced pension plan descriptions for 1,070 firms collected in 1998 and applied to a work history for a hypothetical individual born in 1944 who started work for this firm at ages 25, 35, and 45.

Appendix 8.2: Detailed Descriptions of Covered Samples Underlying Tables in Chapter 8

The samples differ in various ways among the tables presented in this chapter. Although the titles of each table reflect the underlying samples, those who wish to use the HRS data may find a more detailed description of the data underlying each table to be helpful.

Table 8.1. The sample includes respondents who were full-time employees ages 51 to 56 and who also reported a plan type. The early retirement age for DB/DC plans is from the self-reported data in the core survey collected in 1992, 1998, and 2004. The early retirement ages for DC plans were obtained slightly differently in 2004 from 1992 and 1998. In 1992 and 1998, there was only one question asking respondents about the youngest age they are allowed to receive benefits from their DC plan. In 2004, there were separate questions asking respondents with a DC plan whether they are allowed to receive benefits in installments, monthly, or as a lump sum and what is the youngest age they are allowed to receive each of these benefits. In this table, we have selected the youngest age among the possible ages reported.

Table 8.2. The sample includes respondents who were full-time employees ages 51 to 56 who reported a plan type. The normal retirement age for DB plans is from the self-reported data in the core of the 1992, 1998, and 2004 surveys. The HRS did not ask respondents with a DC plan for a normal retirement age. With no actuarial penalty for early retirement, the early retirement date is the only operational date of significance.

Table 8.3. Columns 1, 3, and 5 include values computed for respondents with matched DB plans. (No consideration is given to self-reported plan type.) Columns 2, 4, and 6 also include imputations for those without a matched plan. Only employees are included in this table.

An early retirement date is included if benefits are to be paid before the normal retirement age. If the normal and early retirement ages are the same but early retirement benefit is higher, we consider the age at which early retirement benefits are paid as the early retirement age.

Table 8.4A. The sample includes respondents ages 51 to 56 with a reported early retirement age from their DB/combination plan who have a matched DB/combination plan in 1992.

Table 8.4B. The sample includes respondents ages 51 to 56 with a reported normal retirement age from their DB/combination plan who have a matched DB/combination plan in 1992.

Table 8.5. The sample includes respondents with a reported expected retirement age from their most important plan, whether it is a DB/combination plan or a DC plan, in 1992, 1998, and 2004. Respondents with a DC plan who reported they had the same pension in 1998 as in the previous wave were not asked about their expected age of receiving benefits. Therefore, no values are reported in the first two rows of column 2.

Table 8.6. The table includes respondents ages 51 to 56 who are full-time employees, have reported a plan type, and in addition have reported an expected retirement age for their most important DB/combination or DC plan in 1992, 1998, and 2004.

Table 8.7. The first four rows are for the most important DB plan. The last row is for the DC plan if the respondent reported a DC plan only. Respondents who reported no change in their pension in 1998 were not asked about the age they expected to receive benefits from their DC plans, unless they also reported having a new pension.

Table 8.8. The sample includes 51- to 56-year-old respondents who are full-time employees, have reported a plan type, and have reported an expected retirement age for their most important DB/combination and/or DC plan in 1992, 1998, and 2004. Only a few respondents fall in the DK/RF category.

Table 8.11. The sample includes HRS respondents ages 51 to 61 who reported an expected retirement age for their most important DB/combination plan in 1992 and who have started receiving benefits by 2006. The expected age of receiving benefits and actual age of receiving benefits are grouped in three-year ranges.

Table 8.12. The sample includes HRS respondents with DB/combination plans who have reported values for all three expected ages—age of accepting benefits and early and normal retirement ages—as well as expected and early retirement ages for those with DC plans. Results are very similar when observations for those respondents who reported dates for only one of the categories are also included.

Table 8.13. The sample includes respondents ages 51 to 56 in 1992. There are 337 observations with matched data for the early, normal, expected, and actual ages of benefit receipt. Results are not much changed when the samples are expanded to include 882 observations with matched employer and respondent data for early retirement age, 896 observations with matched employer and respondent data for normal retirement age, and 604 observations providing both expected and actual age of benefit receipt.

9

Pension Values

Having examined pension coverage, plan type, and retirement age, we now turn to the question of what pensions are worth. Given the rapid trends in pensions, and in particular in plan type, it is important to learn how pension values have changed over time and among cohorts in the HRS. It is also interesting to consider differences in plan values by demographic group and among those with different job characteristics. Given the trends observed in previous chapters, special attention is paid to differences in pension values between men and women and how those differences have changed over time.

This chapter begins with respondent reports of pension payments at the expected age of retirement for those with defined benefit (DB) plans and respondent reports of the value in the pension account for those with defined contribution (DC) plans. It then proceeds to place the defined benefit values on the same footing with defined contribution plans, using a prorated measure of the value of the DB pension and calculating its present value. Once the plan valuation is placed on the same footing, we are in a position to add the values of each covered person's DB and DC plan. The discussion then turns to the employer-provided formulas to allow an alternative calculation of the value of DB pensions. Note that employer plan descriptions are not used to value DC plans.[1] In this book, account balances for DC plans are estimated from respondent reports. Once DB plan values based on employer plan descriptions have been generated, a next natural step is to compare those values with the values provided by respondents.

In addition to pension wealth from current jobs, a full accounting of pension wealth must include pensions from previous jobs. We use the HRS to calculate the total value of pensions ever held by respondents. To bring these calculations together, this chapter concludes with tables reporting total pension wealth held by respondents and by households, the share of wealth associated with each plan type, and the share of household pension wealth attributable to men and to women and reporting how these various measures of pension wealth have changed over time.

In the process of discussing pension values, consideration is also given to the question of reporting error and to other indications that respondents are imperfectly informed about what their defined benefit plans will be worth. Imperfect information is measured by differences between benefits computed from plan formulas provided by employers offering defined benefit plans and benefit amounts reported by respondents.[2]

Different Measures of Pension Value

HRS respondents are asked to report plan values differently depending on whether they have a defined benefit or a defined contribution plan. Should they report they have a defined benefit plan, they are asked about expected yearly benefits at a number of different potential retirement dates. For example, those who report that their plan is defined benefit are asked when they expect to first receive their benefits and how much they expect those benefits to be per period (e.g., per month, per year). Benefits are expected to vary with age and years of service at retirement and with earnings in the years before retirement. Thus when asked about a DB plan, respondents provide an estimate of the periodic benefit payments they will receive, covering a period extending well into the future.[3]

Respondents who report a defined contribution plan are asked in each year of the survey to indicate the size of the account held in their name as of the date of the survey. The balance in a defined contribution plan indicates the total value of the pension accumulated from work to date, summing the value of employer and respondent contributions, as well as accumulated investment returns. There is no inherent uncertainty or forecasting required to generate the current balance in the DC account. Knowledge of the balance is required, however.

A number of adjustments are required to place the present value of a defined benefit plan on the same footing as the value of a defined contribution plan. First, the DC plan value is based only on work to date at the time of the survey. Thus the defined benefit plan should be valued only on the basis of work to date.[4] Second, because DB benefits are paid out over many decades and may not begin for a number of years after the survey date, the value of DB benefits should be discounted, reducing the plan value in light of the delay in the timing of receipt. Third, the valuation of DB benefits should include an adjustment to reflect the annuitization of benefits. Benefits are paid only if the respondent continues to survive. Once the DB plan value is adjusted for these factors, the figure obtained represents the stock of money required to generate the benefits promised by the DB plan based on work and earnings to date. This value of the DB plan can then be added to the value of any DC account to obtain the total value of pension wealth on the basis of work to date.

Respondents may not be fully aware of all of the complexities of the benefit formula. Respondents are certainly unlikely to have the formulas associated with various retirement contingencies in their head. Therefore, in addition to reporting respondents' projections of their future benefit amounts, the Health and Retirement Study also provides employer-produced descriptions of the formulas governing benefits. These may be evaluated using special software, applying the benefit formulas to respondents' reports of their earnings histories and their covered tenure under the pension. Use of employer-provided benefit formulas to value DB pensions facilitates comparisons of how benefits vary with the date of claiming, allowing particular attention to be paid to early and normal retirement benefits.

Pension data are not available for the full sample. Some respondents who report having a pension do not report on plan details that are required to fully evaluate their pension plans. Moreover, employer pension plan descriptions are not available for the full sample. To obtain estimates that are representative of the full population, we also explore the effects of imputations on plan values.

A great deal of detail is presented in this chapter, exploring a number of alternative measures of plan values. Our hope is that these detailed findings will be of use to researchers, both when choosing which measures of plan value best suit their needs and, for some, when using the data underlying the tables reported in this chapter.

Respondent Reports of Annual Expected Benefits from Their Most Important DB Plan on Their Current Job

To begin the discussion of benefits from defined benefit plans, Table 9.1A presents summary statistics based on the annual values of expected benefits from the most important defined benefit plan reported by HRS respondents.[5] Benefits are reported by respondents as of the first year the benefit will be received.[6]

Average benefits from DB plans range from around $20,000 per year, as reported by the cohort of those 51 to 56 years old in 1992, to roughly $30,000 per year by those 51 to 56 years old in 2004. To put these benefits into perspective, the table also reports mean annual earnings. Taking the ratio of mean expected benefits to mean earnings, roughly half of earnings are replaced on average. These ratios appear as the bottom number in each column and are identical at 51 percent for each cohort of 51- to 56-year-olds upon their entry into the HRS in 1992, 1998, and 2004.

Looking across the rows in the second, third, and fourth panels of Table 9.1A, that is, looking at how benefits change over time for members of each cohort of 51- to 56-year-olds, cohort members do not report much of a change from wave to wave in the average nominal benefit they ultimately expect to receive. Even though respondents reporting in later years are closer to retirement age, and thus should be better informed about their likely benefits, the average and median benefits they report are not much different from the benefits they reported in earlier waves of the survey. Inflation-adjusted benefits do decline over time, however. Why would benefits fall in real terms over time? One reason is that some respondents have changed jobs over the course of the survey waves, and in their new jobs they will have much lower tenure by the time they retire. It is also likely that a disproportionate share of those with higher benefits will have retired early. The sharp decline in the number of observations as one proceeds along the third row of each panel, across the columns of the table, suggests that selectivity may be a major issue.

Although nominal benefits reported in Table 9.1A differ substantially among cohorts, there is only a very small real increase in benefits among cohorts over time. Average expected annual benefits were reported as $20,200 in 1992 for those 51- to 56-year-old members of the original HRS cohort. Members of the war baby cohort reported average expected benefits of $24,200 at ages 51 to 56 in 1998, while the expected benefit amount increases to $29,900 for those in the early boomer cohort in 2004. However, after adjusting for

Table 9.1A Respondent reports of annual expected benefits, retirement assumed at expected age full-time pension-covered employees will start receiving benefits from their most important DB plan, in thousands of current dollars, and related outcomes (weighted)

Cohort	1992	1994	1996	1998	2000	2002	2004	2006
HRS cohort: ages 51–61 in 1992								
Mean benefits	19.1	19.9	19.8	22.4	27.8	21.6	20.5	21.0
Median benefits	14.1	15.0	14.8	16.8	15.6	15.1	16.8	14.4
No. of observations	1,300	1,117	876	585	407	207	131	68
Mean annual earnings	39.2	43.8	44.1	48.9	51.7	54.1	49.9	55.1
Mean benefits/mean earnings	0.49	0.45	0.45	0.46	0.54	0.40	0.41	0.38
HRS cohort: ages 51–56 in 1992								
Mean benefits	20.2	20.9	20.8	22.6	28.9	21.2	20.5	21.1
Median benefits	15.6	16.8	15.9	15.8	15.6	14.4	16.8	13.3
No. of observations	781	757	655	475	346	173	114	60
Mean annual earnings	39.3	45.3	44.4	48.5	52.1	54.2	52.7	54.7
Mean benefits/mean earnings	0.51	0.46	0.47	0.47	0.55	0.39	0.39	0.39
War baby cohort: ages 51–56 in 1998								
Mean benefits	—	—	—	24.2	27.7	26.4	26.4	24.4
Median benefits	—	—	—	20.4	23.3	21.6	20.2	18.0
No. of observations	—	—	—	419	416	297	259	198
Mean annual earnings	—	—	—	47.4	53.8	57.1	57.9	64.9
Mean benefits/mean earnings	—	—	—	0.51	0.54	0.46	0.46	0.38
Early boomer cohort: ages 51–56 in 2004								
Mean benefits							29.9	30.3
Median benefits							26.2	24.0
No. of observations							381	330
Mean annual earnings							58.6	62.9
Mean benefits/mean earnings							0.51	0.48

Notes: Benefit and earnings amounts are reported in thousands of dollars. Shading highlights values in the year a cohort first entered the study. Additional notes are reported in the appendix.

inflation between 1992 and 2004, real benefits increase by only 6 percent over the entire twelve-year period.

Between 30 and 50 percent of respondents answer "don't know" or refuse to answer when asked the amount of DB benefits they expect to receive. In 1992, 853 out of 1,221 males ages 51 to 56 with pension coverage reported having a DB or combination plan. Out of this group, 588 cases reported an amount for expected benefits. That is, 69 percent have an observed value. This is similar to the match rate of employer plan descriptions that will form the basis for alternative tables presented below. Women are more likely to report that they do not know the benefit amount. In 1992, 672 women ages 51 to 56 indicated that they had a DB or combination plan. Only 338 of them (50 percent) have an observed value for their expected benefits. Similarly, in 1998, 439 out of 772 women ages 51 to 56 reported having a DB or combination plan. About 60 percent of them (265/439) reported an amount for their expected benefits.

Effects of Increasing Labor Force Participation of Women on Trends in DB Pension Values

Changes in the composition of the sample might be expected to shape the differences in benefit amounts reported by members of different cohorts summarized in Table 9.1A. Recent years have witnessed an enormous increase not only in the labor force participation of women but in their pension plans as well. Thus as seen in Table 9.1B, although the real value of annual DB pension benefits expected by men ages 51 to 56 declined by about 7 percent between 1992 and 2004, the real value of DB pension benefits expected by women increased by 57 percent between the same two cohorts over the same period.

Higher and more continuous participation in the labor market affects pensions in a number of ways. Increased participation implies a lower incidence of career interruption, increasing women's wages. Higher wages and longer careers make it more likely that women will be in jobs offering pensions. When they are covered by a pension, higher wages and more continuous spells of full-time work increase the value of women's pensions, both directly and also by encouraging employers to enrich the formulas determining their benefits. All of this said, because women's pensions are less valuable than men's, increasing women's labor force participation exerts a negative influence on the average value of pensions held by all workers with a DB pension, as reported in Table 9.1A.

Table 9.1B   Annual benefits at respondents' expected retirement age from most important DB
plan on a current job, and related outcomes, 1992, 1998, and 2004, respondent data,
full-time employees, thousands of 1992 dollars

Cohort	1992		1998		2004	
	Males	Females	Males	Females	Males	Females
HRS: 51–61 in 1992						
Mean	22.4	12.5	19.2	10.4	12.6	8.3
Median	18.0	8.4	16.2	6.8	10.1	6.1
90/10	9.1	17.3	11.2	12.5	7.3	14.5
No. of observations	840	460	355	230	69	62
HRS: 51–56 in 1992						
Mean	23.8	12.9	19.3	10.6	12.6	7.7
Median	19.2	9.2	15.8	6.8	10.2	6.1
90/10	8.2	18.1	11.3	15.0	7.3	9.6
No. of observations	501	280	291	185	64	50
WBs: 51–56 in 1998						
Mean	—	—	23.3	15.4	17.5	12.8
Median	—	—	20.3	10.2	13.0	8.7
90/10	—	—	11.5	14.2	11.5	13.3
No. of observations	—	—	231	189	145	114
EBs: 51–56 in 2004						
Mean	—	—	—	—	22.2	20.3
Median	—	—	—	—	21.5	17.2
90/10	—	—	—	—	7.9	11.2
No. of observations					216	165

Notes: Benefit values are reported in thousands of dollars. Shading highlights values in the year a cohort
first entered the study. Additional notes are reported in the appendix.

To further characterize changes in the distribution of benefits, Table 9.1B
reports the ratio of annual benefits for those in the ninetieth percentile of benefits compared with the tenth percentile. In 1992, the expected benefits for the
ninetieth percentile of 51- to 56-year-old men were about 8.2 times the benefits expected by those in the tenth percentile. There seems to be little systematic change in the ratio between the HRS cohort and the early boomer
cohort.

In contrast, as labor force participation increased for women and their
patterns of participation became more consistent throughout their lifetimes,
instances of very low benefits for some due to discontinuous patterns of partici-

pation became less common. The 90/10 ratio of benefits for 51- to 56-year-old women, initially more than twice as large as the comparable ratio for men, falls from 18.1 for the HRS cohort in 1992 to 11.2 for female members of the early boomer cohort in 2004. Comparing the 90/10 ratios of men and women over time, the narrowing of the distribution of benefits for women in newer cohorts brings the dispersion of their benefits much closer to men's by 2004, although the dispersion of women's benefits is still somewhat wider.

Discussion in this chapter periodically returns to the theme of changing relative pension benefits and pension values between men and women. On most dimensions examined in this and other chapters, the closing of the gap in pensions between men and women is substantial and of considerable interest.

Respondent Reports of DC Account Balances from All Plans on Their Current Jobs

Account balances are reported in Table 9.2 for those who indicate that they have a defined contribution plan. In this table, values are reported in current rather than constant dollars. Members of the HRS cohort who were 51 to 56 in 1992 had average balances of $43,900 when they entered the survey. By 2004, those 51 to 56 (early boomers) had nominal balances of $89,500, roughly double the balance of members of the cohort that preceded them twelve years earlier.

Comparing the means and medians, account balances are clearly skewed, with disproportionately large accounts raising the mean relative to the median. This introduces the question of whether some of the accounts are so small that they should be disregarded. This question is also relevant to evaluating the importance of pension coverage. When we arbitrarily set a lower limit on account values of $1,000 in current year dollars, we find that as of 2004, 5 percent of the DC plans had balances below this minimum. These balances are likely to be added to before most of the 51- to 56-year-old respondents reach retirement age. This suggests that with regard to DC plans held on current jobs, there is a wide spread in plan balances but that very few plans have balances that are so low they should be ignored. There is one caveat here. Although only 2 percent of the plans held by men have a balance below $1,000, 10 percent of the accounts held by women fall below $1,000 (that is up from 9 percent of women's accounts in 1992). Thus the importance of the level of coverage of women by DC pensions may be overstated, although the strong trend in coverage of women is not affected much by these small accounts.

Table 9.2 Respondent reports of DC account balances in all plans on current job, and related outcomes, full-time employees, thousands of current dollars

Cohort	1992	1994	1996	1998	2000	2002	2004	2006
HRS: 51–61 in 1992								
Mean	44.2	50.8	64.9	88.7	105.2	97.8	106.5	160.2
Median	17.0	20.0	23.0	30.0	30.0	30.0	40.0	55.0
No. of observations	1,347	926	875	653	512	289	232	147
HRS: 51–56 in 1992								
Mean	43.9	50.7	63.4	91.2	110.7	104.9	118.3	175.9
Median	15.0	20.0	24.0	30.0	30.0	30.0	45.0	56.0
No. of observations	852	641	638	531	439	249	197	127
WBs: 51–56 in 1998								
Mean	—	—	—	73.4	87.2	106.8	97.6	125.3
Median	—	—	—	27.0	30.0	40.0	42.0	58.0
No. of observations	—	—	—	596	507	405	375	284
EBs: 51–56 in 2004								
Mean	—	—	—	—	—	—	89.5	88.4
Median	—	—	—	—	—	—	36.0	30.0
No. of observations	—	—	—	—	—	—	633	515

Notes: Benefit values are reported in thousands of dollars. Shading highlights values in the year a cohort first entered the study.

As we have emphasized, defined contribution balances reported here are based on a different concept from the expected DB benefits reported in Table 9.1A. Reported DC account balances are the account values held by the respondent at the time of the survey. DB values are reported at the time of retirement and in all following years. This has consequences for changes in reported DB and DC values over time. DC balances held by a particular respondent grow between the survey date and the retirement date as contributions and investment returns mount. Expected DB amounts are as of the expected retirement date. If predictions of earnings and retirement date were accurate, if no one retired or changed jobs between periods so that the sample did not change between surveys with selected retirements, and if reporting of expected benefits did not vary with the value of the dollar in the year of the survey, expected DB amounts might not change from survey to survey, while DC amounts would continue to change.

It is not easy to follow changes in benefit amounts from wave to wave. For example, as seen in Table 9.2A, there were 147 respondents from the original HRS cohort who reported a balance in 2006. Looking back to 1998 along the second row from the bottom, 81 (147 − 66) of the 147 respondents who reported a balance in 2006 did not report a balance in the earlier year. Looking down the first column of the table, ten were not interviewed in 1998, six were not working, twenty-two reported no pension in 1998, and twenty-five reported that they did not have a defined contribution plan. Similarly, from the second row from the bottom in Table 9.2B, of the 284 members of the war baby sample who reported a positive DC account balance in 2006, only 148 reported a positive balance in 1998. Reporting error may be one reason for these discrepancies.

Effects of Increasing Labor Force Participation of Women on Trends in DC Pension Values

Returning to the theme of the strong trend in women's pensions throughout the period covered by the HRS, DC plan values are also reported separately for men and women in Table 9.2C. Comparing the means of account balances, measured in constant (1992) dollars, in the first row of the second panel in Table 9.2C, we see that in 1992 men ages 51 to 56 had account values that were 2.7 (58.7/21.8) times the value of the accounts held by women. By 2004, on average the account values held by men 51 to 56 years old amounted to 1.6

Table 9.2A   Status in 1998, 2000, 2002, and 2004 of the original HRS sample with positive account balances in 2006

Respondents' status	1998	2000	2002	2004	2006
Not interviewed	10	9	5	6	0
Not working	6	3	3	2	0
No pension	22	21	15	12	0
No DCs	25	19	20	20	0
DK on balances	18	12	29	22	0
With positive account balances	66	83	75	85	147
Total	147	147	147	147	147

Table 9.2B   Status in 1998, 2000, 2002, and 2004 of the original war baby sample with positive account balances in 2006

Respondents' status	1998	2000	2002	2004	2006
Not interviewed	24	23	19	11	0
Not working	4	10	10	4	0
No pension	39	31	20	21	0
No DCs	36	50	47	34	0
DK on balances	33	21	34	43	0
With positive account balances	148	149	154	171	284
Total	284	284	284	284	284

(75.2/48.1) times the balances held by women. Thus as expected, there was much higher growth in the values of the accounts held by women. Indeed, the average account value held by women in the 2004 cohort of 51- to 56-year-olds, as observed in the year 2004, was 2.2 (48.1/21.8) times the value of the accounts held by women 51 to 56 in 1992, when observed in 1992. Comparable account values held by men increased by 28 (75.2/58.7) percent over this period.

We repeat the format of Table 9.2C in Table 9.2D. The difference is that Table 9.2D includes only those with a DC plan only, thus eliminating secondary DC plans for those holding both a DB and a DC plan. In 1992, men 51 to 56 who were full-time employees with primary DC plans had account values that were 4 (63.5/15.9) times the value of the accounts held by women. By 2004, on average the account values in primary DC plans held by men 51 to 56 years old amounted to 1.7 (68.5/40.4) times the balances held by women. Thus when only primary DC accounts are examined, there was even higher growth

Table 9.2C Total DC account balances and related outcomes on current job, 1992, 1998, and 2004, respondent data, full-time employees, thousands of 1992 dollars

Cohort	1992		1998		2004	
	Males	Females	Males	Females	Males	Females
HRS: 51–61 in 1992						
Mean	57.9	23.9	81.4	33.4	55.8	52.2
Median	22.6	10.0	32.1	12.1	25.4	15.2
90/10	75.0	65.0	96.7	114.0	90.0	40.0
No. of observations	782	565	394	259	123	109
HRS: 51–56 in 1992						
Mean	58.7	21.8	84.1	34.5	63.0	56.7
Median	23.0	10.0	34.2	13.5	26.4	15.2
90/10	80.0	58.9	90.0	115.0	79.6	50.0
No. of observations	482	370	312	219	104	93
WBs: 51–56 in 1998						
Mean	—	—	77.4	42.2	69.6	45.1
Median	—	—	29.7	16.9	30.2	21.1
90/10	—	—	132.0	75.3	92.9	42.5
No. of observations	—	—	292	304	179	196
EBs: 51–56 in 2004						
Mean	—	—	—	—	75.2	48.1
Median	—	—	—	—	36.0	15.8
90/10	—	—	—	—	56.0	200.0
No. of observations	—	—	—	—	346	287

Note: Benefit values are reported in thousands of dollars.

in the values of the accounts held by women and slower growth in the real value of the accounts held by men. Indeed, the average account value held by women in the 2004 cohort of 51- to 56-year-olds, as observed in the year 2004, was 2.54 (40.4/15.9) times the value of the accounts held by women 51 to 56 in 1992, when observed in 1992. Comparable account values held by men increased by 8 (68.5/63.5) percent over this period.

There has been strong growth in coverage by DC plans. As a result, a large number of those covered by a DC plan in the HRS have been covered by a DC plan for relatively few years. These respondents have relatively low balances. Others who were covered by DC plans for decades have high balances. The effect of mixing these two groups is to cause the ratio of benefits between those at the ninetieth and tenth percentiles of the distribution of pension balances

Table 9.2D   Total DC account balances and related outcomes on current job, 1992, 1998, and 2004, respondent data, with DC plan(s) only, full-time employees, thousands of 1992 dollars (weighted)

Cohort	1992		1998		2004	
	Males	Females	Males	Females	Males	Females
HRS: 51–61 in 1992						
Mean	59.4	17.7	80.1	28.4	58.3	56.2
Median	20.0	7.0	21.4	9.1	20.3	15.2
90/10	75.0	56.3	118.7	101.4	100.0	34.6
No. of observations	363	310	257	182	88	81
HRS: 51–56 in 1992						
Mean	63.5	15.9	83.6	29.1	65.5	60.9
Median	20.0	8.0	21.4	9.2	25.4	15.2
90/10	106.7	47.8	150.1	100.1	80.0	33.3
No. of observations	223	210	193	152	75	71
WBs: 51–56 in 1998						
Mean	—	—	62.7	28.8	66.9	39.0
Median	—	—	20.3	9.3	19.3	16.9
90/10	—	—	166.7	62.2	150.0	45.5
No. of observations	—	—	137	188	105	141
EBs: 51–56 in 2004						
Mean	—	—	—	—	68.5	40.4
Median	—	—	—	—	25.8	10.4
90/10	—	—	—	—	55.0	194.5
No. of observations	—	—	—	—	202	187

Note: Benefit values are reported in thousands of dollars.

shown in Tables 9.2C and 9.2D to vary over time and between samples. These ratios move around a great deal because they are very sensitive to the size of the denominator, the value of the pension for those in the tenth percentile. This low number, a value between $1,000 and $3,000, changes a great deal over time and varies between cohorts, causing large changes in the 90/10 differential.

The Present Value of Defined Benefit Plans—Current Plan, Respondent Data

So far, the value of a defined benefit plan has been represented by a flow, the value of the benefit to be received in each year if the respondent retires at the expected time. In contrast, the value of the defined contribution plan is represented by a stock, the cumulated total of employer plus employee contributions plus earnings from investments, represented by the balance in the account. To put the values of DB and DC plans on the same footing, one must begin by summing the values of the yearly benefits to be paid by the defined benefit plans, discounting to adjust for the difference in when benefits will be available, and weighting the probability of payment by a measure of life expectancy.[7]

As discussed in Chapter 2, pension wealth is the name given to the present value of the expected benefit payments from a defined benefit plan. Pension wealth is calculated in Table 9.3 first by summing the discounted values of each year of benefit receipt back to the age of expected retirement. Benefits are then further discounted back to the indicated calendar year. Thus benefits are discounted back to 1992 for members of the original HRS cohort, to 1998 for war babies, and to 2004 for early boomers. Finally, to express benefits in constant 1992 dollars, thereby facilitating comparisons across cohorts, present values for members of the 1998 and 2004 cohorts are discounted back to 1992 using only the cost of living.[8]

Looking across the rows in Table 9.3, the present values of DB benefits from current jobs for those within each cohort decline over time. Two reasons for this decline may be noted. Those with higher benefits may retire first, and plans in pay status are not included in this table. Thus the number of observations declines sharply as each cohort is followed over time. In addition, some who continue to work full time on a job offering a pension will have left their long-term job and as a result will be receiving a lower wage and a lower pension.

Once again, consistent with the strong trend in women's pensions, when comparing DB benefits across cohorts for men and for women, there is almost no change for 51- to 56-year-old men but a considerable growth in benefits for women. The present value of men's benefits grows slightly in constant 1992 dollars from $165,300 in 1992 to $170,500 in 2004. In contrast, the present value of women's pensions increases from $97,800 for those 51 to 56 in 1992 to $147,400 in 2004. The ratio of the present values of pensions between men and women ages 51 to 56 falls from 1.69 to 1 (165.3/97.8) in 1992, to 1.16 to 1 (170.5/147.4) in 2004. That is, by 2004, there is only a 16 percent difference in the value of DB pensions held by men and women who are approaching retirement.

Within groups of men and women, over time the distribution of present values of the most important DB plan has been widening slightly for men and

Table 9.3 Present value of benefits from most important DB plan on current job at expected age of benefit receipt and related outcomes, respondent report, full-time employees, by cohort and gender, thousands of 1992 dollars (weighted), 1992, 1998, and 2004

Cohort	1992		1998		2004	
	Males	Females	Males	Females	Males	Females
HRS: 51–61 in 1992						
Mean	163.5	100.4	152.5	94.6	95.5	80.2
Median	131.3	61.6	129.9	67.0	78.3	56.0
90/10	12.0	23.6	12.3	15.7	17.0	15.6
No. of observations	853	476	369	242	73	61
HRS: 51–56 in 1992						
Mean	165.3	97.8	152.5	95.0	97.9	74.3
Median	131.9	60.2	129.0	64.8	81.0	59.3
90/10	10.7	27.4	12.3	16.7	11.2	11.6
No. of observations	512	294	304	197	68	51
WBs: 51–56 in 1998						
Mean	—	—	165.5	125.7	128.3	117.7
Median	—	—	136.4	89.0	97.8	89.5
90/10	—	—	14.5	18.9	16.3	13.2
No. of observations	—	—	249	202	150	116
EBs: 51–56 in 2004						
Mean	—	—	—	—	170.5	147.4
Median	—	—	—	—	138.2	110.3
90/10	—	—	—	—	12.8	15.3
No. of observations	—	—	—	—	218	171

Note: Benefit values are reported in thousands of dollars.

narrowing sharply for women. Thus for women, Table 9.3 shows that the ratio of benefits between those at the ninetieth and tenth percentiles has fallen from 27.4 for those who were 51 to 56 in 1992, to 15.3 for those who were 51 to 56 in 2004. The comparable change for men is from 10.7 to 12.8.

Prorated Value of DB Pension Wealth, Respondent Data

When comparing pension values between defined benefit and defined contribution plans, one has to make adjustments for the differences between plan types in the timing of benefits and the timing and availability of future accruals. These considerations are in addition to any delay in payment until the covered worker qualifies for receipt of retirement benefits. A DC plan provides an account that has an unambiguous immediate market value, even if the benefit is not available for some time. But the current DC balance does not include the value of any future benefits that will be earned by work from the survey period through retirement. In contrast, a DB plan promises a yearly benefit flow, and the value of that flow depends not only on years of coverage and salary to date but also on how many future years of work will be provided until the expected retirement date and at what wage. Thus, for example, the present values of defined benefit plans reported in Table 9.3 assume that the individual works until the reported expected date of retirement. It evaluates the benefit using years of service that will eventually be accrued by the time of the expected retirement date as well as the projected salary at that retirement date.

One step toward putting the reported values of DB plans on the same footing as those of DC plans is to prorate the DB benefits based on work to date. As discussed previously, this compromise approach allows the years of service accumulated to date to be evaluated using the wage that would be paid assuming the worker remained until the specified retirement date, rather than the wage accumulated to the date of the survey. At the same time, the years of service used in calculating the DB benefit do not assume any future employment.

Prorated benefits are reported in Table 9.4. Figures in Table 9.4 were obtained by multiplying the values in Table 9.3 by the ratio of years of service accumulated to date, divided by years of service that would be accumulated by the expected retirement date. For example, if a person had worked fifteen years through 1992 and expected to work another ten years until 2002, the benefit is computed as if the person worked through 2002, but that benefit is then multiplied by 15/25. Thus the present values reported in Table 9.4, where benefits are prorated, are lower than those reported in Table 9.3, where benefits are not prorated.

Table 9.4 reports an average prorated value of DB plans of $129,600 for 51- to 56 year-old covered, full-time, male workers in 1992 (row 1, column 1 of the second panel). That is about 78 percent of the value that uses expected eventual tenure in computing the benefit ($165,300), as reported in the same location in Table 9.3. For 51- to 56-year-old covered women, the prorated value in 1992 is $73,500, about 75 percent of the comparable value ($97,800) in Table 9.3. By 2004, the present value of expected DB benefits at expected retirement age for men is $170,500, while the prorated value for the DB plan

Table 9.4   Prorated present value of benefits from most important DB plan on current job and related outcomes, respondent report, full-time employees, by cohort and gender, thousands of 1992 dollars, 1992, 1998, and 2004

	1992		1998		2004	
Cohort	Males	Females	Males	Females	Males	Females
HRS: 51–61 in 1992						
Mean	133.7	79.2	132.7	81.9	87.6	75.9
Median	96.8	44.1	111.1	60.6	73.8	54.1
90/10	18.6	44.8	16.3	21.8	16.2	16.7
No. of observations	837	471	365	240	72	61
HRS: 51–56 in 1992						
Mean	129.6	73.5	130.1	80.9	89.8	69.1
Median	89.6	36.0	110.3	56.7	73.8	56.5
90/10	19.4	49.4	17.8	23.6	14.8	13.4
No. of observations	503	291	302	196	67	51
WBs: 51–56 in 1998						
Mean	—	—	128.9	92.8	110.0	103.0
Median	—	—	98.6	59.3	77.9	68.8
90/10	—	—	26.8	30.9	20.6	24.0
No. of observations	—	—	247	199	149	113
EBs: 51–56 in 2004						
Mean	—	—	—	—	130.4	106.1
Median	—	—	—	—	89.9	63.3
90/10	—	—	—	—	28.6	33.1
No. of observations					214	170

Notes: Benefit values are reported in thousands of dollars. Additional notes are reported in the appendix.

for men is $130,400 (column 5, first row, bottom panel). Comparable figures for women are $147,400 and $106,100. Thus for those 51 to 56 in 2004, the prorated value for men is 76 percent of the full value, while the prorated value for women is about 72 percent of the full value.

The next step is to compare the prorated value of the most important DB pension on current jobs from Table 9.4 with the value for the total of all DC plans held by respondents on their current jobs from Table 9.2C. As reported, the prorated value of DB plans held by 51- to 56-year-old males in 1992 was $129,600. Table 9.2C reports defined contribution plans on their current jobs in 1992 held by male respondents 51 to 56 summed to $58,700 on average. Thus the most important DB plan on the current job held by men in 1992 was worth about 2.2 times the value of all DC plans held on current jobs. For women 51 to 56 in 1992, their DB plans on current jobs were worth 3.37 (73.5/21.8) times the value of their DC plans. Remember these comparisons are between pension values for those covered by a DB plan and pension values for those covered by a DC plan. To compare the total value of DB pensions with those of DC pensions, these values must be weighted by the numbers of respondents holding each plan type. In Table 9.19, we will compare the average values of DB and DC pensions held by members of different cohorts.

With the spread of DC plans over time, and the increasing length of time available for covered workers to have contributed to DC plans as the plans became more mature, one would expect this situation to have changed. The ratio of values of DB to DC benefits for men 51 to 56 in 2004 fell to 1.73 to 1 (130.4/75.2). By 2004, the ratio of DB to DC values had fallen to 2.21 to 1 (106.1/48.1) for women.

To begin the process of determining the full worth of all pension benefits, Table 9.5 adds the prorated value of DB plans to DC account balances. Primary and secondary DC plan values are added to the values of primary DB plans. The average values of pensions reported in Table 9.5 are below the values of primary DB plans reported in Table 9.4. The reason is that many of the respondents who have a DC plan only, and are included in Table 9.5 but not 9.4, have plans with relatively low values.

Once again, we find that although pension values for women remain below those for men, the gap has narrowed over time. In 1992, the ratio of pension values between men 51 to 56 and women of the same age was 2.25 to 1 (117.2/52.0). By 2004, the ratio had narrowed to 1.47 to 1 (117.3/79.8). The gap in total pension values between pension-covered men and women is wider than the gap in values of defined benefit plans found in Table 9.4.

The increase in the relative number of jobs in the public sector held by women contributes to the narrowing of the gap in pension wealth between men and women. Although, as seen in Table 6.1A and B, in 2006 DB plans comprised 44 percent of pension-covered men and 32 percent of pension-covered women in the private sector, DB plans comprised 80 percent of pension-covered men and 72 percent of pension-covered women in the public sector. Thirty-six

Table 9.5   Prorated present value of benefits from most important DB plan plus balances in all
DC plans from pension on current job, and related outcomes, respondent report, by
cohort and gender, full-time employees, thousands of 1992 dollars, 1992, 1998, and
2004

	1992		1998		2004	
Cohort	Males	Females	Males	Females	Males	Females
HRS: 51–61 in 1992						
Mean	120.5	57.2	123.7	62.2	75.9	67.1
Median	71.6	23.4	68.4	31.7	41.7	24.9
90/10	57.3	94.7	57.1	73.5	49.3	58.6
No. of observations	1,312	885	659	450	171	154
HRS: 51–56 in 1992						
Mean	117.2	52.0	125.7	62.8	81.9	65.8
Median	67.0	19.6	71.3	32.1	47.9	25.4
90/10	53.6	90.2	57.9	73.5	40.7	59.5
No. of observations	803	566	528	372	151	132
WBs: 51–56 in 1998						
Mean	—	—	131.7	71.4	104.6	70.5
Median	—	—	76.3	25.9	48.5	33.9
90/10	—	—	145.7	87.9	55.3	55.4
No. of observations	—	—	416	440	279	282
EBs: 51–56 in 2004						
Mean	—	—	—	—	117.3	79.8
Median	—	—	—	—	61.5	33.7
90/10	—	—	—	—	50.1	159.0
No. of observations	—	—	—	—	457	395

Note: Benefit values are reported in thousands of dollars. Additional notes are reported in the appendix.

percent of the jobs with pensions held by women in 2006 are in the public sector, whereas the corresponding number for men is 28 percent.

In contrast, the growth of DC plans has helped to widen the gap in pension
wealth between men and women who are covered by pensions. To be sure, DC
plans held by women have increased in value more rapidly than have plans held
by men. However, as we have seen, the gap in the value between DC plans
held by men and women is much wider than it is for DB plans. As more men
and women are counted in the ranks of those with DC plans only, and fewer
men and women have a DB plan, the difference in the average value of pensions between men and women widens as a result.

Pension Values Disaggregated by Demographic and Labor Market Characteristics, Respondent Reports

The next step is to present pension values from work on the current job separately for different demographic and employment groups. In the process we also present the results separately according to the type of pension a respondent holds. Table 9.6 meets these two purposes. Before turning to the data, it should be noted that the population underlying Table 9.6 differs from that represented by earlier tables in this chapter in two respects: it includes those who are partially retired, and it also includes the self-employed.

By 2004, the plans of those who had both a defined benefit and a defined contribution plan together were worth $205,000 (in 1992 dollars), with the DB plan worth $130,000 on average and the DC plan(s) worth $75,000 (Table 9.6, row 1, column 9 plus column 12). In contrast, those with a DB plan alone had a plan worth $112,000 in 2004 (row 1, column 3). Those with a DC plan alone had a plan worth $61,000 in 2004 (row 1, column 6).

Comparing pension values between men and women, the pensions held by men are always more valuable. However, we again see that women have closed the gap in the value of their DB plans. DB plans held by women increased in value between the early boomer and original HRS cohorts by 33 percent for women with DB plans only and by 37 percent for women with both DB and DC plans. For men the comparable changes were 11 and -3 percent, respectively. Similarly, DC pensions increased in value by 131 percent for women with DC plans only and by 74 percent for women who had a DB plan in addition to their DC plans. The comparable figures for men were 1 percent and 53 percent, again allowing women to close the gap in the value of their DC pensions relative to men.

We saw previously the changing patterns of plan coverage between blacks and whites. By 2004, the patterns of change in plan value were uneven. Blacks with a DB plan only had plans worth about 12 percent less than those held by whites, but the DB plans held by blacks who also had a DC plan were worth 22 percent more than the comparable DB plans held by whites. DC plans held by blacks with a DC plan only were worth 21 percent less than the DC plans held by whites, while the DC plans held by blacks were only 4 percent less valuable than the DC plans held by whites when both also had a DB plan.

Among the other differentials shown in the table, the differences in the values of pensions held by college graduates relative to high school graduates

Table 9.6 Prorated DB values for most important DB plan and DC values from all DC account balances in a current job, and related outcomes, by cohort and plan type, disaggregated for various subgroups, respondent reports, thousands of 1992 dollars

| | DB only | | | DC only | | | Both | | | | | | | | |
| | | | | | | | DB plan | | | DC plan | | | Don't know/refuse | | |
Subgroups	1992	1998	2004	1992	1998	2004	1992	1998	2004	1992	1998	2004	1992	1998	2004
All	97	114	112	50	48	61	126	126	130	47	81	75	29	67	72
Males	115	131	128	78	66	79	147	138	143	55	93	84	30	59	72
Females	70	90	93	16	28	37	79	99	108	34	60	59	28	103	72
White	96	117	116	54	49	65	129	124	128	49	84	78	12	55	73
Black	110	102	102	13	13	46	116	147	156	27	56	75	57	95	72
Hispanic	85	112	87	21	53	31	115	105	118	26	51	24	—	80	53
Other	113	59	66	32	53	38	80	192	174	47	39	65	68	—	—
Married	99	115	107	49	55	72	129	135	139	51	86	80	29	92	68
Not married	89	110	128	51	25	32	119	99	98	37	60	58	—	2	81
Less than high school	64	57	78	17	19	17	79	43	64	15	20	173[a]	—	—	53
High school graduate	76	92	74	36	33	27	92	93	103	30	65	48	12	14	53

Some college	110	108	74	30	46	47	115	115	85	59	66	81	—	118	120
College graduate	101	148	104	58	52	71	188	147	175	58	127	69	63	—	15
More than 16 years	155	142	180	150	82	125	139	175	170	54	93	91	10	68	89
Union	107	123	129	33	58	54	114	112	146	36	77	52	29	143	95
Not union	83	103	86	42	43	55	122	135	120	51	80	89	23	59	67
Large firm	105	123	118	45	54	65	137	134	127	50	93	73	35	103	68
Medium firm	89	94	122	62	53	43	104	79	137	27	47	85	6	160	66
Small firm	81	131	112	50	42	66	106	138	144	61	50	42	26	80	—
Employee	97	115	108	40	45	54	119	127	130	46	79	75	24	92	72
Self-employed[b]	184	121	283	232	77	159	456	110	183	177	149	11	57	—	—

Notes: Benefit values are reported in thousands of dollars. Additional notes are reported in the appendix.

a. There are only three respondents in the sample.

b. There were fifty-five cases in 1992 who were self-employed and reported a pension. Only eight cases out of this group reported type both/combination plans. In 1998, there were fifty respondents who were self-employed with a pension. Only six cases reported their plan type as combination/both in Wave 4. About fifty-six cases in 2004 were self-employed with a pension, and three cases reported having both plans.

are substantial, as would be expected given the differences in earnings. In 2004, for those with a DC plan only, there is almost no difference in the values of DC pensions held by union versus nonunion members, while there is a 50 percent difference in favor of union members in the value of DB plans among those who report having a DB plan only. Except for differences in the value of DC plans held by those with both plan types, differences in the values of pensions held by employees of large versus small firms are relatively modest.

It is useful to consider the results from Table 9.6 in light of our earlier findings indicating how demographic and other factors are related to pension coverage. As seen in Table 5.4, women's participation rates in a pension on their current job increased by 7.6 percent between cohorts of 51- to 56-year-olds interviewed in 1992 and 2004. Moreover, in Chapter 6 we saw that the demographic and industry factors in Table 9.6 are also related to the likelihood of holding a DB rather than a DC plan. Because Table 9.6 conditions both on coverage and on plan type, the relative differences in pension values between members of these different industry and demographic groups will be wider than the differences shown in this table.

Pension Values of DB Plans from Employer-Provided Pension Plan Descriptions

Given the complexities of the formula determining benefits under a defined benefit plan, and the resulting potential of reporting error on the part of the respondent, it is useful to consider additional evidence on plan values. As an alternative to using respondent reports of expected DB benefits, we base estimates of the present value of defined benefit pensions on employer-provided pension plan descriptions. The formulas coded by the HRS from employer-produced documents are applied to the coverage and earnings histories reported by the respondent. The benefits reported in Table 9.7 are not prorated and thus are produced using the same methodology as used for the present values based on self-reports reported in Table 9.3.

Once again, the data suggest that women, although receiving lower benefits than men, are closing the gap. Thus for cohorts ages 51 to 56, average benefits measured in 1992 dollars for men exceed those for women. From the HRS to the early boomer cohorts, benefits are roughly unchanged for men, growing slightly from \$173,000 to \$175,000. For women benefits increase from \$129,000 to \$166,000.

Table 9.7   Present value of benefits from most important DB plan at expected age of benefit receipt, based on firm report, by cohort and gender, full-time employees, thousands of 1992 dollars (weighted), 1992, 1998, and 2004

Cohort	1992		1998		2004	
	Males	Females	Males	Females	Males	Females
HRS: 51–61 in 1992						
Mean	179	125	151	114	120	108
Median	122	86	114	83	85	80
90/10	11.6	12.5	10.5	4.4	57.8	20.6
No. of observations	775	550	219	204	52	77
HRS: 51–56 in 1992						
Mean	173	129	145	118	108	102
Median	116	86	107	87	85	74
90/10	10.6	12.3	9.7	14.0	37.6	24.8
No. of observations	468	364	177	160	46	74
WBs: 51–56 in 1998						
Mean	—	—	163	136	160	136
Median	—	—	127	98	115	87
90/10	—	—	9.8	11.7	9.5	15.3
No. of observations	—	—	167	192	106	131
EBs: 51–56 in 2004						
Mean	—	—	—	—	175	166
Median	—	—	—	—	147	120
90/10	—	—	—	—	7.7	10.4
No. of observations	—	—	—	—	164	204

Note: Benefit values are reported in thousands of dollars. Additional notes are reported in the appendix.

In general, the present values computed with employer-provided data are higher than the benefits from self-reported data in Table 9.3. However, the samples are not comparable. We will compare plan values based on self-reports and firm reports for comparable samples in later tables.

Comparing Benefits at Early, Normal, and Expected Retirement Ages

The employer-provided data are well suited for comparing benefits at alternative retirement ages—expected retirement age, early retirement age, and normal retirement age. These relationships are reported separately for those with DB plans only and combination plans in Table 9.8. The pension software produces benefits at alternative ages, so the comparisons are relatively straightforward to generate. Looking down each column, comparing the values in the first row of the first and third panels, and then in the first row of the second and fourth panels, the present values of benefits at normal retirement age exceed those at early retirement age by substantial amounts. Comparing results in the third and fifth panels and the fourth and sixth panels, more often than not, benefits at the expected retirement age are seen to exceed those at the normal retirement age.

In addition to reporting on benefits at expected, early, and normal ages, Table 9.9 reports average benefits at retirement ages of 50, 55, 60, and 65. It also reports benefits separately for men and women. Again, benefits are higher in younger cohorts for women, with much smaller differences by cohort for men. Comparing values in row 8 and row 12 of the last two columns, it appears that benefits increase between early and normal retirement age at a greater rate for women than for men. These differentials are a topic we will explore in greater detail in Chapter 10.

Care must be exercised when comparing pension outcomes across tables. To increase understanding of the role of pensions, we have presented pension values for different groups of workers, measured pension values at different potential retirement dates, and used different sources of data. Thus Table 9.7 includes only full-time employees, while in Table 9.8 anyone with a matched plan is included. Similarly, Table 9.6 includes prorated DB values based on self-reports. Table 9.8 includes DB present values that are not prorated and are from the firm reports. Plan types underlying Table 9.8 (with the exception of expected benefits) are from employer-produced summary plan descriptions, while plan types used in Table 9.6 are self-reported. Outcomes will differ for these different groups when different measures of pension value are used and will also differ due to the differences in underlying sample composition as different respondents from the same cohort report pension outcomes at different times. All of these differences should be borne in mind before outcomes are compared across tables.

Comparing Self-Reports with Employer Reports for DB Plans

To this point we have discussed the results gleaned from respondent reports of plan values and from employer-provided data. Since the samples underlying the self-reported and firm-reported data differ, to compare values from respondent and firm reports the sample should be restricted to those respondents

Present value of DB benefits at early, normal, and expected retirement dates by plan type and cohort, firm reports for respondents with a matched pension plan (weighted), thousands of 1992 dollars

Benefits at early, normal, and expected retirement ages;	HRS: 51–61 in 1992		HRS: 51–56 in 1992		War babies		Early boomers
	1992 (51–61)	1998 (57–67)	1992 (51–56)	1998 (57–62)	1998 (51–56)	2004 (57–62)	2004 (51–56)
Benefits at early retirement age: DB only							
Mean	139.5	56.4	140.2	56.4	88.2	128.2	129.9
Median	70.4	36.7	71.9	36.9	54.5	59.8	59.7
No. of observations	1,137	175	703	148	122	103	153
Benefits at early retirement age: DB or combination							
Mean	121.1	105.3	120.7	102.1	119.7	120.7	125.8
Median	61.5	59.8	62.3	59.8	72.3	65.1	69.2
No. of observations	1,861	600	1159	478	466	315	467
Benefits at normal retirement age: DB only							
Mean	161.2	81.3	161.8	83.4	118.6	147.7	166.7
Median	99.5	58.2	104.1	59.1	87.3	84.0	101.8
No. of observations	1,136	175	703	148	122	103	153
Benefits at normal retirement age: DB or combination							
Mean	141.5	124.3	140.6	122.2	143.6	139.5	156.9
Median	88.8	80.5	92.5	84.3	103.8	91.5	104.2
No. of observations	1,859	600	1,158	478	466	315	467
Benefits at expected retirement age: DB only							
Mean	173.6	82.1	174.2	84.1	115.6	173.6	172.1
Median	115.5	58.2	116.2	58.2	88.1	115.2	133.5
No. of observations	871	135	541	114	100	79	116
Benefits at expected retirement age: DB or combination							
Mean	153.2	125.7	151.8	126.1	147.5	149.2	171.3
Median	101.4	90.5	101.4	95.1	115.3	101.8	131.2
No. of observations	1,407	474	(881)	372	380	239	370

Note: Benefit values are reported in thousands of dollars. Additional notes are reported in the appendix.

Table 9.9 Average present values of benefits at alternative retirement ages from most important DB plan based on firm report, by cohort and gender, full-time employees (weighted), thousands of 1992 dollars

Age of benefit receipt	Cohort	1992 Males	1992 Females	1998 Males	1998 Females	2004 Males	2004 Females
Expected age of benefit receipt	HRS 51–61	179	125	151	114	120	108
	HRS 51–56	173	129	145	118	108	102
	WB 51–56	—	—	163	136	160	136
	EB 51–56	—	—	—	—	175	166
Early retirement age	HRS 51–61	152	90	138	78	107	84
	HRS 51–56	148	92	131	78	95	75
	WB 51–56	—	—	135	107	134	111
	EB 51–56	—	—	—	—	141	109
Normal retirement age	HRS 51–61	171	114	156	100	126	107
	HRS 51–56	166	116	149	101	117	97
	WB 51–56	—	—	158	133	153	129
	EB 51–56	—	—	—	—	163	150
Age 50	HRS 51–61	131	76	121	73	71	70
	HRS 51–56	125	78	107	74	60	65
	WB 51–56	—	—	97	95	205	200
	EB 51–56	—	—	—	—	112	80
Age 55	HRS 51–61	173	103	165	97	108	99
	HRS 51–56	160	103	149	94	101	88
	WB 51–56	—	—	146	113	145	134
	EB 51–56	—	—	—	—	158	121
Age 60	HRS 51–61	172	114	160	109	139	118
	HRS 51–56	164	114	148	106	125	106
	WB 51–56	—	—	152	124	157	138
	EB 51–56	—	—	—	—	167	146
Age 65	HRS 51–61	153	110	139	99	120	110
	HRS 51–56	147	112	131	99	109	102
	WB 51–56	—	—	141	123	142	128
	EB 51–56	—	—	—	—	153	150

for whom both types of data are available. This comparison begins with Table 9.10, where average benefits are reported.

The samples are much larger in 1992 than in 1998 or 2004. In 1992 data, values of pensions, either at the expected retirement age or at the normal retirement age, are higher when based on firm data. That is true for both men and women, but the difference is much larger for women than for men. By 2004, looking at those who were 51 to 56 in that year, the self-reported values are higher than the firm-reported values for men. Values based on firm data remain higher for women than self-reported values.

Having compared the differences between the mean values of pensions reported by respondents and firms, the next three tables are constructed to facilitate comparisons between respondent and firm reports at the level of the individual. The purpose of these tables is to determine the spread of the individual reports around the values obtained from employer plan descriptions. That spread turns out to be substantial.

Begin with Table 9.11A, which reports results for the full HRS cohort ages 51 to 61 in 1992. Thirty-five percent do not report a pension value. The remainder of the observations are arrayed in a table with values based on respondent reports in the column heads and values based on firm reports in the row heads. Only 19 percent of responses lie along the diagonal, indicating agreement between respondent and firm reports. Twenty percent of observations lie above the diagonal, indicating that the value of the respondent report exceeds the value of the firm report, and 24 percent lie below the diagonal because values based on firm reports are higher. Conditioning on the value calculated from firm-provided plan descriptions, there is substantial variation in each row around the amount seen on the diagonal. Similar results are found in Table 9.11B, which is constructed for those 51 to 56 in 1992. In Table 9.12, which is constructed for those 51 to 56 in 1998, 40 percent do not know a key piece of information about their pension, and only 14 percent of the observations lie along the diagonal, indicating rough agreement between respondent and firm reports. Once again, many points lie off the diagonal, some of them quite a distance from the diagonal line. Similar results are found for Table 9.13, which includes respondents ages 51 to 56 in 2004. In that sample, 37 percent do not know a key piece of information, with 16 percent of the observations lying along the diagonal. All of this suggests substantial misreporting of pension values and no tendency for the misreporting to improve over time.

Table 9.10 Comparison of average present values of benefits at alternative retirement ages from most important DB plan based on respondent and firm reports, by cohort and gender (weighted), thousands of 1992 dollars

Age of benefit receipt	Cohort	1992 Males	1992 Females	1998 Males	1998 Females	2004 Males	2004 Females
Expected age of benefit receipt, self-report	HRS 51–61	183 (567)	110 (312)	171 (152)	115 (128)	120 (35)	89 (39)
	HRS 51–56	185 (340)	118 (192)	171 (124)	120 (98)	120 (33)	88 (38)
	WB 51–56	—	—	180 (118)	131 (101)	159 (72)	140 (76)
	EB 51–56	—	—	—	—	188 (116)	157 (121)
Expected age of benefit receipt, firm report	HRS 51–61	203	140	160	131	122	114
	HRS 51–56	195	145	154	135	121	105
	WB 51–56	—	—	170	140	158	180
	EB 51–56	—	—	—	—	182	177
Normal retirement age, self-report	HRS 51–61	165 (577)	137 (284)	181 (28)	110 (12)	161 (35)	98 (30)
	HRS 51–56	186 (352)	132 (170)	185 (23)	120 (9)	178 (29)	87 (24)
	WB 51–56	—	—	200 (88)	136 (48)	167 (67)	142 (64)
	EB 51–56	—	—	—	—	206 (105)	163 (106)
Normal retirement age, firm report	HRS 51–61	213	152	142	150	142	141
	HRS 51–56	205	161	149	168	148	102
	WB 51–56	—	—	184	164	169	181
	EB 51–56	—	—	—	—	178	179

Notes: Benefit values are reported in thousands of dollars. Additional notes are reported in the appendix. Total number of observations is reported in parentheses.

Table 9.11A Respondent-reported versus provider-reported pension values for DB plans, HRS cohort with matched plan descriptions, 1992, HRS respondents ages 51–61

Provider reported	Respondent reported (%)											
	≤20	20–40	40–60	60–80	80–110	110–150	150–190	190–240	240–300	>300	DK	Total
≤20	2	1	0	0	0	0	0	0	0	0	4	7
20–40	2	2	1	1	1	0	0	0	0	0	6	14
40–60	1	2	2	1	1	1	1	0	0	0	6	13
60–80	0	1	1	1	1	1	0	0	0	0	4	9
80–110	0	0	1	1	2	1	1	1	0	0	3	11
110–150	0	0	1	1	2	2	1	0	0	0	4	12
150–190	0	0	0	0	1	1	1	1	1	1	2	8
190–240	0	0	0	0	0	1	1	1	1	1	2	7
240–300	0	0	0	0	0	0	1	1	1	1	1	5
>300	0	0	0	0	0	0	1	2	2	5	2	12
Total	7	6	6	5	7	7	6	7	6	7	35	100 (1,408)

Note: Shaded cells indicate agreement between values from respondents and providers. Total number of observations is reported in parentheses. Total percentages may not add up due to rounding. Additional notes are reported in the appendix.

Table 9.11B Respondent-reported versus provider-reported pension values for DB plans, HRS cohort with matched plan descriptions, 1992, HRS respondents ages 51–56

Provider reported	Respondent reported (%)											
	≤20	20–40	40–60	60–80	80–110	110–150	150–190	190–240	240–300	>300	DK	Total
≤20	2	0	0	0	0	0	0	0	0	0	4	6
20–40	2	2	1	1	0	0	0	0	0	0	7	14
40–60	1	2	2	1	0	1	1	1	0	0	6	14
60–80	0	1	1	1	1	1	0	0	0	0	4	8
80–110	0	1	1	1	2	2	1	1	1	0	3	11
110–150	1	0	1	1	2	2	1	1	0	0	5	12
150–190	0	0	1	0	1	1	1	1	1	1	3	9
190–240	0	0	0	0	0	1	1	1	1	0	2	7
240–300	0	0	0	0	0	0	1	1	1	1	1	6
>300	0	0	0	0	0	0	0	1	2	5	2	12
Total	6	6	6	5	6	7	6	7	7	7	37	100 (881)

Notes: Shaded cells indicate agreement between values from respondents and providers. Total number of observations is reported in parentheses. Total percentages may not add up due to rounding. Additional notes are reported in the appendix.

Table 9.12 Responden-reported versus provider-reported pension values for DB plans, war baby cohort with matched plan descriptions, 1998, ages 51–56

Provider reported	Respondent reported (%)											
	≤20	20–40	40–60	60–80	80–110	110–150	150–190	190–240	240–300	>300	DK	Total
≤20	1	1	0	0	0	0	0	0	0	0	5	8
20–40	1	1	0	1	0	1	1	0	0	0	6	11
40–60	2	2	1	1	1	0	0	0	0	0	4	12
60–80	0	1	1	0	0	1	0	1	0	0	3	8
80–110	1	1	2	1	1	0	1	1	0	0	4	11
110–150	1	0	1	1	1	2	2	1	1	0	5	14
150–190	1	0	0	0	0	1	2	2	1	1	2	8
190–240	0	0	0	1	0	1	1	1	2	1	3	8
240–300	0	0	0	0	0	0	1	1	1	1	2	8
>300	0	0	0	0	0	0	1	1	1	4	2	11
Total	7	6	5	4	4	6	8	7	6	7	40	100 (377)

Note: Shaded cells indicate agreement between values from respondents and providers. Total number of observations is reported in parentheses. Total percentages may not add up due to rounding. Additional notes are reported in the appendix.

Table 9.13 Respondent-reported versus provider-reported pension values for DB plans, early boomer cohort with matched plan descriptions, 2004, ages 51–56

Provider reported	Respondent reported (%)											
	≤20	20–40	40–60	60–80	80–110	110–150	150–190	190–240	240–300	>300	DK	Total
≤20	1	1	0	1	0	0	0	0	0	1	2	5
20–40	2	2	1	1	0	0	0	0	0	0	2	6
40–60	1	1	2	1	1	0	0	1	0	0	4	11
60–80	0	0	1	0	0	1	1	0	0	0	3	7
80–110	0	0	1	1	1	2	0	1	0	1	5	12
110–150	1	1	1	0	1	1	2	1	2	0	5	14
150–190	0	0	1	0	0	2	1	1	1	1	4	10
190–240	0	0	0	1	2	1	2	1	1	1	3	12
240–300	0	0	0	0	0	1	0	1	1	1	2	6
>300	1	0	0	0	1	1	1	1	3	6	4	16
Total	5	4	7	4	6	7	7	6	7	10	37	100 (391)

Notes: Shaded cells indicate agreement between *values* from respondents and providers. Total number of observations is reported in parentheses. Total percentages may not add up due to rounding. Additional notes are reported in the appendix.

In some cases, there is enough information in the panel data to detect errors in the reported values of DB or DC plans. In some cases, there is an obvious error in one year in the location of the decimal place associated with the plan value, so that one year's benefit amount is ten or 100 times the amount reported in surrounding years. Another common error is misreporting of the period over which the benefit is received. For example, what is obviously a yearly benefit may be reported on a monthly basis. Other potential sources of error include misidentification of plan type. Where these errors have been identified, and the evidence is overwhelming that there has been an error, we eliminate the reported benefit for the particular wave of the survey when it was reported. The relatively few instances where we have done this are reported in Appendix 9.1, which contains the notes to the relevant tables.

Results with Imputed Values

An outstanding question is how the preceding findings are affected by missing data. The four tables in Appendix 9.2 redo key calculations from the present chapter, imputing results for missing observations.[9] While the number of imputations varies by year and cohort, there are many more imputations for women than for men. Typically, more than half the observations for women are imputed. Average annual benefits from DB plans and mean account balances are very close between the samples with and without imputations (Table 9.1B vs. Table 9.21 and Table 9.2C vs. Table 9.22). If the imputations are working correctly, that suggests that those who are missing observations are not very different from those for whom values are being imputed. There is a larger difference between samples with and without imputed results when prorated present values are compared (Table 9.4 vs. Table 9.23). Present values are systematically lower for the sample that includes imputations.

To provide an overview of the effects of imputations of present values, Table 9.14 reports mean present discounted values for DB benefits (not prorated) for samples with and without imputations. The comparisons are made for both respondent and employer reports. The second, fourth, sixth, and eighth blocks of data include the imputed results. The first, third, fifth, and seventh blocks of data exclude them. The values reported include the yearly benefits at the expected age of benefit receipt, average account balances in DC plans, present values of DB benefits at expected retirement age (not prorated) based on self-reported

Table 9.14 Comparing observed plus imputed with observed values of pensions on current job based on respondent and firm reports, by cohort and gender, full-time employees, thousands of 1992 dollars, 1992, 1998, and 2004 (weighted)

Sample	Cohort	1992		1998		2004	
		Males	Females	Males	Females	Males	Females
Sample with observations of average benefit at expected age of benefit receipt, respondent report	HRS 51–61	22.4	12.5	19.2	10.4	12.6	8.3
	HRS 51–56	23.8	12.9	19.3	10.6	12.6	7.7
	WB 51–56	—	—	23.3	15.4	17.5	12.8
	EB 51–56	—	—	—	—	22.2	20.3
Observed plus imputed sample of average benefit at expected age of benefit receipt, respondent report	HRS 51–61	21.0	11.4	18.5	10.3	11.8	7.9
	HRS 51–56	22.2	11.6	18.6	10.6	12.5	7.6
	WB 51–56	—	—	21.5	15.6	17.2	11.2
	EB 51–56	—	—	—	—	23.2	19.9
Sample with observations of average account balances, respondent report	HRS 51–61	57.9	23.9	81.4	33.4	55.8	52.2
	HRS 51–56	58.7	21.8	84.1	34.5	63.0	56.7
	WB 51–56	—	—	77.4	42.2	69.6	45.1
	EB 51–56	—	—	—	—	75.2	48.1
Observed plus imputed sample, average account balances, respondent report	HRS 51–61	59.9	23.8	75.9	33.7	55.1	42.9
	HRS 51–56	59.9	21.6	77.9	34.3	60.0	45.3
	WB 51–56	—	—	77.3	50.3	75.9	41.2
	EB 51–56	—	—	—	—	76.6	46.8

Sample with observations of present value of benefit at expected age of benefit receipt, respondent report	HRS 51–61	163.5	99.3	152.5	94.6	95.5	80.2
	HRS 51–56	165.3	97.8	152.4	95.0	97.9	74.3
	WB 51–56	—	—	165.5	125.7	128.3	117.8
	EB 51–56	—	—	—	—	170.5	147.4
Observed plus imputed sample present value of benefit at expected age of benefit receipt, respondent report	HRS 51–61	149.6	88.8	132.8	80.5	91.4	72.0
	HRS 51–56	151.8	85.6	133.4	82.1	93.8	68.1
	WB 51–56	—	—	156.0	112.6	127.7	94.4
	EB 51–56	—	—	—	—	159.7	131.7
Sample with observations of present value of benefit at expected age of benefit receipt, firm report	HRS 51–61	178.7	125.0	151.3	114.1	120.2	107.7
	HRS 51–56	173.4	128.7	144.9	118.0	108.0	101.8
	WB 51–56	—	—	162.8	136.0	159.7	136.4
	EB 51–56	—	—	—	—	175.0	166.3
Observed plus imputed sample present value of benefit at expected age of benefit receipt, firm report	HRS 51–61	167.1	111.7	126.0	97.2	93.2	96.0
	HRS 51–56	164.1	117.1	124.7	98.6	84.4	86.9
	WB 51–56	—	—	160.8	131.2	148.3	124.2
	EB 51–56	—	—	—	—	160.0	152.6

Note: Shading highlights values in the year a cohort first entered the study. Additional notes are reported in the appendix.

data, and present values of DB benefits (not prorated) at expected retirement age based on firm-reported data.

Again we can see in the summary tables that yearly DB values and DC account balances do not differ significantly when imputations are added to the sample. Adding imputations to the sample does reduce the average present values of benefits, whether the present values are based on respondent observations or employer-produced benefit formulas. Nevertheless, the differences in values are not very large. This is useful to know, especially for those who would use the observed values in behavioral models and are reluctant to use imputations.

Total Value of Pensions from Current, Last, and Previous Jobs

To this point we have discussed the value of pensions on current jobs. We now expand these measures to include realized and expected pensions from past jobs, counting both DB and DC plan values. In this section, pension values from last or previous jobs are based on self-reported data.

Before turning to the data, it is useful to consider the methodology used to generate values from any current, last, and previous jobs.[10] As we have explained, the pension value from a current job includes the prorated projected pension value from the most important DB plan, plus current account balances from all DC plans. For plans not yet in pay status, defined benefit plans are valued as of the expected retirement age and then discounted back to the base year for the particular cohort. Next, the pension values from respondents' last job and up to three previous pension jobs are included. When counting the present value of the most important DB plan on each job, plan value is adjusted to reflect whether the plan was in pay status. If the plan was reported to be in pay status, the DB plan value includes only the remaining benefits. Current account balances are included if accounts were left to accumulate. Pensions that are cashed out, rolled over, annuitized, or lost are not included.[11]

Values of both pensions from current jobs and those earned on jobs held previously are expressed as of the base year for the cohort, 1992 for the HRS cohort, 1998 for the war babies, and 2004 for the early boomers. Once all values are discounted back to the appropriate base year for the respondent, as in other calculations of values we have undertaken, amounts are further converted to 1992 dollars. Specifically, the benefits in 1998 and 2004 are discounted back to 1992 dollars by 2.8 percent for each of the years between 1992 and 1998 for 1998 values, and between 1992 and 2004 for 2004 values.

To illustrate the nature of the adjustments to the base year for pensions from last or previous jobs, consider an age-eligible member of the HRS cohort. Account balances and projected benefits from dormant DB plans from last and previous jobs are adjusted upward by 5.8 percent for each year from the year those jobs ended through 1992. For plans that are in pay status, the calculations are also adjusted to include only the remaining portion of the benefit as of the base year. The adjustments for pension benefits from last and previous jobs held by members of the war baby and early boomer cohorts are analogous, except that 1998 and 2004 are the base years for these cohorts. There is an additional exception when calculating pension benefits for younger spouses of age-eligible members of the HRS or war baby cohorts who were first interviewed in 1992 or 1998 but became age eligible only in 1998 or 2004. Benefits from their last and previous jobs are adjusted by 5.8 percent for each of the years between the time when those jobs ended and the base year of their cohort, 1998 or 2004.

It also should be noted that pension benefits have not been adjusted to incorporate updated information from periodic reports collected by the HRS about dormant pensions. This information is available in several surveys (1996, 1998, 2002, 2004, and 2006) where respondents were asked about the status of dormant pensions (DB plans that will pay benefits in the future and DC accounts left to accumulate) from their last and previous jobs reported when first interviewed or from jobs left after their initial interviews.

A strong word of caution is in order for those who would compare plan values reported by respondents in different waves of the HRS. One should not expect to find fully consistent results from one wave to another. There are many reasons to expect reporting errors:

1. As we have documented in Chapter 7, plan type reported by the respondent may differ from one wave to another, even if the respondent reports no job change.
2. Pension coverage reported by the respondent may differ from one wave to another, even though the respondent reports no job change.
3. Pension values may not be consistently reported from wave to wave.

Over 51 percent of the respondents to the original HRS cohort were covered by at least one live pension as of the date of the initial survey. According to the data in Table 9.15A, column 3, 38.1 percent reported pension wealth from current jobs, and 19.3 (6.4+12.9) percent reported pension wealth from a last or previous job. The difference between the sum of the percentages with current, last, and previous jobs and the total with nonzero pension wealth implies that 5.9 (57.4−51.5) percent of respondents enjoy a pension from more than one category, current, last, and previous job. Among the 51.5 percent of respondents who are covered by one or more live pensions from a current or previous job, on average the plans are worth $124,252 in 1992 dollars (column 4, row 4). The median plan value is $62,823. If in order to eliminate the potential effects of outliers and misreported values respondents with the top and bottom 1 percent of observed pension values are eliminated from the sample, the mean pension value on the current job falls from $101,398 (row 1, column 4) to $87,934 (row 1, column 6).

Turning now to the bottom panel of Table 9.15A, 66.4 percent of households with at least one person age 51 to 61 in 1992 had a live pension in 1992 (bottom row, column 3). The mean value of pensions in households with at least one plan was $154,071, with a median value of $86,642. Notice that households may count the pensions of spouses who are out of the age range (e.g., 51 to 61 for Table 9.15A), so more pensions are being counted when we consider pension wealth held by households than when we consider pension wealth held by individuals who are within the specified age range.

To consider differences among cohorts, begin with pension values for those ages 51 to 56 in the original HRS cohort, reported in Table 9.15B. Those values may be compared with values for those 51 to 56 in 1998 in Table 9.15C and those 51 to 56 in 2004 in Table 9.15D. Coverage for individuals who are 51 to 56 in 2004 is higher than in 1992 by 4.3 percentage points. Average pensions held by individuals 51 to 56 in the early boomer sample are worth $126,164, which is $13,411 (126,494−113,083) more than the value of pensions held by 51- to 56-year-old individuals in the original HRS sample. At $161,494, the total value of pensions in covered households, with at least one resident 51 to 56 years old, is $11,741 higher in 2004 than in 1992.[12]

Table 9.15E standardizes for the effect of including more detailed data on pensions from last and previous jobs. These data first became available in 2002. To allow consistent comparisons over time, Table 9.15E limits the information used to that information that was available in previous waves. Specifically, Table 9.15E includes only the most important plan from last and previous jobs (corresponding to Sections K and L of the HRS). In addition, information from brackets is not used in the imputation process in Table 9.15E. It is used in

Table 9.15 Cumulative values of pensions throughout the life cycle: observed plus imputed pension values from current, past, and previous jobs among individuals and households upon entry to the HRS, 1992 dollars, respondent data (weighted)

Table 9.15A HRS cohort ages 51–61, respondent data

Job on which pension was earned	Mean	Percent nonzero	Among nonzero observations		
			Mean	Median	Mean: excluding top and bottom 1%
All individuals ages 51–61					
Current job	38,620	38.1	101,398	45,000	87,934
Last job	9,893	6.4	155,319	103,396	136,906
Previous jobs	15,484	12.9	120,391	51,331	98,938
Total pension	63,998	51.5	124,252	62,823	106,318
All households with an individual age 51–61					
Current job	58,802	49.0	119,988	55,452	106,651
Last job	18,402	12.1	152,268	101,810	139,208
Previous jobs	25,059	20.3	123,657	58,000	105,534
Total pension	102,263	66.4	154,071	86,642	136,068

Note: Observations for all individuals totaled 9,623, while the total for all households was 7,392. Additional notes are reported in the appendix.

Table 9.15B HRS cohort ages 51–56, respondent data

Job on which pension was earned	Mean	Percent nonzero	Among nonzero observations		
			Mean	Median	Mean: excluding top and bottom 1%
All individuals ages 51–56					
Current job	39,778	42.1	94,475	39,870	81,314
Last job	6,242	4.4	141,348	80,661	134,249
Previous jobs	13,349	12.0	111,552	41,495	87,223
Total pension	59,368	52.5	113,083	48,984	95,966
All households with an individual age 51–56					
Current job	63,950	54.9	116,375	51,917	106,039
Last job	15,860	9.0	175,865	106,089	148,673
Previous jobs	22,182	19.4	114,074	48,340	95,514
Total pension	101,992	68.1	149,753	79,322	132,078

Note: Observations for all individuals totaled 5,449, while the total for all households was 4,533. Additional notes are reported in the appendix.

Table 9.15C War baby cohort ages 51–56, in constant 1992 dollars, respondent data

			Among nonzero observations		
Job on which pension was earned	Mean	Percent nonzero	Mean	Median	Mean: excluding top and bottom 1%
All individuals ages 51–56					
Current job	48,774	43.4	112,312	45,970	96,201
Last job	4,788	3.6	131,937	87,459	124,075
Previous jobs	14,496	14.9	97,459	29,882	85,964
Total pension	68,059	54.6	124,672	54,784	107,708
All households with an individual age 51–56					
Current job	68,161	51.9	131,213	59,615	117,289
Last job	6,707	5.2	129,101	79,099	125,427
Previous jobs	26,990	21.1	128,079	47,449	113,470
Total pension	101,857	64.3	158,432	77,423	141,525

Note: Observations for all individuals totaled 3,126, while the total for all households was 2,622. Additional notes are reported in the appendix.

Table 9.15D Early boomer cohort ages 51–56, in constant 1992 dollars, respondent data

			Among nonzero observations		
Job on which pension was earned	Mean	Percent nonzero	Mean	Median	Mean: excluding top and bottom 1%
All individuals ages 51–56					
Current job	49,924	46.1	108,235	43,076	92,812
Last job	6,182	3.3	185,266	82,562	97,699
Previous jobs	15,530	16.9	91,820	41,972	88,857
Total pension	71.636	56.8	126,164	59,693	107,544
All households with an individual age 51–56					
Current job	67,591	53.3	126,849	57,881	113,200
Last job	8,015	4.4	180,439	82,562	109,990
Previous jobs	29,305	24.0	121,862	56,760	112,601
Total pension	104,911	65.0	161,494	85,183	141,815

Note: Observations for all individuals totaled 3,326, while the total for all households was 2,759. Additional notes are reported in the appendix.

Table 9.15E   Early boomer cohort ages 51–56, in constant 1992 dollars, with one
plan from last and previous jobs, respondent data

Job on which pension was earned	Mean	Percent Nonzero	Among nonzero observations Mean	Among nonzero observations Median	Among nonzero observations Mean: excluding top and bottom 1%
All individuals ages 51–56					
Current job	49,924	46.1	108,235	43,076	92,962
Last job	5,592	3.3	171,986	82,562	95,215
Previous jobs	14,206	16.3	91,849	37,131	84,822
Total pension	69,721	56.4	124,932	58,785	105,986
All households with an individual age 51–56					
Current job	67,591	53.3	126,849	57,881	112,490
Last job	7,297	4.4	166,445	77,537	111,722
Previous jobs	27,767	23.3	119,050	55,063	109,353
Total pension	102,656	64.7	158,722	82,562	139,502

Note: Observations for all individuals totaled 3,326, while the total for all households was 2,759. Additional notes are reported in the appendix.

Table 9.15D. The bottom line is that this adjustment for the changing methodology adopted by the survey seems to have only a minor effect on the average pension values.

The increase between 1992 and 2004 in real pension values held by households with a respondent 51 to 56 is due almost entirely to women. As seen in Table 9.16, for households with at least one member age 51 to 56, the value of total household pensions attributable to men decreased slightly from $118,560 to $110,537 (column 2, rows 2 and 4). In contrast, the value of total household pensions attributable to women increased from $31,194 to $50,957 (column 3, rows 2 and 4). This increases the share of household pensions attributable to women from 21 percent in 1992 to 32 percent in 2004.

Turn now to results that calculate the value of defined benefit pensions by using employer-provided plan descriptions matched with respondent reports on work and earnings history. These calculations are reported as of the respondent's date of entry into the Health and Retirement Study. Once again we examine trends in pension values among cohorts, differences between men and women in total pension values, and the values of pensions in the

Table 9.16 Observed plus imputed pension values from current, past, and previous jobs per household, by source of pension by gender, 1992, 1998, and 2004, in 1992 dollars, respondent data (weighted)

Cohort	Total HH pension	Total pension due to men	Total pension due to women	% of total HH pension due to women
HRS: 51–61	154,071 (4,762)	119,030	35,040	23%
HRS: 51–56	149,753 (3,003)	118,560	31,194	21%
WBs: 51–56	158,432 (1,758)	114,997	43,435	27%
EBs: 51–56	161,494 (1,709)	110,537	50,957	32%

Note: Total number of observations is in parentheses. Additional notes are reported in the appendix.

household. Unlike Tables 9.15A–E and Table 9.16, which restrict reported coverage of previous pensions to those plans that were "live"—that is, plans on current jobs, dormant plans that had not yet paid benefits, and plans in pay status—Tables 9.17A–C and Table 9.18 also include the value of plans that were cashed out, rolled over, annuitized, or in other ways disposed of by the time the respondent entered the survey. Thus they represent the total value of pensions earned rather than the value of pensions still live at the time of the survey. Pension wealth figures are presented here for the original HRS cohort and for the war baby cohort. Required employer data on pensions from last and previous jobs were not available for 2004 as of the time of this writing. Although values of DB pensions are taken from employer-produced reports, values of DC pensions are based on self-reported data.

When using employer-produced pension formulas, because expected retirement age is not available for last and previous jobs, for these jobs DB benefits are calculated using the actual age the job was terminated. DB benefits are prorated for current jobs. The total prorated value of DB wealth is then added to the current account balances from the DC plans to generate the total value of pension wealth reported in the table. Values are imputed when observations are missing.

Comparing the three tables based on employer data (9.17A–C) with the tables based on respondent data (9.15A–C), differences between firm and respondent data seem to vary among the cohorts and according to age group. Most differences are modest.[13]

Table 9.17 Observed plus imputed pension values from current, past, and previous jobs among individuals and households upon entry to the HRS, 1992 dollars: firm data for DB, respondent data for DC (weighted)

Table 9.17A HRS cohort ages 51–61

			Among nonzero observations		
Job on which pension was earned	Mean	Percent nonzero	Mean	Median	Mean: excluding top and bottom 1%
All individuals ages 51–61					
Current Job	40,424	37.8	106,867	47,868	95,746
Last Job	11,833	6.6	179,009	110,152	156,624
Previous Jobs	22,548	15.4	146,235	39,551	108,868
Total Pension	74,805	52.8	141,562	64,310	119,255
All households with an individual age 51–61					
Current job	62,063	48.7	127,412	58,165	113,967
Last job	25,184	12.2	206,246	131,137	182,471
Previous jobs	38,101	23.7	160,606	50,755	137,714
Total pension	125,348	67.6	185,448	93,674	162,720

Note: Observations for all individuals totaled 9,623, while the total for all households was 7,392. Additional notes are reported in the appendix.

Table 9.17B HRS cohort ages 51–56: firm data for DB, respondent data for DC

			Among nonzero observations		
Job on which pension was earned	Mean	Percent nonzero	Mean	Median	Mean: excluding top and bottom 1%
All individuals ages 51–56					
Current job	43,262	42.0	102,891	45,307	92,465
Last job	6,406	4.7	137,457	72,682	127,318
Previous jobs	20,069	15.2	132,341	30,934	90,299
Total pension	69,737	54.4	128,122	57,161	106,886
All households with an individual age 51–56					
Current job	69,334	54.9	126,337	59,684	113,970
Last job	18,699	9.3	201,945	120,255	169,739
Previous jobs	33,544	23.8	140,699	37,971	119,284
Total pension	121,577	70.1	173,426	85,000	151,643

Note: Observations for all individuals totaled 5,449, while the total for all households was 4,533. Additional notes are reported in the appendix.

Table 9.17C   War baby cohort ages 51–56: firm data for DB, respondent data for
DC, in constant 1992 dollars

Job on which pension was earned	Mean	Percent nonzero	Among nonzero observations		
			Mean	Median	Mean: excluding top and bottom 1%
All individuals ages 51–56					
Current job	50,818	44.8	113,313	58,892	100,569
Last job	4,176	4.1	102,661	58,473	98,665
Previous jobs	13,637	14.1	96,603	32,328	81,841
Total pension	68,630	55.8	122,884	61,665	108,371
All households with an individual age 51–56					
Current job	70,614	53.8	131,218	70,059	122,249
Last job	6,262	6.1	102,558	56,246	90,677
Previous jobs	19,533	19.0	102,775	33,750	83,934
Total pension	96,410	65.9	146,380	76,258	131,486

Note: Observations for all individuals totaled 3,126, while the total for all households was
2,662. Additional notes are reported in the appendix.

As we did with respondent data, Table 9.18 calculates the share of total
wealth attributable to women in a sample based on employer data. Once again,
data are not available for the early boomer cohort, so the results are reported
only for the original HRS cohort and for war babies. These results suggest a
trend of about 7 percentage points between 1992 and 1998 in the share of pension wealth attributable to women, just one point higher than the trend found
in Table 9.16 based on self-reported data.

The next set of tables in this chapter explores how the share of pension
wealth due to defined contribution plans has grown over time, while the share
of pension wealth due to defined benefit plans has declined. Table 9.19 presents results based on respondent reports. The denominator in the first three
columns is the total number of households with a pension, indicated by the
parenthetical figure in column 1. The average value of wealth from pensions,
taken over all households with a pension, has grown by 8 percent between the
1992 and 2004 cohorts of 51- to 56-year-olds (from $149,753 in 1992 to
$161,490 in 2004). Pension values due to defined benefit plans per pension-
covered household have been declining, falling by 10 percent (from $112,480

Table 9.18 Observed plus imputed pension values from current, past, and previous jobs per household, by source of pension by gender, 1992 and 1998, in 1992 dollars: firm data for DB, respondent data for DC (weighted)

Cohort	Total HH pension	Total pension due to men	Total pension due to women	% of total HH pension due to women
HRS: 51–61	185,448 (4,843)	140,007	45,442	25%
HRS: 51–56	173,426 (3,087)	130,652	42,773	25%
WBs: 51–56	146,380 (1,705)	98,858	47,521	32%

Note: Total number of observations is reported in parentheses. Additional notes are reported in the appendix.

Table 9.19 Observed plus imputed pension values from current, past, and previous jobs per household, by source of pension by plan type, 1992, 1998, and 2004, in 1992 dollars, respondent data (weighted)

Cohort	Total HH pension	Total pension due to DBs	Total pension due to DCs	% of total HH pension due to DCs
HRS: 51–61	154,070 (4,762)	117,671	36,400	24%
HRS: 51–56	149,753 (3,003)	112,480	37,274	25%
WBs: 51–56	158,432 (1,758)	103,230	55,202	35%
EBs: 51–56	161,490 (1,709)	101,095	60,399	37%

Note: Total number of observations is reported in parentheses. Additional notes are reported in the appendix.

to $101,095) between these cohorts. In contrast, pension values due to defined contribution plans have grown from $37,274 per pension-covered household to $60,399. For the 1992 cohort of 51- to 56-year-olds, DC pensions accounted for 25 percent of total pension wealth. By 2004, DC pensions accounted for 37 percent of total pension wealth.

With DB pensions still accounting for 63 percent of total pension wealth in 2004, any study of wealth, saving, or retirement still must consider explicitly the role of DB pensions in total wealth.

Table 9.20   Observed plus imputed pension values from current, past, and previous
jobs per household, by source of pension by plan type, 1992, 1998, and
2004, in 1992 dollars, firm data (weighted)

Cohort	Total HH pension	Total pension due to DBs	Total pension due to DCs	% of total HH pension due to DCs
HRS: 51–61	185,448 (4,843)	149,705	35,744	19%
HRS: 51–56	173,426 (3,087)	137,214	36,212	21%
WBs: 51–56	146,380 (1,705)	93,449	52,931	36%
EBs: 51–56	—	—	—	—

Note: Total number of observations is reported in parentheses. Additional notes are
reported in the appendix.

Turning now to analogous results based on employer data, the data in
Table 9.20 tell a similar story of growth in the share of pension wealth due to
DC plans, but it remains a situation where DB pensions are more valuable
than DC plans as a source of household pension wealth.

Conclusions

This chapter has explored various measures of pension value. The defined benefit plans covering HRS respondents on their current jobs would replace about
half their yearly earnings at their expected retirement age. By 2004, real benefits (from the most important DB plan on their current jobs, in constant 1992
dollars) expected by men age 51 to 56 averaged $22,200, while real benefits
expected by women averaged about $20,300. Although the real value of an-
nual DB pension benefits expected by men ages 51 to 56 declined by about
7 percent between 1992 and 2004, the real value of DB pension benefits expected by women increased by 57 percent between the same two cohorts over
the same period. Measuring account balances in DC plans in constant (1992)
dollars, there was much higher growth in the values of the accounts held by
women. Nevertheless, by 2004, account balances in DC plans held by men
amounted to about $75,200 in 1992 dollars, while women's account balances
were about $48,100. In 1992, men 51 to 56 had account values that were 2.7
times the value of the accounts held by women. By 2004, the accounts held

by men 51 to 56 years old were 1.56 times the balances in accounts held by women.

Calculating the present value of benefits in constant 1992 dollars, the most important DB plan reported by 51- to 56-year-old men in 2004 was worth $170,500. The present value of pensions reported by 51- to 56-year-old women was $147,400 in 2004. The ratio of present values of pensions between men and women ages 51 to 56 fell from 1.69 to 1 in 1992, to 1.16 to 1 in 2004.

Prorating DB benefits so that they reflected the value accumulated only from work to date facilitates their comparison with DC benefits. Prorating reduces the present value of DB benefits by a little over one-quarter. By 2004, the prorated value in constant 1992 dollars of DB benefits expected by 51- to 56-year-old men was $130,400. The comparable figure for women was $106,100.

Comparing the prorated present value of DB plans with account balances in DC plans, the most important DB plan on the current job reported by men 51 to 56 in 2004 was worth about 1.73 (130.4/ 75.2) times the value of all DC plans held by men on their current jobs. For women 51 to 56 in 2004, their DB plans on current jobs were worth 2.21 (106.1/48.1) times the value of their DC plans.

Once the valuations of DB and DC plans are placed on the same footing, we are in a position to add the values of each covered person's DB and DC plan. By 2004, broadening the sample to include those 51 to 56 with all types of pensions, the average male respondent with a pension reported a value from either a DB or a DC plan, or both, averaging $117,300, and the average female respondent reported a value of $79,800. The ratio of male to female benefits narrowed from 2.25 to 1 (117.2/52.0) in 1992, to 1.46 to 1 (117.3/79.8) in 2004.

We next compared DB pension values between respondent reports of plan values and the values obtained from applying employer-provided plan descriptions to respondent reports of their earnings history. When compared on an individual basis, there is wide variation between the values calculated from the employer plan description and the respondent's report. For example, in the full HRS cohort ages 51 to 61 in 1992, responses from only 19 percent of respondents lie along a diagonal indicating agreement between respondent and firm reports.

Our investigation of the effects of imputing for missing observations provides a number of examples where reported values differ from the values that include imputations. But on the whole, imputations do not change the patterns of outcomes observed when missing values are not imputed.

Considering pension wealth from jobs held in the past as well as those currently held, 56.8 percent of all respondents 51 to 56 in 2004—that is, more than half the age-eligible population (not of full-time workers, as in many tables from earlier chapters, but among the entire population)—report being covered by a pension. Inclusion of past pensions raises the average value of pensions among the covered population to $126,164 in 1992 dollars. Expanding the analysis to households, 65 percent of households with at least one person age 51 to 56 in 2004 had a pension. The mean value of pensions in households with at least one plan is $161,494.

The big stories in these data are the continuing importance of pension wealth; despite the rapid growth of DC plans, the continuing importance of wealth from defined benefit plans; and the increasing importance of women's pensions. By 2004, women accounted for 32 percent of all pension wealth in households with at least one respondent 51 to 56 years old, up from 21 percent in 1992. As of 2004, in self-reported data DB plans still accounted for 63 percent of the value of pensions held by households with at least one member 51 to 56 years old.

Appendix 9.1: Detailed Descriptions of Covered Samples Underlying Tables in Chapter 9

Table 9.1A. The sample includes all full-time employees who have reported a DB or combination DB/DC plan and have an observed value for the amount of benefits they expect to receive in the future. Respondents who report their expected ages of retirement and DB benefits are included. DKs and RFs are excluded. Full-time status was defined earlier.

The average benefit at the expected retirement age is calculated from respondent reports of the most important DB plan for those covered by a DB or combination plan. The value reported in each year represents the report of expected benefit at the year the respondent expects to retire.

Unlike the tables reporting present values in the remainder of the chapter, pension values in Tables 9.1A and B are assumed to be reported in survey year dollars. Thus a benefit received in 2014 and reported in 2004 is assumed to be reported in 2004 dollars. In all subsequent tables, it is assumed that benefits reported for receipt in 2014 would be reported in 2014 dollars, and thus are discounted for inflation between 2004 and 2014.

When a respondent reports future benefits as a percentage of earnings just prior to retirement, future earnings must be projected. To calculate future earnings, current earnings are multiplied by the Social Security Administration's projection of the intermediate future inflation rate plus the real wage growth rate (2.8+1.1=3.9). After using calculated final earnings to compute the benefit in the year of expected retirement, benefits are then discounted back to the year the question was asked.

Each wave's reported DB benefits are compared with the average of benefits from all waves. Respondents with extreme values relative to their own mean over the course of the panel are excluded from the following waves: six cases from Wave 1, five cases from Wave 2, four cases from Wave 3, seven cases from Wave 4, three cases from Wave 5, two cases from Wave 6, four cases from Wave 7, and six cases from Wave 8. In most cases, the extreme values appear to result from a mistake in the "per" variable—for example, a value that would be consistent with observations from other years if it were per year is instead said to represent the benefit the respondent will receive per week or per month.

In 2000, one respondent's reported expected DB benefits of $45,000 per month has been changed to $4,500 per month. That respondent's reported expected benefit in 1998 is $4,500 per month and is $3,000 per month in 2002. That respondent reported working at the same employment in 2000 and 2002 as in 1998 and reported a comparable annual income in those years.

The number of observations with observed annual earnings is less than the sample with a reported expected benefit in each survey year by two to fifteen cases.

In 1992 and 2004, it is possible to use the earnings at retirement and the normal retirement age to adjust the earnings for cases where expected benefits are reported in terms of a percentage of earnings at retirement. But since the information is not available for other waves, for consistency we have not used that information in 1992 and 2004.

In the 2006 data, we changed one observation due to a better than tenfold jump in earnings compared with earlier years as a result of an apparent error in the reporting of the period over which earnings were received, with the report mistakenly indicating receipt on a monthly rather than yearly basis.

Table 9.1B. Retirement assumed at expected age pension-covered employees will start receiving benefits, weighted.

Table 9.2. For full-time employees with DC plans, weighted.

The composition of the samples is different in each wave. One case from 1996 and 1998 and two cases from 2004 are excluded from the 1996, 1998, and 2006 data, respectively. Those cases have reported account balances in those years that are inconsistent with their report of their DC account balances in other survey years.

In Wave 2, there are three cases with a value of $9,999,994 for their account balances. This value represents $9,999,994 or more. The $9,999,994 has been included in the calculation of the mean.

In Wave 3, there is one case with three DC plans each with a $6,000,000 balance. The respondent reported $1,000,000 in Wave 2 and $3,500,000 in Wave 4. But the respondent is not a full-time employee. Therefore the balance is not affecting the means.

In Wave 6, one respondent reported $10,000,000 for his account balances. In Waves 5 and 7, his DC balances are $1,000,000. The Wave 6 figure has been converted to $1,000,000.

Table 9.3. Retirement is assumed at the expected age full-time pension-covered employees will start receiving benefits.

DB values are as of 1992 for the HRS cohort, as of 1998 for the war baby cohort in 1992 dollars, and as of 2004 for the early boomer cohort in 1992 dollars. The future amount reported is discounted at 5.8 percent back to the year the question was asked. The discount rate of 5.8 percent is taken from Social Security Administration projections of the intermediate future inflation rate of 2.8 percent and a real interest rate of 3.0 percent. Whenever benefits are discounted, the inflation portion of the adjustment is always 2.8 percent, even when adjusting over historical periods where a different inflation rate was realized. By standardizing for the inflation rate over the period, we hope to eliminate changes in values resulting from projecting and discounting at different underlying inflation rates.

All present values in this table are based on the weighted sample. However, the numbers of observations presented are unweighted.

Between 30 and 50 percent of respondents answer "don't know" or refused to answer when asked the amount of benefits.

Table 9.4. Retirement is assumed to take place at the expected age pension-covered employees will start receiving benefits from their most important DB plan. Data are weighted.

Table 9.5. Retirement is assumed at expected age pension-covered employees will start receiving benefits from their most important DB plan. Data are weighted. See also appendix notes on Tables 9.1A and 9.1B.

Table 9.6. Retirement is assumed at the expected age pension-covered employees will start receiving benefits from their most important DB plan. Data are weighted.

Plan values for DB plans are the prorated DB benefits from the respondent's expected retirement age. The 1998 and 2004 benefits are in 1992 dollars. DC values include account balances from all DC plans in a current job.

Data are for respondents who were between 51 and 56 years of age in 1992, 1998, and 2004. Although respondents may have answered "don't know" in response to questions about their plan type, the HRS has collected information sufficient to calculate values. Respondents who reported DK on the plan type question in 1992 were asked follow-up questions as if the plan was a DB plan. In 1998 and 2004, respondents who answered DK in response to the plan type question were then asked questions as if they had reported having both a DB and a DC plan. With very few observations under the DK category, reported values in the last three columns should not be given much credence.

Table 9.8. Combination plans include those who report coverage by "both" plan types. We also label as a combination plan the case where a respondent has two plans, one a DB plan and the other a DC plan.

Respondents with a zero DB benefit at the early, normal, or expected age of retirement are not included.

The 1998 data are in 1992 dollars. When discounting to 1992, we use a rate of 5.8 percent for members of the HRS cohort and 2.8 percent for members of the war baby cohort.

In the 1992 data, one case with very large earnings (compared with his earnings when full-time status in other waves) is excluded. Earnings are used when calculating DB benefits if the respondent reports benefits as a proportion of income.

In all but one case, the DB benefits at early, normal, and expected retirement ages in 1998 are lower than those benefits in 1992. This is contrary to what one expects. We screened the data for both survey years and restricted the sample to those who were working at the same employment since 1992 and had firm plan documents in both years. This sample indicated that DB benefits in 1998 are higher than those in 1992, as expected. We can conclude that the implausible trend between 1992 and 2004 is due to a changing mix of observations between the samples.

Table 9.9. Data are for full-time employees and weighted.

Table 9.10. The sample is restricted to full-time employees who have data for both the self- and firm report for their benefits at their expected and normal retirement age. Respondents with zero benefits at the early, normal, or expected retirement ages are excluded. The table reports mean benefits, with the number of observations in parentheses.

Table 9.11A and B. DB values are the amounts of DB benefits at the expected age of retirement.

Table 9.12. DB values are the amounts of DB benefits at the expected age of retirement.

Table 9.13. DB values are the amounts of DB benefits at the expected age of retirement.

Table 9.14. Data are for full-time employees and weighted. The 1998 and 2004 data are in 1992 dollars.

Table 9.15. All respondents or households are included in Tables 9.15A–E. Defined benefit pension values from current jobs are projected to the expected retirement age and prorated to 1992. For the last and previous jobs, pension values include respondents who reported expecting some future benefits or were currently receiving benefits. The values of plans that are cashed out, rolled over into an IRA, converted to an annuity, or where benefits were lost are not included in these tables. Plan values realized before the survey date are excluded. Respondents' weights are used for individuals; household weights, for households. Defined benefit values are the calculated values from respondents' self-reports. Pension values are imputed for those respondents who reported expecting future benefits or receiving benefits and had missing values for the amount of the benefits. Defined contribution benefits are also from the self-reported data. Account balances are imputed for respondents who reported a DC/combination plan and were missing their current account balances. Defined contribution benefits include the sum of the account balances from any number of DC plans individuals may have reported. Respondents who reported zero for the number of plans, zero account balances, or prorated defined benefits are excluded. Current, last, and previous jobs correspond to jobs in Sections F, G, and H of HRS Wave 1; G, GG, and GH in Wave 4; and J, K, and L in Wave 7. Last job is the most recent job held by those who are currently not working. Previous job is the job of at least five years' duration held before either the current job for those who are working or the last job for those who are not, and all earlier jobs that offered a pension. In Waves 1 and 4, respondents with a plan type "Both" from their last and previous jobs were asked about that plan's account balance when they left that job. They were not asked about the disposition of that plan and its current balances (in 1992 or in 1998) if it was left to accumulate. For such plans, we have assumed those accounts have been left to accumulate and they have grown by the nominal interest rate for each of the years between the year those jobs ended and 1992 or 1998, as applicable. In 2004, respondents were asked about their current account balances for both DC and combination plans. In Table 9.15C and 9.15D, values are discounted to 1998 and 2004 (respectively) and then expressed as current 1992 dollars.

Missing responses for the amount of expected benefits and benefits received have been imputed. In the imputation process, if the sample size was large enough to make a regression possible and meaningful, we have used a set of covariates. For smaller samples, the imputations involve two steps. First, the ratio of benefits to earnings is calculated and imputed through hot decking where necessary for respondents with missing benefit amounts. Second, the imputed benefit to earnings ratio is multiplied by earnings to calculate the missing amount of benefits. Where necessary, earnings are imputed for respondents with missing earnings information.

Table 9.15C. Some respondents who were between 51 and 56 years of age in 1998 were first interviewed in 1992 as the spouse of an age-eligible HRS respondent. Although they were younger than 51 years of age at the time of their initial interview, any benefits from current/last and previous pension jobs were recorded in 1992, not 1998. The values recorded in 1992 are used for these respondents when they are added to the 1998 sample of war babies.

Table 9.15D. This table is different from earlier tables in this series in two ways. First, in 2004, the plan values include pension values from more than one plan (up to four plans) from last and previous jobs (K and L sections of the HRS). In 1992 and 1998, respondents were asked about only one plan from those jobs. Therefore pension values from last and previous jobs in Tables 9.15A–C include pension values from only one plan from each of those jobs. Second, in 2004, bracket questions were asked of respondents who did not know or refused to report the amount of benefits they expected from their DB plans. Information from those bracket questions is used in the imputation of missing expected benefits from DB plans in 2004 in Table 9.15D.

For consistency, we have not used the information from brackets in Table 9.15E. Therefore, Table 9.15D and 9.15E are different in two ways: First, Table 9.15E includes the most important plan from last and previous jobs (K and L sections of the HRS), whereas Table 9.15D includes all four plans from those jobs. Second, information from brackets is not used in the imputation process in Table 9.15E, whereas it is in Table 9.15D.

Table 9.16. Only households with pensions are included in this table.

Table 9.17. Defined benefit pension values from current jobs are projected to the expected retirement age and prorated to 1992. For the last and previous jobs, pension values are estimated at the termination dates of those jobs. All values are weighted. Respondent weights are used for individuals and household weights for households. Defined benefit values are the calculated values from plan documents. Pension values are imputed for those respondents without a matched pension plan who reported a DB/combination plan, regardless of the reported disposition of that plan. Defined contribution benefits are from the self-reported data. Account balances are imputed for respondents who reported a DC/combination plan and were missing their current account balances. Defined contribution benefits include the sum of the account balances from any number of DC plans individuals may have reported. Respondents with a reported zero number of plans, zero account balances, or prorated defined benefits are excluded. In Waves 1 and 4, respondents with a plan type "Both" from their last and previous jobs were asked about that plan's account balance when they left that job. They were not asked about the disposition of that plan and its current balances (in 1992 or in 1998) if it was left to accumulate. For such plans, we have assumed that those accounts have been left to accumulate and that they have grown by the nominal interest rate for each of the years between the year those jobs ended and 1992 or 1998, as applicable. In 2004, respondents were asked about their current account balances for both DC and combination plans. In Table 9.17C, values are discounted to 1998 and then expressed as current 1992 dollars.

Table 9.18. Only households with pensions are included in this table. The table uses household weights. See notes to Table 9.17 for further details on the pension wealth calculations.

Table 9.19. Households with pension are included in this table.

Table 9.20. Households with pension are included in this table. Note that in comparison with Table 9.19, the DB values reported here include DB wealth ever earned, so that plans that were rolled over, cashed out, used to purchase an annuity, or lost are counted here but not in Table 9.19. In addition, this table includes the value of last and previous pensions paid before the survey dates in 1992 and 1998, while the data in Table 9.19 do not. The 2004 firm survey data for previous and last jobs are not available.

Table 9.21. Full-time employees, retirement assumed at expected age pension-covered employees will start receiving benefits from their most important DB plan, weighted, in thousands of 1992 dollars.

Table 9.22. Full-time employees, weighted, in thousands of 1992 dollars.

Table 9.23. Respondent data, for full-time employees; retirement assumed at expected age full-time pension-covered employees will start receiving benefits from their most important DB plan; weighted, in thousands of 1992 dollars.

Table 9.24. Firm data, full-time employees; retirement assumed at expected age full-time pension-covered employees will start receiving benefits from their most important DB plan; weighted, in thousands of 1992 dollars.

Appendix 9.2. Findings with Imputations

Table 9.21 Imputed plus reported values of expected annual pension benefits, 1992, 1998, and 2004, respondent data, by gender, most important DB plan on a current job, full-time employees, thousands of 1992 dollars

Cohort	1992		1998		2004	
	Males	Females	Males	Females	Males	Females
HRS: 51–61 in 1992						
Mean	21.0	11.4	18.5	10.3	11.8	7.9
Median	16.8	8.1	13.8	6.8	9.9	6.1
90/10	10.8	15.9	10.9	20.3	12.0	15.0
No. of observations	1,336	1,004	601	465	136	145
HRS: 51–56 in 1992						
Mean	22.2	11.6	18.6	10.6	12.5	7.6
Median	17.5	8.3	14.0	6.7	10.1	6.1
90/10	9.9	14.9	10.8	19.7	9.1	15.0
No. of observations	817	642	494	379	116	126
WBs: 51–56 in 1998						
Mean	—	—	21.5	15.6	17.2	11.2
Median	—	—	17.1	10.3	14.5	8.0
90/10	—	—	13.3	13.5	9.0	10.7
No. of observations	—	—	378	415	226	236
EBs: 51–56 in 2004						
Mean	—	—	—	—	23.2	19.9
Median	—	—	—	—	19.8	13.4
90/10	—	—	—	—	8.9	10.3
No. of observations	—	—	—	—	357	364

Note: Benefit values are reported in thousands of dollars. Additional notes are reported in the appendix.

Table 9.22   Imputed plus reported values of DC account balances from all DC plans from current job, respondent data, full-time employees, by gender, 1992, 1998, and 2004

Cohort	1992		1998		2004	
	Males	Females	Males	Females	Males	Females
HRS: 51–61 in 1992						
Mean	59.9	23.8	75.9	33.7	55.1	42.9
Median	22.6	10.0	29.2	11.4	22.8	15.2
90/10	75.0	60.0	83.3	80.0	79.8	49.4
No. of observations	1,046	763	538	407	185	177
HRS: 51–56 in 1992						
Mean	59.9	21.6	77.9	34.3	60.0	45.3
Median	22.6	10.0	32.1	11.4	25.4	14.2
90/10	78.0	58.0	83.4	120.1	100.0	49.4
No. of observations	653	500	432	341	154	152
WBs: 51–56 in 1998						
Mean	—	—	77.3	50.3	75.3	37.8
Median	—	—	30.5	16.9	26.0	14.3
90/10	—	—	112.5	106.7	81.3	70.0
No. of observations	—	—	402	433	255	326
EBs: 51–56 in 2004						
Mean	—	—	—	—	76.6	46.8
Median	—	—	—	—	28.7	15.8
90/10	—	—	—	—	65.1	150.0
No. of observations	—	—	—	—	490	497

Note: Benefit values are reported in thousands of dollars. Additional notes are reported in the appendix.

Table 9.23 Imputed plus reported prorated present values of expected benefits from DB plan on current job, based on respondent report, by cohort and gender, 1992, 1998, and 2004

Cohort	1992		1998		2004	
	Males	Females	Males	Females	Males	Females
HRS: 51–61 in 1992						
Mean	117.5	65.5	113.0	66.9	82.9	66.3
Median	78.9	32.1	79.6	39.5	61.8	43.8
90/10	29.2	57.3	22.4	32.3	25.8	42.7
No. of observations	1,335	1004	601	463	136	144
HRS: 51–56 in 1992						
Mean	112.4	58.9	111.8	66.9	84.6	61.5
Median	74.0	26.5	75.5	37.7	64.0	42.2
90/10	33.4	87.3	26.0	32.8	25.4	28.0
No. of observations	817	642	494	377	116	125
WBs: 51–56 in 1998						
Mean	—	—	114.8	79.2	107.6	74.3
Median	—	—	82.1	38.8	76.2	43.6
90/10	—	—	30.2	54.6	23.8	33.7
No. of observations	—	—	377	413	226	235
EBs: 51–56 in 2004						
Mean	—	—	—	—	115.8	86.5
Median	—	—	—	—	72.9	52.7
90/10	—	—	—	—	27.1	57.3
No. of observations	—	—	—	—	355	362

Note: Benefit values are reported in thousands of dollars. Additional notes are reported in the appendix.

Table 9.24   Imputed plus reported prorated present value of benefits from most important DB plan on current job, at expected age of benefit receipt, based on employer report, by cohort and gender, 1992, 1998, and 2004

Cohort	1992		1998		2004	
	Males	Females	Males	Females	Males	Females
HRS: 51–61 in 1992						
Mean	129.0	82.2	104.5	80.1	79.7	89.1
Median	76.9	44.6	69.7	51.6	48.6	68.4
90/10	25.6	38.0	39.4	37.5	45.9	32.3
No. of observations	1,336	1,004	601	463	136	144
HRS: 51–56 in 1992						
Mean	124.1	77.4	103.1	79.8	72.5	80.5
Median	73.4	43.3	66.5	51.6	47.1	54.8
90/10	29.9	57.3	31.8	36.4	45.9	45.7
No. of observations	817	642	494	377	116	125
WBs: 51–56 in 1998						
Mean	—	—	118.1	93.7	124.9	100.2
Median	—	—	82.8	53.0	88.1	66.9
90/10	—	—	24.6	43.3	17.8	32.7
No. of observations	—	—	377	413	226	235
EBs: 51–56 in 2004						
Mean	—	—	—	—	110.4	104.1
Median	—	—	—	—	73.9	61.9
90/10	—	—	—	—	27.3	43.7
No. of observations	—	—	—	—	355	362

Note: Benefit values are reported in thousands of dollars. Additional notes are reported in the appendix.

10

Retirement Incentives from Defined Benefit Pensions

Researchers have long known that benefits from defined benefit (DB) plans accumulate very unevenly for covered workers.[1] Benefit accrual is calculated as the change in the present value of benefits from another year of work. There is a spike in benefit accrual when benefits are first vested, when the covered worker qualifies for early retirement, and/or when the worker qualifies for normal retirement benefits. Thus when graphing the rate of benefit accrual against age and years of service for a particular respondent, the change in benefits with another year of work appears to spike at these key ages.

Any number of plan features may be responsible for the spikes in benefit accrual at key ages. The benefit formula itself may be changed and increased in generosity. For those qualifying for early retirement benefits, a lower rate may be used to reduce benefits for each year preceding eligibility for a normal retirement benefit when the person has retired before reaching eligibility—for example, instead of reducing benefits by, say, 6 percent for each year the individual has retired before normal retirement age, once a person qualifies for early retirement, benefits might be reduced by 3 percent for each year before qualifying for normal retirement. Or benefits may be supplemented temporarily to substitute for Social Security until the person becomes eligible for Social Security benefits. Other DB plan features may also contribute to the benefit spikes.[2]

Once having qualified for early retirement benefits, the rate of accrual in the present value of benefits may spike again, but less sharply, upon qualifying for normal retirement benefits. If a person does not qualify for early retirement benefits, the spike at normal retirement age may be quite sharp. After normal retirement age, the present value of defined benefit pensions frequently declines and thus the accrual often becomes negative.[3]

For those who are within a few years of qualifying for early retirement benefits, the looming spike in benefits creates a strong incentive to postpone leaving the labor force until qualifying. Once having qualified for the extra benefits generating the spike at early retirement age, DB pensions will contribute only a modest additional incentive to continue working, if they do not create a disincentive in these later years. Thus upon becoming eligible for early retirement benefits, those who postponed retiring only because of the extra compensation associated with the benefit spike will feel free to retire. Others, who in any case would have waited to retire until after early retirement age, will find their retirement decision governed as in the standard model of retirement. They will weigh the value of their basic compensation for continued work against the value of leisure. Additional increases in pension values from postponing retirement further will be relatively modest in size. As a result, they will not play a prominent role in shaping the retirement decision.

The last few chapters have demonstrated how much trouble respondents have in describing their plan type, retirement ages, and plan values. Spikes in benefit accrual rates are even more difficult for respondents to describe (Gustman and Steinmeier, 2004b). Among the basic information required to convey benefit accrual rates, respondents must understand and report how the formula or benefit reduction rate changes upon qualifying for early and normal retirement, which means reporting the change in benefit reduction rates before and after qualifying for early and normal retirement, as well as any special early retirement benefits. Although they may know the value of benefits to be received upon qualifying for early retirement, they simply cannot convey with any accuracy the benefit reduction rates or other features that are responsible for the spikes.[4]

As a result, employer-provided pension plan descriptions are particularly important for describing the retirement incentives generated by DB plans. Fortunately, because detailed plan descriptions are available for an important fraction of HRS respondents, the researcher can measure how benefits from DB plans accrue with age and service and how benefits change at the point of eligibility for early and normal retirement benefits. Using benefit formulas collected in 1992, 1998, and 2004, plan descriptions can be used to analyze changes in benefit levels and accruals by year and cohort; how the rates at which benefits accrue differ between men and women; and whether, over time, those who report continuing coverage by the same plan nevertheless experience differences in the rates at which their plans accrue benefits.[5] These issues are the subject of the remainder of this chapter.

Ages of Eligibility for Retirement Benefits

The analysis in Chapter 8 of early and normal retirement ages in DB plans suggested that men qualify for early retirement about a year before women. There also was a suggestion of a slight trend between 1992 and 2004, amounting to perhaps a half-year increase in the early retirement age of men.

Further data on early retirement age under DB plans can be found in the employer-provided plan descriptions reported in Table 10.1. In considering changes in these data between groups that were 51 to 56 years old in 1992, 1998, and 2004, remember that the sample mix is changing over time. DB plans are becoming less common, and those from younger cohorts are employed in a different group of industries than are those from older cohorts. In addition, the employing industries are different between women and men, and over time work histories and jobs are changing rapidly for women.

Summing the figures in the first two rows of Table 10.1, column 2, we see that in 1992, 72.2 percent of those 51 to 56 years of age with a DB plan qualified for an early retirement benefit by age 55. By 1998, the figure was 73.2 percent. By 2004, 74.1 percent qualified for early retirement benefits by age 55. From the next to last row of the table, we see that mean values of early retirement age declined slightly between 1998 and 2004. Normal retirement ages also declined, from 62.4 for those 51 to 56 in 1992 to 61.7 in 2004. The fraction of respondents who qualified for normal retirement benefits at age 65 declined from 51.2 percent in 1992 to 36.7 percent in 2004. Among those who were not eligible for early retirement, or whose plans did not offer an early retirement benefit, normal retirement age also decreased very slightly between 1992 and 2004.

Pension Wealth Values by Age and Cohort

Before turning to an analysis of the rates at which benefits accrue under each covered worker's specific plan, it is useful to summarize the course of average benefits by age. The present values of DB benefits are reported assuming the

Table 10.1 Distribution of early and normal retirement ages of DB plans

Age	Early retirement age				Normal retirement age				Normal retirement age: Rs without ER			
	51–61 1992	51–56 1992	51–56 1998	51–56 2004	51–61 1992	51–56 1992	51–56 1998	51–56 2004	51–61 1992	51–56 1992	51–56 1998	51–56 2004
< 55	21.9	22.4	24.2	28.5	1.1	1.4	2.0	2.2	22.2	27.5	18.7	19.0
55	48.2	49.8	49.0	45.6	3.5	4.0	5.9	5.8	16.0	19.9	19.4	31.8
56	4.4	4.6	2.9	2.4	1.3	1.6	1.6	3.4	1.2	2.1	2.2	1.8
57	3.9	4.1	3.1	1.8	1.6	1.8	4.0	2.9	1.4	1.4	—	1.5
58	2.9	2.6	2.9	2.7	2.1	2.1	2.9	2.9	0.9	1.2	0.9	0.7
59	3.4	2.9	2.9	0.8	1.7	1.3	2.0	1.3	1.8	2.1	—	1.0
60	10.1	9.3	9.3	8.5	19.6	19.1	15.6	19.0	15.6	13.9	33.5	24.1
61	1.9	1.9	0.7	0.7	1.4	1.2	0.9	0.9	3.9	3.6	5.6	0.6
62	2.2	1.7	3.5	7.5	14.8	15.2	15.1	19.9	17.0	14.7	10.2	7.8
63	0.5	0.3	1.0	0.7	0.5	0.4	2.7	2.5	1.5	0.8	1.7	2.6
64	0.7	0.3	0.5	0.7	0.6	0.5	0.6	1.3	1.7	1.5	—	0.9
65	0	0	0	0	51.8	51.2	46.8	36.7	13.8	10.0	7.0	7.0
> 65	0	0	0	0	0.1	0.1	0	1.1	3.0	1.3	0.8	1.1
Average	55.0	54.9	54.9	54.6	62.5	62.4	62.1	61.7	58.2	57.1	57.7	56.9
No. of observations	1,317	843	357	297	1,317	843	357	297	410	237	85	172

Notes: Retirement age calculations are based on SPD data as applied to information provided by HRS respondents on work and earnings history. All observations are weighted. The sample includes full-time employees.

Table 10.2   Pension wealth values by age and cohort, in thousands of 1992 dollars

Sample statistics	50	55	60	65	70	1992/ 1998/ 2004	ER age	NR age	NR age w/o ER
			Age 51–61 in 1992 (1,221 observations)						
Mean	110	164	179	164	133	152	125	149	142
Median	52	101	131	122	98	86	64	96	90
			Age 51–56 in 1992 (805 observations)						
Mean	107	153	169	155	125	130	121	143	150
Median	51	96	124	115	93	66	63	95	97
			Age 51–56 in 1998 (334 observations)						
Mean	97	149	166	155	125	121	118	146	143
Median	53	108	137	126	106	68	71	106	116
			Age 51–56 in 2004 (374 observations)						
Mean	96	153	177	171	144	131	105	149	117
Median	57	103	137	145	123	76	62	109	69

Notes: Pension value calculations are based on SPD data as applied to information provided by HRS respondents on work and earnings history, using the projected liability method. All observations are weighted. The sample includes only those plan documents that are from current jobs.

individual retired and claimed benefits at alternative ages, 50, 55, 60, 65, 70, the year the respondent qualifies for early benefits, and the year the respondent qualifies for normal retirement. Benefit amounts are also reported assuming individuals terminated their employment in the base year the respondent joined the HRS—1992 for members of the HRS cohort, 1998 for war babies, and 2004 for early boomers.

Table 10.2 indicates the rate at which the present value of DB benefits rise with age. Among the five-year intervals chosen, benefits peak at around age 60. Median benefits are well below average benefits. By age 55, the present value of benefits averages over $150,000. By the 2004 cohort, benefits are 42 percent higher at normal than at early retirement age.

Aggregated findings in Chapter 9 show that DB pension values are substantially higher for men than for women, while benefits grow much more rapidly over time for women than for men. In exploring the pattern of benefits by age for men and women, the results in Table 10.3 reflect these earlier findings. They also report how the present value of benefits changes as the age of retirement is changed for each person with a matched employer summary plan description.

Table 10.3 Pension wealth values by gender, age, and cohort, in thousands of 1992 dollars

Sample statistics	50	55	60	65	70	1992/ 1998/ 2004	ER age	NR age	NR age w/o ER
Males 51–61 in 1992 (727 observations)									
Mean	131	190	200	178	141	176	148	169	175
Median	62	121	145	133	102	102	80	110	130
Females 51–61 in 1992 (494 observations)									
Mean	76	120	143	140	120	111	88	118	103
Median	41	71	104	105	95	67	46	79	62
Males 51–56 in 1992 (472 observations)									
Mean	125	173	185	165	130	149	142	161	183
Median	58	105	138	122	93	76	79	109	137
Females 51–56 in 1992 (333 observations)									
Mean	72	121	142	137	117	100	88	117	113
Median	41	71	104	105	91	55	43	74	68
Males 51–56 in 1998 (156 observations)									
Mean	98	159	177	161	127	126	135	159	140
Median	55	132	145	127	106	80	100	119	116
Females 51–56 in 1998 (178 observations)									
Mean	95	137	153	147	124	116	98	129	145
Median	48	79	113	119	108	64	55	91	117
Males 51–56 in 2004 (115 observations)									
Mean	110	169	184	169	135	146	118	149	113
Median	73	130	154	148	122	110	73	126	69
Females 51–56 in 2004 (182 observations)									
Mean	80	138	171	173	152	117	95	150	122
Median	42	83	120	133	123	65	52	102	58

For both men and women ages 51 to 61 in 1992, the present value of benefits is higher at age 60 than at either 55 or 65. This pattern continues to hold for those 51 to 56 in 1992 and 1998 and for men in 2004. For women 51 to 56 in 2004, benefits are slightly higher at age 65 than at age 60. For those whose plans offer early retirement benefits and who qualify for such benefits, retiring at normal retirement age offers higher benefits than does retiring at early retirement age.

At normal retirement age, benefits for men 51 to 56 years old in 1992 are about 38 percent (161/117) higher than they are for women. By 2004, the difference in the present value of benefits between 51- to 56-year-old men and women disappears entirely.

There is a stronger incentive to continue working until qualifying for normal retirement benefits for women than for men. For women 51 to 56 years old in 1992, benefits at normal retirement age are 33 percent (117/88) higher than at early retirement age. For men, the difference is 13 percent (161/142). In 2004, the present value of women's benefits at normal retirement age is 58 percent (150/95) higher than their benefits if they leave at early retirement age. Benefits for men increase between early and normal retirement ages by 26 percent (149/118) in 2004.

Benefit Accrual Profiles

The preceding data on the present value of benefits by age and upon qualifying for early and normal retirement benefits provide a hint as to the location and size of retirement incentives created by pensions. But the incentive we directly measure is simply the difference in average benefits between early and normal retirement ages. It is possible to generate much more precise information by measuring the spikes in the benefit accrual profiles around the key early and normal retirement ages. That is, instead of focusing on average benefits at each year of age, the next set of tables measures incentives by aligning the early retirement ages for each HRS respondent and the normal ages for each respondent and asking how benefits change in the years during which the individual qualifies for early and normal retirement benefits. For example, one measure indicates the change in the present value of benefits from working the year during which a person becomes eligible for early retirement benefits. For a person with an early retirement age of 55, this measure is calculated as the difference in benefits from retiring at ages 54 and 55. But for a person with an early retirement age of 60, the change in present value is calculated between the ages of 59 and 60.

The estimated pension accrual profiles reported here are again based on formulas from employer-produced summary plan descriptions as applied to information provided by HRS respondents on their work and earnings histories. All data are weighted

Changes in benefits are calculated for four different time periods. They are defined as follows:

Preretirement years: the third through first year before qualifying for early retirement benefits, if available, or the analogous period before normal retirement age if there is no early retirement.

ER age: the year during which the individual qualifies for early retirement benefits.

ER–NR age: the period between the year during which the individual qualifies for early retirement benefits and the year during which the individual qualifies for normal retirement benefits.

NR age: the year during which the individual qualifies for normal retirement benefits.

After NR age: the year after the individual qualifies for normal retirement benefits.

Values for each of these periods are reported for members of each of the cohorts in Table 10.4. Accrual rates are reported in dollar amounts at the top of the table and as a share of yearly wages at the bottom of the table. Working the final year until qualifying for early retirement benefits, as shown in column 2 of Table 10.4, increases the present value of benefits by $41,500 for members of the HRS cohort ages 51 to 56 in 1992 and by $27,200 for 51- to 56-year-old members of the early boomer cohort. These increases in benefits, as seen in the bottom panel of Table 10.4, are roughly worth about one year's pay. More specifically, in 1992 a 51- to 56-year-old respondent with a DB pension would increase the present value of benefits by 99 percent of one year's wages by working the year before qualifying for early retirement benefits. The reward for working increases to 100 percent of one year's wage for those ages 51 to 56 in 2004 who work the year before qualifying for early retirement benefits.

Although the dollar value of the increment in benefits from qualifying for early retirement declines by over 30 percent between those 51 to 56 in the HRS and early boomer cohorts, there is a much smaller increase in the share of wages represented by these benefits. This suggests that those with DB plans in 1992 and 2004 are employed by different industries and occupations. In particular, wages are lower for those covered by DB plans in 2004.

Continuing with the data in Table 10.4, column 1 shows that each year of work in the two years before the year that would qualify a covered worker for early retirement benefits is worth 18 percent to 24 percent of one year's pay. Work between early and normal retirement age increases in value from $3,100 for those 51 to 56 in 1992 to $6,100 per year for those 51 to 56 in 2004. These values amount to 9 percent and 18 percent of one year's pay, respectively. For those whose pension allows them to qualify for early retirement benefits, column 4 shows the size of the secondary spike from working the one year until

Table 10.4 Pension accruals for DB plans

Sample statistics	Preretirement	Plans with early retirement ER age	Plans with early retirement ER–NR age	Plans with early retirement NR age	Plans w/o ER NR age	After NR age
		In thousands of 1992 dollars				
		Age 51–61 in 1992				
Mean	7.3	42.1	3.2	4.2	48.5	−5.8
Median	4.2	12.3	2.6	1.4	18.2	−1.5
No. of observations	1,727	1,317	1,276	1,317	410	1,727
		Age 51–56 in 1992				
Mean	6.8	41.5	3.1	4.8	56.2	−5.6
Median	4.0	11.9	2.6	1.3	20.8	−1.5
No. of observations	1,080	843	818	843	237	1,080
		Age 51–56 in 1998				
Mean	7.2	46.7	3.9	4.2	40.3	−2.5
Median	4.7	11.5	2.5	1.0	16.8	−1.3
No. of observations	409	331	302	331	78	409
		Age 51–56 in 2004				
Mean	8.9	27.2	6.1	6.7	31.3	−1.9
Median	5.4	7.4	5.0	3.4	14.1	−0.5
No. of observations	421	270	251	270	151	421
		Pension accruals/wage accruals				
		Age 51–61 in 1992				
Mean	0.19	1.01	0.10	0.14	1.24	−0.12
Median	0.13	0.38	0.09	0.05	0.46	−0.05
		Age 51–56 in 1992				
Mean	0.18	0.99	0.09	0.15	1.37	−0.12
Median	0.12	0.35	0.09	0.05	0.52	−0.05
		Age 51–56 in 1998				
Mean	0.19	1.06	0.11	0.12	1.11	−0.06
Median	0.15	0.30	0.10	0.05	0.49	−0.05
		Age 51–56 in 2004				
Mean	0.24	1.00	0.18	0.18	0.85	−0.09
Median	0.17	0.22	0.16	0.12	0.50	−0.02

Notes: Pension accrual calculations are based on SPD data as applied to information provided by HRS respondents on work and earnings history. All observations are weighted. The sample includes full-time employees. It does not include any imputations.

Preretirement years refers to the third through first year before qualifying for early retirement benefits, if available, or to the three years before normal retirement age if there is no early retirement.

ER age is the year during which the individual qualifies for early retirement benefits.

ER–NR age refers to the years between early retirement and the year before qualifying for normal retirement.

NR age is the year just before qualifying for normal retirement benefits.

The values for preretirement and ER–NR age are the average values per year. The sample in the ER–NR age column is smaller because some of the respondents had less than one year between their early and normal retirement ages.

qualifying for normal retirement benefits. The normal retirement spike is worth $4,800 to those 51 to 56 in 1992 and $6,700 to those 51 to 56 in 2004, which amounts to 15 percent and 18 percent of annual pay, respectively.

The next to last column includes those respondents whose plan does not offer an early retirement benefit or who because of their date of hire have an early retirement date that coincides with their normal retirement date. The spike from working that last year until qualifying for normal retirement benefits amounts to 137 percent of one year's pay for those 51 to 56 in 1992 and 85 percent of one year's pay for those 51 to 56 in 2004. Working after qualifying for normal retirement benefits is associated with a decline in the present value of benefits. This decline, shown in the final column of Table 10.4, is fairly modest, ranging from 12 percent of one year's pay for those 51 to 56 in 1992 to 9 percent of one year's pay for those 51 to 56 in 2004.

Cohort Differences in Rates of Benefit Accrual

There are few differences between cohorts in the rate of benefit accrual. Again Table 10.4 can be used to compare accrual rates between members of the original HRS cohort, 51 to 56 in 1992, and members of the early boomer cohort, 51 to 56 in 2004. The spike in early retirement benefits as a share of yearly earnings is slightly lower in 2004, increasing from 99 percent to 100 percent of one year's pay. But the basic reward remains at about one year's pay for staying the year until qualifying for early retirement benefits. The increase from staying the year before qualifying for normal retirement benefits for those in a plan offering early retirement increased slightly, from 15 percent of one year's pay for the HRS cohort to 18 percent of one year's pay for the early boomers. Again, there is no major change over the twelve-year period. Rewards for work in years that are not related to eligibility for early or normal benefits increased, with the reward for working between the years when one qualifies for early and normal benefits increasing from 9 percent to 18 percent of one year's pay. Last, the penalty for working after normal retirement age has declined in absolute terms, from –12 percent of annual pay for those 51 to 56 in 1992 to –9 percent of annual pay for those 51 to 56 in 2004.

These are very modest changes in overall retirement incentives, especially in those crucial years associated with working the year before qualifying for early and normal retirement benefits and the year after qualifying for normal retirement benefits. Although the dollar values of these benefits have changed, that appears to be due to a change in the mix of workers covered by defined benefit plans between the 1992 and 2004 cohorts of the HRS. Because the incentives affecting the retirement decisions of those with DB pensions have not changed sharply over this twelve-year period, any difference in the effects of DB pensions on the retirement behavior of members of these cohorts might reflect changes in DB coverage, or differences in the retirement behavior associated with the changing mix of industries of those with DB plans, but not changes in the incentives associated with the DB plans per se.

Differences in Benefit Accruals between Men and Women

The measured differences in pension incentives over time are averages of values for men and women. The next step is to focus on any differences in incentives facing men and women from their DB plans. Accordingly, Tables 10.5 and 10.6 report pension accrual profiles separately for men and women.

Given the higher wage levels enjoyed by men and their greater number of years of job tenure, benefit accruals are higher for men than for women. Men have higher benefit accruals whether benefits are measured in dollar terms or as a proportion of salary. Higher accruals for men are particularly evident when examining the very sharp increases in pension values for working the year during which the individual qualifies for early retirement benefits. Conversely, benefit accrual in the years during which the individual attains eligibility for normal retirement benefits, for those who have qualified for early benefits, are higher for women than for men. The spike at early retirement ranges from $37,500 to $54,900 for men, 112 to 160 percent of final year's pay. For women, the early retirement spike ranges from $18,800 to $35,900, 49 percent to 96 percent of one year's pay. Although men and women both face a strong incentive to work the last year that qualifies them for their early retirement benefit (or normal retirement benefit if there is no early benefit), as a proportion of pay the incentive is much higher for men than for women.

Men face a stronger penalty for working after normal retirement age than do women. For men the penalty ranges from 8 to 18 percent of one year's pay. For women the penalty is much lower, ranging from a penalty of 6 percent of one year's pay to a bonus of 1 percent of one year's pay.

Table 10.5 Pension accruals for DB plans, males

Sample statistics	Preretirement	Plans with early retirement			Plans w/o ER	
		ER age	ER age– NR age	NR age	NR age	After NR age
In thousands of 1992 dollars						
Age 51–61 in 1992						
Mean	7.6	53.8	2.9	1.5	63.4	−8.0
Median	4.4	16.8	2.5	0.6	24.7	−2.6
No. of observations	986	765	742	765	221	986
Age 51–56 in 1992						
Mean	7.0	52.7	2.6	2.6	74.4	−7.8
Median	4.1	16.0	2.4	0.38	27.7	−2.6
No. of observations	602	477	463	477	125	602
Age 51–56 in 1998						
Mean	7.8	54.9	3.7	4.3	49.8	−3.7
Median	4.6	15.2	2.0	0.45	23.3	−2.7
No. of observations	190	160	147	160	30	190
Age 51–56 in 2004						
Mean	10.0	37.5	4.8	3.5	32.8	−4.5
Median	5.7	8.8	5.0	2.1	14.8	−1.6
No. of observations	182	107	98	107	75	182
Pension accruals/wage accruals						
Age 51–61 in 1992						
Mean	0.17	1.18	0.07	0.06	1.46	−0.17
Median	0.12	0.48	0.07	0.02	0.58	−0.08
Age 51–56 in 1992						
Mean	0.16	1.12	0.07	0.08	1.68	−0.16
Median	0.11	0.46	0.07	0.01	0.80	−0.07
Age 51–56 in 1998						
Mean	0.18	1.14	0.09	0.10	1.36	−0.08
Median	0.13	0.41	0.07	0.01	0.49	−0.07
Age 51–56 in 2004						
Mean	0.25	1.60	0.14	0.09	0.83	−0.18
Median	0.15	0.25	0.13	0.08	0.54	−0.04

Notes: Pension accrual calculations are based on SPD data as applied to information provided by HRS respondents on work and earnings history. All observations are weighted. The sample includes full-time employees. It does not include any imputations.

Preretirement years refers to the third through first year before qualifying for early retirement benefits, if available, or to the three years before normal retirement age if there is no early retirement.

ER age is the year during which the individual qualifies for early retirement benefits.

ER–NR age refers to the years between early retirement and the year before qualifying for normal retirement.

NR age is the year just before qualifying for normal retirement benefits.

The values for preretirement and ER–NR age are the average values per year. The sample in the ER–NR age column is smaller because some of the respondents had less than one year between their early and normal retirement ages.

Table 10.6 Pension accruals for DB plans, females

Sample statistics	Preretirement	Plans with early retirement			Plans w/o ER	After NR age
		ER age	ER age– NR age	NR age	NR age	
		In thousands of 1992 dollars				
		Age 51–61 in 1992				
Mean	6.8	23.9	3.8	8.3	31.2	−2.6
Median	3.8	7.9	3.0	2.5	12.8	−0.4
No. of observations	741	552	534	552	189	741
		Age 51–56 in 1992				
Mean	6.4	24.7	3.8	8.1	35.6	−2.6
Median	3.8	7.3	2.9	2.3	13.3	−0.42
No. of observations	478	366	355	366	112	478
		Age 51–56 in 1998				
Mean	6.4	35.9	4.2	4.1	32.5	−1.1
Median	4.7	6.4	2.8	1.6	13.9	−0.62
No. of observations	219	171	155	171	48	219
		Age 51–56 in 2004				
Mean	7.9	18.8	7.1	9.4	29.7	0.46
Median	5.1	6.2	5.0	3.9	13.1	0.21
No. of observations	239	163	153	163	76	239
		Pension accruals/wage accruals				
		Age 51–61 in 1992				
Mean	0.22	0.77	0.13	0.26	0.97	−0.06
Median	0.16	0.28	0.12	0.12	0.39	−0.02
		Age 51–56 in 1992				
Mean	0.20	0.78	0.13	0.25	1.02	−0.06
Median	0.16	0.26	0.12	0.11	0.37	−0.02
		Age 51–56 in 1998				
Mean	0.20	0.96	0.14	0.14	0.90	−0.03
Median	0.17	0.26	0.12	0.09	0.42	−0.03
		Age 51–56 in 2004				
Mean	0.24	0.47	0.21	0.25	0.87	0.01
Median	0.19	0.19	0.20	0.16	0.43	0.07

Notes: Pension accrual calculations are based on SPD data as applied to information provided by HRS respondents on work and earnings history. All observations are weighted. The sample includes full-time employees. It does not include any imputations.

Preretirement years refers to the third through first year before qualifying for early retirement benefits, if available, or to the three years before normal retirement age if there is no early retirement.

ER age is the year during which the individual qualifies for early retirement benefits.

ER–NR age refers to the years between early retirement and the year before qualifying for normal retirement.

NR age is the year just before qualifying for normal retirement benefits.

The values for preretirement and ER–NR age are the average values per year. The sample in the ER–NR age column is smaller because some of the respondents had less than one year between their early and normal retirement ages.

Changes in Benefit Accrual Experienced by
Individuals over Time

Employer-provided pension plan descriptions are available for both 1992 and 1998 for a select group of employees who were 51 to 56 in 1992 and remained at the same firm for the next six years. These data, reported in Table 10.7, provide some indication of how pensions change for the same individual over time.[6]

To be sure, individuals who remain covered by a pension at the same employer are not representative of the full sample of respondents with a pension in 1992.[7] Pension values are somewhat higher as of 1992 for those respondents who have a plan description in both years than for the full sample reported for 1992 in Tables 10.2 and 10.3.[8] For example, at age 60, the mean pension for those 51 to 56 in 1992 with a matched sample is $188,000 in Table 10.7, while for the full sample reported in Table 10.2, the comparable figure is $179,000. Nevertheless, it is of interest to explore the differences in pensions within this limited sample.

For those with continuing coverage on the same job, pension wealth values calculated using the plan descriptions from 1998 are lower than the pension values calculated using 1992 plan descriptions. This can be seen by comparing values between the first two rows of each panel in Table 10.7. Thus for the full sample of 164 respondents 51 to 56 with matched plan descriptions in both years, pensions at age 60 are worth $188,000 when they are valued using plan descriptions and wages in 1992 and are worth $166,000 when valued at the same age when using plan descriptions and wages from 1998.

Table 10.8 reports differences in benefit accruals between 1992 and 1998 for the sample of 51- to 56-year-old respondents with matched plans in both years. There are three notable changes. Benefit accruals are higher at early retirement age when using plan descriptions from 1998 rather than 1992, especially when reported as a share of yearly earnings. Among those who are eligible for an early retirement benefit, benefit accruals at normal retirement age are lower when using 1998 plan descriptions. For those without an early retirement benefit, benefit accruals at normal retirement are also higher when using the 1998 plan descriptions. Similar results are found when these calculations are made separately for men and women.

Table 10.7 Pension wealth values from DB plans by age of receipt, in thousands of 1992 dollars, for those 51–56 in 1992 who had a matched employer-provided pension plan description and the same job in 1992 and 1998

Sample statistics	50	55	60	65	70	1992/1998	ER age	NR age	NR w/o ER
Males and females									
Mean in 1992	110	164	188	175	145	136	133	162	144
Mean in 1998	95	142	166	154	128	161	113	136	129
1992/1998 ratio	1.21	1.12	1.10	1.12	1.13	0.73	1.20	1.14	1.09
Median in 1992	58	102	139	136	105	78	72	102	97
Median in 1998	62	105	140	130	106	135	69	104	118
No. of observations	164	164	164	164	164	164	149	149	22
Males									
Mean in 1992	129	190	206	186	149	155	163	185	188
Mean in 1998	109	160	175	155	124	173	135	151	144
1992/1998 ratio	1.19	1.16	1.15	1.18	1.20	0.77	1.22	1.16	1.21
Median in 1992	65	104	149	138	106	81	91	128	152
Median in 1998	67	133	148	134	106	150	92	113	153
No. of observations	96	96	96	96	96	96	81	81	12
Females									
Mean in 1992	80	121	157	157	139	104	95	132	96
Mean in 1998	72	113	150	153	135	144	85	118	112
1992/1998 ratio	1.25	1.04	1.02	1.02	1.02	0.65	1.17	1.12	0.95
Median in 1992	47	82	120	122	103	69	42	95	80
Median in 1998	49	85	122	122	106	118	48	83	103
No. of observations	68	68	68	68	68	68	68	68	10

Table 10.8 Pension accruals for DB plans, in thousands of 1992 dollars, for those 51–56 in 1992 who had a matched employer-provided pension plan description and the same job in 1992 and 1998

Sample statistics	Preretirement	Plans with early retirement			Plans w/o ER	
		ER age	ER age– NR age	NR age	NR age	After NR age
Pension accrual ($000)						
Mean in 1992	8.6	43.3	3.6	6.4	32.9	−5.4
Mean in 1998	7.6	44.4	3.0	2.9	35.7	−0.87
Median in 1992	4.4	15.7	3.0	2.0	11.8	−0.77
Median in 1998	5.6	9.5	2.2	1.0	13.9	−0.70
No. of observations	218	139	135	139	32	218
Pension/wage accrual (%)						
Mean in 1992	0.21	1.04	0.11	0.17	0.81	−0.11
Mean in 1998	0.23	1.15	0.11	0.13	1.06	−0.01
Median in 1992	0.15	0.41	0.09	0.08	0.37	−0.03
Median in 1998	0.19	0.38	0.10	0.05	0.48	−0.03

Conclusions

This chapter has focused on the incentives created by defined benefit pensions to continue at work or to retire. Detailed information about the underlying plan formula and the respondent's work and earnings history are required to determine the size of these incentives. When plan formulas are evaluated, the incentives they generate are sizable.

Almost three-quarters of respondents with a DB plan who work full time qualify for an early retirement benefit by age 55, with a present value of about $150,000 in 1992 dollars. There is a stronger incentive to continue working until qualifying for normal retirement benefits for women than for men. For women 51 to 56 years old in 1992, benefits at normal retirement age are 32 percent higher than at early retirement age. For men, the difference is 13 percent. For the cohorts 51 to 56 years old in 2004, the difference reached 57 percent for women, while it was 26 percent for men. The larger initial period difference in benefits between normal and early retirement age for women is consistent with their lower job tenure. Once having qualified for benefits at the early retirement age, it appears that the incentive to stay additional years until reaching normal retirement age is declining both for men and for women.

The increase in benefits from working the year during which the individual qualifies for early retirement provides the strongest of the incentives to remain at work created by pensions. When the early and normal retirement ages are aligned for each HRS respondent, the present value of benefits increases from working the final year until qualifying for early retirement by $41,500 for those 51 to 56 in 1992, with the increment in benefits falling to $27,200 for those 51 to 56 in 2004. Working the year the individual qualifies for early retirement increases the present value of benefits by roughly the equivalent of one year's pay.

Because of their higher salaries, the dollar value of benefit accruals for working the year early retirement eligibility is attained is higher for men than for women. The spike at early retirement is $52,700 for men 51 to 56 in 1992, falling to $37,500 for those 51 to 56 in 2004. For men, these increments in benefits from qualifying for early retirement amount to 112 and 160 percent of final year's pay, respectively. For women, working the year before qualifying for early retirement benefits is worth $24,700 for those 51 to 56 in 1992 and $18,800 for those 51 to 56 in 2004. These amount to 78 percent and 49 percent of one year's pay for women 51 to 56 in 1992 and 2004, respectively.

Changes in pension values and pension incentives were also analyzed for those employees who were 51 to 56 in 1992 and remained at the same firm between 1992 and 1998. At the same retirement age, pension values based on 1992 plan formulas are 10 to 20 percent higher when evaluated using 1992 plan descriptions and wages than when evaluated using the plan descriptions and wages from 1998. Despite the difference in level of benefits, benefit accruals at early retirement age are higher when using plan descriptions from 1998 rather than 1992.

11

Disposition of Pensions upon Leaving a Job and Pension Incomes in Retirement

This chapter describes what happens to the pensions covering HRS respondents when they leave their jobs. This requires descriptions of pension coverage, plan type, and plan values for job leavers as well as a detailed description of the fate of those pensions. In this chapter we also investigate pension incomes as reported in the assets and income section of the Health and Retirement Study.

The HRS is designed to help paint a more complete picture of the importance of pensions as a source of retirement income. When first interviewed, a respondent who reports having had a pension on a previous job is asked a battery of questions that is conditioned on plan type. The respondent is asked whether a defined benefit (DB) plan is paying or is expected to pay benefits; whether a defined contribution (DC) plan is continuing as an account, was annuitized, or rolled over to a new employer; or whether either plan type was rolled over into an IRA or cashed out. A similar battery of questions is asked when, during a subsequent wave, a respondent reports having left a pension job held when last interviewed. From these data it is possible to estimate the importance of DB and DC pensions for each cohort of HRS respondents as they transition into retirement.

Among our findings, defined benefit pensions continue to be a very important source of retirement income, even for members of younger HRS cohorts. In addition, analyses of the importance of pension wealth in retirement wealth are likely to paint a different picture of the importance of pensions than are studies focusing on pension incomes in retirement.

Defined benefit plans are more likely to be retained in the form of a pension into retirement than are defined contribution plans. At retirement, some assets originating in pensions are rolled over into an IRA, an annuity, or some other saving vehicle. To be sure, upon leaving their jobs some will have cashed out their pension plans and spent the proceeds on increased consumption. Nevertheless, as a result of the transformation of pensions into other assets when leaving a job, there will be a tendency to underestimate the importance of pensions as a source of retirement income, especially in the case of defined contribution plans.

Disposition of Pensions from Last or Previous Jobs

To begin the discussion of the disposition of pensions, Table 11.1 shows the frequency with which respondents from different cohorts report holding a last or previous job at the time they entered the HRS survey.[1] Among members of the original HRS cohort, 68.4 percent of respondents held a last or previous job upon entering the HRS. Exactly half of this group, 34.2 percent of respondents, had at least one pension from a last or previous job. Comparing outcomes among cohorts ages 51 to 56, between the 1992 and 2004 cohorts, the share of respondents reporting a last or previous job declined from 65.9 percent to 51.9 percent. There was a much smaller decline in the fraction of members of each cohort who reported a pension from a last or previous job. About 32.6 percent of those 51 to 56 in 1992 and 30.4 percent of those 51 to 56 in 2004 reported having a pension from a last or previous job.

The values of pensions from last or previous jobs are larger for members of younger cohorts.[2] As expected from the pervasive trend in plan type, the share of benefits from defined benefit plans has been falling and the share of benefits from defined contribution plans rising. The values of pensions from last or previous jobs, by plan type, in 1992 dollars, are reported for the HRS cohorts in Table 11.2. Pensions earned from last or previous jobs by members of the original HRS cohort were worth $30,225 per HRS respondent. The total from DB plans is $25,340 per HRS respondent, while DC plans were worth $4,885 per HRS respondent. Examining changes among cohorts of 51- to 56-year-olds, the value of pensions from last or previous jobs per HRS respondent increased from $24,096 in 1992 to $26,250 in 2004. Between the cohorts of those 51 to 56 years old in 1992 and in 2004, the value of benefits per HRS respondent

Table 11.1   Percentage of respondents with last and/or previous job and pension in
1992, 1998, and 2004 (weighted)

Last or previous job and pension status	51–61	51–56		
	1992	1992	1998	2004
% of respondents with last job	26.7	22.6	15.1	14.6
% of respondents with pension from last job	9.1	6.8	6.0	5.2
% of respondents with at least 1 previous job	51.4	51.1	43.1	43.9
% of respondents with at least 1 pension from a previous job	26.6	26.9	25.1	26.6
% of respondents with a last or previous job	68.4	65.9	52.4	51.9
% of respondents with at least 1 pension from a last or previous job	34.2	32.6	29.7	30.4
No. of respondents	9,623	5,449	3,126	3,326

Note: A last job is a job held in the past by a person who is no longer employed. A previous job is a job held before the current job or the last job.

Table 11.2   Values of pensions from last or previous jobs per HRS respondent in the
indicated cohort, in 1992 dollars

Plan type	51–61	51–56		
	1992	1992	1998	2004
DB plans	25,340	20,146	15,602	14,119
DC plans	4,885	3,950	7,574	12,131
Total pensions	30,225	24,096	23,176	26,250

from DB plans from last or previous jobs fell from \$20,146 to \$14,119, while the value of DC plans increased from \$3,950 to \$12,131.

Clearly members of the cohorts thus far sampled by the HRS have not suffered great losses in the values of their pensions from last or previous jobs. Roughly speaking, total plan values have grown by 9 percent over twelve years, with the decline in value of DB plans more than offset by the increase in value of DC plans.

HRS respondents' reports of the disposition of their pensions from their last or previous jobs are summarized in Tables 11.3A through 11.3D. There is one table for each cohort. The first column of each table reports the dollar value of each outcome divided by the total number of HRS respondents. Thus

Table 11.3A Disposition of all pensions (observed and imputed) from last and previous jobs, HRS, 51–61 in 1992, respondent data (weighted)

Disposition of pension	Overall mean (1992 dollars)	% nonzero observations	Mean of nonzero observations (1992 dollars)
	Defined benefit		
Expect future benefit	5,705	7.3	78,178
Receive current benefit	16,520	9.1	180,728
Received cash settlement	2,756	7.9	35,079
Rolled into IRA	359	0.4	98,123[a]
	Defined contribution		
Amount in account	3,153	4.4	71,219
Rolled into IRA	995	1.9	53,730
Converted to annuity	104	0.2	63,765
Transferred to new employer	89	0.3	29,722
Withdrew the money[b]	544	3.2	16,996
No. of observations: ages 51–61		9,623	

Notes: The sample includes respondents with observed and imputed values. Percent nonzero observations is the ratio of the number of nonzero observations to the total sample size.

a. The sample includes one respondent with $1,000,000 in benefits rolled over into an IRA. If that case is excluded, the mean drops to $44,437.

b. The category "Withdrew the money" was not included as a separate category in the list of options for the disposition of DC pensions from previous pension jobs. However, it is possible to use the comment coding to identify those within the "other" category who withdrew their money. Thus, in this table, those who withdrew the money are respondents in the "other" category who reported they "received cash—spent it, saved it, or paid debts or bills."

row 1, column 1, of Table 11.3A reports that when averaged across all respondents in the original HRS cohort, pensions from last or previous jobs that were expected to pay future benefits were worth $5,705 per HRS respondent in 1992 dollars. Altogether, 7.3 percent of respondents from the original cohort reported that they expected to receive a benefit from a defined benefit plan held in a last or previous job. For the average respondent who expected future benefits from a DB plan held on a last or previous job, the present value of future benefits expected from last or previous job was $78,178.

Having a defined benefit plan in pay status is the highest valued outcome reported by members of the original HRS cohort for a pension from a last or previous job. This outcome, shown in column 1, row 2, of Table 11.3A, is worth $16,520 per HRS respondent. For the original cohort, 9.1 percent of all respondents have a DB pension in pay status from a last or previous job. The present value averages $180,728 per respondent with a plan in pay status.

The frequency of respondents reporting a DB plan from a last or previous job in pay status is lower among members of younger cohorts. It is lower for those 51 to 56 than it is for those 51 to 61, and it falls from 5.0 percent of 51- to 56-year-old respondents in 1992 (Table 11.3B) to 4.4 percent of 51- to 56-year-old respondents in 1998 (Table 11.3C), and to 2.8 percent of 51- to 56-year-old respondents in 2004 (Table 11.3D). Pension values per respondent from DB plans in pay status fall from $11,240 for those 51 to 56 in 1992 (Table 11.3B, column 1, row 2) to $9,656 in 1998 (Table 11.3C, column 1, row 2), and to $6,558 in 2004 (Table 11.3D, column 1, row 2). Thus with a value of around $225,000 per 51- to 56-year-old recipient in each of the three HRS cohorts, the average value of benefits received from DB pensions in pay status per HRS respondent falls over time because this outcome is becoming less common, not because a DB plan in pay status is worth less to those from younger cohorts who are entitled to this benefit.

Table 11.3B   Disposition of all pensions (observed and imputed) from last and previous jobs, HRS, 51–56 in 1992, respondent data (weighted)

Disposition of pension	Overall mean (1992 dollars)	% nonzero observations	Mean of nonzero observations (1992 dollars)
	Defined benefit		
Expect future benefit	6,256	8.5	73,593
Receive current benefit	11,240	5.0	224,766
Received cash settlement	2,154	8.2	26,357
Rolled into IRA	496	0.5	109,683[a]
	Defined contribution		
Amount in account	2,094	4.4	47,295
Rolled into IRA	1,183	1.8	65,768
Converted to annuity	99	0.1	78,041
Transferred to new employer	61	0.3	21,627
Withdrew the money	513	3.3	15,640
No. of observations: ages 51–56		5,449	

a. The sample includes one respondent with $1,000,000 in benefits rolled over into an IRA. If that case is excluded, the mean drops to $31,197.

Table 11.3C Disposition of all pensions (observed and imputed) from last and previous jobs, war babies in 1998, respondent data (weighted)

Disposition of pension	Overall mean (1992 dollars)	% nonzero observations	Mean of nonzero observations (1992 dollars)
	Defined benefit		
Expect future benefit	4,373	8.6	50,769
Receive current benefit	9,656	4.4	220,215
Received cash settlement	1,222	4.7	25,919
Rolled into IRA	351	0.3	35,139
	Defined contribution		
Amount left in account	2,530	4.3	59,122
Rolled into IRA	2,602	4.5	57,511
Converted to annuity	620	0.5	135,270
Transferred to new employer	560	0.7	76,718
Withdrew the money	1,262	4.7	27,060
No. of observations: ages 51–56		3,126	

Table 11.3D Disposition of all pensions (observed and imputed) from last and previous jobs, early boomers in 2004, respondent data (weighted)

Disposition of pension	Overall mean (1992 dollars)	% nonzero observations	Mean of nonzero observations (1992 dollars)
	Defined benefit		
Expect future benefit	5,088	7.9	64,022
Receive current benefit	6,558	2.8	232,737
Received cash settlement	1,421	4.1	34,640
Rolled into IRA	1,052	2.4	44,345
	Defined contribution		
Amount left in account	4,752	7.0	68,326
Rolled into IRA	5,496	6.6	83,698
Converted to annuity	334	0.3	108,000
Transferred to new employer	319	0.9	37,234
Withdrew the money	1,230	6.2	19,986
No. of observations: ages 51–56		3,326	

Notes: In 2004, brackets were added for respondents who answered "don't know" or who refused to answer questions about the amount of benefits they expected to receive from their defined benefit plan at retirement, the amount of benefits if receiving benefits currently, and the amount of cash settlements from their DB plan. Brackets were also added when a respondent answered "don't know" or refused to answer when asked about the amount in a DC account at the time the respondent left the job as well as about the account balance at the time of the survey.

Additionally, among those 51 to 56 in 1992 through 2004, 8 to 8.6 percent of respondents expected future benefits from a defined benefit plan from a last or previous job. The average value of these plans per HRS respondent falls slightly from $6,256 in 1992 to $5,088 in 2004.

Within the original HRS cohort ages 51 to 56, 8.2 percent of respondents cashed out a DB plan on a last or previous job (Table 11.3B, row 3, column 2). Examining the 2004 cohort of 51- to 56-year-olds, we see that 4.1 percent of respondents indicated that they received a cash settlement from a DB plan (Table 11.3D, row 3, column 2). By 2004, an additional 2.4 percent of respondents rolled their DB benefit into an IRA.

As the overall value of DB plans declines among cohorts, the level of benefits accounted for by cash-outs and rollovers of DB plans remains relatively constant in (1992) dollar terms. The share of DB benefits accounted for by cash-outs and rollovers increased from 13.2 percent (2,154+496)/(6,256+11,240+2,154+496) for those 51 to 56 in 1992 to 17.5 percent (1,421+1,052)/(5,088+6,558+1,421+1,052) for those 51 to 56 in 2004. Nevertheless, by 2004, more than four-fifths of the dollar value of DB pensions from last or previous jobs for this most recent of HRS cohorts continues in a form that allows the origin of the funds to be identified as a DB pension.

Those who held a DC plan on a last or previous job are much less likely to report that their plan continued in the form of a pension. Among 51- to 56-year-old members of the original HRS cohort in 1992, 5.2 percent of respondents reported having a DC pension from a last or previous job that was rolled over or converted to an annuity, or where the balance was withdrawn. A little less than half of those with a DC plan on a last or previous job, representing 4.7 percent of respondents, reported that the amount was left in the account with a current employer or transferred to a new employer. For the 1992 cohort of 51- to 56-year-olds, the amount left in the account averaged $2,094 per HRS respondent. With the rise in defined contribution plans, by 2004, among those 51 to 56, 7.9 percent of respondents reported leaving their funds in a DC plan with a previous employer or transferring it to a new employer. However, with 13.1 percent of respondents reporting their plans were rolled over, cashed out, or otherwise no longer held as a DC plan, over 62 percent of those with a DC plan from a last or previous job no longer held their balances in the form of a pension. By 2004, about 42 percent of the value of benefits received per respondent from a DC plan on a last or previous job remained in a form that can be identified as originating from a defined contribution plan.

These finding suggest that surveys that record the value of pensions from individuals who have left their pension jobs will understate the values of DB and DC pensions from last or previous jobs. In 1992, about 82 percent of the assets originating from pensions held on a last or previous job by those 51 to 56 years of age could be identified as originating from a pension plan even after the respondent had left the firm. By 2004, 64 percent of the assets originating from pensions held on last or previous jobs by those 51 to 56 years of age could be identified as originating with a pension plan after the respondent had left the firm. Surveys of retirees that measure the share of assets originating from pensions will greatly understate the importance of pensions as a source of retirement incomes. Moreover, as DC plans continue to grow in importance, this amount of understatement will increase.

Disposition of Pensions from Jobs Held in Previous Waves

Having analyzed the form and amounts of pension payouts in jobs held before a respondent began participating in the HRS, we turn to comparable data on jobs left sometime after the respondent began participating in the HRS. Data on the disposition and value of pensions left during the course of the survey are collected in the wave following the termination of employment from a pension-covered job. A little over two-thirds of the total value of DB and DC pensions disposed of by members of the original cohort (35,323/52,246) remained in the form of DB pensions, with $28,558 represented by DB plans in pay status.

These and related results can be seen in Table 11.4A. As seen in row 2 of the table, 18.2 percent of respondents from the original HRS cohort report receiving a benefit from a defined benefit plan sometime during the course of the survey. On average, the plans of those receiving a DB benefit are worth $160,362. When divided by the number of respondents in the original HRS cohort (9,623), the defined benefit pension plans that are in pay status are worth $28,588 per respondent, the figure referred to above.

Expecting future benefits from a defined benefit plan is the second most valuable mode of disposition for a pension held by members of the original HRS cohort. Adding the values of DB plans expected by 5.8 percent of respondents to eventually pay benefits, and dividing by the total number of respondents in the cohort, yields a value of $6,735 per respondent in the original HRS cohort. This is the average value, per respondent in the cohort, of DB plans that are expected to pay future benefits.

Table 11.4A Disposition of all pensions (observed and imputed) by type of payout upon leaving pension-covered jobs, HRS, 51–61 in 1992, respondent data (weighted)

Disposition of pension	Overall mean (1992 dollars)	% nonzero observations	Mean of nonzero observations (1992 dollars)
	Defined benefit		
Expect future benefit	6,735	5.8	115,782
Receive current benefit	28,588	18.2	160,362
Received cash settlement	1,820	3.3	54,813
Rolled into IRA	1,233	1.3	92,312
	Defined contribution		
Amount in account	6,237	9.0	69,650
Rolled into IRA	5,195	7.3	70,957
Converted to annuity	1,411	1.0	133,455
Transferred to new employer	5	0.09	4,945
Withdrew the money	790	3.4	19,713
Received/receiving installments	232	0.2	1,126
No. of observations: ages 51–61		9,623	

Notes: The sample includes respondents with observed and imputed values. Percent nonzero observations is the ratio of the number of nonzero observations to the total sample size.

Samples in each payout category include respondents with an observed value plus imputations for respondents with missing values. We have used information from brackets for questions that had brackets in the imputation process. For imputing "account balances" when an employee left the job, we have used current account balances in the sorting process when hot decking. For current account balances we have used "account balances" when left in the hot-decking process. For other payout options where no information from brackets was available, the imputation involves two steps. First, the ratio of benefits to earnings is calculated and imputed through hot decking where necessary for respondents with missing benefit amounts. Second, the imputed benefit to earnings ratio is multiplied by earnings to calculate the missing amount of benefits. Where necessary, earnings are imputed for respondents with missing earnings information.

Pension values for all outcomes are present discounted values of plan values in 1992 dollars. The discount rate is 5.8 percent within each cohort and 2.8 percent between cohorts.

Pension values indicate the value of pension plans in various forms of payout from jobs respondents left after their initial interview. Pension values from last (reported in the G, GG, and K sections of the HRS) and previous jobs (reported in the H, GH, and L sections), which respondents were asked about when they were interviewed for the first time, are not included in this table and Tables 11.4B–11.4D.

Nine percent of respondents in the original cohort reported that they left their money in a DC account administered by their former employer, with the accounts worth $6,237 per respondent in the original cohort. An additional 7.3 percent of respondents report having a DC plan that was rolled over into an IRA, with a value of $5,195 per HRS respondent. DB plans were cashed out by 3.3 percent of respondents. Among those who cashed out a DB plan, the plan on average was worth $54,813. This is about one-third of the value of DB plans that entered into pay status, per respondent with a nonzero observation. When averaged over all respondents in the original cohort, cash settlements of DB plans were worth $1,820 per HRS respondent. For DC plans, 3.4 percent of all respondents withdrew money worth a total of $790 per HRS respondent in 1992.

For members from the original HRS cohort, with only minor exceptions for cash-outs and for transfers to a new employer, the value in each category of pensions disposed of during the course of the HRS survey period per HRS respondent (Table 11.4A) exceeds the comparable value per HRS respondent of pensions disposed of before entering the survey (Table 11.3A). This need not have been the case. As shown in the third column of Table 11.3A, the DB plans of those who retired before entering the HRS and were receiving benefits were worth $180,728, compared with $160,362 for those who retired during the course of the survey and immediately began collecting DB benefits. Similarly, those retiring before entering the HRS who left a DC account with the firm had an account value of $71,219. In contrast, those who left during the course of the survey had $69,650 in their account.

Despite the fact that in the major categories, the mean of nonzero observations is higher for those who left before joining the HRS than for those who left during the course of the survey, the total value of plans is higher for those who left during the course of the survey. The basic reason is that twice as many (18.2 vs. 9.1 percent) respondents received current benefits upon leaving with a DB plan during the course of the survey than when leaving with a DB plan before joining the HRS. Similarly, more than twice (9.0 vs. 4.4 percent) as many respondents with a DC plan left the balance to accumulate in their employer's plan upon leaving during the course of the survey as when leaving before joining the HRS. The comparable frequencies are 7.3 percent versus 1.9 percent for those who rolled a DC plan into an IRA.

The simple comparisons made between plan values calculated before a person enters the HRS compared with leaving after having joined the survey are affected by changes in methodology used by the HRS to value pensions over time. At first the HRS asked about only a single pension. The number of pensions asked about was increased in subsequent waves.[3] In addition, bracketing was adopted in later waves. That is, a person who answered "don't know" or who refused to answer when asked about pension value is presented with a series of bracketed answers and asked whether the value falls within the specified range. While we address the effects of bracketing in the next section, these differences in procedures over time make it hazardous to compare pension values upon leaving the job for members of different cohorts.

Thus we now turn to the information on the disposition of pensions among cohorts but advise caution in interpreting Tables 11.4B to 11.4D. If one compares the values in column 2 across the three tables, the issue becomes obvious. As seen in column 2 of Table 11.4B, because those in the 1992 cohort of 51- to 56-year-olds have had eight waves of the survey to dispose of their pensions, virtually all of them have done so. Conversely, those 51 to 56 in 2004 had only one wave to dispose of their pensions. As a result, the percentage of nonzero observations in each category amounts to only 1 or 2 percent of the sample and

Table 11.4B Disposition of all pensions (observed and imputed) by type of payout upon leaving pension-covered jobs, HRS, 51–56 in 1992, respondent data (weighted)

Disposition of pension	Overall mean (1992 dollars)	% nonzero observations	Mean of nonzero observations (1992 dollars)
	Defined benefit		
Expect future benefit	8,276	7.3	112,546
Receive current benefit	31,223	18.6	171,192
Received cash settlement	2,273	3.6	61,797
Rolled into IRA	1,533	1.5	98,262
	Defined contribution		
Amount in account	7,968	11.2	71,735
Rolled into IRA	6,475	8.8	73,990
Converted to annuity	1,648	1.0	164,209
Transferred to new employer	7	0.2	4,533
Withdrew the money	985	4.8	20,410
Received/receiving installments	257	0.2	1,133
No. of observations: ages 51–56		5,449	

Note: The sample includes respondents with observed and imputed values.

Table 11.4C Disposition of all pensions (observed and imputed) by type of payout upon leaving pension-covered jobs, war babies, 51–56 in 1998, respondent data (weighted)

Disposition of pension	Overall mean (1992 dollars)	% nonzero observations	Mean of nonzero observations (1992 dollars)
	Defined benefit		
Expect future benefit	7,129	6.5	109,473
Receive current benefit	26,414	11.1	237,389
Received cash settlement	2,185	2.3	93,516
Rolled into IRA	2,130	2.0	103,136
	Defined contribution		
Amount in account	7,445	9.6	77,898
Rolled into IRA	5,791	6.6	87,356
Converted to annuity	3,293	0.9	363,983
Transferred to new employer	402	0.5	76,643
Withdrew the money	712	3.5	20,383
Received/receiving installments	20	0.4	4,863
No. of observations: ages 51–56		3,126	

Table 11.4D Disposition of all pensions (observed and imputed) by type of payout upon leaving pension-covered jobs, early boomers, 51–56 in 2004, respondent data (weighted)

Disposition of pension	Overall mean (1992 dollars)	% nonzero observations	Mean of nonzero observations (1992 dollars)
	Defined benefit		
Expect future benefit	1,055	1.0	107,136
Receive current benefit	4,392	1.1	383,896
Received cash settlement	177	0.2	80,850
Rolled into IRA	40	0.1	41,719
	Defined contribution		
Amount in account	1,863	1.9	96,639
Rolled into IRA	260	0.3	77,961
Converted to annuity	92	0.05	199,408
Transferred to new employer	56	0.2	25,451
Withdrew the money	50	0.9	5,775
Received/receiving installments	1	0.1	1,050
No. of observations: ages 51–56		3,233	

sometimes less. Nevertheless, even for the cohort 51 to 56 in 2004, it is as likely that DB plans will be preserved in their current form, either paying or expecting to pay DB benefits to 2.1 percent of respondents, as it is that DC plans will be preserved in their current form, remaining in the account or transferred to a new employer.

Tables 11.7A–C in Appendix 11.1 allow interested researchers to compare outcomes not only by cohort, but by cohort and year. However, the value of this exercise is limited by the small cell sizes found in these tables.

An additional complication is suggested by evidence that those who do not take benefits from their pensions until later waves have less valuable pensions. The older cohorts will have had more years to realize turnover in their pensions, which will mean pensions of lower value are more likely to be included in figures on disposition of pensions for older than for younger cohorts.

All of this said, it is obvious from the data on disposition of pensions that despite the trend to DC plans, DB plans continue to play an important role as a source of income in retirement.

Effects of Bracketing

The results presented in this chapter use all the information available in the survey. Because more comprehensive measures were used in later waves than in earlier waves, this could create a problem for interpreting trends. Perhaps of greatest potential importance, brackets were not used in calculating benefit amounts for the HRS cohort in 1992 and for the war baby cohort in 1998, but they were introduced in this sequence for DC plans in 2000. For expected future benefits, receiving benefit amounts, and cash settlement amounts for DB plans, brackets were introduced in 2002. Brackets are used for all the results in 2004.[4]

Table 11.5 provides information regarding the potential effects on trends of introducing brackets. Using data from 2004 and 2006, Table 11.5 reports calculated values for the various types of payouts both with and without brackets. These values suggest that increasing reliance on brackets over time did not introduce a consistent trend in reported pension values. Although there are some differences between values depending on whether bracketed amounts are included, these differences vary between cohorts and differ by whether the calculation was made in 2004 or 2006. In some cases brackets reduce the value of DB plans and increase the value of DC plans, but these patterns are not consistent.

Table 11.5   Average value of nonzero observations by type of payout upon leaving pension-covered jobs by whether values are calculated with brackets or without brackets, in thousands of 1992 dollars (weighted)

Disposition of pension	2004		2006	
	With brackets	Without brackets	With brackets	Without brackets
Ages 51–61 in 1992				
Expect future benefits	45 (25)	64 (25)	40 (16)	40 (16)
Receive current benefits	113 (136)	108 (136)	92 (98)	100 (98)
Cash settlement	32 (15)	34 (15)	22 (17)	37 (17)
Amount left in account	48 (83)	49 (83)	46 (54)	31 (54)
Ages 51–56 in 1992				
Expect future benefits	40 (22)	56 (22)	43 (15)	43 (15)
Receive current benefits	115 (115)	109 (115)	100 (82)	107 (82)
Cash settlement	39 (12)	42 (12)	24 (15)	41 (15)
Amount left in account	60 (71)	48 (71)	52 (47)	34 (47)
Ages 51–56 in 1998				
Expect future benefits	88 (46)	103 (46)	89 (32)	92 (32)
Receive current benefits	189 (106)	194 (106)	176 (105)	179 (105)
Cash settlement	36 (13)	35 (13)	102 (8)	102 (8)
Amount left in account	43 (73)	38 (73)	81 (52)	82 (52)
Ages 51–56 in 2004				
Expect future benefits	—	—	112 (44)	110 (44)
Receive current benefits	—	—	369 (39)	380 (39)
Cash settlement	—	—	114 (9)	130 (9)
Amount left in account	—	—	56 (63)	56 (63)

Note: Total number of observations is in parentheses.

Pension Incomes in Retirement

To this point, we have explored statistics indicating the disposition of pensions when a covered worker leaves a firm. Now we turn to the assets and income section of the HRS to measure reported incomes from pensions among those whose plans are in pay status.

Before turning to these data, it is useful to reiterate a number of issues related to measuring income due to pensions. First, there is a conceptual issue that arises because assets originating as pensions often do not continue in that form. As we have seen, they often are transformed into some other asset type or are spent, reducing the share of retirement income that will appear to originate from a pension plan. Similar to other surveys of retirees, the assets and income section of the HRS does not distinguish the original source of reported income. If an asset had been transformed from a pension to some other form, the income will be reported as emanating from the transformed asset. Tracing retirement incomes to the original pension asset would be very difficult and at some levels impossible. Once dollars from a pension plan are mixed with other assets, it is arbitrary to label some of the assets as having been consumed in the past and other assets as having been saved in some other form and thus the source of income in retirement. For example, if a lump sum settlement from a pension were deposited in a bank account and mixed with other funds, and some of the money in the account had been spent on consumption over the years, it would not be possible to decide which dollars currently in the bank account had their roots in the pension plan and which came from some other source.

Also affecting measurement of pension incomes, there were a number of changes over the years in the pension questions asked in the HRS assets and income section.[5] As a result, once again one must exercise considerable care in interpreting changes in reported incomes from pensions over time. For example, in its early years, the income section asked about only one pension and then asked about more plans in later years. The reported number of plans per household would be expected to increase over time as a result, whether or not the number of plans held by members of each household was in fact increasing. Comparing the values in the initial year a 51- to 56-year-old cohort entered the survey, the number of plans per household increases from 1.0 to 1.1 between 1992 and 2004. This increase may reflect both the changes in the survey questions as well as actual changes in the number of pensions held per household.

Turning now to the data reporting household incomes from pensions, Table 11.6 shows monthly incomes from pensions for each of the four cohort groups. The sum of monthly pension incomes from pensions held by both spouses is reported. The monthly value of income from pensions averages $1,031 for members of the original HRS cohort who were 51 to 61 upon entering the survey. Looking across row 2 in the first panel of Table 11.6, we see that the monthly value of pensions per household in receipt of a pension benefit declines over time, with an average monthly pension income of $1,031 in 1992, falling to $794 in 2006. One can see from row 3 that the number of households from the original HRS cohort reporting a pension income increases over time, rising from 1,241 in 1992 to 2,036 in 2006. These two sets

Table 11.6 Monthly income from pensions in 1992 dollars (weighted)

Measures of prevalence and value of pensions	1992	1994	1996	1998	2000	2002	2004	2006
Ages 51–61 in 1992								
Total no. of plans per HH with pension income	1.0	1.2	1.3	1.2	1.3	1.3	1.3	1.3
Total value of payments from plans per HH with pension income	1,031	1,343	1,100	942	915	846	844	794
No. of HHs with pension income	1,241	1,558	1,833	1,712	2,090	2,152	2,227	2,036
Sample size: HH with at least 1 member	7,324	6,693	6,461	6,321	6,015	5,895	5,658	5,304
Ages 51–56 in 1992								
Total no. of plans per HH with pension income	1.0	1.1	1.2	1.2	1.2	1.3	1.3	1.3
Total value of payments from plans per HH with pension income	1,073	1,511	1,265	1,032	1,041	945	925	817
No. of HHs with pension income	520	696	851	914	1,189	1,285	1,418	1,183
Sample size: HH with at least 1 member	4,494	4,128	3,994	3,976	3,785	3,724	3,612	3,172
Ages 51–56 in 1998								
Total no. of plans per HH with pension income	—	—	—	1.1	1.1	1.2	1.2	1.2
Total value of payments from plans per HH with pension income	—	—	—	1,118	1,200	1,164	1,131	1,023
No. of HHs with pension income	—	—	—	324	451	545	659	535
Sample size: HH with at least 1 member	—	—	—	2,612	2,524	2,472	2,448	2,367
Ages 51–56 in 2004								
Total no. of plans per HH with pension income	—	—	—	—	—	—	1.1	1.1
Total value of payments from plans per HH with pension income	—	—	—	—	—	—	1,302	1,095
No. of HHs with pension income	—	—	—	—	—	—	246	303
Sample size: HH with at least 1 member	—	—	—	—	—	—	2,739	2,531

Note: Pension incomes are from the assets and income section of the HRS.

of numbers together suggest that households who first report their pension incomes in later years of the survey have less generous benefits. Another possibility is that pension incomes per household decline as the primary beneficiary dies and the spouse continues to receive a reduced benefit.

We turn now to the three panels reporting pension incomes for the three cohorts of 51- to 56-year-olds. In the year of entry into the survey, monthly household income from pensions increases from $1,073 for members of the original HRS cohort to $1,302 for members of the early boomer cohort.

Terms of payment over the lifetime are not reported in the assets and income section. For example, we do not know the terms of the annuity underlying any monthly payments. There is no report of whether it is a single payer annuity, 50 percent survivor benefit, 100 percent survivor benefit, ten-year certain (a guarantee that benefits will be paid for at least ten years), or what. If, for argument's sake, these plans were all defined benefit and the proper annuity factor were ten, the present values of lifetime benefits would range from $130,000 to $156,000 for those receiving their benefits immediately. In Tables 11.3B and 11.3D, we found present values of benefits from last or previous jobs ranging from $225,000 to $233,000 for those who were in receipt of DB benefits at the time they were first surveyed by the HRS.

Conclusions

This chapter has used data on the disposition of pensions upon leaving a job to determine the extent to which pensions are retained into retirement and directly generate retirement incomes. Our findings demonstrate the continuing importance of defined benefit pensions among the retirement age population, even into the youngest of the HRS cohorts. Pensions from last or previous jobs held by members of the cohort 51 to 56 years old in 2004 are worth $26,250 (in 1992 dollars) per respondent in the cohort. They are worth $2,154 more, per respondent, than are comparable pensions held by those 51 to 56 in 1992. Between these cohorts, DB plans have fallen in value by about $6,000 per respondent in the cohort, while DC plans per respondent have increased in value by a little over $8,000 per respondent.

Not all pensions continue in a form that is easily connected back to its origin as a pension. Although defined benefit plans are much more likely to be preserved in a form that is directly recognizable as originating from a pension plan, defined contribution plans are not.

The fact that only a fraction of both plan types continues in some form easily recognized as originating as a pension has a further consequence. It is easy to underestimate the importance of pensions when asking retirees about the source of their income. The role of pensions will be understated in surveys of retiree incomes by source. This may explain why the frequency of pension incomes among retirees and the value of income from pensions received by retirees are typically so much smaller than are comparable figures reporting the coverage and value of plans held by those who are still employed. The differences between pension values reported for workers and retirees are too large to be explained by rising incomes over time and resulting cohort differences in earnings.

When we consider both the smaller share of DC plans that continue in the form of a pension, together with the trend to defined contribution plans, this suggests a factor that will continue to reduce the fraction of retired respondents who will report that they are receiving income from a pension plan and the share of retiree incomes measured as originating from pensions.

Appendix 11.1: Year-by-Year Measures of the Disposition of Pensions during the Course of the Survey

This appendix provides more detail on the findings in Tables 11.4A through 11.4D. It reports the form and amount of pension payouts separately for each wave of the survey. Only a limited number of pensions are disposed of each year. That means that the cells showing what happened to each plan type for each cohort in each year are sometimes quite thin. This increases the variance of the data presented in this appendix.

It is clear from data in these appendix tables that the most valuable pensions are cashed out early. Those who do not take benefits from their pensions until later waves have less valuable pensions. Appendix Tables 11.7A to 11.7C allow the reader to compare plan values while controlling for the age of the respondent. For example, compare the outcomes in 1994 for those 51 to 56 in 1992 in the HRS cohort with outcomes in 2000 for those 51 to 56 in 1998 from the war baby cohort, and for 2006 for those 51 to 56 in 2004 for the early boomer cohort.

Table 11.7A Average value of nonzero observations by type of payout upon leaving pension-covered jobs, HRS, 51–61 in 1992, in thousands of 1992 dollars (weighted)

Disposition of pensions	1994	1996	1998	2000	2002	2004	2006
Defined benefit plans							
Expect future benefits	116	163	87	87	71	45	40
	(138)	(108)	(112)	(84)	(68)	(25)	(16)
Receive current benefits	210	176	138	114	132	113	92
	(215)	(300)	(273)	(256)	(288)	(136)	(98)
Cash settlement	67	47	86	56	32	32	22
	(56)	(57)	(53)	(32)	(52)	(15)	(17)
Rolled into IRA	56	75	187	163	63	38	28
	(17)	(18)	(18)	(15)	(17)	(12)	(9)
No. leaving jobs with DB or combination pension	428	495	407	376	401	174	119
Defined contribution plans							
Amount left in account	34	62	68	65	69	48	46
	(75)	(120)	(112)	(145)	(145)	(83)	(54)
Rolled into IRA	31	60	101	71	65	60	41
	(42)	(104)	(111)	(104)	(128)	(50)	(53)
Convert to annuity	161	103	56	62	147	60	319
	(9)	(17)	(12)	(10)	(23)	(10)	(11)
Transferred to new employer	—	—	—	4	14	4	—
				(1)	(3)	(3)	
Withdrew the money	7	13	18	15	17	19	20
	(42)	(34)	(58)	(64)	(87)	(57)	(33)
Received/receiving installments	—	—	—	—	—	—	1
							(18)
No. leaving jobs with DC or combination pension	178	322	320	332	367	201	152

Notes: Pension values that were reported "lost" or reported in the "other" category are not included. All multiple responses regarding disposition of pension plans are taken into account in calculating the pension values. Samples in each payout category include respondents with an observed value plus imputations for respondents with missing values. We have used information from brackets for questions that had brackets in the imputation process. For imputing "account balances" when the employee left the job, in addition, we have used current account balances in the sorting process when hot decking. For current account balances we have used "account balances" when left in the hot-decking process. For other payout options where there was no information from brackets available, the imputations involve two steps. First, the ratio of benefits to earnings is calculated and imputed through hot decking where necessary for respondents with missing benefit amounts. Second, the imputed benefit to earnings ratio is multiplied by earnings to calculate the missing amount of benefits. Where necessary, earnings are imputed for respondents with missing earnings information.

Pension values for all outcomes are present discounted values of plan values in thousands of 1992 dollars. The discount rate is 5.8 percent within each cohort and 2.8 percent between cohorts. Pension values indicate the value of pension plans in various forms of payouts from jobs respondents left after their initial interview. Pension values from last (reported in the G, GG, and K sections of the HRS) and previous jobs (reported in the H, GH, and L sections) where respondents were asked about these when they were interviewed for the first time are not included here. Total number of observations is reported in parentheses.

Table 11.7B   Average value of nonzero observations by type of payout upon leaving pension-covered jobs, HRS, 51–56 in 1992, in thousands of 1992 dollars (weighted)

Disposition of pensions	1994	1996	1998	2000	2002	2004	2006
Defined benefit plans							
Expect future benefits	135	132	90	93	69	40	43
	(84)	(74)	(76)	(65)	(62)	(22)	(15)
Receive current benefits	290	238	163	118	132	115	100
	(85)	(114)	(119)	(173)	(219)	(115)	(82)
Cash settlement	58	36	114	63	39	39	24
	(34)	(29)	(34)	(17)	(32)	(12)	(15)
Rolled into IRA	76	41	265	163	73	33	17
	(7)	(10)	(10)	(12)	(13)	(10)	(7)
No. leaving jobs with DB or combination pension	215	238	216	258	311	148	101
Defined contribution plans							
Amount left in account	24	64	41	61	80	47	52
	(38)	(76)	(62)	(112)	(111)	(71)	(47)
Rolled into IRA	40	68	101	66	72	64	41
	(21)	(54)	(68)	(78)	(105)	(35)	(51)
Converted to annuity	356	128	69	28	157	47	256
	(3)	(6)	(4)	(3)	(17)	(7)	(9)
Transferred to new employer	—	—	—	4	14	2	—
				(1)	(3)	(2)	
Withdrew the money	5	8	16	11	17	20	19
	(24)	(17)	(26)	(45)	(69)	(47)	(26)
Received/receiving installments	—	—	—	—	—	—	1
							(14)
No. leaving jobs with DC or combination pension	93	187	171	242	287	159	131

Note: See notes to Table 11.7A.

Table 11.7C　Average value of nonzero observations by type of payout upon leaving pension-covered jobs, for war baby cohort ages 51–56 in 1998 and early boomer cohort ages 51–56 in 2004, in thousands of 1992 dollars (weighted)

Disposition of pensions	WBs				EBs
	2000	2002	2004	2006	2006
Defined benefit plans					
Expect future benefits	111	77	88	89	112
	(39)	(70)	(46)	(32)	(44)
Receive current benefits	270	264	189	176	369
	(53)	(93)	(106)	(105)	(39)
Cash settlement	77	100	36	102	114
	(18)	(26)	(13)	(8)	(9)
Rolled into IRA	72	125	103	33	69
	(6)	(22)	(18)	(11)	(8)
No. leaving jobs with DB or combination pension	126	207	178	153	103
Defined contribution plans					
Amount left in account	46	63	43	81	56
	(69)	(94)	(73)	(52)	(63)
Rolled into IRA	79	67	124	47	67
	(66)	(58)	(35)	(46)	(39)
Converted to annuity	187	398	172	530	453
	(2)	(5)	(6)	(14)	(8)
Transferred to new employer	62	6	154	2	25
	(5)	(4)	(3)	(1)	(5)
Withdrew the money	6	25	36	3	6
	(24)	(36)	(39)	(19)	(28)
Received/receiving installments	—	—	—	5	1
				(14)	(4)
No. leaving jobs with DC or combination pension	161	187	153	135	148

Note: See notes to Table 11.7A.

12

The Changing Role of Pensions in Total Wealth

A next natural step is to consider pensions in the context of the total wealth accumulated by the retirement age population. Analogous to the treatment of defined benefit (DB) plans, the annual flow of Social Security benefits can be discounted and summed to form Social Security wealth, which turns out on average to be the most valuable of all retirement assets.[1] Among others, additional assets include home equity, financial wealth, business and real estate wealth, and individual retirement accounts.

Before turning to the data, some methodological issues should be mentioned. At the level of the individual, there is no ambiguity when respondents are classified into one cohort or another according to their age at the time of the survey. There is, however, a question of how to identify which cohort a household belongs to. Most obviously, if two spouses are from two different cohorts, the household is associated with both cohorts. Although it is possible to define the affiliation of a household so that it is linked to only a single cohort, for example, by arbitrarily classifying a household in accordance with the age of the older spouse or the age of the financially knowledgeable respondent, we will not take that approach. Rather, a household will be included with a particular cohort if at least one member of the household falls within the age range specified for the cohort, so that some households are counted with two different cohorts.

Another issue concerns discounting. A problem arises when two spouses are from different cohorts. When dealing with individuals, the procedure we have adopted is to discount pensions to the base year of the individual's cohort by using a nominal interest rate (5.8 percent in our analysis). Benefits are discounted to 1992 for members of the HRS cohort, to 1998 for war babies, and to 2004 for early boomers. A 2.8 percent discount rate is then used to restate values in 1992 dollars for the war babies and early boomers, facilitating comparisons of wealth between cohorts.[2]

In contrast to the treatment of individuals, when a household has members from different cohorts, there are two base years. In calculating household wealth, we will discount the benefits and other assets of both spouses to the birth year of the spouse who has determined the household's cohort. For example, a household with one member 51 to 56 in 1992 and another 51 to 56 in 1998 will have all pensions discounted (at 5.8 percent) to 1992 when the household is being counted as part of the 1992 cohort. When the household is counted as part of the 1998 cohort, the pensions of both the husband and wife will be discounted to 1998 at a 5.8 percent discount rate, even though the husband when considered as an individual is part of the 1992 cohort. Assets will be similarly centered, so when the household is counted as part of the 1992 cohort, all asset values are as of 1992. When the household is part of the 1998 cohort, all asset values are as of 1998. Once household wealth is determined as of 1998, the dollar values will be adjusted for the effects of cost of living changes, discounting by 2.8 percent over the six-year period between 1998 and 1992. As a result, the pension wealth calculated for a household may not be the simple sum of the pension wealth figures derived when each spouse is considered as a separate individual.

Baseline Results

Baseline results are reported in Table 12.1A for members of the original HRS cohort, with at least one member of the household 51 to 61 in 1992. On average, pension wealth accounts for 23.7 percent of the entire retirement wealth accumulated by households from this cohort. Pensions represent 19.7 percent of retirement wealth for the median 10 percent of wealth-holding households. Note that pension wealth is based on respondent reports of defined contribution (DC) plan balances and prorated present values of respondent reports of expected yearly retirement benefits from DB plans.

Social Security wealth is more important than pension wealth, accounting for 30.9 percent of the total wealth of the original HRS cohort. Pensions and

Table 12.1A   Components of mean wealth and wealth for median 10 percent of
wealth-holding households, HRS 51–61 (in 1992 dollars)

Source of wealth	Mean		Mean for the median 10 percent of wealth-holding households	
	Value ($)	% of total	Value ($)	% of total
Total	421,578	100	326,165	100
House value	74,179	17.6	60,970	18.7
Real estate	26,604	6.3	8,151	2.5
Business assets	21,308	5.3	6,010	1.8
Financial assets	41,634	9.3	20,139	6.2
IRA assets	17,569	3.8	9,723	3.0
Social Security	129,122	30.9	144,986	44.5
Pension value	98,216	23.7	64,261	19.7
Net value of vehicles	12,945	3.3	11,925	3.7
No. of observations	7,245			

Notes: The figures in this table are based on the authors' calculations. Net wealth is defined as net worth, assets less liabilities. Pension value is based on self-reported data and includes pension values from any current/last and previous jobs. The pension value from a current job includes the calculated prorated projected pension value from the most important DB plan and current account balances from all DC plans. Pension values from last (G section) and previous jobs (H section) include projected pension values from those jobs if the pensions had not yet entered pay status, as well as remaining pension values in 1992 for pensions that were in pay status in 1992. Current account balances in 1992 from last and/or previous jobs are also included. The median 10 percent of wealth-holding households are those with net wealth in the forty-fifth to fifty-fifth percentiles. All data are weighted by RAND household weights. Households with the top and bottom 1 percent of total wealth are excluded.

Social Security together account for 54.6 percent of the total retirement wealth for the members of this cohort. For the median wealth-holding households, Social Security accounts for 44.5 percent of total wealth, so that pensions and Social Security together account for almost two-thirds of total retirement wealth.

Housing represents another 17.6 percent of average household wealth or 18.7 percent of median household wealth. The remaining 28.5 percent of average household wealth (17.2 percent of median household wealth) is accounted for by other financial assets, IRAs (which as seen in Chapter 11 benefit from the rollover of pensions), and business, real estate, and other assets.

The Changing Role of Pensions in Total Wealth

Trends in Pensions and Other Components of Retirement Wealth

A number of trends in pensions discussed in earlier chapters are reflected in the values of pensions at the household level. These include the expansion of coverage; the trend in plan type, modified by the continuing importance of DB plans for the retirement age population along with the incomplete maturation of 401(k) plans; the effect of the growth in stock prices on assets in DC plans; and increasing benefits earned by women.

Growth in housing prices has caused housing wealth to be higher for younger cohorts. Similarly, growth in stock prices would cause the value of equities as well as IRA balances to increase. IRAs would further increase as 401(k) plans mature and workers from younger cohorts, who are covered for a greater share of their work lives, increase the size of rollovers from 401(k) balances over time.

Trends in components of retirement wealth can be seen in Tables 12.1B–D, which report outcomes for those aged 51 to 56 in 1992, 1998, and 2004. Between 1992 and 2004, total retirement wealth grew by 12 percent, increasing from $409,765 to $458,846. The wealth of the median 10 percent of households increased by 5.3 percent over the same period. Pension wealth grew at at about the same rate as did total wealth, so that the share of household wealth accounted for by pensions fell only very slightly from 24.0 percent in 1992 to 23.7 percent in 2004. For households with the median 10 percent of total wealth, the share of household wealth represented by pensions increased over the period, from 19.4 percent to 21.6 percent.

Real Social Security wealth declined slightly between 1992 and 2004, but a slightly higher real interest rate was used in discounting benefits for members of the younger cohort (see note 2).

IRA assets grew from 3.8 percent of total wealth to 5.9 percent. House values also grew as a share of total wealth from 17.6 percent to 20.3 percent. Financial assets grew from 9.4 percent to 11.5 percent of total assets, while real estate and business assets declined both absolutely and relatively, with real estate falling from 6.4 percent to 4.4 percent of total wealth and business assets falling from 5.3 percent to 3.7 percent of total wealth.

Table 12.1B   Components of mean wealth and wealth for median 10 percent of wealth-holding households, HRS 51–56 in 1992 (in 1992 dollars)

Source of wealth	Mean		Mean for the median 10% of wealth-holding households	
	Value ($)	% of total	Value ($)	% of total
Total	409,765	100	312,253	100
House value	72,171	17.6	57,499	18.4
Real estate	26,048	6.4	9,297	3.0
Business assets	21,919	5.3	6,155	2.0
Financial assets	38,536	9.4	19,238	6.2
IRA assets	15,569	3.8	10,218	3.3
Social Security	123,953	30.2	135,859	43.5
Pension value	98,186	24.0	60,493	19.4
Net value of vehicles	13,383	3.3	13,494	4.3
No. of observations	4,442			

Notes: The figures in this table are based on the authors' calculations. Net wealth is defined as net worth, assets less liabilities. Pension value is based on self-reported data and includes pension values from any current/last and previous jobs. The pension value from a current job includes the calculated prorated projected pension value from the most important DB plan and current account balances from all DC plans. Pension values from last (G section) and previous jobs (H section) include projected pension values from those jobs if the pensions had not yet entered pay status, as well as remaining pension values in 1992 for pensions that were in pay status in 1992. Current account balances in 1992 from last and/or previous jobs are also included. The median 10 percent of wealth-holding households are those with net wealth in the forty-fifth to fifty-fifth percentiles. All data are weighted by RAND household weights. Households with the top and bottom 1 percent of total wealth are excluded.

Table 12.1C   Components of mean wealth and wealth for median 10 percent of
wealth-holding households, war babies 51–56 in 1998 (in 1992 dollars)

Source of wealth	Mean		Mean for the median 10% of wealth-holding households	
	Value ($)	% of total	Value ($)	% of total
Total	427,728	100	303,144	100
House value	65,926	15.4	52,675	17.4
Real estate	24,816	5.8	9,390	3.1
Business assets	21,951	5.1	4,807	1.6
Financial assets	48,834	11.4	18,790	6.2
IRA assets	27,456	6.4	11,495	3.8
Social Security	117,156	27.4	131,919	43.5
Pension value	109,270	25.5	62,782	20.7
Net value of vehicles	12,320	2.9	11,288	3.7
No. of observations	2,602			

Notes: Pension value is based on self-reported data. It includes pension values from any current/last and previous jobs. The pension value from a current job includes the calculated prorated projected pension value from the most important DB plan and current account balances from all DC plans. Pension values from last (GG section) and previous jobs (GH section) include projected pension values from those jobs for dormant pensions, remaining pension values in 1998 for pensions that were in pay status in 1998, and current account balances in 1998. The pension values from last and previous jobs for respondents who were age eligible in 1998 (and their spouses) but were first interviewed in 1992 are from the G and H sections in 1992. For respondents in this group, benefits from a job that was terminated after their initial interview are also included. The account balances and projected benefits from dormant DB plans are adjusted by 5.8 percent for each year from the year first reported to 1998. For plans that are in pay status, the remaining portion of the benefit as of 1998 is included. The benefits are discounted back to 1992 dollars by 2.8 percent for each of the years between 1992 and 1998. Households with the top and bottom 1 percent of total wealth are excluded.

Table 12.1D   Components of mean wealth and wealth for median 10 percent of wealth-holding households, early boomers 51–56 in 2004 (in 1992 dollars)

Source of wealth	Mean		Mean for the median 10% of wealth-holding households	
	Value ($)	% of total	Value ($)	% of total
Total	458,846	100	328,844	100
House value	93,328	20.3	66,068	20.1
Real estate	20,385	4.4	7,318	2.2
Business assets	16,842	3.7	4,679	1.4
Financial assets	52,689	11.5	14,596	4.4
IRA assets	27,229	5.9	13,964	4.2
Social Security	127,843	27.9	140,266	42.7
Pension value	108,896	23.7	71,131	21.6
Net value of vehicles	11,632	2.5	10,822	3.3
No. of observations	2,708			

Notes: The methodology used in this table is analogous to that described in the note to Table 12.1C, where in this case the relevant base year is 2004 rather than 1998. Households with the top and bottom 1 percent of total wealth are excluded.

Trends in Wealth by Household Demographic Structure

The next step is to consider trends in household wealth separately for single males, single females, and couples. Table 12.2 reports results by household demographic structure.[3]

Once again, the findings highlight the rapidly changing status of women.[4] Consider the difference in total wealth between 1992 and 2004, for comparably structured households with at least one member 51 to 56 years old. Among households consisting of single men, total wealth decreased by 2.3 percent. In contrast, total wealth increased by 16.0 percent for couple households and by 24.9 percent in households consisting of single women. In 1992, 51- to 56-year-old households consisting of a single male had 55.2 percent more wealth than did households with a single female, and couple households had 2.71 times the wealth of households with a single female. By 2004, the gap, measured by the ratio of total wealth of single-male to single-female households, was reduced to 21.4 percent from 55.2 percent twelve years earlier.

Table 12.2 Total wealth, pension wealth, and Social Security wealth by household members, ages 51–56 in 1992, 1998, and 2004, weighted (in 1992 dollars)

Household members	1992	1998	2004
One-member HH (males)			
Total wealth	277,352	252,924	271,063
Pension wealth	78,709	59,021	52,862
SS wealth	71,528	65,185	67,807
No. of HHs	402	190	307
One-member HH (females)			
Total wealth	178,752	202,410	223,259
Pension wealth	33,071	44,434	49,293
SS wealth	54,307	53,192	61,574
No. of HHs	793	383	614
Two-member HH			
Total wealth	485,183	519,016	562,963
Pension wealth	116,695	135,530	136,866
SS wealth	148,616	143,485	158,508
No. of HHs	3,247	2,029	1,787

Notes: Married respondents whose spouses were not interviewed are included in the two-member household category. Households with the top and bottom 1 percent of total wealth are excluded.

By 2004, two-earner households had 2.52 times the wealth of households headed by a single woman, down from a ratio of 2.71 to 1 in 1992.

Pension wealth in 2004 was 33.0 percent lower than in 1992 for single men, 17.3 percent higher in 2004 than in 1992 for two-earner households, and 49.1 percent higher in 2004 for single women. Differences in Social Security wealth between cohorts were somewhat smaller but still moved substantially in favor of single-women households.

Wealth Differences between Households with and without Pensions

Households with pensions have higher wealth than do those without pensions. The difference in wealth is about $213,286 for those in the original HRS cohort, 51 to 61 years old in 1992. Comparing Tables 12.3A and 12.3B, total wealth of households with pensions is $492,216 versus $278,930 for households without pensions. The difference in wealth is, of course, not simply due to a difference in

Table 12.3A Components of mean wealth and wealth for median 10 percent of wealth-holding households, HRS 51–61 in 1992 (in 1992 dollars), households with pensions

Source of wealth	Mean Value ($)	Mean % of total	Mean for the median 10% of wealth-holding households Value ($)	Mean for the median 10% of wealth-holding households % of total
Total	492,216	100	404,012	100
House value	80,193	16.3	69,473	17.2
Real estate	23,314	4.7	9,391	2.3
Business assets	14,394	2.9	5,686	1.4
Financial assets	45,693	9.3	23,805	5.9
IRA assets	19,996	4.1	11,342	2.8
Social Security	147,817	30.0	159,951	39.6
Pension value	146,852	29.8	110,727	27.4
Net value of vehicles	13,959	2.8	13,636	3.4
No. of observations	4,712			

Notes: At least one member of the household has a pension. Households with the top and bottom 1 percent of total wealth are excluded.

Table 12.3B Components of mean wealth and wealth for median 10 percent of wealth-holding households, HRS 51–61 in 1992 (in 1992 dollars), households without pensions

Source of wealth	Mean Value ($)	Mean % of total	Mean for the median 10% of wealth-holding households Value ($)	Mean for the median 10% of wealth-holding households % of total
Total	278,930	100	147,884	100
House value	62,035	22.2	31,794	21.5
Real estate	33,251	11.9	3,257	2.2
Business assets	35,271	12.6	3,807	2.6
Financial assets	33,437	12.0	7,078	4.8
IRA assets	12,666	4.5	2,734	1.8
Social Security	91,370	32.8	92,166	62.3
Pension value	0	0	0	0
Net value of vehicles	10,899	3.9	7,047	4.8
No. of observations	2,533			

Notes: None of the household members has a pension. Households with the top and bottom 1 percent of total wealth are excluded.

pensions. Employers are more likely to provide pensions to households with higher incomes and wealth, and such households are more likely to demand pensions of higher value. Overall, the difference in total wealth between households with and without pensions exceeds the value of the pension, $146,852. For households with a pension, the pension accounts for 29.8 percent of total wealth.

Households with pensions have much higher covered earnings than do households without pensions. Thus, in 1992, Social Security wealth, which is a direct reflection of the household's covered earnings, averages $147,817 for households with pensions and $91,370 for households without pensions. Not all HRS households without pensions were poorer than households with pensions, however. As can be seen between Tables 12.3A and 12.3B, in 1992 both real estate wealth and business wealth are considerably higher for households without pensions. These assets are not evenly distributed among households. Rather, a few households without a covered earnings history owned significant wealth, often from an owned business that did not offer a pension.[5]

Many other households without pensions come from the lower end of the earnings distribution. Low-wage workers are less likely to be in jobs that offer pensions. For many of those from low-income households, Social Security provides what they perceive to be an adequate retirement benefit. Further details on the role of self-employment and business wealth in creating wealth differences between households with and without pensions can be found in Gustman and Steinmeier (1999b).

Detailed descriptions of trends in total wealth, pensions, and Social Security between households with and without pensions are reported in the appendix to this chapter. Tables 12.5A through Table 12.5F report results for households with at least one member 51 to 56 years old.

A word of caution is in order before briefly summarizing the data contained in these tables. Over the period between 1992 and 2004, it has become easier for small firms and the self-employed to adopt a pension plan. As a result, the composition of the two groups, those with and without pensions, may be systematically different in 2004 than in 1992, with more self-employed falling in the group with pensions in the latter period. Those without pensions have lower business wealth in the second period.

Total wealth owned by households with pensions in 2004 is 20.6 percent higher than the wealth owned by households with pensions in 1992. Despite higher pension wealth in 2004, the share of total wealth represented by pensions in households with pensions is slightly lower in 2004 than in 1992, 28.4 percent in 2004 and 30.3 percent in 1992.

In contrast, trends for households without pensions were not nearly as favorable. The total wealth of 51- to 56-year-old households without pensions was lower in 2004 than in 1992, decreasing in real (1992) dollars from $273,075 in 1992 to $230,964. Most of the decline was in the value of real estate and business assets held by households without pensions. In contrast, there was virtually no decline in the value of real estate and business assets held by households with pensions between 1992 and 2004. This suggests a change in the composition of the group without pensions. Specifically, by 2004 fewer business owners may fall within the group of households without pensions.

By 2004, the gap in total wealth between households with and without pensions had widened to $338,499, so that households with pensions had 147 percent more wealth than did households without pensions. Nevertheless, the value of pensions held by households with pensions in 2004, $161,756, represents less than half the gap in total wealth between households with and without pensions. The difference in Social Security benefits is substantial. In 2004, households with a pension had 88.7 percent higher Social Security wealth than did households without pensions, again suggesting that much of the difference in total wealth between households with and without pensions simply reflects lower lifetime earnings by those without pensions.

Pensions, Social Security, and the Distribution of Retirement Wealth

Households with lower wealth are likely to be most dependent on Social Security. Those with higher wealth will have increasing shares of their wealth held in the form of other assets. Most important, pensions complement Social Security. As Social Security accounts for a decreasing share of total wealth as wealth increases, pensions fill the gap.

These relations can be seen in Tables 12.4A to 12.4D, which report the components of wealth for those falling into different deciles of the wealth distribution for members of different HRS cohorts. Thus as seen in Table 12.4A, row 5, the present value of the household's future Social Security benefits falls from 87.3 percent of total wealth for members of the lowest wealth decile to 14.0 percent for members of the highest wealth decile. As the share of wealth accounted for by Social Security declines, the share of total wealth accounted

Table 12.4A Distribution of wealth values from pensions and Social Security by wealth decile, HRS 51–61 in 1992 (in thousands of 1992 dollars)

Sources of wealth	Source of wealth by indicated total wealth decile										Total
	1–10	11–20	21–30	31–40	41–50	51–60	61–70	71–80	81–90	91–100	
Total wealth	34.6	96.5	160.3	224.4	291.7	363.0	450.8	562.1	738.8	1,292.7	421.58
Total pension wealth	0.7	6.2	18.3	30.5	50.5	78.7	112.5	153.3	223.2	308.0	98.2
Total pension wealth/total wealth (%)	2.0	6.4	11.4	13.6	17.3	21.7	25.0	27.3	30.2	23.8	23.3
Total Social Security wealth	30.2	71.2	96.9	124.4	137.7	151.8	158.7	169.1	170.0	181.0	129.12
Total Social Security wealth/total wealth (%)	87.3	73.8	60.4	55.4	47.2	41.8	35.2	30.1	23.0	14.0	30.6
Total pension wealth plus Social Security wealth	30.9	77.4	115.3	154.9	188.2	230.5	271.2	322.4	393.2	489.0	227.34
Total pension wealth plus Social Security/total wealth (%)	89.3	80.2	71.9	69.0	64.5	63.5	60.2	57.4	53.2	37.8	53.9

Note: Households with the top and bottom 1 percent of total wealth are excluded.

Table 12.4B Distribution of wealth values from pensions and Social Security by wealth decile, HRS 51–56 in 1992 (in thousands of 1992 dollars)

Sources of wealth	Source of wealth by indicated total wealth decile										
	1–10	11–20	21–30	31–40	41–50	51–60	61–70	71–80	81–90	91–100	Total
Total wealth	35.8	96.9	155.7	215.7	279.2	347.5	430.7	540.7	711.6	1,281.8	409.8
Total pension wealth	1.0	6.8	14.8	29.2	44.8	77.8	107.8	154.2	225.1	319.8	98.2
Total pension wealth/total wealth (%)	2.8	7.0	9.5	13.5	16.0	22.4	25.0	28.5	31.6	24.9	24.0
Total Social Security wealth	33.1	73.2	96.7	121.3	134.1	144.6	151.2	158.0	160.3	166.8	124.0
Total Social Security wealth/total wealth (%)	92.5	75.5	62.1	56.2	48.0	41.6	35.1	29.2	22.5	13.0	30.3
Total pension wealth plus Social Security wealth	34.1	80.0	111.5	150.4	178.8	222.4	259.0	312.2	385.4	486.7	222.1
Total pension wealth plus Social Security/total wealth (%)	95.3	82.6	71.6	69.7	64.0	64.0	60.1	57.7	54.2	38.0	54.2

Note: Households with the top and bottom 1 percent of total wealth are excluded.

Table 12.4C Distribution of wealth values from pensions and Social Security by wealth decile, war babies 51–56 in 1998 (in thousands of 1992 dollars)

Sources of wealth	Source of wealth by indicated total wealth decile										
	1–10	11–20	21–30	31–40	41–50	51–60	61–70	71–80	81–90	91–100	Total
Total wealth	36.6	89.6	147.9	203.8	264.7	345.7	434.9	564.0	760.8	1,426.0	427.7
Total pension wealth	0.9	5.4	14.8	28.4	49.8	77.5	108.6	184.3	257.4	364.6	109.3
Total pension wealth/total wealth (%)	2.5	6.0	10.0	13.9	18.8	22.4	25.0	32.7	33.8	25.6	25.6
Total Social Security wealth	31.2	66.2	89.3	108.2	121.4	135.8	146.3	149.9	152.4	170.6	117.2
Total Social Security wealth/total wealth (%)	85.2	73.9	60.4	53.1	45.9	39.3	33.6	26.6	20.0	12.0	27.4
Total pension wealth plus Social Security wealth	32.1	71.6	104.2	136.5	171.2	213.3	254.8	334.1	409.7	535.2	226.4
Total pension wealth plus Social Security/total wealth (%)	87.7	79.9	70.5	67.0	64.7	61.7	58.6	59.2	53.9	37.5	52.9

Note: Households with the top and bottom 1 percent of total wealth are excluded.

Table 12.4D Distribution of wealth values from pensions and Social Security by wealth decile, early boomers 51–56 in 2004 (in thousands of 1992 dollars)

Sources of wealth	Source of wealth by indicated total wealth decile										
	1–10	11–20	21–30	31–40	41–50	51–60	61–70	71–80	81–90	91–100	Total
Total wealth	28.8	81.2	139.6	212.4	286.6	377.9	481.3	617.8	843.5	1,517.5	458.8
Total pension wealth	0.9	2.5	12.1	30.0	49.8	85.0	124.3	163.2	232.5	388.3	108.9
Total pension wealth/total wealth (%)	3.1	3.1	8.7	14.1	17.4	22.5	25.8	26.4	27.6	25.6	23.7
Total Social Security wealth	27.2	64.2	91.3	118.9	138.1	148.4	156.5	165.7	181.9	185.7	127.8
Total Social Security wealth/total wealth (%)	94.4	79.1	65.4	56.0	48.2	39.3	32.5	26.8	21.6	12.2	27.9
Total pension wealth plus Social Security wealth	28.1	66.7	103.4	148.9	188.0	233.4	280.8	328.8	414.4	574.1	236.7
Total pension wealth plus Social Security/total wealth (%)	97.6	82.1	74.1	70.1	65.6	61.8	58.3	53.2	49.1	37.8	51.6

Note: Households with the top and bottom 1 percent of total wealth are excluded.

for by pensions increases. This can be seen in row 3, where pension wealth increases as a share of total wealth from the first through the ninth decile. From the third to the ninth decile, the share of total wealth due to pensions plus Social Security falls from 71.9 percent to 53.2 percent, with the share of total wealth accounted for by other assets slowly increasing.

The trend in the distribution of Social Security and pension wealth can be seen in Tables 12.4B to 12.4D, which compare values for the three HRS cohorts ages 51 to 56. From row 5 of Tables 12.4B and 12.4D, the overall share of total wealth due to Social Security has decreased by about 2.4 percentage points. It looks like Social Security accounts for a larger share of total wealth in 2004 than in 1992 for those in the bottom half of the wealth distribution, while accounting for a smaller share of total wealth for those in the top half of the wealth distribution. The share of total wealth due to pensions across the wealth distribution does not differ systematically between cohorts.

Conclusions

Even in the period before the financial crisis of 2008, the press was commonly reporting that there had been a deterioration in retirement saving and retirement preparation. There is no evidence of such deterioration within the HRS data; rather, cohorts approaching retirement age near the end of the period between 1992 and 2004 have maintained their retirement preparedness. Indeed, those 51 to 56 in 2004 had accumulated 12 percent more real wealth in the run-up to retirement than did those who were 51 to 56 in 1992.

Although there were many changes in pensions that supposedly undermined pension saving, pensions represented only a three-tenths of 1 percent smaller share of total wealth in 2004 than in 1992, accounting for 23.7 percent of retirement wealth in 2004. In particular, the wealth position of pension-covered workers was not substantially undermined during the period of partial transition from DB to DC plans.

Gains enjoyed by women are strongly reflected in the gains of both single women and of couple households. Although very wide gaps in total wealth, pension wealth, and Social Security wealth between single men and single women were readily apparent in 1992, these gaps closed rapidly over the next twelve years.

By 2004, households with pensions had about 2.47 times the wealth of households without pensions. The gap in total wealth is much larger than the value of the pensions held by those with benefits and reflects a wide difference in earnings. The difference in total wealth between households with and without pensions has grown wider over the 1992–2004 period, with the ratio of total wealth of households with pensions to total wealth of households without pensions increasing from 1.73 to 2.47. Much of this change appears to be the result of changes in the composition of each group, with pensions spreading to households that would not have had one in earlier years.

Disaggregating the results among those falling into different wealth deciles, it is clear that as the share of total wealth accounted for by Social Security declines as one moves up the wealth distribution, the share of total wealth due to pensions increases. As a result, the share of total wealth due to pensions and Social Security declines very gently as one proceeds up the wealth distribution, with an especially slow rate of decline from the third to the eighth decile of the wealth distribution.

Of course, these data stop before the financial decline of 2008–2009. Nevertheless, we have developed enough information in this chapter to begin to sketch a picture of the likely effects of the financial downturn of 2008–2009 on the assets of the population on the verge of retirement. The final chapter of this book will include a preliminary discussion of that issue.

Appendix 12.1: Differences in the Composition of Wealth between Households with and without Pensions

Tables 12.5A–12.5F describe the distribution of components of wealth among 51- to 56-year-old households. Results are presented separately for households with and without pensions for 1992, 1998, and 2004.

Table 12.5A   Components of mean wealth and wealth for median 10 percent of
wealth-holding households, HRS 51–56 in 1992 (in 1992 dollars),
households with pensions

Source of wealth	Mean		Mean for the median 10% of wealth-holding households	
	Value ($)	% of total	Value ($)	% of total
Total	472,273	100	382,398	100
House value	76,089	16.1	68,173	17.8
Real estate	23,398	5.0	9,304	2.4
Business assets	15,276	3.2	4,972	1.3
Financial assets	41,744	8.8	20,160	5.3
IRA assets	17,519	3.7	10,388	2.7
Social Security	140,756	29.8	153,390	40.1
Pension value	143,086	30.3	102,926	26.9
Net value of vehicles	14,403	3.0	13,085	3.4
No. of observations	2,969			

Notes: At least one member of the household has a pension. Households with the top and
bottom 1 percent of total wealth are excluded.

Table 12.5B   Components of mean wealth and wealth for median 10 percent of
wealth-holding households, HRS 51–56 in 1992 (in 1992 dollars),
households without pensions

Source of wealth	Mean		Mean for the median 10% of wealth-holding households	
	Value ($)	% of total	Value ($)	% of total
Total	273,075	100	142,002	100
House value	63,602	23.3	29,577	20.8
Real estate	31,842	11.7	1,050	0.7
Business assets	36,446	13.3	4,468	3.1
Financial assets	31,520	11.5	5,126	3.6
IRA assets	11,303	4.1	2,311	1.6
Social Security	87,208	31.9	91,360	64.3
Pension value	0	0	0	0
Net value of vehicles	11,153	4.1	8,110	5.7
No. of observations	1,473			

Notes: None of the household members has a pension. Households with the top and bottom
1 percent of total wealth are excluded.

Table 12.5C Components of mean wealth and wealth for median 10 percent of wealth-holding households, war babies 51–56 in 1998 (in 1992 dollars), households with pensions

Source of wealth	Mean Value ($)	Mean % of total	Mean for the median 10% of wealth-holding households Value ($)	Mean for the median 10% of wealth-holding households % of total
Total	508,662	100	409,922	100
House value	72,735	14.3	66,097	16.1
Real estate	22,204	4.4	13,517	3.3
Business assets	16,423	3.2	9,256	2.3
Financial assets	58,644	11.5	30,297	7.4
IRA assets	31,094	6.1	14,623	3.6
Social Security	133,230	26.2	144,104	35.2
Pension value	160,094	31.5	117,472	28.7
Net value of vehicles	14,237	2.8	14,556	3.6
No. of observations	1,818			

Notes: At least one member of the household has a pension. Households with the top and bottom 1 percent of total wealth are excluded.

Table 12.5D Components of mean wealth and wealth for median 10 percent of wealth-holding households, war babies 51–56 in 1998 (in 1992 dollars), households without pensions

Source of wealth	Mean Value ($)	Mean % of total	Mean for the median 10% of wealth-holding households Value ($)	Mean for the median 10% of wealth-holding households % of total
Total	253,720	100	137,975	100
House value	51,286	20.2	38,780	28.1
Real estate	30,432	12.0	1,119	0.8
Business assets	33,835	13.3	336	0.2
Financial assets	27,741	10.9	−725	−0.5
IRA assets	19,632	7.7	2,904	2.1
Social Security	82,596	32.6	90,126	65.3
Pension value	0	0	0	0
Net value of vehicles	8,198	3.2	5,435	3.9
No. of observations	783			

Notes: None of the household members has a pension. Households with the top and bottom 1 percent of total wealth are excluded.

Table 12.5E Components of mean wealth and wealth for median 10 percent of
wealth-holding households, early boomers 51–56 in 2004 (in 1992
dollars), households with pensions

	Mean		Mean for the median 10% of wealth-holding households	
Source of wealth	Value ($)	% of total	Value ($)	% of total
Total	569,463	100	420,308	100
House value	109,217	19.2	82,033	19.5
Real estate	21,378	3.8	11,763	2.8
Business assets	15,380	2.7	3,880	0.9
Financial assets	64,300	11.3	28,539	6.8
IRA assets	33,141	5.8	15,244	3.6
Social Security	151,038	26.5	157,631	37.5
Pension value	161,756	28.4	107,753	25.6
Net value of vehicles	13,251	2.3	13,465	3.2
No. of observations	1,736			

Notes: At least one member of the household has a pension. Households with the top and
bottom 1 percent of total wealth are excluded.

Table 12.5F Components of mean wealth and wealth for median 10 percent of
wealth-holding households, early boomers 51–56 in 2004 (in 1992
dollars), households without pensions

	Mean		Mean for the median 10% of wealth-holding households	
Source of wealth	Value ($)	% of total	Value ($)	% of total
Total	230,964	100	99,180	100
House value	60,596	26.2	18,864	19.0
Real estate	18,340	7.9	0	0
Business assets	19,853	8.6	640	0.6
Financial assets	28,769	12.5	3,657	3.7
IRA assets	15,051	6.5	1,554	1.6
Social Security	80,058	34.7	70,486	71.1
Pension value	0	0	0	0
Net value of vehicles	8,297	3.6	3,979	4.0
No. of observations	972			

Notes: None of the household members has a pension. Households with the top and bottom
1 percent of total wealth are excluded.

13

Conclusions

In this book, we have taken advantage of the scope and depth of the pension data reported by the Health and Retirement Study to paint a rich and detailed picture of the pensions held by the retirement age population. The period from 1992 through 2006 has witnessed significant changes in pensions, and these are reflected in the HRS data. Using complementary information from the HRS, it also has been possible to relate our findings about the pensions held by the HRS population to their other sources of retirement wealth.

Major findings have been summarized at the end of each chapter. Accordingly, by way of final discussion, we provide an overview of the wide range of pension outcomes analyzed in this book and then turn to a few major areas of policy concern. We indicate the relevance of our findings to those policy topics. Following that is a preliminary analysis of the vulnerability of the HRS population to the financial downturn of 2008–2009. We conclude with a word to researchers who would use the HRS pension data.

The HRS Paints an Extraordinarily Rich Picture of Pensions

As we have seen, the Health and Retirement Study is uniquely suited to an analysis of the pensions held by the retirement age population. Participation in pensions, plan type, other plan characteristics, ages of eligibility for benefits, annual and lifetime benefit amounts promised by pensions, account balances, retirement incentives created by pensions, transformation of pensions upon leaving the job, and the value of pensions as a percentage of household wealth are among the many pension outcomes we have analyzed. Because the HRS includes a large number of respondents, it has been possible to compare pension outcomes among important subgroups of the population. A survey design that collects information separately from each spouse has made it possible to include a full picture at the household level while avoiding the kind of reporting error and missing variable problems that arise when only one spouse is interviewed about the pensions and work history of both husband and wife.

The panel design of the HRS both follows respondents over time and collects retrospective information on status before the survey began. With this information, we have been able to trace the accumulation of pensions over each respondent's work life, including information for those who changed jobs as well as for those who remained in the same job over time. For those who have changed jobs, either before participating in the HRS or during the course of the survey, information has been collected on the history of participation in pensions, the course of continued coverage, and the value of pensions from previous and current employment. At the same time, it has been possible to trace changes in pensions by those who remain in the same job and to understand how pensions are transformed upon termination of employment.

Comparisons among cohorts highlight trends in pension offerings, including major transitions such as the trend to defined contribution (DC) plans. Detailed evidence about the transitions can be seen in such outcomes as the narrowing of the gap between job tenure and tenure under the pension, tracing the continuing but as yet incomplete adjustment to the spread of the 401(k) and other DC plan innovations. Data collected from succeeding cohorts also increase our understanding of the different circumstances facing those who entered the labor market only twelve years apart. Differences by cohort in the sources of retirement income and in the role of pensions in financing retirement are well documented by the HRS.

Employer-produced plan descriptions collected for HRS respondents have proven useful for a number of different analyses. Covered workers can describe only imperfectly what benefits would be at alternative ages of retirement, especially along the retirement paths that were available but not chosen by the respondent. As a result, the detailed employer plan descriptions provided by the HRS allow us to document the retirement incentives created by defined benefit (DB) plans, where descriptions of these incentives based on respondent reports would be highly suspect.

Still another advantage of employer data is the help it provides in measuring how well covered workers understand their pensions. Differences in plan type, characteristics, and values between respondent reports and corresponding employer reports are objective indicators of the extent of errors in respondent reporting and respondent misunderstanding of their pensions. Although average values obtained from respondent reports sometimes correspond to comparable outcomes measured from employer data, there are always substantial differences between respondent and firm reports at the level of the individual. These sometimes wide discrepancies between respondent reports and outcomes measured from firm-provided plan descriptions are a direct and useful measure of the level of financial understanding of the respondent. Panel data have provided additional information about reporting errors, allowing us to examine differences in reported plan types by those who claim that their plans have not changed in the panel.

Putting these various dimensions of pensions together, we have been able to paint a broad pension landscape, explore the changes in pensions over time both among cohorts and over the span of the life cycle, examine the pension distribution for individuals as well as households, and at the same time include a great deal of detail that is not available from any other data source.

Some Areas of Policy Concern

In a number of cases, the picture that emerges from the data is quite different from conventional wisdom. Inevitably, the picture is more complex than is normally assumed. This complexity will complicate the job of designing policies aimed at reducing perceived shortcomings in the pension system.

To provide examples, we consider the following four areas of common policy concern.

Participation in Pensions Is Much More Extensive Than Is Commonly Portrayed

Responding to concerns that participation in pensions is inadequate, there have been many proposals for regulations and changes in pension law that would increase pension coverage and encourage more workers to participate in pensions when they are covered. Yet at least among the HRS retirement age population, our results suggest that pension participation is much higher than is commonly recognized.

When estimating participation in pensions, some surveys take account of pensions on current jobs but they do not include pensions from jobs held previously, nor do they mention pensions that have been rolled over or otherwise transformed into a different type of saving. In addition, because household assets are treated collectively, it seems fair to argue that members of the same household are covered by a pension when either spouse is covered. Yet most pension surveys collect information at the level of the individual or individual employee but do not collect the data needed to analyze coverage at the household level. Some of these considerations make a major difference in estimates of coverage.

Consider the shortcoming of focusing only on pensions from a current job. A 50 percent coverage rate is often reported as the share of current employees covered by a pension. Adjusting for the age of HRS respondents, a simple prior would have 60 percent of employees who are approaching retirement age participating in a pension. If the employment rate were 75 percent (in 2004, the employment rate for 51- to 56-year-old men was 79 percent, while for women it was 71 percent), with a 60 percent coverage rate, 45 percent of respondents would be covered by a pension. Such figures generate a concern that more than half the population seems not to be covered by a pension.

In contrast, when we realize that coverage may come not only from current jobs but from jobs held in the past, 56.6 percent of all HRS respondents 51 to 56 in 2004 are covered by a live pension—so they will receive benefits from a current job, are receiving benefits from a pension from a current or previous job already in pay status, or will receive benefits from a plan from a previous job that is scheduled to pay benefits at some future date. Labeling a household as covered if either the husband or the wife has a pension, 65 percent of respondent households with at least one member 51 to 56 in 2004 have at least one member with a live pension. Including those who have rolled over their plans or cashed them out raises the total to 78 percent of respondent households with at least one member 51 to 56 in 2004 having had a pension at some time over his or her work life. Similarly, over 80 percent of respondents have been covered by a pension from their own job at some time in their work life or had a spouse who was covered by a pension. As we have seen, some of the balances may be quite low, with 5 percent of the respondents with a DC account on their current job in 2004 having a balance below $1,000. Nevertheless, the extent of pension coverage is much higher than is recognized in policy discussions about extending pension coverage to a larger share of the population.

Analogous problems arise when pension coverage and share of retirement income from pensions are measured by asking retirees to report what part of their retirement income is due to pensions. As we have seen in Chapter 11, many pensions will have been transformed into some other financial instrument at the time the individual leaves the job. Once retired, this income will not be attributed to a pension, even though it originated from a pension plan.

Another dimension of participation is the number of plans an employee holds. Covered full-time employees average between 1.2 and 1.4 pension plans on their current jobs. Among those age 51 to 56 in 2004, about 21 percent of respondents with a pension from their last job reported having more than one plan from that job. About 17 percent of early boomers with pension coverage reported having more than one plan from their most recent previous pension job.

With four-fifths of the population having been covered by a pension at some time during their lifetime, either from their own work or their spouse's work, any policy to increase coverage should carefully determine the reasons why the remainder is uncovered. Among those without a pension, a significant fraction will have concluded that Social Security provides an adequate retirement income and therefore will not wish to participate in a pension. This will be especially true for those whose earnings are below average. For example, among those in the second wealth decile in 2004, roughly four-fifths of the household's wealth is due to Social Security. For those with modest earnings, the replacement rate may be deemed by the family to be adequate.

Defined Contribution Plans Remain Immature for the HRS Retirement Age Population

A clear finding in HRS data is that the transition to DC plans is incomplete.[1] Yet some policy analysts on both sides of the debate ignore that evidence when marshalling their arguments as to whether the trend to DC plans is a good thing or a bad thing and whether this trend should be encouraged or discouraged by policy intervention.

Until the recent downturn in the stock market, a topic we will return to later, the transition to DC plans has not had a major effect on the adequacy of benefits held by the current population approaching retirement age. In 2004, pensions accounted for 23.7 percent of the retirement wealth of all HRS households ages 51 to 56. In 1992 the comparable figure was 24.0 percent. Adding pension wealth from jobs held in the past to those currently held, the total value of all pensions among 51- to 56-year-old households with pensions in 2004 is $161,756 (in 1992 dollars and excluding the top 1 percent of wealth holding households), accounting for 28.4 percent of the total wealth of households with pensions.

To be sure, by 2004 a much larger share of pension wealth was held in defined contribution (DC) plans than in the past. Nevertheless, DB plans still accounted for 63 percent of the pension wealth of the retirement age population.

HRS data suggest a number of reasons for the continuing importance of DB plans within the retirement age population. Most important, DB pensions are concentrated in union, large-firm, and public sector employment, where because of seniority rules, older workers hold a disproportionate share of the jobs; younger workers tend to hold different jobs with employers that are more likely to offer defined contribution plans. That is, the trend to DC plans has not been manifested by the simple replacement of DB plans with DC plans. Rather, employment in jobs offering DB plans is declining, and jobs offering DB plans are much more likely to be held by older workers. This further complicates any policy-related arguments that pretend there has been some simple substitution of DC for DB plans.

Consider, for example, an argument against DC plans based on evidence that current retirees seem to have inadequate benefits from their (currently immature) DC plans. Any such argument that ignores the continuing role of DB plans and the immaturity of DC plans for the current generation of retirees would be misplaced. Rather than cite any evidence based on current or recent retirees, the proper grounds for considering how the trend to DC plans affects retirement adequacy is how that trend affects benefits in the long run.[2]

Some would promote DC plans on the grounds that—the immaturity of these plans notwithstanding—they are primarily responsible for the turn-around in the trend to earlier retirement already observed in the data, and as widely recognized, public policy should promote an increase in the retirement age. Many forces, including changes in Social Security incentives, trends to multiearner families, and early exit into the disability program, are shaping trends in retirement behavior for older members of the population. One thing is certain. To the extent that retiree behavior is shaped by pensions, the retirement decisions of those who have recently reached retirement age are still heavily influenced by incentives in their DB plans. Indeed, one can expect DB plans to continue to influence retirement behavior for a number of years to come. Thus it will be incumbent on the HRS to continue to collect detailed data indicating the value and incentives created by defined benefit plans if policy makers are to understand the influence of the different forces shaping retirement behavior.

More generally, before designing policies that would encourage adoption of one plan type or another, advocates for policies that would influence plan type need to understand the story that the HRS data have to tell.

Women's Pensions Are Improving Rapidly

There has been continuing concern with pensions held by women. A first concern is with the adequacy of women's pensions from their own work, including both pension coverage and plan values resulting from employment the woman herself has held. A second concern is with spouse or survivor benefits. Divorce or death of a spouse propel many older women into poverty. This issue is one of property rights within the family and has been addressed through legislation.[3]

Our analysis has confirmed that in the early years of the HRS, women's pensions due to their own labor lagged well behind those of men. But over the twelve years between 1992 and 2004, although women's pensions have not achieved parity with those of men, gains in coverage and plan value are closing the gap between men's and women's pensions.

Over the 1992–2004 period, participation in pensions by women respondents to the HRS, ages 51 to 56, increased from 35.8 percent to 43.4 percent, an increase of 21 percent. Participation by men stayed roughly the same, declining from 50.9 percent of all male respondents to 50.4 percent over the period. The lower employment rate of women is a major reason for the continuing gap between the pensions held by male and female respondents to the HRS. Seventy-four percent of male respondents to the HRS but only 58 percent of female respondents report working full time. Among employed 51- to 56-year-olds and those working full time, there is no gap in pension coverage on current jobs and only a modest gap in terms of pension coverage from past employment.

Between 1992 and 2004, participation in pensions by employed women increased from 55 percent to 61 percent, while increasing among employed men from 61 percent to 63 percent. Similarly, participation in a pension was on a par for men and women who worked full time, with 66 percent of full-time men and 68 percent of full-time women participating in a pension. Looking back over respondent work histories, in 2004, among those 51 to 56 years of age, 73.1 percent of men and 63.1 percent of women had been covered by a pension on a current or previously held job. Coverage for men had declined from 75.2 percent in 1992, while coverage for women had increased from 50.8 percent in 1992, representing a rise of over 24 percent.

The trend toward DC plans had a similar impact on the types of pensions held by men and women. By 2004, men and women had very similar distributions of plan type. In 1992, 70 percent of men 51 to 56 years old with a pension had a DB plan, compared with 64 percent of women. By 2004, 51 percent of men and 48 percent of women had a DB plan. Sixty percent of men had a DC plan in 1992, while 54 percent of women had a DC plan that same year. By 2004, 75 percent of men and 69 percent of women had a DC plan.

Although differences between men and women in plan type and in age of retirement are relatively minor, differences in plan values are still a major consideration. While rising plan values for women have closed the gap with men, especially in terms of the value of DB plans, DC plans held by women remain less valuable than DC plans held by men.

Yearly benefits expected by 51- to 56-year-old employed men with DB plans hardly changed between 1992 and 2004. In 1992, expected benefits were $23,800 per year, slightly more than the value in constant (1992) dollars stated in 2004 of $22,200. In contrast, among 51- to 56-year-old employed women, expected yearly benefits from DB plans increased from $12,900 in 1992 to $20,300 in 2004. Similarly, the present value of DB payments from the most important DB plan remained roughly constant over time for 51- to 56-year-old fully employed men. In 1992, the value was $165,300; by 2004, the value was $170,500. In contrast, the present value of expected DB benefits increased by more than 50 percent for 51- to 56-year-old employed women, from $97,800 in 1992 to $147,400 in 2004. Thus the ratio of the present values of expected DB benefits of women to men increased from 59 percent in 1992 to 86 percent in 2004.

The gap in DC plan values between men and women has been much slower to close. In 1992, the value of DC plans held by full-time working men on current jobs (in 1992 dollars) was $58,700. By 2004, the value, in 1992 dollars, had increased by 28 percent to $75,200. The corresponding balances for women in 1992 and 2004 were $21,800 and $48,100, respectively. While DC balances held by women increased by 120 percent, they continue to lag behind the DC plan balances in plans covering men, with women's DC plan balances amounting to 64 percent of those of men.

Given the rapid progress in women's pensions, it is not surprising that almost the entire growth in the value of real pensions held by households with a respondent 51 to 56 is due to women. The value of total household pensions due to men 51 to 56 years old declined in constant 1992 dollars from $118,560 to $110,537. In contrast, the value of total household pensions due to women increased from $31,194 to $50,957. This increased the share of household pensions due to women from 21 percent in 1992 to 32 percent in 2004.

Contributing to the narrowing of the gap in pension wealth between men and women, jobs in the public sector have increased for women. Thirty-six percent of jobs with pensions held by women are in the public sector, whereas 28 percent of jobs with pensions held by men are in public sector employment.

Despite the Trend to DC Plans, There Is Only Limited Vulnerability of the Retirement Age Population to the Stock Market Decline

It is possible to use the data on the sources of total wealth in 2006, together with information on the share of IRAs invested in stocks in 2006, the value of stocks held directly in the respondent's financial portfolio in that year, and the share of DC wealth from current jobs that is held in stocks, to estimate the potential vulnerability of the retirement age population to the stock market decline of 2008–2009.[4]

The components of household wealth in 2006 are reported in Table 13.1. For purposes of comparison with our findings in Chapter 12, these results are reported in 1992 dollars. To reduce measurement error, the table eliminates the highest and lowest 1 percent of wealth-holding households from the sample.

In 2006, 34.9 percent of total pension wealth (41,863/119,879) was held in DC accounts. Since data are not available on the share of DC pensions from past employment held in stocks, we use the fraction of current DC accounts that are held in stocks as an approximation. Among those with a DC pension on their current job, about 61.7 percent of plan balances are in stocks (18,662/30,235). Altogether in 2006, pensions account for 23.0 percent of total wealth (119,879/521,028). As a result of stockholdings in IRAs, direct stockholdings, and DC plans held in stocks (DC plans from both current and previous jobs), in 2006 $79,169 was held in stocks. This amounts to 15.2 percent of total assets. If the stock market declines by one-third from peak to trough and does not recover for some time, 5.1 percent of total wealth would be lost. Apparently, the trend to defined contribution plans combined with the fall in the stock market will not affect the wealth holdings of the retirement age population to an extent that would be life changing.

Table 13.1   Components of wealth and wealth for all households and median 10
             percent of wealth-holding households, respondents ages 53–58 in 2006
             (in 1992 dollars)

Source of wealth	Mean		Mean for the median 10% of wealth-holding households	
	Value ($)	% of total	Value ($)	% of total
Total	521,028	100	364,811	100
House value	114,872	22.0	81,454	22.3
Real estate	24,593	4.7	11,894	3.3
Business assets	27,040	5.2	5,722	1.6
Financial assets	51,056	9.8	18,399	5.0
Net value of vehicles	12,100	2.3	11,874	3.3
Social Security	135,979	26.1	146,448	40.1
Pension value	119,879	23.0	71,917	19.7
DB value	78,016	15.0	50,320	13.8
DC value	41,863	8.0	21,596	5.9
Current DC balances	30,235	5.8	16,315	4.5
Current DC in stocks	18,662	3.6	10,924	3.0
IRA assets	35,510	6.8	17,104	4.7
IRA in stocks value	26,122	5.0	12,373	3.4
Direct stockholdings	26,687	5.1	6,532	1.8
IRA plus stockholdings plus DC in stocks	79,169	15.2	33,535	9.2
Pension plus Social Security	255,857	49.1	218,364	59.9
Number of observations	2,493			

Note: Households with top and bottom 1 percent of total wealth are excluded.

The reduction in total wealth from the stock market decline is relatively small because the share of total wealth held in stocks is so limited. Older workers rely on other components of retirement wealth. The effect is to have cushioned the early boomer cohort against the financial downturn. At the top of the list, Social Security accounts for 26.1 percent of total retirement wealth. With a quarter of retirement wealth in the form of Social Security, a form that is not at all affected by the financial decline, 51- to 56-year-old households enjoyed a substantial cushion against the financial downturn.

The continuing importance of defined benefit plans also cushions the retirement assets of the retirement age population against the direct effects of an asset decline brought about by a stock market fall. Although defined benefit plans are reacting to the financial downturn, the reaction will be slower than the immediate decline in equity prices. Moreover, those close to retirement age will have become entitled to a good part of their benefits, and firms that do not go through bankruptcy will be unable to take most of those benefits away. In addition, a large part of the benefits that private sector workers are entitled to is covered by government insurance. As a result, the influence of DB plans will continue to stabilize the total size of the portfolio held by the retirement age population.

Altogether, our findings suggest that most of the retirement age population will be able to weather the recent financial downturn without suffering a very large change in their standard of living. To be sure, there will be many exceptions, with some individuals, especially the wealthiest, experiencing very sharp drops in their retirement assets. However, on average the losses will be manageable.

There are, of course, other challenges arising for the retirement age population from the recession. With the bursting of the housing bubble, assets held in the form of a house have declined in value. A 20 percent decline in the value of the average house amounts to a loss of 4.4 percent of total retirement wealth $(0.2 \times 114,872/521,028)$. Those who borrowed heavily on their homes are particularly vulnerable. However, many in the retirement age population have paid off a large share of their mortgage, have been in their residence for many years, and will not sell their homes until forced to do so in later years by health problems or the loss of a spouse. These individuals will be less vulnerable to the recent decline in house values and will have a number of years to recover.

Job loss also presents a major challenge to the retirement age population. With wide layoffs, seniority does not provide as much protection as it does in more stable times. Seniors who have lost a long-term job have great difficulty returning to the labor market at or near the wage they were earning on a job they held for many years. Even those who have not yet left a long-term job have only a limited scope for adjusting to an unexpected decline in the value of pensions and other retirement assets.

All of these factors considered, the decline in the stock market will have less of a direct effect on the wealth of those on the cusp of retiring than is often suggested. (For further analysis, see Gustman, Steinmeier, and Tabatabai, forthcoming.)

A Word to Pension Data Users

We would like to end with a word to pension data users. HRS pension data are readily available to researchers. Detailed software has been constructed to encourage the use of employer-provided pension plan descriptions. Nevertheless, the HRS pension data still require considerable effort to use. Tracing the pensions through the waves of the survey, keeping track of dormant or previous pensions, imputing missing pension variables or variables required to evaluate pensions, and weighting the observations appropriately when conducting analyses among cohorts of different sizes are all complex and time-consuming tasks. An important aim of this book and the accompanying data files is to make the HRS pension data easier to use and thereby to encourage their use. We hope our results will provide benchmarks for those who would undertake these complex tasks themselves. It always helps to have road signs along the way.

We also hope that by making HRS pension data easier to use, they will receive even more use in policy studies, in emerging areas of behavioral research, and perhaps even in personal financial advising. Moreover, as seen in Chapter 12 and in this final chapter, when studying household wealth, researchers who ignore pension and Social Security wealth do so at their own peril. With measures of pension and Social Security wealth available on the HRS Web site, there is no longer an excuse to represent pensions by measures of coverage or plan type alone when studying these important issues, or to count only the value of DC plans while ignoring DB plans. Nor can one rely only on measures of liquid assets or other incomplete measures of household wealth and still obtain an accurate picture of the consequences of events unfolding in the economy or of proposed policies meant to affect saving, retirement, or related outcomes.

This book has used the Health and Retirement Study to examine in considerable depth just one of the subjects included in this important survey, pensions of our older population. The HRS includes detailed information on many other economic outcomes, including work, earnings, and retirement. As the most recent and comprehensive data available on the U.S. population over age 50, it also includes in-depth descriptions of health status, its determinants and consequences, psychological well-being, family relationships, living arrangements, and complex financial and nonfinancial linkages within and between generations. Thus the HRS is an important resource not just for economists but for the medical community, gerontologists, sociologists, demographers, and other behavioral analysts concerned with the older population. Today the HRS covers the generations immediately preceding the baby boomers as well as the oldest members of the baby boom generation. With the wave of respondents to be added in 2010, it will incorporate the boomers born in the middle of that generation. The analyses that have been and will be conducted with the HRS provide a solid foundation for those designing the policies that affect the older members of our population. They also provide the opportunity for researchers to conduct the kind of in-depth analysis of the health and welfare of the U.S. population over the age of 50 that cannot be undertaken with any other data source.

Appendix: Constructed Files

In the course of our work for the Health and Retirement Study we have created a number of data files that have been made available to users of the survey. This appendix briefly describes four of those files.[1] They are available on the HRS Web site (hrson line.isr.umich.edu). In addition, our intention upon publication of this book is to make the data files underlying each of the tables in the book available to qualified users.[2]

Skipped (Carry Forward) Variable Files

When a worker continues with the same employer, and especially if s/he continues in the same job, skip patterns in the HRS questionnaire are based on the assumption that some job-related variables have not changed (in order to save the time needed to re-ask them). For others who may have changed jobs since Wave 1, the new information is collected when they are first interviewed after starting the new job. For example, if a respondent changed jobs after Wave 2 and before Wave 3, the details of his/her new employment was collected in Wave 3. The schedule is to ask every fourth wave of those who remained on the same job about their industry, job title, occupation, when the respondent started this type of work, certain benefits, job responsibilities, firm size at location and all locations, union or government employment, required education, and coverage by FICA, and to request a list of job requirements.

In order to reduce the complexity that skip patterns create for users, we have created files that "carry forward" these skipped variables from the wave when the relevant question was last asked. The result is a rectangular array of data that provides observations for the skipped variables. These carry forward variables are not only helpful in updating the full array of labor market outcomes by wave, but they are important for evaluating pensions. Thus pension wealth calculations may make use of a number of the carry forward variables.

In addition to carrying forward the skipped values, we have tried to unify the code frames when possible. The code frames for some of the questions are different in different waves. For some questions different codes may stand for the same response, and for others the same code may have a different meaning in different waves. An example of different codes representing the same response is the "firm size at all locations" question. In this question the response indicating "only one location" is represented by different codes depending on the survey year. It is 999,995 in Wave 1, 99,997 in Wave 2, 9,999,995 in Wave 3, and 9,999,995 in Wave 4. The unification of this code involves converting those codes to "9,999,995," designating "only one location" for all waves.

As an example of a question where the same code has a different meaning in different waves, consider the question of "the number of years of education needed for the job." In this question the code "96" indicates "no education needed" in Wave 2 but "Missing/Inap" in Wave 1. The unification of this code involves converting the code "96" in Wave 1 to "blank" for "Missing/Inap" and in Wave 2 to "0" for "no education needed" responses.

Respondents Pension Tracker Data File

In each wave, this file identifies respondents with a pension plan and also pensions from all reported jobs since the respondent's first interview. The pension coverage information from all previous interview waves is brought forward to subsequent interview waves. There is one data file for each wave. At the same time, information gathered about dormant pensions in the old pension sequence is taken backward to earlier waves to identify those plans that were cashed out before a current wave. Those plans that were cashed out are excluded from the list of live pension plans in that wave and later waves. Each file includes variables indicating pension coverage from each job, identified by the job on which the pension is or was held, and the number of pension plans from current and previous employment. Each data file also includes an index identifying each of the previous pension plans that are dormant (i.e., not in pay status, not cashed out, rolled over, converted to an annuity, or lost), the number of pension plans from the current job, the total number of previous pension plans through a current interview date, and the number of dormant pension plans that a respondent is entitled to (has active claim on) as of that interview date.

There is also a flag variable constructed to indicate the source of each of those plans (i.e., each plan is represented by a flag indicating if that plan is from a job): for example, in the H section of Wave 1, the FB section of Wave 2, or a current job in Wave 5. There are also two additional variables in each wave: total number of pension plans and total number of live pension plans that a respondent has reported since being first interviewed.

Employer Pension Tracker File

This file identifies employees with self-reported pension coverage and matched summary plan descriptions. This data file also contains indices indicating whether respondents had pension coverage in indicated years from current, last, and/or previous jobs; whether respondents worked in an employment with twenty-five or more employees at all locations; and whether respondents' employer contact information was available. The file identifies the sources of SPDs (the employer survey, DoL files, Web search, 5500 data, experiment Y, or its extension). Other indices include whether the respondents' employer was interviewed and whether matched plans were obtained through that interview for the respondent. The file also contains HHID (household identifier), PN (person number), HHIDPN (household identifier person number), ASUBHH (1992 sub-household identifier), and FSUBHH (1998 sub-household identifier). These identifiers are used for merging with other HRS data files. The information in this file is useful for those who have access to the (restricted) SPD files, as well as for those who are deciding whether to request access to these files.

Imputations for Pension-Related Variables

Where necessary to evaluate pensions, several pension-related variables from current, last, and previous jobs are imputed. In addition, measures of account balances and pension wealth from DB plans have been imputed where the aim is to obtain population-relevant estimates.

Various methods are used to impute pension-related variables. The choice of method depends in part on the availability of covariates. Methods used include a mixed method when a large sample is available. Here a multiple regression is estimated for observations where the dependent variable is available, with covariates such as firm size, industry, union, and personal characteristics. The regression is then used to predict the value of the dependent variable for all observations, including when the respondent answered "don't know" or refused to answer, and those observations with missing values. The predicted dependent variable is in turn used to sort the observations. Missing variables are then replaced with values from the preceding adjacent observation. Where the samples are small and covariates are not available, imputation is based on a hot-decking method, or if the sample is small enough or the structure of the questionnaire requires, by simple replacement. The hot-decking procedure involves assigning a random number to each of the cases, then sorting the data by the random number in descending order, and finally replacing a missing value by the neighboring observed value.

Imputed variables include pension coverage, number of pension plans, type of pension plan, account balances for type both (DC balances when a person has both plan types), account balances for type DC only, expected age of retirement, and present values of DB benefits at expected age of retirement. Dispositions of DB, DC, or both types of plans are imputed, as are the amounts of cash settlement and the amounts of any rollover. There is a flag constructed for each of the imputed variables indicating cases that have imputations.

Notes

1. Introduction

1. There is an extensive literature discussing the problems facing Social Security. See the report of the President's Commission (President's Commission to Strengthen Social Security, 2001), the Report of the Trustees (U.S. Social Security Administration, 2003, and reports issued annually), and numerous academic studies such as the series of volumes edited by Martin Feldstein and his colleagues at the National Bureau of Economic Research (Feldstein, 1998; Feldstein and Liebman, 2002; Campbell and Feldstein, 2001). See also Schieber and Shoven (1999) and Diamond and Orszag (2004), among many others.

   Medicare and supplementary health insurance are an important, but sometimes ignored, fourth leg of the stool. Skinner (2007) discusses the uncertainty for income security in retirement due to potential health expenditures as a retiree. The baby boomers' welfare in retirement will also depend on their housing wealth and other saving, as well as on various types of government payments and support from family members.

2. Given the similarity of the problems created by the aging populations of many countries across the globe, the HRS has become a model for surveys adopted in England (ELSA, English Longitudinal Study of Aging), the European Union (SHARE, Survey of Health, Aging and Retirement in Europe), Mexico, South Korea, China, India, and New Zealand. A detailed description of the HRS and relevant data files derived from the HRS and fielded in other countries can be found at http://hrsonline.isr.umich.edu.

3. In addition, cohorts were added to include those who were older than 61 in 1992 so that currently the HRS is representative of the U.S. population over the age of 50. However, only limited information is provided on the pensions of the members of those older cohorts, which is why we focus only on those born in 1931 and later.

4. Chapter 9 presents calculations of pension wealth in the HRS, the present value of the benefits that will accrue to holders of defined benefit plans.

5. Vesting may be immediate (after a specified waiting period) or gradual. If benefits are not vested in the years after coverage begins, full and immediate vesting (cliff vesting) is required under law after five years of coverage. Graded vesting under a schedule where the person owns an increasing share of the pension with time on the job is also permitted. Until benefits are vested, the benefit is zero. It then sharply increases in the year of vesting.

6. For a summary of the literature that preceded the Health and Retirement Study, see Gustman and Juster (1996). Among the studies based on the Health and Retirement Study that include pensions and Social Security as part of wealth, see Moore and Mitchell (2000); Gustman and Steinmeier (1999b); Engen, Gale, and Uccello (2004); and Scholz, Seshadri, and Khitatrakun (2006).

7. A small panel data set of pensions could be created by combining the 1983 and 1989 Surveys of Consumer Finances. See Gustman and Steinmeier (1999a).

8. To be sure, it was possible to approximate incentives from pensions in a panel study. For example, Gustman and Steinmeier (1986a, 1986b) imputed pension incentives by merging information from the Retirement History Study, including respondent reports of when they would be eligible for early retirement, with reports of pension incentives by industry obtained from separate surveys of firms conducted by the Urban Institute.

9. These studies ask respondents, in differing detail, for the many plan characteristics required to evaluate their pensions while also asking respondents for the name and address of their employer. The employer information is then used to secure a detailed description of the pension plan offered by the respondent's employer. Gustman and Steinmeier (1989, 2000a), for example, describe the reward structures created by the pensions covering respondents to the Survey of Consumer Finances, the Health and Retirement Study, and the National Longitudinal Survey of Mature Women.

10. Note that the coverage rates for full-time employees in Figure 1.1 do not include the self-employed. In contrast, Table 6.1, which provides a more detailed description of coverage rates, does include the self-employed.

11. One other requirement of a cash balance plan may be noted. Covered workers must be offered the option of receiving benefits in the form of an annuity. That is not required of a defined contribution plan.

12. Beginning with the 2008 wave of the HRS, additional criteria are used to identify plan type. Also beginning with the 2008 wave, many fewer questions are conditioned on reported plan type.

2. Theories Explaining Pensions

1. Gustman, Mitchell, and Steinmeier (1994) and Parsons (1996) review the pension literature from the 1970s through the early 1990s.
2. Gustman and Steinmeier (1999b) find very little substitution between pensions and nonpension, non–Social Security wealth. Roughly speaking, those with more generous pension plans do not reduce their saving in other forms to compensate for the increase in retirement saving in the form of the pension. Other studies find significant substitution of pensions for saving only among those with higher levels of income and/or education.

   There are a number of possible explanations. Those who highly value current over future consumption (those who have a high time preference rate) may find pensions to be an imperfect substitute for wealth in hand. Alternatively, some have attributed the presence of pensions throughout the firm to demands for pensions by middle management, who indeed wish to take advantage of the tax benefits pensions provide. To meet pension discrimination rules requiring balanced participation by low- as well as high-earning employees, firms may introduce incentives for lower wage workers to participate in pensions. In that case, low wage workers (and those with high time preference rates) may be encouraged, through matching provisions or other rewards, to hold a level of pensions that, together with their Social Security, exceeds in value their total desired saving. Higher pensions would not reduce retirement saving if other retirement saving were already reduced to low levels. There may be some nonpension, non–Social Security saving for liquidity and precautionary purposes, but after generous pension incentives are introduced, there may be no need for additional retirement saving.

   Another explanation has been advanced to explain the finding that pensions are imperfect substitutes for other forms of saving. Pensions may lead workers to become aware of a basic need for retirement saving (Cagan, 1965). This would lead to a positive association between pensions and other forms of saving. Still another explanation for the lack of association between pensions and other forms of retirement saving has to do with differences in worker preferences for retirement. Feldstein (1974) argues that those with pensions intend to retire earlier than do those without. This induces those with pensions to increase saving in preparation for retirement relative to a person of the same age who does not have a pension and will be retiring at a later age.
3. The demand for annuities is relatively weak, and this remains a puzzle. In attempting to explain this phenomenon, Brown et al. (2008) argue that consumers evaluate annuities using an "investment frame" that focuses on risk and return, rather than using a consumption frame that considers the consequences of an annuity for lifetime consumption. That is, when consumers focus only on the evaluation of risk and reward from purchasing an annuity and ignore the value of consumption smoothing, they find the risk of annuities to be high

relative to the returns and so choose not to purchase annuities. For evaluations of other theories attempting to explain the weak demand for annuities, see Brown (2007).

4. Relevant empirical studies include Burkhauser (1979), Barnow and Ehrenberg (1979), Bulow (1981, 1982), Kotlikoff and Smith (1983), Blinder (1981), Gordon and Blinder (1980), Kotlikoff and Wise (1985, 1987), Ippolito (1986), and Gustman and Steinmeier (1989).

5. Burkhauser (1979), Fields and Mitchell (1984), Stock and Wise (1990a, 1990b), and Lumsdaine, Stock, and Wise (1990, 1992, 1994). This literature is summarized in Quinn, Burkhauser, and Meyers (1990) and Lumsdaine and Mitchell (1999).

6. It is sometimes argued that workers self-select into particular jobs based on the early retirement age offered by the plan. If true, this phenomenon would be of interest because statistical studies of retirement showing that retirement outcomes are related to pension plan features such as the early retirement age might have the causality backward. Those who want to retire early might select jobs offering an early retirement age. However, we are skeptical of an argument that selection into jobs is made on the basis of a pension early retirement age. We do not think this is a very important phenomenon, at least not for the HRS cohorts. A number of considerations have led to our skepticism.

The first argument against employment selection based on pension early retirement age is that members of the HRS cohort experienced very large changes in early retirement age between their ages of hire and retirement. Even though those covered by pensions were unlikely to change their jobs, in the end the early retirement age observed for a plan is very different from the early retirement age specified at the time of hire. More important, at the time the members of the HRS selected their long-term jobs, the early retirement ages mandated by their plans were not only much higher than they are today but much less variable than the ages in place when the employees finally did retire. Since the early retirement age was not an important plan feature when they joined the firm, and there was not much choice regarding early retirement age, they would not have paid much attention to it at the time. They certainly would not have considered the early retirement age to be an important factor shaping their choice of employment at a young age.

Empirically, we observe a very large decline in early and normal retirement ages over the period from the late 1960s through the early 1980s. This is the same period that members of the HRS cohort would have been employed in their long-term jobs, the ones offering pensions. It is the time when rules of 75, ten-year vesting, and explicit reductions in early retirement age were widely adopted. For example, 40 percent of the sample of workers from the Retirement History Study reported that they would qualify for early retirement benefits by age 60; whereas three-fourths of those with pensions in the 1983 Survey of

Consumer Finances reported qualifying for early retirement benefits by age 60. Anderson, Gustman, and Steinmeier (1999) present a variety of evidence documenting the changes in plan rules over this period and their effects on retirement.

A second argument has to do with the role of rents and resulting queues for high-wage jobs in shaping employment patterns. The important fact to remember for members of the HRS cohort is that pensions were commonly offered on jobs in which a rent was an important part of compensation (Ellwood, 1985). Here a rent, which may also be paid to enhance productivity or reduce hiring or supervision costs, is defined as the difference between the wage on the job and in the next best alternative available to the worker. It is much less likely that occupational choice was determined by pension plan features than by salary differentials (Gustman and Steinmeier, 1993b). It is even less likely that second-order features of the pension, such as the expected early retirement age offered by the pension at the time of initial job selection, shaped occupational choice.

Finally, the findings on imperfect knowledge of pensions in Chapter 7 provide convincing evidence that HRS respondents and members of neighboring cohorts had very little idea of the (misleading) early retirement date at the time they joined the firm. The original HRS cohort had long job tenure and took jobs offering pensions many years before they would be eligible for retirement. People in their twenties and thirties were largely unaware of pension benefits, let alone ages of early retirement. Thus they were unlikely to be motivated to accept a job decades before their retirement on the basis of an early retirement age that they were unlikely to understand.

To be sure, there are some jobs where selection based on early retirement age is probably important. The military and police and fire professions come to mind. But compared with the overall stock of union and large firm workers in the HRS, this must be a minor phenomenon.

7. See also Hutchens (1987) on delayed payment contracts.

8. This explanation carries more force when applied to those who are nearing retirement age than for those who are many years away from retiring. It is clear that those who have only a few years until they qualify for early retirement benefits will pay a heavy penalty if they leave a firm offering a defined benefit plan before qualifying. However, pensions do not create a sufficiently large penalty to keep those in their thirties, or even in their forties, from leaving the firm. It is easy to offset the cost to a younger worker of the foregone pension benefits that would otherwise accrue at older ages had the person remained at the job. All it takes is a modest raise in pay on the new job (Gustman and Steinmeier, 1993b, 1995).

9. In a test of the implicit pension contract story, Stern and Todd (2000) find that during the time mandatory retirement provisions were legal, employers of half

the labor force did not adopt mandatory retirement. This is a puzzling finding if defined benefit pensions were adopted to facilitate retirement by workers who were covered by an implicit employment contract. Stern and Todd also contend that workers who are subject to mandatory retirement should be less likely to retire early than those who are not. Again this prediction is not consistent with the data.

10. Munnell and Soto (2007b) and Munnell et al. (2008) provide data on recent trends in plan type in the state and local government sector.

11. Banks, Blundell, and Tanner (1998), Bernheim, Skinner, and Weinberg (2001), and others argue that there is a sharp drop-off in consumption after retirement. Hurd and Rohwedder (2008a) argue that with the exception of those with very low wealth, once better and more comprehensive consumption data are used, namely, from the Health and Retirement Study, there is only a 5 or 6 percent drop in consumption after retirement, about what one would expect in response to a cessation of work-related expenditures or as a result of other factors consistent with an extended life cycle model.

3. Employment and Retirement in the Health and Retirement Study

1. Because the HRS does not include individuals under the age of 50, it cannot be used to study how those who are decades away from retiring are faring in a world of changing pensions. (For recent studies, see Poterba, Venti, and Wise, 2007a, 2007b, 2008). The pensions held by the population over the age of 50 differ in a variety of ways from the pensions held by those under the age of 50. For example, those over age 50 are more likely to be employed in older industries and thus are more likely to have a defined benefit plan than are younger workers.

2. A number of our recent studies use HRS pension data to determine how pensions affect retirement. See, for example, Gustman and Steinmeier (2004a, 2005b, 2008).

3. A special edition of the *Journal of Human Resources* edited by Juster and Suzman (1995) describes the many features of the HRS and the characteristics of the initial HRS cohort in the first year of the survey.

4. Two cohorts of older persons were added to the HRS. The Aging and Health Dynamics (AHEAD) cohort includes those age 70 or older in 1992, while the Children of the Depression (CODA) cohort includes those born from 1924 to 1930. AHEAD data were first collected in 1993; CODA data were first collected in 1998.

5. The constructed age is adjusted by the difference between the month of the interview and the birth month. If the interview month is at least 6 months later than the birth month, the age is increased by one year. If the birth month is later than the interview month by at least six months, the age is reduced by one year.

6. When spouses who were older than age 61 or younger than age 51 are removed from the original sample, in 1992, there were 9,623 respondents from the ages of 51 to 61 and 5,449 from the ages of 51 to 56. In 1998, there were 3,126 respondents aged 51–56. In 2004, 3,326 respondents were ages 51 to 56. Overlap cases are included with the 1992 data. Any respondent ages 51 to 56 in 1998 or 2004 is considered to be a member of the war baby or early boomer cohort, respectively. To be included, a respondent must have undergone a core interview.

7. The differences in the rates at which those falling within the specified age range were sampled in their base years make it necessary to weight the results when reporting outcomes for those falling within a particular age range. Thus the cohort in 1998 of those born from 1942 to 1947 contains a disproportionate number of women. The extra women are from the out of age range group in the HRS cohort.

8. This sampling scheme also means that some households will belong to two cohorts. Thus a household with one member who is born from 1931 to 1941 and a second member born from 1942 to 1947 will be a part of both the HRS cohort and the war baby cohort. As a result, a researcher who wants to include all those who were born from say 1941 to 1947 in a description of an outcome for the war babies cohort will have to be careful to include those who entered the survey in different years.

9. The screener samples for the HRS and war baby cohorts were undertaken in 1992, while the screener sample for the early boomers is from 2004. As a consequence, members of different cohorts are subject to attrition for different periods of time. Weighting is meant to deal with this problem by aligning the composition of the HRS with the composition of the CPS. Some population characteristics are not, however, available on the CPS.

   Although there is some attrition from each wave of the survey, a number of those persons who skip a wave reappear. As a result, Kapteyn et al. (2006) find little evidence in cross-sections that the likelihood of attrition is systematically related to a variety of demographic measures in the HRS.

10. Full-time individuals are those who are working at least 30 hours per week and 1,560 hours per year. Individuals who are working at least 100 hours per year but no more than 25 hours per week or 1,250 hours per year are counted as part time, and individuals not doing any work at all are counted as fully retired. Individuals who fall between full time and part time are classified on the basis of self-reports of their retirement status.

11. HRS data for men in their early sixties are not comparable across years. In 1992, the oldest age for the age-eligible sample was 61, while in later years those ages 62–64 are also included in the category. Thus the employment-population ratio is not shown for men in their early sixties in 1992.

12. On average, covered full-time employees have between 1.2 and 1.4 pension plans at their current job. (Anyone who reports zero as the number of plans, even though having indicated pension coverage, is excluded from this sample.)

13. Hurd and Rohwedder (2008c) suggest that the flow of workers in their early fifties into retirement may not have increased. Rather an increase in disability roles among those of younger age may leave fewer 50-year-olds in the labor force.

4. Pension Data in the Health and Retirement Study

1. During Wave 1 to Wave 4 interviews, respondents were asked about the details of only one pension plan from any previous or last job. In Wave 5, this number was increased to up to three plans and in Wave 6 to up to four plans.

2. The set of questions about old pension plans was asked in the assets and income section of the survey in 1996 and 1998. It was moved to the employment section in 2000.

3. In 1992, pensions were collected from the headquarters of the firm, while in 1998 and 2004, pensions were collected at the plant level. This may be a source of discrepancy between the employer-provided plan descriptions collected in different years.

4. There are twenty-two respondents with coded plan descriptions who did not report pension coverage at their current employment.

5. Out of this group, thirty-seven cases did not report pension coverage in the core survey. Also, three cases who were not interviewed in 1998 had coded plans. They are excluded from the sample. There are forty-five cases with a coded plan, but their firm size is missing or smaller than twenty-five employees. They are included in the sample.

6. The pseudo-R^2 for the probit is 0.15.

7. In addition, earnings records were obtained from the Social Security Administration and matched to respondents. For the initial HRS survey in 1992, a matched record was obtained for three-fourths of the participants. Permissions to obtain Social Security records were again obtained in 2004. These records now provide information on Social Security–covered earnings and on W2 earnings. Bias from systematic failure to match the earnings records does not appear to be a major problem. Gustman and Steinmeier (2004b) found a pseudo-R^2 of .065 when permission to match a Social Security record is related to individual characteristics in a probit equation. Kapteyn et al. (2006) also find a small correlation of match rates with observables. In addition, Gustman and Steinmeier (2004b) find that average indexed yearly earnings on matched respondent records can be predicted from earnings reported by respondents to the survey together with information they provide on employment history. The adjusted R^2 is 60 percent for men and 66 percent for women.

8. Although they have become more commonplace over time, only 6 percent of HRS respondents reported in 2004 that they were covered by a hybrid plan,

that is, a plan with some features of both a DB and a DC plan. One possible reason for the relatively low number reporting a hybrid plan is that some HRS respondents are old enough to have had their eligibility for DB plans grand-fathered. Even though some of their colleagues were forced to switch to a hybrid plan, they were old enough or had sufficient service to be allowed to continue with their original plans.

9. The present value of a DB plan's expected benefits is determined by the plan formula. The values of the DB plans (from self-report) are first computed for the age a respondent reported expecting to start receiving benefits. Those benefits then are prorated and discounted to 1992, 1998, and 2004, respec-tively. The values are prorated based on a respondent's work to date as a share of work from the date of hire until the expected age of retirement. These values are prorated and discounted to allow comparison between individual DB and DC amounts.

10. The 63 percent of respondents reporting an annuity type of benefit from a DC plan seems to be too high. This number agrees with responses to a similar question in the core (62 percent). However, according to Department of Labor figures, fewer than 20 percent of 401(k) plans offer an annuity option. There is some confusion among respondents as to the form that payouts will take.

5. Pension Plan Participation in the Health and Retirement Study

1. Some questions have been raised about the reliability of self- reported participation data, especially for those who are covered by a defined contribu-tion (DC) plan. Turner, Muller, and Vermer (2003) use data from the Survey of Income and Program Participation to explore this issue. Data from respondent reports are matched with data on contributions to 401(k) plans gleaned from W2 reports to judge participation. The W2 data indicate much higher participation than is found in self-reports of coverage for these same individuals. In contrast, payroll and survey data from the Wyatt Corporation examined in Chapter 7 suggest that the degree of underreporting is relatively small. While these two data sets suggest that there is underreporting of participation, they disagree on the extent of underreporting. Another potential source of underreporting should be mentioned. Some who are covered by a DC plan and have an active account but are not contributing during the year the survey is taken will report that they are participating in a plan, while others in the same circumstances will report that they are not. W2 data will not always resolve this source of ambiguity.

2. We also calculated pension participation levels by demographic group after excluding the self-employed. Black-white differences in pension participation are substantially larger within the group of employees than when the self-employed are included. The reason is that the self-employed have much lower

pension participation levels than employees, and whites are more likely to be self-employed.

3. In 1992 and 1994, respondents who reported their plan type as "both" defined benefit (DB) and defined contribution were asked only about the disposition of the DB part of the plan. Thus if the DC part remained dormant, it did not add to the number of respondents with dormant plans. In 1998, the war baby cohort was asked about the disposition of both DB and DC parts of the plan. When we exclude the DC dormant plans originating from type "both," only 8.5 percent of respondents have at least one dormant pension plan. Trends can be discerned by comparing row 2, column 3, with row 3, column 6, in Table 5.5. This comparison suggests a higher frequency of dormant pensions among younger cohorts.

In the HRS survey waves administered from 1992 through 1998, the H/GH and G/GG sections (last and previous pension jobs) asked respondents about only one plan from a previous job. In 2000, respondents were asked about up to three plans. In 2002 and later survey years, those sections asked about up to four plans. As a result, early boomers were asked about several more previous pension plans and their dispositions than were those from earlier cohorts. When we impose the same reporting requirements for the number and type of dormant plans in 2004 as in 1992, the percentage of respondents with at least one dormant plan in 2004 drops to 10.7.

6. Pension Plan Type

1. We focus here on those 51 to 56 in 2004 to provide a smooth transition to the discussion of cohort differences that follows. Data for 2006 are also presented later in this chapter.

2. In defining inclusion in a defined contribution plan, some researchers require the respondent to report a positive account balance. We consider variation in account balances in Chapter 9. Some researchers add a further requirement to distinguish participation in a defined contribution plan. They require that a person make a contribution to a defined contribution plan in the period of observation to be counted as participating in the plan in that period (e.g., see Dushi and Honig, 2007). This requirement is meant to exclude from the ranks of those with a DC plan workers whose firms offer a plan but who do not contribute. Unfortunately, such a requirement also excludes from the list of participants in DC plans those whose employers make the entire contribution to the plan. In 2004, about 11 percent of those 51 to 56 years old with a DC plan in the HRS had the full contribution to their plan made by their employers. In 2004, 17 percent of those 51 to 56 years old who had a DC pension made a contribution although their employers did not, while 58 percent of respondents with a DC plan made contributions and their employers did also. Of the remaining, 12 percent answered "don't know" or refused to answer for questions

on their own and/or their employer's contribution, and 1 percent reported that neither contributed.

3. Gustman and Steinmeier (1993b, 1995) suggest that the lower turnover from jobs offering DB plans is not the result of disincentives to mobility created by the backloading of benefits under DB formulas. Indeed, the financial penalty from terminating benefits under a DB plan is quite small for those who are more than a decade from retirement. Rather, jobs offering a DB plan appear to offer a higher wage premium, the difference in pay on the current job versus the next best opportunity. That wage premium discourages workers from leaving a firm offering a DB plan.

4. The data in Table 6.8, columns 1, 3, and 5, differ slightly from those in Table 6.1. Observations that were included in Table 6.1 are excluded from Table 6.8 if the respondent left the job, or the survey, between 1992 and 1994.

7. Imperfect Knowledge of Pension Plan Type

1. Mitchell (1988); Gustman and Steinmeier (1989); Gustman and Steinmeier (2004b); Chan and Huff Stevens (2006).

2. It appears that retirement behavior conforms to the incentives from pensions only for those who understand how their pensions work (Chan and Huff Stevens, 2008).

3. Willis (2008) discusses reasons for not engaging in financial literacy education.

4. As discussed in detail in the subsequent text, payroll data from Watson Wyatt (Nyce, 2007) suggest that this cannot be the only explanation for any discrepancy between plan type reported by the firm and by respondents. Using payroll data, which are perfectly matched to the respondent, Nyce finds significant discrepancies between respondent- and firm-reported plan type as well as a significant occurrence of DK responses.

5. The match is less precise when the researcher turns to Form 5500 data produced by the Department of Labor. These data are available for many more firms than are the SPDs. The problem is that the basic Form 5500 data do not provide detailed information on the characteristics of workers covered by particular plans. However, such information is sometimes available from supplements to Form 5500 data.

6. As part of the last round of data collection from HRS employers, employer-produced pension plan descriptions are being collected from a number of sources. As part of this effort, some respondents are collecting the descriptions directly from their employers. Presumably, if these respondents sent in all their plans, matching would be exact and up to date. By comparing plans submitted by respondents with those obtained from other sources, it should eventually be possible to determine the extent to which collection of outdated SPDs might account for discrepancies between firm- and respondent-provided plan descriptions.

7. Comparing the column and row totals in Table 7.1A, respondent reports suggest that 29.5 [(7.4 + 17.3)/.836] percent of covered workers have a DC plan. This greatly exceeds the employer-based report that 12 (8.5 + 3.5) percent have a DC plan. The source of the discrepancy is the very high number reporting both types of plans in the respondent data. Otherwise, the proportion of reports indicating a DC plan only, or the total with a DB plan, agree. Adjusting the 7.4 percent figure in column 2, row 4, of Table 7.1A for the fraction who answered "don't know," 8.9 percent of respondents who answered said they had a DC plan only. According to matched employer reports, as seen in row 2, column 5, 8.5 percent had a DC plan only. Moreover, adding the total of respondents who said that they had a DB plan, either because they had a DB plan only or had both types, the fraction of respondents who report a DB plan [(58.9 + 17.3)/.836 = 91.1] is very close to the fraction whose employers reported that they had a DB plan (91.6 = 88.1 + 3.5).

8. One might be concerned about differences in reported plan type between those who report a change in plan type and those who do not. There are some differences, but they do not appear to be of overwhelming importance. In Table 7.2A, where data for the full sample with matched SPDs in 1992 are reported, the percentages of respondents reporting a DB, DC, and both types of plans was 46, 24, and 28 percent, respectively. In Table 7.5A, where plan type is reported among respondents who reported that their plan type has not changed between 1992 and 1998, the percentages of respondents with DB, DC, and both types of plans in 1992 are 52, 28, and 19 percent, respectively. Also note that the subsample of employer-reported plan types for respondents who reported the same pension in 1992 and 1998 in Table 7.5C matches the distribution of employer-reported plan types in Table 7.2A for the larger sample of all respondents with matched pensions in 1992. Thus in Table 7.2A, the percentages reported in employer data of DB, DC, and both types of plans in 1992 are 48, 21, and 31 percent, respectively. In Table 7.5C, the corresponding figures are 48, 20, and 33 percent.

9. Even if the matches obtained were perfect, plan matches are obtained for only two-thirds of HRS respondents who indicate that they are covered by a pension. This means that when generating descriptive data that apply to the overall population, pension plan type based on firm reports has to be imputed for one-third of respondents. In addition, employer responses cannot be used to fulfill another major need. Employer data are not obtained until a year after the respondent survey. As a result, employer data cannot be used to improve identification of plan type in a survey instrument as it is being administered.

10. Some differences between the Watson Wyatt data and the HRS data should be noted. Although some analysis with the Watson Wyatt data suggests that age is not a dominating factor, the Watson Wyatt data cover a full age range while the HRS data cover those over the age of 50. With regard to the definitions of coverage, there is only a slight difference between the Watson

Wyatt and HRS data. We classify the following two cases as DK, while Watson Wyatt data classify them as DC or DB, respectively.

	Have DB	Have DC
1.	DK	Yes
2.	Yes	DK

Our categories for HRS data are DB only, DC only, and both. So if a person gives a DK response to either DB or DC, we cannot tell whether they have both, and so we classify the response as DK.

The two data sets also treat cash balance plans differently, and cash balance plans are more likely to be found in the Watson Wyatt sample of large firms. The HRS treats hybrid plans as DC (they involve an account), while the Watson Wyatt data separate out 401(k) and 403(b) plans, call them DC, and classify hybrid plans as DB. Thus in the Watson Wyatt sample, according to their appendix table A.1 (Nyce, 2007), 73 percent of respondents have a DB plan, which includes hybrid plans, while 28 percent of the sample have a hybrid plan. Thirty-eight percent of Watson Wyatt DB plans are hybrid. It is clear that there are more DB plans in the Watson Wyatt sample of firms than in the HRS and that the HRS is much less successful in identifying hybrid plans in its sample. Note the possibility that with respondents in the HRS sample all over the age of 50, many more in the HRS will have been grandfathered into their old DB plans than would be the case for the younger Watson Wyatt sample.

There also are other differences between the populations surveyed. The Watson Wyatt sample is not nationally representative. Moreover, voluntary respondent participation is lower in the Watson Wyatt sample than in the HRS. Those who participate may be better informed about their pensions than those who refuse to take part in the survey, creating another source of bias.

11. In the HRS data, as we have seen in Table 7.3C, 18 percent of the plan types covering respondents, as indicated by SPDs provided by private firms (i.e., not including public employees in the sample), are DB only, 44 percent are DC only, and 38 percent are both. In the Watson Wyatt sample, 3 percent of respondent-matched plan types from payroll data are DB only, 26 percent are DC only, and 70 percent are both. Thus 56 percent of the HRS firm reports indicate coverage by any DB plan, while for 73 percent of the respondents in the Watson Wyatt sample the payroll data suggest coverage by any DB plan. Hybrid plans are not nearly numerous enough to account for this difference. Similarly, in the HRS sample, 82 percent of private firm reports involve any DC plan, while in the Watson Wyatt sample, the analogous figure is 96 percent.

12. Changes in plan type observed in panel data provide only part of the story. Selectivity bias creates an additional problem. The sample is confined to those

who report that their plan is unchanged. Those with pensions that change between waves may be in less stable employment, may be located in firms that have switched to cash balance or other hybrid plans, or may be covered by plans that are more suitable for job changers, or their plans may differ for other reasons from those who remain in the same job with an unchanging pension. There also is a question about how having experienced a recent plan change affects knowledge or learning about one's pension. Those whose plans are unchanged from period to period may have a longer period to learn about their pension. Conversely, those with a recent pension change may have just recently been made more aware of their plan type by their employer.

13. Much of the analysis in Chan and Huff Stevens (2006) refers to measures of the value of the pension. There is a question of whether respondent reports allow a consistent comparison between pension values reported before leaving the job with pension values reported after respondents leave their job. Pension benefits reported by respondents before they retire typically are estimated using the standard formula for a single annuity. For those who annuitize benefits, typically those with a DB plan, pension value in retirement depends on the type of annuity chosen. The amounts vary a great deal between a joint and survivor benefit, which for married persons is required by law, compared with the single annuity reported when the benefit is not yet in receipt. This may generate some of the differences observed between values reported pre- and postretirement. Second, annuities may differ for other reasons from those expected before retirement or analogously from the stated benefit contained in the SPD. For example, a person may ask for a ten- or twenty-year certain payment, that is, a payment that is guaranteed to be paid for a minimum number of years (such as ten or twenty years) whether the covered worker survives for that period or not. Having the minimum payment period guaranteed reduces the annual benefit payments in retirement. Third, if the individual has taken some of the benefit in the form of a lump sum, that will reduce the value of the benefit actually received after retirement.

14. If the firm reports were collected at a different time than the respondent reports, and the plan had changed in the meantime, this would reduce the degree of correspondence between respondent and firm reports. Given the short period between respondent and firm reports, compared with the periods being analyzed between when respondent and firm reports of plan type are solicited, any lag in the collection of plan descriptions from the firm should have only a limited effect.

15. These questions were contained in the Pension Characteristics Module and administered to all those in the survey who reported having a pension.

16. An additional approach to correcting errors in plan type is suggested by the work of Gary Engelhardt and his colleagues. Comparisons of W2 data with Social Security earnings data allowed Cunningham and Engelhardt (2002) and Cunningham, Engelhardt, and Kumar (2007) to identify many of those

with defined contribution plans. Recent versions of W2 data being matched to HRS respondents provide even more precise identification of plan type for those respondents making contributions to their DC pension plans. In some cases, it will be possible to unambiguously identify respondents who have misreported plan type and to correct their response. Of course, this will not help to send them down the correct DB or DC branch of the pension questionnaire if they have been asked the wrong pension sequence in a previous wave of the survey.

17. The ability of respondents to identify plan type will only deteriorate further with the increasing complexity of pensions and the inclusion of DC plan features in DB plans, and vice versa.

18. For further discussion, see Gustman and Tabatabai (2006).

8. Pension Retirement Ages

1. The Pension Protection Act, Section 905, contains a provision allowing the partial payment of pension benefits after age 62 to those with a defined benefit plan. Our data cover the period through 2006, so that even if implemented, this provision would not affect observed behavior in our sample. The Department of Labor continues to receive testimony suggesting that this provision has not been widely implemented.

2. A DC plan is actuarially fair when it comes to choosing the initial withdrawal date. If one postpones withdrawing from a DC plan for one year, the remaining balance is spread over fewer years, raising the feasible withdrawal in each year. Once the benefits are vested, a DC plan does not impose a special penalty should a covered worker leave the year before qualifying for early retirement. To be sure, after the covered worker leaves the firm, a contribution will not be made by the worker or the firm, but the account will continue to accumulate interest. Of course, increased liquidity at early retirement age may also affect the retirement behavior of those with a DB plan.

3. Obviously, expected age of benefit receipt increases over time when it is calculated only among those who have not yet retired. The resulting differences in expected age of benefit receipt can be seen in the last column of Table 8.5, where the calendar year is held constant at 2004 but the cohort is allowed to vary. Those who were 51 to 56 in 1992, and thus were 63 to 68 in 2004, and were still working full time in 2004 had an expected retirement age of 66.9. This is in contrast to the expected age of benefit receipt among those 51 to 56 and still working full time in 2004 of 62.6.

4. Another reason for the trend to a later expected age of benefit receipt is the increase in the weight given to defined contribution plans over time. Those with a DC plan only account for 29 percent of full-time pension-covered workers ages 51 to 56 in 1992 (530/1,834), but they account for 44 percent of 51- to 56-year-old full-time pension-covered workers in 2004 (521/1,160).

5. Table 8.11 was constructed as follows. In the assets and income section of the HRS, the financial respondents are asked whether they and/or their spouses are currently receiving any pension benefits. If the response is affirmative, they are asked when they/their spouses started receiving that benefit and the amount of the benefit they received last month. These questions are asked about the largest pension they currently receive and then the second largest plan. Table 8.11 compares the expected age for the most important DB/combination plan reported in 1992 (from the employment section) with the actual age when the benefits first started (from the assets and income section) reported in the 2006 survey. The sample includes all respondents who in Wave 1 reported that they were expecting to receive some future pension benefits and in Wave 8 said that they were receiving some benefits.

9. Pension Values

1. Cunningham and Engelhardt (2002) have developed ingenious techniques for estimating the values of defined contribution plans from employer-provided plan formulas for DC plans and indicators of respondent contributions obtained either from self-reports or from tax (W2) data. Cunningham, Engelhardt, and Kumar (2007) argue that high levels of imputations are required to project DC pension values from self-reports, making estimates based on plan formulas and W2 data even more attractive.

   There is, however, an important drawback to using W2 data and DC plan formulas to evaluate DC balances. It is not sufficient to know the formulas determining employer contributions, their relation to respondent contributions to the pension over time, and the level of respondent contributions. One must also know the investment choices made for plan assets and returns to those investments over time. This information is not available in the HRS. Two other problems should be noted. Matched employer data describing employer contributions are available for a smaller share of DC plans than for DB plans in the HRS. In addition, at the time of writing of this book, employer plan descriptions for DC plans for 2004 were not as yet coded by the HRS.

2. One might also ask how reporting error in plan type is likely to affect reported DC balances. In Chapter 7 we found that individuals who identify their plans as DB are willing to report plan balances, but these balances do not bear any resemblance to the worth of the DB plan. Thus we can expect balances reported by those who mistakenly report their plans as DC to be subject to potentially large errors. But there is no way to determine the size of these errors. For reasons discussed in the previous note, we do not trust estimates of DC balances based on employer reports. As a result, there is no standard of comparison for DC plans as there is for DB plans, which limits our ability to determine the importance of these errors.

3. Conditional on date of retirement and preretirement earnings, DB pension payments will also depend on whether the formula remains the same between the time of the survey and the time when the respondent retires. Many respondents will not take potential future changes in plan formula into account when forecasting benefits.

4. There are two approaches to evaluating a DB plan based on work to date. Under a projected liability approach it is assumed that the individual will remain on the job offering the DB plan until reaching retirement age. In that case, when calculating how much of the benefit has been earned by work to date, the plan is evaluated using tenure accumulated to date, not tenure that would be accumulated as of the expected retirement age, while the benefit is calculated using a wage projected through retirement (Ippolito, 1986). In calculating prorated benefits, we use this approach. Respondent reports of expected benefits are readily adjusted to prorate benefits on the basis of work to date. All that is required is to multiply the full expected benefit by the ratio of tenure accumulated by the time of the survey to tenure at the expected retirement date.

   Under a second approach, which calculates the employer's legal liability under the plan, it is assumed that employment ends immediately. This concept is relevant should the person terminate employment immediately or should the plan be terminated immediately. In the event of immediate termination, the value of the yearly DB pension is again based on tenure accumulated to date, but the wage used in the benefit formula is based on earnings to date, rather than on projected earnings through the retirement date (Bulow, 1981, 1982).

   The values calculated under the projected and legal liability methods are quite different for those with only a few years of tenure, but the difference declines with increasing tenure on the job. Both methods result in a lower pension value than when employment is treated as if it will last with certainty until the expected date of retirement, and the benefit is calculated as the current value of the benefit that will be realized as of that retirement date, including the value of future work in the benefit value. Pension wealth can also be calculated using information on expected turnover from the job, a calculation of particular interest to the actuarial evaluation of the benefit promised by a plan (Gustman and Steinmeier, 1989).

5. Throughout this chapter we have reported the value of the most important defined benefit plan. In the subsequent discussion in the text, we report the sum of the values for all DC plans. We have not included the value of the second DB plan both because there is higher likelihood of confusion among respondents reporting two DB plans and because of analytical problems that will be created when we attempt to use matched employer-provided descriptions of DB plans. In 1992, there were 71 cases out of 2,980 respondents with

any DB plan, whether held alone or in combination with a DC plan, where the respondent reported having two DB plans. All values in this chapter are averaged over all respondents who reported inclusion in the relevant plan under discussion and a positive value for their plan.

6. To adjust for differences in the year of expected retirement reported by different respondents, Table 9.1A discounts the reported values from the year the benefit will first be received back to the year the benefit was reported. That is, the benefit amounts reported in Table 9.1A are in current year dollars as of the year of the survey. The discount rate used is 5.8 percentage points and is based on the long-run projections of the Social Security Administration.

7. Thus the further in the future a benefit will be received, the smaller the contribution that yearly benefit will make to pension wealth. Pension wealth is lower the higher the interest rate used to adjust the value of the future benefit payment.

8. When discounting within cohorts, we use 5.8 percent as a discount rate. This figure is consistent with long-run Social Security Administration projections. When making comparisons across cohorts, we report all benefits in 1992 dollars. Thus in Table 9.3, the value of DB benefits for members of the early boomer cohort are discounted back to 2004 at the 5.8 percent interest rate and are further discounted from 2004 back to 1992 using only the inflation rate of 2.8 percent.

9. Table 9.21 in Appendix 9.2 reports yearly pension payments expected by respondents if they retire at their expected retirement age and is comparable to Table 9.1B. Table 9.22 in this appendix reports DC account balances obtained from respondents in 1992 dollars and is comparable to 9.2C; Table 9.23 reports the present value of the most important DB plan based on respondent reports and is comparable to Table 9.4. We have also imputed prorated present values based on employer reports in Table 9.24. The imputations are based on a variety of methods. When sufficient observations are available, a nearest neighbor methodology is used. Detailed descriptions of the imputation methodology are on the HRS Web site, https://ssl.isr.umich.edu/hrs/files.php?versid=64.

10. If respondents are not working at the time of their initial interview, they are asked about their last job prior to that interview. That job is referred to as "last job." Whether or not respondents are working at their initial interview, they are also asked about up to three previous pension jobs. Those jobs are referred to as "previous jobs."

11. Pensions from a last job are reported in Section G of the 1992 survey, Section GG of the 1998 survey, and Section K of the 2004 survey. Pensions from previous jobs are reported in Section H of the 1992 survey, Section GH of the 1998 survey, and Section L of the 2004 survey. The pension values from last and previous jobs for respondents (and their spouses) who were age eligible in 1998 but were first interviewed in 1992 are from Sections G and H in 1992.

These are the younger spouses of respondents who were age eligible in 1992. Similarly, for respondents who were age eligible in 2004 (and their spouses) but were first interviewed in 1998, their pension values from their last and previous jobs are from Sections GG and GH in 1998. For respondents in these two groups, benefits from a job that was terminated after their initial interview are also included.

12. One household may be included in more than one cohort. For example, a household that includes a respondent who was within the age range of the HRS cohort in 1992, with a spouse who was within the age range of the war baby cohort in 1998, will be counted in the household data as part of both the HRS and war baby cohorts.

When considering the data indicating the change in the total value of pensions over time, note the effect on average pensions of the changing household structure over time in favor of one-person households. Thus in the weighted HRS data for those 51 to 56 in 1992, households with one member account for 28 percent of all households. By Wave 7, they account for 36 percent of all households. Among households with a pension, the share of households with one member increases from 21 percent to 27 percent over that period. The increase in the proportion of single-person households will reduce the average value of pensions in each household over time.

13. Older members of the original HRS cohort (those 57 to 61) are more likely to have left their pension jobs at the time of the initial survey than are those ages 51 to 56. As a result, more previous employers must be located if their plan descriptions are to be obtained. For a variety of reasons, it is much harder to locate pension plan descriptions from previous than from current employers. As a result, there is a much greater rate of imputation for pensions from last or previous jobs in the employer data when those in the full age of the original HRS cohort are included in the sample.

10. Retirement Incentives from Defined Benefit Pensions

1. See the discussion in Chapter 2. For a review of the long literature exploring the retirement incentives created by defined benefit pensions, see Gustman, Mitchell, and Steinmeier (1994).

2. Retiree health benefits may also become available upon qualifying for pension benefits. Retiree health benefits are becoming much less common, but where they are available they most often are provided by firms that also offer defined benefit plans. Retiree health benefits are particularly valuable in the years before a retiree qualifies for Medicare. For an analysis of the relation of retiree health benefits to retirement wealth, see Gustman and Steinmeier (2000b) and Blau and Gilleskie (2006).

3. As noted in Chapter 2, the negative decline in the present value of benefits after normal retirement age was once very sharp. Before mandatory retirement

was outlawed and concerns about age discrimination curbed certain pension practices, once a person reached normal retirement age, benefits were frozen. No additional credit was given either for wage growth or for additional years of tenure from work beyond the normal retirement age. As a result, a person who worked after normal retirement age would forego current benefits but would not receive higher yearly benefits once retired to compensate for all or part of the lost benefits. Antidiscrimination rules now require some adjustment in yearly benefits paid so that when a person works after the normal retirement age, the present value of benefits decreases much more slowly today than in the past.

4. Although respondents cannot describe the accrual profile in detail, their retirement behavior has been shown to respond to the location of spikes in the accrual profile. Presumably as they approach, say, the early retirement age, they learn that waiting another year to retire will result in a substantial increase in benefits, leading them to postpone their retirement.

5. In recent years, both the coding of plan documents for the Health and Retirement Study and the maintenance and updating of pension software have been under the supervision of Helena Stolyarova. We are grateful for her help in dealing with issues that have arisen during the course of our analysis.

6. One difference between these and earlier results should be noted. For members of the 1992 cohort with continuing pensions through 1998, pensions valued in 1998 are discounted back to 1992 at a 5.8 percent discount rate. When the pensions of members of younger cohorts, those 51 to 56 in 1998, were analyzed in earlier chapters, their benefits as of 1998 were converted into 1992 dollars using an inflation rate of 2.8 percent. Benefits were not further discounted to account for the 3.0 real interest rate used in our analyses. This allowed comparisons of real pension benefits between cohorts when members reached the same age.

7. To limit the extent of selection bias in this sample, we restrict the sample to those who were 51 to 56 years old in 1992, rather than considering the changes in pensions for the full age range of the sample, 51 to 61. Older individuals from the original HRS cohort who remained with a DB plan might be even more different from typical workers experiencing a change in their pension over time.

8. Another difference from earlier tables should be noted. Table 10.7 compares values for the same person in two different years, while the earlier tables compared pension values for members of different cohorts. In Tables 10.1 to 10.6, the values reported in 1992, 1998, and 2004 are for cross-sections of 51- to 56-year-olds in the three years. In Tables 10.7 and 10.8, the changes from 1992 to 1998 pertain to respondents who were 51 to 56 in 1992, and who, when the plan description for 1998 was matched, were 57 to 62 years old.

11. Disposition of Pensions upon Leaving a Job and Pension Incomes in Retirement

1. Recall that a last job is a job held in the past by a person who is no longer employed. A previous job is a job held before the current job or the last job.
2. As discussed in the section on bracketing, changes in the design of the HRS survey over time may be responsible for a slight exaggeration in the estimated size of this trend.
3. Some of the changes in methodology across waves of the HRS when calculating the disposition of pensions include the following:

   In 1994, 1996, and 1998, respondents did not have the option to report whether they had transferred their account to the new employer.

   In 1994, respondents were not asked about the disposition of the account part of their combination plan. The value of that part of their pension is not included in Tables 11.4A and B.

   For the first time in 2006, respondents were asked about their DC account distributions in the form of installments.

   In 1994, 1996, and 1998, respondents were asked about only one pension plan from their previous job. Since 2000, they have been asked about up to three pension plans. Therefore, plan values for the 1994, 1996, and 1998 survey years represent the values from only one pension plan; but in the 2000–2006 survey years, plan values represent the sum of all plans (up to four) from each payout option.

   Pension values that were reported "lost" or reported in the "other" category are not included.

   All multiple responses regarding disposition of pension plans are taken into account in calculating the pension values.

4. Another factor affecting the measurement of trends is a change in the number of plans asked about in the sequence of questions on the disposition of the previous pension. In the Wave 1 to Wave 4 interviews, the respondent was asked about only one pension plan from any previous or past job. In Wave 5, the number was increased to up to three plans. In Waves 6 to 8, the respondent was asked about up to four plans. In this chapter, values are calculated for all plans asked about in the particular wave of the survey. This creates a potential upward bias in the estimated trend in plan values over time.
5. In 1992, respondents were asked whether they (the respondent/spouse/partner) received any pension income in the previous year (i.e., in 1991). If the response was affirmative, they were asked about the total value of the income from a pension they received in 1991, that is, in the year before the survey. The reported values are converted to an amount per month to conform with the data on pension incomes reported in later waves. Pension income is reported separately for the financial respondent and his/her spouse.

From 1994 forward, respondents were asked whether they (the respondent/ spouse/partner) were currently receiving any income from retirement pensions. If they answered yes, they were asked about the number of plans they were receiving benefits from. Pension income is described in terms of the amount they received last month. Respondents with more than two plans were asked about each of the most important two plans and then about the sum of last month's income from any additional pension plans.

From 1996 forward, a set of unfolding questions was put to respondents if they answered "don't know" or refused to answer when asked to report the amount of their pension income. These unfolding questions present brackets and ask whether the income from pensions falls with the specified ranges. Beginning in 2002, unfolding questions were asked for the additional plans beyond the first two plans.

Because pension incomes are reported on a per month (last month) basis, if the length of the period over which pension benefits are paid is longer than one month, the amount will be recorded if the month before the survey happens to be the month in which a payment was made. If not, an amount will not be recorded for the respondent. This does not necessarily lead to any bias in the average values of pensions reported in the survey but will lead to an understatement of the number of workers receiving a pension income over the year.

There is no indication as to whether the benefits are from a DB or DC plan. Reported incomes are most likely to be from DB plans, but respondents who receive a regular installment from a DC plan may also have received a benefit in the previous month. Respondents are asked about benefits from an annuitized DC account following these questions.

The data include imputations for respondents with missing values. Imputations for 1992–2004 surveys were produced by HRS staff. The 2006 imputations were produced by RAND.

Pension incomes are weighted and are in 1992 dollars. Pension incomes from spouses/partners who were not a member of the survey because they refused to respond and for whom values were not provided by a proxy are excluded from these tables.

12. The Changing Role of Pensions in Total Wealth

1. Social Security wealth measures used in this book were constructed by the HRS under the supervision of Kandice Kapinos and her colleagues (Kapinos et al., 2008). We are especially grateful to Kapinos and her coauthors, Charlie Brown, Michael Nolte, Helena Stolyarova, and David Weir for providing us with these data. Social Security wealth is equal to the expected present value of all benefits, including own, spouse, and survivor benefits for each member of the household.

2. Note that the nominal interest rate used by Kapinos et al. (2008) in discounting differs slightly from the 5.8 percent rate we use throughout. For discounting to

1992 and 1998, they use a 6.3 percent interest rate. For discounting to 2004, they use the same 5.8 percent rate that we do. The real interest rates they use are 2.2 percent for those in the 1992 cohort, 2.7 percent for those in the 1998 cohort, and 2.9 percent for those in the 2004 cohort. Using a higher real interest rate reduces Social Security wealth for members of younger cohorts.

3. Notice the change between 1992 and 1998 in the raw numbers of observations falling within each household type. There are two-thirds as many couple households in 1998 as in 1992 but only half as many single-female households and a similar fraction for single-male households. As discussed in Chapter 3, the war baby and early boomer cohorts were substantially smaller than the HRS cohort, but younger, out-of-age-range spouses originally interviewed in 1992 were counted as part of the war baby cohort in couple households in 1998. In the case of households with single men or single women, households are always first included in the year the individual entered the survey. As a result, the smaller size of the 1998 war baby sample is reflected directly in the number of one-person households observed in 1998, creating a larger decline in the number of one-person households between 1992 and 1998 than in the number of two-person households.

   When observations are weighted, however, the differences in the raw numbers of households of each type between cohorts have no effect on the proportion of households of each type. Thus the percentage of female-headed households increases from 17.1 percent to 18.6 percent between 1992 and 1998, while the percentage of couple households declines from 71.8 percent to 69.2 percent.

4. Changes in the number of households of each type do not have a major effect on the differences in total wealth held by households of different types in different years. There is only a small change in the proportion of households of each type between 1992 and 2004. Between 1992 and 2004, the percentage of households consisting of a single male increased from 11.0 percent to 12.9 percent. The percentage of households with a single female increased from 17.1 to 19.6 percent, while the percentage of couple households declined from 71.8 percent to 67.6 percent.

5. For further analysis of the relation between various forms of wealth, self-employment, and pensions, see Gustman and Steinmeier (1999b).

13. Conclusions

1. Those with DC plans have been on the job for three fewer years than those with DB plans, and time spent covered by a DC pension is equal to only 70 percent of the time spent on the job that is sponsoring the DC plan. In contrast, those with DB plans have been covered by a pension for virtually the entire time they have spent with their employer. For members of the cohort that was 51 to 56 in 2004, those with a defined benefit plan had spent 16.8 years on average at their current employment, while those with a defined contribution plan had spent

13.8 years with their current employer. In 2004, HRS respondents with a DB plan had been covered by the plan for 16.3 years, while those with a DC plan had been covered for 9.7 years. Fewer years of coverage mean that DC plans are less valuable than they would be under a more mature system where the covered workforce exhibits a stable, steady-state age structure.

2. Thus it may be that, as some argue, in the long run the trend to DC plans will undermine the contribution to retirement wealth from pensions. Samwick and Skinner (2004) disagree with this idea, however. Their analysis suggests that once the adverse effect of turnover on the value of DB pensions is considered, DC plans will do at least as good a job as DB plans in replacing the earnings of covered workers. Poterba, Venti, and Wise (2007a, 2007b) predict a very rapid rise in the value of DC plans to be enjoyed by members of younger cohorts when they reach retirement age. But these scenarios are based on the long term. They do not yet apply to the current retirement age population.

3. The Pension Equity Act and related legislation have addressed the question of the extent of ownership of pensions by a spouse and the provision of adequate survivor benefits. Legislation has also addressed the division of pensions at divorce and the use of unisex survival tables.

4. For DC plans we have information only on the share held in stocks for plans offered on the current job. Our approximations will assume that respondents hold the same portfolio mix in DC pensions from last and previous jobs as they do on current jobs. The actual share of assets held in stocks at the time of the stock market decline also depends on the adjustments the respondent may have made in the portfolio after 2006. Some investors who suspected a stock market decline was imminent adjusted their portfolios. Others adjusted their portfolios after the market decline began but before the market hit bottom. Still others will have sold at the market's bottom and failed to enjoy subsequent gains. This means that the complete effect of the stock market decline on the HRS population cannot be determined until data are collected in 2010.

Appendix

1. Note that other data files are also available on the HRS Web site or are available on a restricted basis to those who have obtained the proper permission. Among the most important of the files available on the HRS Web site are: software designed to evaluate employer-provided pension plan descriptions (Pension Estimation Program by Peticolas and Stolyarova), files that include present values of pensions from Wave 1 of the survey (Pension Present Value Database by Peticolas and Steinmeier), and files with present values of Social Security wealth measures (Social Security Wealth Measures by Kapinos with Brown, Nolte, Stolyarova, and Weir).

2. Files that are based on tables that include only respondent-reported data will be made available to all users. The files underlying tables that are based in part on restricted pension or Social Security data will require the user to qualify for access to restricted data by following the procedures described on the HRS Web site.

References

Anderson, Patricia M., Alan L. Gustman, and Thomas L. Steinmeier. 1999. "Trends in Male Labor Force Participation and Retirement: Some Evidence on the Role of Pension and Social Security in the 1970s and 1980s." *Journal of Labor Economics* 17(4), Part 1: 757–783.

Banks, James, Richard Blundell, and Sarah Tanner. 1998. "Is There a Retirement Saving Puzzle?" *American Economic Review* 88(4): 769–788.

Barnow, Burt S., and Ronald G. Ehrenberg. 1979. "The Costs of Defined Benefit Pension Plans and Firm Adjustments." *Quarterly Journal of Economics* 93: 523–540.

Bayer, Patrick J., B. Douglas Bernheim, and John Karl Scholz. 1996. "The Effects of Financial Education in the Workplace: Evidence from a Survey of Employers." NBER Working Paper No. 5655. Cambridge, MA: National Bureau of Economic Research.

Beller, Daniel J. 2005. "Transition Provisions in Large Converted Cash Balance Pension Plans." Report 2005-13. Washington, DC: AARP Public Policy Institute.

Bellman, Lutz, and Florian Janik. 2007. "Firms and Early Retirement: Offers That One Does Not Refuse." IZA Working Paper No. 2931, July. Bonn, Germany: Institute for the Study of Labor.

Benitez-Silva, Hugo, Moshe Buchinsky, Hiu-Man Chan, John Rust, and Sophia Sheivasser. 1999. "An Empirical Analysis of the Social Security Disability Application, Appeal and Award Process." *Labour Economics* 6: 147–178.

Benitez-Silva, Hugo, Moshe Buchinsky, and John Rust. 2001. "Dynamic Models of Retirement and Disability." Paper presented at the Winter Meetings of the Econometric Society, New Orleans, January.

Bernheim, B. Douglas. 1988. "Social Security Benefits: An Empirical Study of Expectations and Realizations." In R. R. Campbell and E. Lazear, eds., *Issues in Contemporary Retirement*. Stanford, CA: Hoover Institution Press, 312–335.

————. 1989. "The Timing of Retirement: A Comparison of Expectations and Realizations." In David A. Wise, ed., *The Economics of Aging*. Chicago: University of Chicago Press for National Bureau of Economic Research, 335–355.

————. 1990. "How Do the Elderly Form Expectations? An Analysis of Responses to New Information." In David A. Wise, ed., *Issues in the Economics of Aging*. Chicago: University of Chicago Press for National Bureau of Economic Research, 259–283.

Bernheim, B. Douglas, and Daniel M. Garrett. 1996. "The Determinants and Consequences of Financial Education in the Workplace: Evidence from a Survey of Households." NBER Working Paper No. 5667. Cambridge, MA: National Bureau of Economic Research.

Bernheim, B. Douglas, Jonathan S. Skinner, and Steven Weinberg. 2001. "What Accounts for the Variation in Retirement Saving across U.S. Households?" *American Economic Review* 91(4): 832–857.

Blau, David, and Donna Gilleskie. 2006. "Health Insurance and Retirement of Married Couples." *Journal of Applied Econometrics* 21: 935–953.

Blinder, Alan S. 1981. *Private Pensions and Public Pensions: Theory and Fact*. W. S. Woytinshky Lecture No. 5. Ann Arbor: University of Michigan, December.

Bodie, Zvi. 1990. "Pensions as Retirement Income Insurance." *Journal of Economic Literature* 28(1): 28–49.

Bound, John, Todd R. Stinebrickner, and Timothy Waidmann. 2007. "Health, Economic Resources and the Work Decisions of Older Men." NBER Working Paper No. 13657. Cambridge, MA: National Bureau of Economic Research.

Brown, Jeffrey R. 2007. "Rational and Behavioral Perspectives on the Role of Annuities in Retirement Planning." NBER Working Paper No. 13537. Cambridge, MA: National Bureau of Economic Research.

Brown, Jeffrey R., Jeffrey R. Kling, Sendhil Mullainathan, and Marian V. Wrobel. 2008. "Why Don't People Insure Late Life Consumption? A Framing Explanation of the Under-Annuitization Puzzle." NBER Working Paper No. 13748. Cambridge, MA: National Bureau of Economic Research.

Brown, Jeffrey R., Nellie Liang, and Scott Weisbenner. 2007. "Individual Account Investment Options and Portfolio Choice: Behavioral Lessons from 401(k) Plans." NBER Working Paper No. 13169. Cambridge, MA: National Bureau of Economic Research.

Bulow, Jeremy. 1981. "Early Retirement Pension Benefits." NBER Working Paper No. 654. Cambridge, MA: National Bureau of Economic Research.

————. 1982. "What Are Corporate Pension Liabilities?" *Quarterly Journal of Economics* 97(3): 435–452.

Burkhauser, Richard V. 1979. "The Pension Acceptance Decision of Older Workers." *Journal of Human Resources* 14(1): 63–75.

Burtless, Gary, and Robert Moffitt. 1984. "The Joint Choice of Retirement Age and Postretirement Hours of Work." *Journal of Labor Economics* 3(2): 209–236.

Cagan, Phillip. 1965. *The Effect of Pension Plans on Aggregate Savings.* New York: National Bureau of Economic Research.

Campbell, John Y., and Martin Feldstein, eds. 2001. *Risk Aspects of Investment-Based Social Security Reform.* Chicago: University of Chicago Press for National Bureau of Economic Research.

Chan, Sewin, and Ann Huff Stevens. 2006. "New Measures of Pension Knowledge." Unpublished manuscript, New York University.

———. 2008. "What You Don't Know Can't Help You: Pension Knowledge and Retirement Decision Making." *Review of Economics and Statistics* 92(2): 253–266.

Choi, James J., David Laibson, Brigitte Madrian, and Andrew Metrick. 2004. "For Better or Worse: Default Effects and 401(k) Savings Behavior." In David A. Wise, ed., *Perspectives on the Economics of Aging.* Chicago: University of Chicago Press for National Bureau of Economic Research, 81–121.

———. 2005. "Passive Decisions and Potent Defaults." In David A. Wise, ed., *Analyses in the Economics of Aging.* Chicago: University of Chicago Press for National Bureau of Economic Research, 59–78.

Clark, Robert L., and Ann A. McDermed. 1990. *The Choice of Pension Plans in a Changing Regulatory Environment.* Washington, DC: American Enterprise Institute.

Clark, Robert L., and Sylvester J. Schieber. 1998. "Factors Affecting Participation Rates and Contribution Levels in 401(k) Plans." In Olivia S. Mitchell and Sylvester J. Schieber, eds., *Living with Defined Contribution Pensions.* Philadelphia: University of Pennsylvania Press for the Pension Research Council, 69–97.

———. 2001. "The Emergence of Hybrid Pensions and Their Implications for Retirement Income Security in the Twenty First Century." Paper presented at the annual meeting of the Society of Actuaries, May 31, Dallas, Texas.

———. 2002. "Taking the Subsidy out of Early Retirement: The Story behind the Conversion to Hybrid Pensions." In O. Mitchell, Z. Bodie, B. Hammond, and S. Zeldes, eds., *Innovations in Retirement Financing.* Philadelphia: University of Pennsylvania Press, 149–174.

———. 2004. "An Empirical Analysis of the Transition to Hybrid Pension Plans in the United States." In William Gale, John Shoven, and Mark Warshawsky, eds., *Private Pensions and Public Policies.* Washington, DC: Brookings Institution Press, 11–42.

Cunningham, Christopher, and Gary Engelhardt. 2002. "Federal Tax Policy, Employer Matching and 401(k) Savings. Evidence from HRS W2 Records." *National Tax Journal* 55(3): 617–645.

Cunningham, Christopher, Gary Engelhardt, and Anil Kumar. 2007. "Measuring Pension Wealth." In Brigitte Madrain, Olivia S. Mitchell, and Beth J. Soldo, eds., *Redefining Retirement: How Will Boomers Fare?* Oxford: Oxford University Press, 211–233.

Cutler, David M., Jeffrey B. Liebman, and Seamus Smyth. 2006. "How Fast Should the Social Security Eligibility Age Rise?" National Bureau of Economic Research,

Retirement Research Center Working Paper NB04-05. Cambridge, MA: National Bureau of Economic Research.

Delavande, Adeline, and Robert J. Willis. 2007. "Managing the Risk of Life." University of Michigan Retirement Research Center Research Paper No. UM WP 2007-167. Ann Arbor: University of Michigan, Retirement Research Center.

Diamond, Peter A., and Botond Koszegi. 2003. "Quasi-Hyperbolic Discounting and Retirement." *Journal of Public Economics* 87(9–10): 1839–1872.

Diamond, Peter A., and Peter R. Orszag. 2004. *Saving Social Security: A Balanced Approach.* Washington, DC: Brookings Institution Press.

Dominitz, J., C. F. Manski, and J. Heinz. 2001. "Social Security Expectations and Retirement Savings Decisions." Pittsburgh: Carnegie Mellon University, H. J. Heinz School of Public Policy.

Dorsey, Stuart, Christopher Cornwell, and David Macpherson. 1998. *Pensions and Productivity.* Kalamazoo, MI: Upjohn Institute for Employment Research.

Dushi, Irena, and Marjorie Honig. 2007. "Are 401(k) Saving Rates Changing? Cohort/Period Evidence from the Health and Retirement Study." University of Michigan Retirement Research Center, Working Paper No. 2007-160. Ann Arbor: University of Michigan, Retirement Research Center.

Ellwood, David. 1985. "Pensions and the Labor Market." In David A. Wise, ed., *Pensions, Labor, and Individual Choice.* Chicago: University of Chicago Press, 19–53.

Employee Benefit Research Institute. 2004. "The 14th Retirement Confidence Survey, 2004." Issue Brief Number 268, April. Washington, DC: Employee Benefit Research Institute.

Engelhardt, Gary V., and Anil Kumar. 2006a. "Employer Matching and 401(k) Saving: Evidence from the Health and Retirement Study." Unpublished manuscript, Syracuse University.

———. 2006b. "Pensions and Household Wealth Accumulation." Unpublished manuscript, Syracuse University.

Engen, Eric M., William G. Gale, and Cori Uccello. 2004. "Lifetime Earnings, Social Security Benefits and the Adequacy of Retirement Wealth Accumulation." Working Paper No. 2004-10. Boston: Center for Retirement Research at Boston College.

Farber, Henry S. 1998. "Are Lifetime Jobs Disappearing? Job Duration in the United States, 1973–1993." In John Haltewanger, Marilyn Manser, and Robert Topel, eds., *Labor Statistics Measurement Issues.* Chicago: University of Chicago Press, 157–203.

———. 2000. "Trends in Long-Term Employment in the United States: 1979–1996." In Samuel Estreicher, ed., *Global Competition and the American Employment Landscape as We Enter the 21st Century: Proceedings of New York University 52nd Annual Conference on Labor.* New York: Kluwer Law International, 63–98.

————. 2008. "Employment Insecurity: The Decline in Worker-Firm Attachment in the United States." Working Paper No. 530. Princeton, NJ: Princeton University Industrial Relations Section.

Feldstein, Martin S. 1974. "Social Security, Induced Retirement, and Aggregate Capital Accumulation." *Journal of Political Economy* 84: 905–926.

————, ed. 1998. *Privatizing Social Security.* Chicago: University of Chicago Press for National Bureau of Economic Research.

Feldstein, Martin S., and Jeffrey B. Liebman, eds. 2002. *The Distributional Aspects of Social Security.* Chicago: University of Chicago Press for National Bureau of Economic Research.

Fields, Gary S., and Olivia S. Mitchell. 1984. *Retirement, Pensions, and Social Security.* Cambridge, MA: MIT Press.

French, Eric. 2005. "The Effects of Health, Wealth, and Wages on Labor Supply and Retirement Behavior." *Review of Economic Studies* 72(2): 395–427.

Friedberg, Leora. 2001. "The Impact of Technological Change on Older Workers: Evidence from Data on Computer Use." NBER Working Paper No. 8297. Cambridge, MA: National Bureau of Economic Research.

Friedberg, Leora, and Michael T. Owyang. 2002. "Explaining the Evolution of Pension Structure and Job Tenure." Working Paper No. 2002-022A. St. Louis: Federal Reserve Bank of St. Louis, October.

Gale, William G. 1998. "The Effects of Pensions on Household Wealth: A Reevaluation of Theory and Evidence." *Journal of Political Economy* 106(4): 706–723.

Gordon, Roger H., and Alan S. Blinder. 1980. "Market Wages, Reservation Wages and Retirement." *Journal of Public Economics* 14: 277–308.

Gustman, Alan L., and F. Thomas Juster. 1996. "Income and Wealth of Older American Households: Modeling Issues for Public Policy Analysis." In Eric Hanushek and Nancy L. Maritato, eds., *Assessing Knowledge of Retirement Behavior.* Washington, DC: National Academy Press, 11–60.

Gustman, Alan L., Olivia S. Mitchell, Andrew A. Samwick, and Thomas L. Steinmeier. 1999. "Pension and Social Security Wealth in the Health and Retirement Study." In James Smith and Robert Willis, eds., *Wealth, Work, and Health: Innovations in Measurement in the Social Sciences.* Ann Arbor: University of Michigan Press, 150–208.

Gustman, Alan L., Olivia S. Mitchell, and Thomas L. Steinmeier. 1994. "The Role of Pensions in the Labor Market: A Survey of the Literature." *Industrial and Labor Relations Review* 47(3): 417–438.

————. 1995. "Older Union and Nonunion Workers and Their Jobs in the Health and Retirement Survey." *Proceedings of the Forty-Seventh Annual Meeting: Industrial Relations Research Association Series, January 6–8, 1995,* 44–53.

Gustman, Alan L., and Martin Segal. 1977a. "Interstate Variations in Teachers' Pensions." *Industrial Relations* 16(3): 335–344.

———. 1977b. "Teachers' Salary Structures . . . Some Analytical and Empirical Aspects of the Impact of Collective Bargaining." *Proceedings of the Thirtieth Annual Winter Meeting: Industrial Relations Research Association Series, December 28–30, 1977,* 437–445.

Gustman, Alan L., and Thomas L. Steinmeier. 1986a. "A Disaggregated Structural Analysis of Retirement by Race, Difficulty of Work and Health." *Review of Economics and Statistics* 67(3): 509–513.

———. 1986b. "A Structural Retirement Model." *Econometrica* 54(3): 555–584.

———. 1989. "An Analysis of Pension Benefit Formulas, Pension Wealth and Incentives from Pensions." *Research in Labor Economics* 10: 53–106.

———. 1992. "The Stampede toward Defined Contribution Pension Plans: Fact or Fiction?" *Industrial Relations* 31(2): 361–369.

———.1993a. "Cost-of-Living Adjustments in Pensions." In Olivia S. Mitchell, ed., *As the Workforce Ages: Costs, Benefits, and Policy Challenges.* Ithaca, NY: ILR Press, 147–180.

———. 1993b. "Pension Portability and Labor Mobility: Evidence from the Survey of Income and Program Participation." *Journal of Public Economics* 50: 299–323.

———. 1995. *Pension Incentives and Job Mobility.* Kalamazoo, MI: Upjohn Institute for Employment Research.

———. 1999a. "Changing Pensions in Cross-Section and Panel Data: Analysis with Employer Provided Plan Descriptions." *Proceedings, National Tax Association, Ninety-First Annual Conference 1998, Austin, Texas,* 371–377.

———. 1999b. "Effects of Pensions on Savings: Analysis with Data from the Health and Retirement Study." *Carnegie-Rochester Conference Series* 50: 271–326.

———. 2000a. "Employer Provided Pension Data in the NLS Mature Women's Survey and in the Health and Retirement Study." *Research in Labor Economics* 19: 215–252.

———. 2000b. "Pensions and Retiree Health Benefits in Household Wealth: Changes from 1969 to 1992." *Journal of Human Resources* 35(1): 30–50.

———. 2000c. "Retirement in Dual-Career Families: A Structural Model." *Journal of Labor Economics* 18(3): 503–545.

———. 2001. "How Effective Is Redistribution under the Social Security Benefit Formula?" *Journal of Public Economics* 82 (1): 1–28.

———. 2002. "Retirement and the Stock Market Bubble." NBER Working Paper No. 9404. Cambridge, MA: National Bureau of Economic Research.

———. 2004a. "Social Security, Pensions and Retirement Behavior within the Family." *Journal of Applied Econometrics* 19(6): 723–738.

———. 2004b. "What People Don't Know about Their Pensions and Social Security: An Analysis Using Linked Data from the Health and Retirement Study." In William G. Gale, John B. Shoven, and Mark J. Warshawsky, eds., *Private Pensions and Public Policies.* Washington, DC: Brookings Institution Press, 57–119.

———. 2005a. "Imperfect Knowledge of Social Security and Pensions." *Industrial Relations* 44(2): 373–397.

———. 2005b. "Retirement Effects of Proposals by the President's Commission to Strengthen Social Security." *National Tax Journal* 58(1): 27–49.

———. 2006. "Social Security and Retirement Dynamics." University of Michigan Retirement Research Center Working Paper No. 2006-121. Ann Arbor: University of Michigan, Retirement Research Center.

———. 2008. "How Does Modeling of Retirement Decisions at the Family Level Affect Estimates of the Impact of Social Security Policies on Retirement?" University of Michigan Retirement Research Center Working Paper No. 2008-179. Ann Arbor: University of Michigan, Retirement Research Center.

———. 2009. "How Changes in Social Security Affect Recent Retirement Trends." *Research on Aging* 31(2): 261–290.

Gustman, Alan L., Thomas L. Steinmeier, and Nahid Tabatabai. 2008. "Do Workers Know about Their Pensions? Comparing Workers' and Employers' Pension Information." In Anna Lusardi, ed., *Overcoming the Saving Slump; How to Increase the Effectiveness of Financial Education and Saving Programs.* Chicago: University of Chicago Press, 47–81.

———. Forthcoming. "The Retirement Age Population and the Stock Market Decline." *Journal of Economic Perspectives.*

Gustman, Alan L., and Nahid Tabatabai. 2006. "Determining Plan Type in the HRS Pension Sequence." Hanover, NH: Unpublished report to the Health and Retirement Study.

Huberman, Gur, and Wei Jiang. 2006. "Offering vs. Choices in 401(k) Plans: Equity Exposure and Number of Funds." *Journal of Finance* 41(2): 763–801.

Huff Stevens, Ann. 2005. "The More Things Change, the More They Stay the Same: Trends in Long-Term Employment in the United States, 1969–2002." NBER Working Paper No. 11878. Cambridge, MA: National Bureau of Economic Research.

Hurd, Michael D., and Kathleen McGarry. 1995. "Evaluation of the Subjective Probabilities of Survival in the Health and Retirement Study." *Journal of Human Resources* 30: S268–S292.

———. 2002. "The Predictive Validity of the Subjective Probabilities of Survival." *Economic Journal* 112: 966–985.

Hurd, Michael D., and Susann Rohwedder. 2007. "Trends in Pension Values around Retirement." In Brigitte Madrain, Olivia S. Mitchell, and Beth J. Soldo, eds., *Redefining Retirement: How Will Boomers Fare?* Oxford: Oxford University Press, 234–248.

———. 2008a. "The Retirement Consumption Puzzle: Actual Spending Change in Panel Data." NBER Working Paper No. 13929. Cambridge, MA: National Bureau of Economic Research.

———. 2008b. "Trends in Financial Resources Near Retirement." Unpublished manuscript. Santa Monica, CA: RAND Corporation.

———. 2008c. "Trends in Labor Force Participation: How Much Is Due to Changes in Pensions?" Unpublished manuscript. Santa Monica, CA: RAND Corporation.

Hutchens, Robert. 1987. "A Test of Lazears's Theory of Delayed Payment Contract." *Journal of Labor Economics* 5(4), Part 2: S153–S170.

———. 1999. "Social Security Benefits and Employer Behavior: Evaluating Social Security Early Retirement Benefits as a Form of Unemployment Insurance." *International Economic Review* 40(3): 659–678.

Ippolito, Richard A. 1986. *Pensions, Economics, and Public Policy.* Homewood, IL: Dow Jones–Irwin.

———. 1995. "Explaining the Growth of Defined Contribution Pension Plans." *Industrial Relations* 34: 1–20.

———. 2003. "Tenuous Property Rights: The Unraveling of Defined Benefit Contracts in the U.S." In Onorato Castellino and Elsa Fornero, eds., *Pension Policy in an Integrating Europe.* Northampton, MA: Edward Elgar, 175–197.

Ippolito, Richard A., and John W. Thompson. 2000. "The Survival Rate of Defined-Benefit Pension Plans, 1987–1995." *Industrial Relations* 39(2): 228–245.

Jaeger, David A., and Ann Huff Stevens. 1999. "Is Job Stability in the United States Falling? Reconciling Trends in the Current Population Survey and Panel Study of Income Dynamics." *Journal of Labor Economics* 17(4), Part 2: S1–S28.

Juster, F. Thomas, and Richard Suzman. 1995. "An Overview of the Health and Retirement Study." *Journal of Human Resources* 30 (Suppl.): S57–S83.

Kapinos, Kandice, with Charlie Brown, Michael Nolte, Helena Stolyarova, and David Weir. 2008. "Social Security Wealth Measures, Data Documentation." Ann Arbor, MI, October.

Kapteyn, Arie, Pierre-Carl Michaud, James P. Smith, and Arthur Van Soest. 2006. "Effects of Attrition and Non-Response in the Health and Retirement Study." RAND Working Paper No. WR-407. Santa Monica, CA: RAND Corporation.

Katona, George. 1965. *Private Pensions and Individual Savings.* Ann Arbor: Survey Research Center, Institute for Social Research, University of Michigan.

Kotlikoff, Laurence J., and Daniel Smith. 1983. *Pensions in the American Economy.* Chicago: University of Chicago Press.

Kotlikoff, Laurence J., and David A. Wise. 1985. "Labor Compensation and the Structure of Private Pension Plans: Evidence for Contractual vs. Spot Labor Markets." In David A. Wise, ed., *Pensions, Labor, and Individual Choice.* Chicago: University of Chicago Press, 55–85.

———. 1987. "The Incentive Effects of Private Pension Plans." In Zvi Bodie, John Shoven, and David Wise, eds., *Issues in Pension Economics.* Chicago: University of Chicago Press, 283–336.

Laibson, David. 1997. "Golden Eggs and Hyperbolic Discounting." *Quarterly Journal of Economics* 112: 443–477.

Lazear, Edward P. 1979. "Why Is There Mandatory Retirement?" *Journal of Political Economy* 87(6): 1261–1284.

———. 1983. "Pensions as Severance Pay." In Z. Bodie and J. B. Shoven, eds., *Financial Aspects of the United States Pension System.* Chicago: University of Chicago Press, 57–89.

Lazear, Edward P., and Robert L. Moore. 1988. "Pensions and Mobility." In Zvi Bodie, John Shoven, and David Wise, eds., *Pensions in the U.S. Economy*. Chicago: University of Chicago Press, 163–188.

Lofgren, Eric, Steven A. Nyce, and Sylvester J. Schieber. 2003. "Designing Total Reward Programs for Tight Labor Markets." In Olivia Mitchell, David S. Blitzstein, Michael Gordon, and Judith F. Mazo, eds., *Benefits for the Workplace of the Future*. Philadelphia: University of Pennsylvania Press, 151–177.

Lumsdaine, Robin L., and Olivia S. Mitchell. 1999. "New Developments in the Economic Analysis of Retirement." In Orley Ashenfelter and David Card, eds., *Handbook of Labor Economics*. Amsterdam: North-Holland, 3261–3308.

Lumsdaine, Robin L., James H. Stock, and David A. Wise. 1990. "Efficient Windows and Labor Force Reductions." *Journal of Public Economics* 43(2): 131–159.

———. 1992. "Three Models of Retirement: Computational Complexity versus Predictive Validity." In David Wise, ed., *Topics in the Economics of Aging*. Chicago: University of Chicago Press, 19–57.

———. 1994. "Pension Plan Provisions and Retirement: Men and Women, Medicare, and Models." In David Wise, ed., *Studies in the Economics of Aging*. Chicago: University of Chicago Press, 183–212.

Lusardi, Annamaria. 1999. "Information, Expectations and Savings for Retirement." In Henry Aaron, ed., *Behavioral Dimensions of Retirement Economics*. Washington, DC: Brookings Institution Press, 183–222.

Madrian, Brigitte C., and Dennis F. Shea. 2001. "The Power of Suggestion: Inertia in 401(k) Participation and Savings Behavior." *Quarterly Journal of Economics* 116(4): 1149–1187.

Mitchell, Olivia. 1988. "Worker Knowledge of Pension Provisions." *Journal of Labor Economics* 6(1): 28–39.

Moore, James, and Olivia S. Mitchell. 2000. "Projected Retirement Wealth and Saving Adequacy." In Olivia S. Mitchell, P. Brett Hammond, and Anna M. Rappaport, eds., *Forecasting Retirement Needs and Retirement Wealth*. Philadelphia: University of Pennsylvania Press, Pension Research Council, 68–94.

Munnell, Alicia H., Kelly Haverstick, Mauricio Soto, and Jean-Pierre Aubry. 2008. "What Do We Know about the Universe of State and Local Plans?" Research Paper SLP #4. Boston: Center for Retirement Research at Boston College.

Munnell, Alicia H., and Mauricio Soto. 2007a. "Why Are Companies Freezing Their Pensions?" Paper presented at the meeting of the Retirement Research Centers, Washington, DC, August.

———. 2007b. "Why Have Defined Benefit Plans Survived in the Public Sector?" Research Paper SLP #2. Boston: Center for Retirement Research at Boston College.

Nalebuff, Barry, and Richard J. Zeckhauser. 1985. "Pensions and the Retirement Decision." In David A. Wise, ed., *Pensions, Labor, and Individual Choice*. Chicago: University of Chicago Press, 283–316.

Neumark, David, Daniel Polsky, and Daniel Hansen. 1999. "Has Job Stability Declined Yet? New Evidence for the 1990s." *Journal of Labor Economics* 17(S4): S29–S64.

Nyce, Steven A. 2007. "Behavioral Effects of Employer-Sponsored Retirement Plans." *Journal of Pension Economics and Finance* 6: 251–285.

Nyce, Steven A., and Sylvester J. Schieber. 2002. "The Decade of the Employee: The Workforce Environment in the Coming Decade." *Benefits Quarterly* 18(1): 60–79.

Parsons, Donald. 1996. "Retirement Age and Retirement Income: The Role of the Firm." In Eric A. Hanushek and Nancy L. Maritato, eds., *Assessing Knowledge of Retirement Behavior.* Washington, DC: National Academy Press, 149–195.

Poterba, James, Steven Venti, and David Wise. 2007a. "The Decline of Defined Benefit Retirement Plans and Asset Flows." NBER Working Paper No. 12834. Cambridge, MA: National Bureau of Economic Research.

———. 2007b. "Rise of 401(K) Plans, Lifetime Earnings and Wealth at Retirement." NBER Working Paper No. 13091. Cambridge, MA: National Bureau of Economic Research.

———. 2008. "The Changing Landscape of Pensions in the United States." In Annamaria Lusardi, ed., *Overcoming the Saving Slump.* Chicago: University of Chicago Press, 17–46.

President's Commission to Strengthen Social Security. 2001. "Strengthening Social Security and Creating Personal Wealth for All Americans." Washington, DC, December. http://www.commtostrengthensocsec.gov/reports/Final_report.pdf.

Quinn, Joseph F., Richard V. Burkhauser, and Daniel A. Meyers. 1990. *Passing the Torch: The Influence of Economic Incentives on Work and Retirement.* Kalamazoo, MI: Upjohn Institute for Employment Policy.

RAND HRS Data File. http://hrsonline.isr.umich.edu/modules/meta/rand/index.html.

Rohwedder, Susann. 2003. "Measuring Pension Wealth in the HRS: Employer and Self-Reports." Unpublished manuscript. Santa Monica, CA: RAND Corporation.

Rohwedder, Susann, and Kristin J. Kleinjans. 2006. "Dynamics of Individual Information about Social Security." Unpublished manuscript. Santa Monica, CA: RAND Corporation.

Samwick, Andrew A., and Jonathan S. Skinner. 2004. "How Will 401(k) Plans Affect Retirement Income?" *American Economic Review* 94: 329–343.

Schieber, Sylvester J. 2007. "An Inside Look at Corporate Retirement Plan Restructuring." Paper presented at the 82nd Annual Conference of the Western Economic Association, June 29–July 3, Seattle, Washington.

Schieber, Sylvester J., and John B. Shoven. 1999. *The Real Deal: The History and Future of Social Security.* New Haven, CT: Yale University Press.

Scholz, John Karl, Ananth Seshadri, and Surachai Khitatrakun. 2006. "Are Americans Saving 'Optimally' for Retirement?" *Journal of Political Economy* 114(4): 607–643.

Skinner, Jonathan S. 2007. "Are You Sure You're Saving Enough for Retirement?" *Journal of Economic Perspectives* 21(3): 59–80.

Stern, Steven, and Petra Todd. 2000. "A Test of Lazear's Mandatory Retirement Model." *Research in Labor Economics* 19: 253–273.

Stock, James H., and David A. Wise. 1990a. "The Pension Inducement to Retire: An Option Value Analysis." In David A. Wise, ed., *Issues in the Economics of Aging.* Chicago: University of Chicago Press, 205–224.

———. 1990b. "Pensions, the Option Value of Work, and Retirement." *Econometrica* 58(5): 1151–1180.

Turner, John A., Leslie Muller, and Satyendra K. Verma. 2003. "Defining Participation in Defined Contribution Pension Plans." *Monthly Labor Review* 126: 36–43.

U.S. Social Security Administration. 2003. "The 2003 Annual Report of the Board of Trustees of the Federal Old-Age and Survivors Insurance and Disability Insurance Trust Funds." Washington, DC: U.S. Social Security Administration.

Van der Klaauw, Wilbert, and Kenneth I. Wolpin. 2008. "Social Security and the Retirement and Savings Behavior of Low Income Households." *Journal of Econometrics* 145(1–2): 21–42.

Willis, Lauren E. 2008. "Against Financial Literacy Education." *Iowa Law Review* 94 (November): 199–285.

Index

Retirement ages *(continued)*
157–158; employer provided early versus employee, 162–167, 163*f*, 164–166*t*; estimated versus age of benefit, 178–179, 179*t*; expected age of benefit, 167–171, 168–170*t*; expected early, 158–162, 160–161*t*; information about covered samples, 183–185; pension explanations and, 27–28; pension values by, 209–210, 211*t*, 212*t*, 247–251, 248–249*t*, 250*t*; plans for retirement, 171–175, 172–174*t*

Retirement History Study, 11

Retirement incentives: ages of eligibility, 247; benefit accrual profiles, 9–10, 251–254, 253*t*; changes in individual benefit accrual over time, 258, 259–260*t*; cohort differences in benefit accrual, 254–255; gender differences in benefit accrual, 255, 256–257*t*; overview of, 26–27, 245–247; pension wealth values by retirement ages, 247–251, 248–249*t*, 250*t*; summary, 260–261

Retirement planning, 38, 113

Retirement regulation, 25–28, 31

Rohwedder, Susann, 38, 39, 119, 146, 326n11, 328n13

Rollover of benefits, 8, 91, 262, 279, 280–282*t*, 286. *See also* Individual Retirement Accounts (IRAs)

Samwick, Andrew A., 344n2

Schieber, Sylvester J., 15, 16, 30, 31, 36, 57, 321n1

Scholz, John Karl, 36, 322n6

Sector of employment: and compensation, 34; employment status and, 50–51*t*; pension trends in, 32–34; plan knowledge and, 124*t*, 125*t*, 126; plan type and, 6–7, 6*t*, 8, 29, 97–102, 98–99*t*, 101*t*

Segal, Martin, 32, 34

Self-employment. *See* Employment status

Separate accounts (defined contribution plans), 16

Separation from service. *See* Job tenure

Seshadri, Ananth, 322n6

Shea, Dennis F., 20, 37

Shoven, John B., 321n1

Skinner, Jonathan S., 321n1, 326n11, 344n2

Smith, Daniel, 324n4

Social Security benefits: early retirement and, 158; impact of, 1, 58; pensions, Social Security, and distribution of wealth, 293–298, 294–297*t*; surveys and, 13; total wealth and, 284–285, 285*t*, 291*t*, 292, 300–302*t*; understanding of, 38

Social Security data, 12

Social Security supplements, 8, 26, 158, 245

Soto, Mauricio, 14, 30, 32, 326n10

SPDs. *See* summary plan descriptions (SPDs)

Spouses: cohorts and, 43–44; households and, 283–284, 289–290, 290*t*; plan participation and, 95*t*, 96. *See also* Marital status

Steinmeier, Thomas L., 13, 18, 21, 25, 27, 30, 31, 33, 36, 38, 39, 58, 64, 103, 106, 120, 121*t*, 163, 246, 292, 313, 322nn6,7,8,9, 323nn1,2, 324n4, 325nn6,8, 326n2, 328n7, 331nn1,2, 337n4, 339nn1,2, 343n5

Stern, Steven, 325–326n9

Stock, James H., 324n5

Stock market exposure, 18, 311–314

Stolyarova, Helena, 342n1, 344n1

Summary plan descriptions (SPDs): availability of by sequence and year, 62*t*; collection of, 11–12, 62*t*, 63–64, 119–120, 137; discrepancies of plan knowledge, 20–21; pension formulas and, 157

Survey design, 20, 115–116, 118–119, 151–153, 152*t*